£5-

STUDIES IN
THE HISTORY OF THE
COMMON LAW

STUDIES IN THE HISTORY OF THE COMMON LAW

S.F.C. MILSOM

THE HAMBLEDON PRESS
LONDON AND RONCEVERTE

Published by The Hambledon Press

35 Gloucester Avenue, London NW1 7AX (U.K.)

309 Greenbrier Avenue, Ronceverte
West Virginia 24970 (U.S.A.)

ISBN 0 907628 61 3

© S.F.C. Milsom 1985

British Library Cataloguing in Publication Data

Milsom, S.F.C.
 Studies in the history of the common law.
 — (History series; 44)
 1. Common Law — England — History and criticism
 I. Title II. Series
 344.2'009   KD606

Library of Congress Cataloging in Publication Data

Milsom, S.F.C. (Stroud Francis Charles), 1923-
 Studies in the history of the common law.

 Includes bibliographical references and index.
 1. Common law — Great Britain — History — Addresses, essays, lectures. I. Title
KD671.A75M55 1985   349.42'09   85-5557
ISBN 0 907628 61 3   344.2'009

Printed and Bound in Great Britain by
Robert Hartnoll Ltd., Bodmin, Cornwall

CONTENTS

Acknowledgements		vii
Preface		ix

I. On the Medieval Personal Actions

1	Trespass from Henry III to Edward III	
	Part I: General Writs	1
	Part II: Special Writs	31
	Part III: More Special Writs and Conclusions	61
2	Not Doing is No Trespass: A View of the Boundaries of Case	91
3	Sale of Goods in the Fifteenth Century	105
4	Account Stated in the Action of Debt	133
5	Richard Hunne's 'Praemunire'	145

II. On Legal Development

6	Reason in the Development of the Common Law	149
7	Law and Fact in Legal Development	171
8	An Old Play in Modern Dress: *The Death of Contract* by Grant Gilmore	191
9	The Nature of Blackstone's Achievement	197
10	The Past and the Future of Judge-Made Law	209

III. On the Early Land Law

11	Formedon before *De Donis*	223
12	Inheritance by Women in the Twelfth and Early Thirteenth Centuries	231

IV. Two Legal Historians

13	F.W. Maitland	261
14	T.F.T. Plucknett	279
Table of Cases		295
Table of Statutes and Documents		319
Index		321

ACKNOWLEDGEMENTS

The articles reprinted here first appeared in the following places and are reprinted by the kind permission of the original publishers.

1	*Law Quarterly Review*, 74 (1958), pp. 195-224; 74 (1958), pp. 407-36; 74 (1958), pp. 561-90.
2	*Cambridge Law Journal* [1954], pp. 105-17.
3	*L.Q.R.*, 77 (1961), pp. 257-84.
4	*L.Q.R.*, 82 (1966), pp. 534-45.
5	*English Historical Review*, 76 (1961), pp. 80-2.
6	*L.Q.R.*, 81 (1965), pp. 496-517.
7	*University of Toronto Law Journal*, xvii (1967), pp. 1-19.
8	Reprinted by permission of The Yale Law Journal Company and Fred. B. Rothman & Company from *The Yale Law Journal*, Vol. 84 (1975), pp. 1585-90.
9	The Blackstone Lecture, 1980. Published simultaneously by the Selden Society (1981), and in *The Oxford Journal of Legal Studies*, 1 (1981), pp. 1-12.
10	The Tenth Wilfred Fullagar Memorial Lecture, 1981; *Monash University Law Review*, 8 (1981), pp. 1-14.
11	*L.Q.R.*, 72 (1956), pp. 391-7.
12	*On the Laws and Customs of England: Essays in Honor of Samuel E. Thorne*, ed. M.S. Arnold, T.A. Green, S.A. Scully and S.D. White (University of North Carolina Press, Chapel Hill, 1981), pp. 60-89.
13	British Academy Lecture on a Mastermind, 1980; *Proceedings of the British Academy*, lxvi (1980), pp. 265-81
14	*Proceedings of the British Academy*, li (1965), pp. 505-19.

PREFACE

THE earliest of these papers was written a little over thirty years ago. In history faculties at that time Plucknett's work commanded respect, but was not much followed. And in law faculties the subject was seen as a cultural extra, its uselessness conferring some gentlemanly virtue. Serious enquiry had all but ceased. Indeed it was not supposed that there could be anything important left to inquire about: marked out by Maitland and completed by Holdsworth, the job had been done. Only unworrying details remained unsettled; and generations of students wrote indistinguishable essays summarizing the literature on questions such as the precise manner in which actions on the case developed from the action of trespass.

It was from that question, or a reformulation of it, that the first group of these papers began. And their thrust is perhaps to be explained by something in the writer's own background. To one whose boyhood had been excitedly concentrated upon the natural sciences, and who had been diverted to the law by one accident and then to its history by another, the unsatisfying feature of the subject was the lack of credible connections between phenomena. The forms of action were seen as evolving and competing, hardly even in a market economy but rather in a Darwinian kind of ecological system. It was a vision of law in which you could shout for one side or the other but could not argue, and in which all the reported argument seemed to make little sense. The papers on the personal actions were concerned not just to investigate the working and relationships of the actions, but also to suggest that the argument made more sense if you just listened, instead of demanding answers to your own twentieth-century questions. Most of the argument is about procedure and proof, the central concerns of medieval litigation. But some of it, most obviously argument in terms of "trespass" and "covenant" is not about forms but about elementary legal categories. That was the thesis of the earliest of these papers, "Not Doing is no Trespass", here printed after the later series "Trespass from Henry III to Edward III" which was directed at the early nature of trespass itself as an idea of wrong in general rather than as the particular tort it eventually became. And if the wider thesis was stated in over-simplified form, it still seems helpful.

That thesis was the starting point of the second group into which this collection has been divided, the papers concerned with legal development. Much change, especially in the sixteenth century, came about by a process of reclassification: the rules of contract or property were against you, so you presented your facts as a tort. But that of course is the statement of a result, not of anybody's mental process. There was no sudden plunge into dishonesty. Facts giving rise to claims for compensation for distinct wrongs might include an agreement (to take the most important example) as part of the story: but the agreement was not the cause of action, and the claim was to remedy something other than its breach. And then those facts slowly turned into the fictions deployed when the same actions came to be used to seek redress for breach of the agreement itself. In substance it had become a new contractual remedy, free of the constrictions of the old; and its efficacy depended upon the ability of the jury to give damages for one item of loss when the claim was formally directed at another. But only in the course of the relatively recent paper on Judge-made Law did it dawn upon the writer that this whole process of fictionalisation depended more fundamentally upon the separate roles and sometimes divergent concerns of court and jury in the disposition of a law-suit. One of the difficulties in understanding common law change is precisely that it hardly ever represents anybody's mental process. It is the cumulative result of small interactions, in this case between the initiatives of plaintiffs' lawyers, the inherent force of legal principle weighing with judges, and the common desire of jurors to do what seemed intuitively just (and never mind the judge and his principles).

My slowness in seeing the importance of jury trial in that kind of change seems the more absurd because its importance in the original articulation of rules of law is the second theme of the papers about legal development. First suggested in the paper on Law and Fact, it had probably grown from half-conscious puzzling over the pattern of litigation underlying early formularies like *Novae Narrationes*. By what stages did the law that could be represented in a collection of rigid claims and denials turn into the mass of substantive rules that would be systematised in the nineteenth-century text-books? The first step was the replacement of older modes of trial by the jury (and perhaps in Rome by the *judex*), so that questions could at least be asked about the particular facts of a case. And then there were the various ways in which the questions came to be asked formally, so that courts would rule on them. And then when you have generated lots of substantive rules, there arises the literary question of how to store and present them; and the paper on Blackstone widens this theme into more general reflection on the legal importance of lawyers explaining the law to laymen. But that line of thought has a corollary: perhaps something also happens when lawyers stop trying to explain. And the paper on Judge-made Law indulges more sombre thoughts about the effect of the ending of civil juries on the texture of the law and perhaps on its moral force.

This last change is associated with another, most obviously dramatised in the movement of the law of torts away from its old basis in individual fault and towards new and essentially distributive considerations such as insurance. The reallocation of risks is an aspect of the reallocation of resources. And the two last-mentioned papers, now reaching out from the legal areas growing from the personal actions, touch upon another kind of contemporary change and another theme in legal development. The classical common law, like the Roman, was a system of private law resting upon an idea of private property: it was about relationships between legal equals whose rights were protected by government but were not thought of as dependent upon it. In between the two systems came the centuries of disorder and privation in which feudal structures grew. Land and livelihood were not owned but allocated, conditionally and for a return; and the important legal relationships were not between man and man but between man and lord. Work upon the final disappearance in England of any feudal reality, upon the small stages by which the dependent tenant turned into an independent owner, prompted reflection upon the small stages by which economic pressures are turning us back into a managed society, dependent upon benefits allocated by a new kind of lord. Most of the important legal questions for ordinary English people today arise between themselves and authority, not between each other. Our mixed law is more pervasive than our mixed economy, and the new vertical structures slowly push private law into irrelevance. Consider the land law itself. Legal historians of the future may admire, as evidence of relatively painless adjustment, the persistence with which the tenant in fee still uses his feudal name, unreal for centuries, as he sinks into a second unreality. He had long since become an owner: and the rent officer and the planning officer do not question his ownership, just reallocate much of the economic benefit. Nobody ever questioned lordship either.

There is no unity between the two papers directly concerned with the history of the land law itself. My interest in the subject came relatively late. What had been no more than a despairing dissatisfaction had to be analysed when writing the introduction to a new edition of "Pollock and Maitland". A solution suggested itself, and was most fully set out in lectures published as *The Legal Framework of English Feudalism* (and most simply in the second edition of *Historical Foundations of the Common Law*). The paper on Inheritance by Women was a continuation of that line of thought, and seemed appropriate in a volume for Professor Thorne who had had a not dissimilar thought. The paper on Formedon is much earlier, and was written only to record a find made in a plea roll while working on the personal actions. Another such find was recorded in the paper on Richard Hunne, here placed with the group on the personal actions because it is relevant to the history of defamation.

Nor is there much unity, except admiration, between the two papers on legal historians. That on Plucknett was an obituary, written soon after his death, of a man I had at least met. It had to set out the main facts of his life; and the important facts are that he was intellectually a self-made man and that what he made himself, determinedly and unambiguously, was a historian. Although employed in law faculties all his working life, Plucknett had no legal training. He came to the subject from constitutional history, and his most interesting work was that which treated it as a part of social history. Legal argument was something with which he never much concerned himself; and he primly dismissed as a dismal aberration Maitland's thought that lawyers might advance legal history.

But a lawyer, seeking to analyse Maitland's unique position as a writer of history, could not help wondering whether his quality as a lawyer might not have had something to do with it. Dead almost eighty years, his greatest book was published now ninety years ago; and it still compels. What other history book of such an age is even read as a work of scholarship rather than as literature or as itself a piece of historical evidence? What other historian's interpretation of his materials has survived him by any comparable period? A part of the explanation lies in the readership. Historians are increasingly turning to legal sources for details of social and economic history, and they continue to study courts and other legal institutions: but it is still rare for them to venture into the law itself and consider the formal framework of society for its own sake. The paper, of course, was mainly concerned with that part of the explanation that lay in the author, with the dramatist's sympathy that compels in detail by representing large themes through the mouths of imaginary real people, and with the rare lawyer's ability to discern and impose compelling overall patterns. Such a paper was not easy for one who is both devoted and an unbeliever; and no doubt it was ill done. But the present *apologia* may end by bringing some threads together. Another part of the explanation for the durability of Maitland's essentially static and Bractonian vision lies in the material itself. Legal development and legal change happen in ways which are hardly ever obvious at the time or easily discernible afterwards. Words slowly change their meaning, procedures their function; but there is no signal – no challenge to bring home to those affected how their social and economic situation is altering, and consequently no barrier to alert historians when they carry later legal usages and later social assumptions back through the change.

A personal obligation remains. The publisher has acknowledged our debt to the original publishers of these papers; and I should like to record a different kind of debt to the late Arthur Goodhart who as editor of the *Law Quarterly Review* gave singular encouragement when it was needed.

Cambridge
January 1985

S.F.C. Milsom

TRESPASS FROM HENRY III TO EDWARD III
PART I: GENERAL WRITS

"HER progeny throve and multiplied, until a time came when, the older forms having been neglected, an action for damages, an action which traced descent from the *breve de transgressione*, seemed to be almost the only remedy offered by the common law." [1] Maitland could thus look forward and mark the importance of this newcomer, trespass; but the lawyers of the time could not look forward, and to them trespass was not important. It was something peripheral to their learning,[2] and nobody wrote down the answers to questions which have come to matter. How did trespass come into being? How and when were its progeny born? What, if any, were the principles of liability?

These articles are concerned, not with the answers to these questions, but with the terms in which they are asked. What was trespass? Maitland assumed, as have most other writers, that it was from the beginning what it is today; and the picture which he drew for those lucky classes who heard him lecture on the forms of action [3] has been generally accepted. Some may think, with Professor Woodbine, that trespass descended from novel disseisin rather than appeal of felony; some may think, with Miss Dix and Mr. Fifoot, that case in its turn grew out of trespass through the action of the judges rather than the *in consimili casu* clause [4]; but all agree that what came into being in the thirteenth century was a single entity, a definite tort with the essential ingredient of direct forcible injury, and that out of or around this entity there developed, by a process beginning in the late fourteenth century, the mass of actions on the case.

It is this picture that the writer seeks to question. He does not believe that there was in the thirteenth or fourteenth century an entity equivalent to the modern trespass, or that the word trespass at that time ever meant anything narrower than just wrong. The concept was unlimited. Limitation came from without rather than within: the question was not whether a wrong qualified as a trespass, but whether it was the kind of trespass which the royal court could or would handle.

---

[1] Pollock and Maitland, *History of English Law* (2nd ed.), II, p. 525.
[2] Professor Hamson once suggested to the writer that trespass in its early days may have seemed rather an administrative than a strictly legal matter.
[3] *The Forms of Action at Common Law*, Lectures IV to VI.
[4] Stat.Westm. II, c. 24.

The kinds of trespass which the royal court most commonly handled were, of course, those which we should call trespass today; and this is why our concept has generally seemed to fit when projected back in time. That it does not always fit is the narrow point to be established. Reliance will chiefly be placed upon two sorts of evidence. One consists of a range of writs, to be set out in a later article, beginning with forms which were for direct forcible injuries, and ending with forms which were not; and it will be seen that there is no discernible boundary, and that all were treated alike and all called trespass.[5] Secondly, there will be included in this article material which tends to show that the standard writs, which we should identify as the writs of trespass *par excellence*, were sometimes available when there had been no direct forcible injury.

This point is destructive only, but none the less important. The assumption that trespass was a concept involving direct force is the essence of the received views not only of the origin of trespass but also of the origin and development of case. If we can dispose of it, we shall no longer be obliged to regard the transformation of the law referred to by Maitland as a process in which the permanent difficulty was in stretching analogies with a central fixed point, like a goat at the end of its chain.

Can any other view be offered? A picture will, it is hoped, become discernible; but the writer's chief constructive ambition is to present facts about the development of the various kinds of trespass writ. Mr. Hall has recently printed examples from thirteenth-century registers [6]; those which follow come mostly from the rolls of the King's Bench and the Common Pleas. These rolls were selected as being the least likely to contain irregularities; and for the same reason cases known to have begun by bill were excluded. There seems, however, to be no ground for the common suspicion of irregularity in proceedings by bill,[7] and this is relevant because it is not always possible to tell whether there was a writ or not. Some forms of entry are peculiar to writs and some to bills, but there are some appropriate to both [8]; so that while

---

[5] The purely terminological evidence must always be inconclusive: where trespass is used in a context where its modern sense will not fit, it can be argued that it was not meant technically. When the early existence of the modern sense is once questioned, this argument does not seem likely; but it cannot be met except by Ockham's razor.

[6] " Some early writs of ' Trespass ' " (1957) 73 L.Q.R., p. 65.

[7] See now Professor Sayles in *Sel.Cas. in K.B.*, IV, at p. lxxxv.

[8] Richardson and Sayles, *Select Cases of Procedure without Writ*, pp. xlvii, 1, 125 (the case on p. 15 is a doubtful example); *cf.* Sayles, *Sel.Cas. in K.B.*, III, pp. 84, 87, 104. See also now Professor Sayles's introduction to Vol. IV of the latter work, at p. lxxiv.

queat vi coatoo petitioon
How way appeat pestiie
By what means before

uliteo quadan via cam teneat
use way r holds
heaps

ulloa teorem neem deA queam
land his frome which

in ea habeoe non debeet ut
vot keep
from
someone

diuteo
it may be proclaimed.

identified plaints have been put aside, a few may have made their way in undetected.

A rough classification has been imposed upon the material for ease of handling, the primary division being into general and special writs. These terms are found in the sources and must be considered later; for the present let it be said only that *general* writs are those in which the defendant is required to answer why he did the act complained of without more, while *special* writs set out special matter showing why his act was wrongful. Within these categories the classification depends upon the nature of the complaint: the nature of the defendant's act in the case of general writs, and of the special matter in the case of special writs. Something is said of almost all the main kinds of trespass writ, whether or not they are of immediate interest; and suggestions raised by the material are sometimes pursued even when they do not serve the narrower purpose of the inquiry. For these digressions the excuse is that anything is relevant which shows to what purposes the writs were put, and whether trespass was an entity or a generic term. A large omission is cases which appear to have been predominantly criminal in character. The importance of these appears very clearly from Mr. Hall's article [9]; but the writer is chiefly interested in the development of civil liability, and has felt himself excused by the privilege of reading an account by Mr. Alan Harding which it is hoped will soon be published.

The material in this first article consists entirely of general writs. To save space proper names have been replaced throughout by capital letters: P is the plaintiff, D the defendant, and their plurals are PP and DD; other characters are X, Y, Z; and places are A, B, C. Sums of money are expressed in figures instead of words, £ being used for pounds, m. for marks, and s. for shillings.

1. Wrongs to Land

Introductory

In a case of 1234, of which more later, the defendant had done nothing but come onto the plaintiff's land [10]:

> *quare vi & contra justiciam utitur quadam via & eam tenet ultra terram suam de A quam in ea habere non debet ut dicitur;*

but generally he had come and done something, and the wrong lay not in his coming but in what he did. The category of wrongs to land is thus largely artificial; we need expect few common

---

[9] *Op. cit.*
[10] *Bracton's Note Book*, pl. 843. See also pp. 11-12, *infra*.

elements; and it will be a matter of taste whether or not we include, for example, cases in which the defendant came onto the plaintiff's land and beat him or took away his goods. These are in fact postponed in order that they may be compared with ordinary writs of battery and *de bonis asportatis* later. This comparison will provide what justification there is for treating wrongs to land as a category: under Henry III the phrase *vi et armis* seems to be associated with the invasion of the plaintiff's land. There was no rule; but entries alleging an invasion had *vi et armis* more often than not, and others more often than not lacked it.

Ejectment

The word is not meant in its technical sense. But the proper remedy for an ejected freeholder was novel disseisin, and only one example has been noted in which a trespass writ was brought; it dates from 1240 [11]:

> *quare vi & armis & contra pacem domini Regis ejecerunt predictam P de uno mesuagio in A in quod ipsa P se posuit post mortem X consanguinee predicte P cujus heres ipsa P est.*

Possibly the plaintiff had not acquired seisin; but it may be doubted whether Bracton would have approved of her action.[12] In the following case the proper remedy would presumably have been not novel disseisin but the viscontiel writ *de quarentina habenda*,[13] perhaps not yet invented in 1255 [14]:

> *quare vi & armis fregerunt hostia & fenestras domus predicte P in A quam tenuit per quarantenam suam post decessum X quondam viri sui secundum legem & consuetudinem Anglie, & ipsam P & familiam suam ab eadem domo violenter ejecerunt & eandem P verberaverunt & maletractaverunt & Y servientem ipsius P ibidem ceperunt & imprisonaverunt contra pacem &c.*

To this the substantive plea was that X had held only for life. The entry goes on to show the plaintiff proceeding against two other defendants *de placito quare predictam transgressionem preceperunt*: but it is decided that they need not answer *donec factum convincatur*.[15]

Of *ejectio firme* itself the writer has noted five examples under

---

[11] KB. 26/121, m. 1, now *Curia Regis Rolls*, xvi, pl. 1174.
[12] *Bracton*, f. 413.
[13] *Reg.Omn.Brev.* (1634), f. 175d; Fitzherbert, *Natura Brevium* (1588), f. 161E. It also has the key words *violenter ejecit*. *Cf.* Stat.Merton, c. 1; *Placitorum Abbreviatio*, p. 223a (1290).
[14] KB. 26/155, m. 3.
[15] *Cf.* KB. 26/168 (1260), m. 1; *Plac.Abb.*, p. 268a (1277).

Henry III, divisible into two classes. First are actions to which the lessor was defendant, as in this from 1254 [16]:

> *quare contra pacem domini Regis ejecerunt eandem P de libera firma sua quam tenuit de predicto D* (principal defendant) *in A ad terminum qui nondum preteriit.*

In this case *vi et armis* appears only in the count; but it is in the writ in a case of 1260, also against the lessor, the lease being recited as special matter in a *cum* clause.[17] The other three examples are actions against persons claiming by title paramount, and are all of 1259–60. One of the writs is in special form, but is largely obscured by damage to the membrane.[18] Another was this [19]:

> *quare vi & armis ejecerunt ipsum P de manerio de A cum pertinenciis quod X ei dimisit ad terminum qui nondum preteriit contra pacem &c.;*

to which the defendants, husband and wife, pleaded that X had held only as guardian of the wife. The third was [20]:

> *quare ipsi ex precepto Y vi & armis venerunt ad domum ipsius P in A quam habuit ex dimissione X ad terminum qui nondum preteriit & hostia & fenestras ejusdem domus fregerunt & in ipsum insultum fecerunt & ipsum & totam familiam suam violenter & viliter ab eadem domo expulerunt & catalla & blada sua ad valenciam 20 m. devastaverunt contra pacem &c.*

This time the defendants claimed that X had died leaving an infant heir, so that the wardship belonged to Y.[21]

The early appearance of *ejectio firme* may explain Bracton's assertion that *quare ejecit* lay against *quoscunque dejectores*.[22] What follows is only a guess about the relation between the two actions, but it will at least assemble some relevant facts; it turns upon the unsettled practice of the time over specific remedies,[23] of which more will be said in connection with special writs. In 1224 a lessee sued his lessor and others *quare intruserunt se*[24]; if analysed at all, this was probably thought of as covenant in substance, but formulated with an eye to the co-defendants. Its

---

[16] KB. 26/154 (C.P.), mm. 31, 33. *Cf. ibid.*, m. 13, which may be another example but the language is ambiguous.
[17] KB. 26/168, m. 16d. *Cf. Select Cases of Procedure without Writ*, pp. 104, 127 (1260–61).
[18] KB. 26/161, m. 15. The facts appear broadly similar to KB. 26/167 (1260), m. 1, which is formally *de bonis asportatis* by the lessee, but substantially *ejectio firme*.
[19] KB. 26/161, m. 3. *Cf. Select Cases of Procedure without Writ*, p. 97 (1259).
[20] KB. 26/161, m. 12.
[21] *Cf.* Britton (ed. Nichols) I, p. 418.
[22] f. 220.
[23] *Cf.* Maitland, *Collected Papers*, II, pp. 153–154.
[24] *Curia Regis Rolls* (hereafter referred to as C.R.R.), XI, pl. 2594.

quare form,²⁵ however, enabled Raleigh to adapt it for use against the lessor's grantee; this is the classical *quare ejecit, occasione cujus venditionis*, and it is found in 1235–36.²⁶ The conjecture is that the proliferation of *quare* writs then obscured its ancestry, making it look like just one kind of possessory protection for the termor, and producing the position represented by Bracton's account ²⁷: *ejectio firme*, with *quare ejecit* conceived as a frequent special case, would be to the termor what novel disseisin was to the freeholder. All would be well in cases like that of 1254, when the lessor himself was principal defendant; but when the defendant claimed by title paramount, as in 1259–60, difficult problems would arise. A reaction caused by these difficulties would explain Britton's account, even more puzzling than Bracton's, in which he seems to deny the existence of *quare ejecit* itself, and despairingly advises lessees not to let themselves be thrown out.²⁸ If, indeed, *quare ejecit* was under Edward I jeopardised by its association with *ejectio firme*, that danger did not last long ²⁹; but what was still doubtful in the early years of the next reign, and exciting to a Year Book reporter, was whether and when a plaintiff in *quare ejecit* could get his term back.³⁰ This would be a likely result of the association with *ejectio firme*, because it was then beginning to be settled that specific relief could not be had in trespass writs.³¹

A later confusion may also be relevant. Fitzherbert supposed *ejectio firme* to be the original entity,³² and he thought that *quare ejecit* had been derived from it ³³ under the powers of the *in consimili casu* clause. He has his own tale explaining why this should have been necessary; but the idea that *quare ejecit* was invented to fill a gap left by *ejectio firme* appears in Year Book reports as early as 1364 ³⁴ and 1374.³⁵ In each case the action was trespass *vi et armis* brought by a lessee against the lessor who had ejected him; and the lessor challenged the writ on the ground, among others, that since the freehold was in him, he could not come with force and arms and against the peace. In each case this was supported by a reference to *quare ejecit*: that writ was

---

²⁵ Bracton gives also a *praecipe* form for *quare ejecit*; f. 220.
²⁶ *Bracton's Note Book*, pl. 1140.
²⁷ f. 220.
²⁸ (Ed. Nichols), I, p. 417.
²⁹ Examples are found in 1271, KB. 26/201, m. 8d; and 1275, CP. 40/8, mm. 14, 38; and again in 1302, YB. 30–31 Ed. I, R.S., p. 282. Nichols dates *Britton* at 1291–92 (I, p. xviii).
³⁰ YB. 4 Ed. II, Seld.Soc., Vol. 42, p. 181. *Cf. Casus Placitorum*, p. 42.
³¹ *Cf. Plac.Abb.*, p. 346b; Maitland, *Coll.Papers*, II, pp. 153–154.
³² Fitzherbert, *Natura Brevium*, f. 198A.
³³ By the legendary William of Merton; *cf. Reg.Omn.Brev.*, f. 227.
³⁴ YB. Mich. 38 Ed. III, f. 33d.
³⁵ YB. Hil. 48 Ed. III, pl. 12, f. 6d.

framed without *vi et armis* and *contra pacem*, it is said, because the defendant would be the freeholder; and if trespass *vi et armis* had been available against the freeholder, there would have been no need to invent *quare ejecit*. What we have been taught to regard as a fundamental distinction between the two remedies seems still blurred; and when we learn that in 1389, only a little later, a termor is found recovering his term by *ejectio firme*,[36] we may wonder whether it was ever clear.

The argument made against the writ in 1364 and 1374 will be considered elsewhere. The writ itself, which can be deduced from the 1374 report, recited the lease as special matter in a *cum* clause, and was in all essentials the same as one of 1260 mentioned above.[37] A related writ, rather similar in form but not *vi et armis*, was that by which the executors of a lessee sued the lessor who had entered. The writer has seen a specimen of 1371 [38] substantially in the form in the Register.[39]

Reaping crops, etc.

A case is found, alleging force but not arms, in 1224 [40]:

quare vi messuerunt blada sua viridia & succiderunt arbores suas in A & ea asportaverunt &c.;

and it is, incidentally, among the relatively few early cases in which we know for certain that there was a writ.[41] In 1237 both force and arms were alleged, together with *contra pacem* at the beginning of the writ [42]; and four years later are a number of entries in the general terms of this one [43]:

quare vi & armis intraverunt mariscum ipsius P de A & arbores ipsius P in eodem marisco inventas prostraverunt & extirpaverunt & asportaverunt sine licencia ipsius P & alia dampna & gravamina ei intulerunt contra pacem &c.

The *alia dampna et gravamina* have yet to separate into *alia enormia* and a separate allegation of damage; and this is the form found under Edward I. As late as 1283 an entry is found without *vi et armis*,[44] but this allegation, always more common than not, was probably standard by the end of the reign.[45]

[36] Plucknett, *Concise History* (5th ed.), p. 373, n. 5. See also the remarkable reasoning in *Vieux Natura Brevium* (1584), f. 123r & d: it is said that you cannot get the term back in *ejectio firme, nient pluis que . . . home recovera damages pur trepas nient fait, mes a feser.*
[37] *Supra*, p. 5, n. 17. [38] CP. 40/443, m. 122.
[39] *Reg.Omn.Brev.*, ff. 97, 102d.; Fitzherbert, *Natura Brevium*, f. 92G.
[40] C.R.R., XI, pl. 2211.
[41] *Ibid.*, pl. 2806.
[42] C.R.R. XVI, pl. 36.
[43] C.R.R., XVI pl. 1254; cf. pll. 1180 1583, 1719, 1824.
[44] CP. 40/48, m. 21d.
[45] *Placita Coram Rege, 1297* (British Record Soc.), pp. 6, 61.

A point remains. In three nicely spaced cases, in 1230,[46] 1254,[47] and 1272,[48] the defendant's answer to the action was that the land upon which the trees, or whatever it was, grew was his own. This ended the matter; in the words of the last case, *liberum tenementum non potest per hoc breve de transgressione terminari*, and the plaintiff must get a writ of novel disseisin if he wants. None of these cases alleged *vi et armis*, and one wonders whether this is coincidence.

Depasturing

Dr. Glanville Williams[49] noted a case as early as 1214,[50] and then none until Edward I; and the next seen by the present writer was a plaint in 1237, which has been printed by Mr. Richardson and Professor Sayles.[51] In 1241, however, there is an entry not unlike the common form of later years[52]:

> *quare vi & armis intraverunt manerium ipsius P de A & prata sua cum animalibus suis pascaverunt & fenum suum conculcaverunt & alia dampna ei intulerunt contra pacem &c.*

In 1270 *alia dampna ei intulerunt* has become *alia enormia ei intulerunt ad grave dampnum*[53]; and apart from cases where a figure is named for damage[54] as in the following example, there is no further substantial change. A typical, though simple, entry comes from 1274[55]:

> *quare blada predicti P in terris suis apud A cum averiis suis vi & armis depasti fuerunt & alia enormia ei ibidem intulerunt ad dampnum ipsius P £40 & contra pacem &c.*

To this last action there were more than fifty defendants; and it seems clear that down to the time of Edward I at any rate the most frequent use of the writ was against persons asserting rights of common.[56] The proprietary remedies for and against one who claimed a right of common were, respectively, a writ of right or a *quod permittat* in the *debet*, and the writ *quo jure*. Possessory

---

[46] *Bracton's Note Book*, pl. 378 and C.R.R. XIII pl. 2350.
[47] *Plac.Abb.*, p. 142a.
[48] *Ibid.*, p. 262a.
[49] *Liability for Animals*, p. 130.
[50] C.R.R., VII, p. 206: not a straightforward case.
[51] *Select Cases of Procedure without Writ*, p. 23.
[52] C.R.R., XVI, pl. 1308.*Cf. Reg.Omn.Brev.*, ff. 94–96 *passim*, 99, 101d, 108d, 110.
[53] KB. 26/200A (C.P.), m. 9 (several pasture from which defendants had also driven plaintiff's own animals).
[54] *Cf., e.g., Sel.Cas. in K.B.*, II, p. 84 (1292); III, p. 134 (1304). Examples of another form, setting a value on the crops, are *Placita Coram Rege, 1297*, pp. 1, 187.
[55] CP. 40/5, m. 19d.
[56] See, *e.g., Sel.Cas. in K.B.*, II, p. 84; III, p. 134. An example of this use in 1337 is CP. 40/312, m. 189.

protection of the commoner was secured by other varieties of *quod permittat*, or, in certain circumstances, novel disseisin; but there was no special possessory action against the assertion of such a right.[57] This work was done by writs of trespass; and the actions now under consideration and some of those under the next following heading are examples of it.

Dr. Glanville Williams[58] remarked some variation in registers of Edward I, but *vi et armis* seems to appear more often than not in the plea rolls. The action, however, is too rare to be confident. A specimen entry lacking it is of 1274[59]:

> *quare ipsi contra pacem domini Regis cum bidentibus suis pascebant pasturam dicti P in A que posita fuit in defensione ad boves dicti P & ad boves aliorum qui in dicta pastura habent communam & hoc fecerunt ad grave dampnum suum.*

Two questions may be asked. First, was genuine violence ever necessary? Occasionally a writ may disclose the use of force, for example by alleging also a battery on the plaintiff or his servant.[60] The count under Edward III always recited a blood-curdling list of weapons, but we shall see that this was just common form. Under Edward I such lists are sometimes found[61]; but if they mean anything it may be equally significant that some counts do not even repeat *vi et armis*,[62] and others repeat it but contain no other indication of violence or threat of violence.[63] Sometimes, again, a count will show that the depasturing continued for a long period.[64] It seems clear that no violence was necessary.

If this is right, the second question arises: Would the action lie when the depasturing was not the deliberate act of the animals' owner? Dr. Glanville Williams thought not.[65] His reasons were firstly the words of the writ, alleging that the defendant had done the wrong "with" his animals; secondly the nature of trespass as a direct injury; and thirdly the apparent novelty of a case in 1353,[66] after which the liability for an escape was clear. The

---

[57] Many cases were settled in replevin after a distress damage feasant.
[58] *Op. cit.*, p. 131.
[59] CP. 40/5, m. 78. In 1348 it is stated that the commoner himself cannot have the action; 22 *Lib.Ass.*, pl. 48, f. 95d.
[60] *e.g.*, *Placita Coram Rege, 1297*, p. 1; CP. 40/370 (1352), m. 3; KB. 27/380 (1855), m. 33d.
[61] *e.g.*, CP. 40/50 (1283), m. 17.
[62] *Sel.Cas. in K.B.*, II, p. 84 (1292); *Placita Coram Rege, 1297*, p. 187.
[63] *e.g.*, *Sel.Cas. in K.B.*, III, p. 134 (1304).
[64] *e.g.*, *ibid.*, II, p. 84 (a week); III, p. 134 (a month); and CP. 40/399 (1359), m. 155d (3 years).
[65] *Op. cit.*, p. 131.
[66] 27 *Lib.Ass.*, pl. 56, f. 141.

writer cannot set much store by the first of these points,[67] or any by the second; the 1353 case, however, is strong evidence, the only doubt being whether the difficulty was indeed a novel use of the action, or just the terms of the special verdict that the depasturing was not *contra pacem*. That the latter may be the explanation is suggested by a writ of the previous year [68]:

> *quare vi & armis muros grangie ipsius P apud A cum quibusdam porcis fregit & blada sua in eadem grangia ad valenciam £20 cum eisdem porcis depastus fuit conculcavit & consumpsit & alia enormia ei intulit ad grave dampnum ipsius P & contra pacem &c.*

The defendant had surely not set his pigs to charge those walls; they did it on their own initiative. All he had done was to put them where they could get at the plaintiff's property; and this raises a further point. Reflection will suggest that in the possible fact situations, except the frequent one of a right of common being asserted, making liability depend upon intention would have been difficult to work.

Be this as it may, the doubt is about the scope of the action, not the liability of the owner of the animals: the injured party could certainly distrain damage feasant, or proceed in a local court.[69] Moreover, whether or not the action lay for an escape before 1353, there is no doubt about it after that date [70]; and lawyers have had difficulty in reconciling this with our idea of trespass. Other uses of trespass writs in this period, also anomalous to our eyes, will appear below; but this one is exceptional in that it was not later cut down to make an honest writ on the case.

Hunting, shooting and fishing

Fishing will be taken first, because the action was put to the same sort of use as in the depasturing cases. The most interesting are two from 1234 printed in *Bracton's Note Book*. In the first the defendants were to answer a complaint [71]—

> *quod ... vi & armis & contra pacem domini Regis piscati fuerunt in piscaria ipsius P inter* [two named bridges] *ubi piscari non debent nec solent & asportaverunt palos palatii ipsius P;*

---

[67] Cf. the writ *infra*, at n. 68. In 1359 there were two pleasing writs demanding *quare pratum cum quibusdam porcis subvertit*; CP. 40/399, mm. 46, 151; cf. *Reg.Omn.Brev.*, f. 108d.
[68] CP. 40/371, m. 25. See also 22 *Lib.Ass.*, pl. 51, f. 96.
[69] Glanville Williams, *op. cit.*, p. 127.
[70] CP. 40/399 (1359), m. 168 (plea that plaintiff had not fenced as he should, and it was his own fault). Cf. Glanville Williams, *op. cit.*, pp. 132–133.
[71] *Bracton's Note Book*, pl. 835. There had been a writ; but these may not be the *ipsissima verba*.

and in the second, in which the plaintiff was a guardian, the defendants were to answer [72]:

> *quare vi & armis venerunt in liberam piscariam ipsius heredis in A & in ea piscati sunt contra justiciam desicut illi nullam communam habuerunt in piscaria illa die quo predictus X pater ipsius heredis obiit ut dicitur.*

In each case the defendants' lord comes and warrants their fishing as done in his right, and claims that he is entitled to fish with the plaintiff. This claim forms the real issue in both actions, and in the former it led, somewhat to Maitland's bewilderment,[73] to a grand assize.

Closer examination of these two cases may be profitable. In the first, the plaintiff speaks in terms of *debet et solet*; in the second, he counts that his ward's father *fuit seisitus anno & die quo fuit vivus & mortuus sine communa quam predicti homines ibi habere debeant*. The former phrase is reminiscent of a proprietary *quod permittat*[74] and the latter of a *quod permittat* in the nature of *mort d'ancestor*, brought by persons asserting rights of common. In substance what the plaintiffs in these two cases are doing is the converse; they are attacking the assertion of rights of common. It was remarked in connection with depasturing that there was no special possessory protection against such an assertion, that work being done by trespass writs. The second of the cases under discussion is an early and elaborate example of this, and is of the same nature as many depasturing cases. But what of the first case, with its *debent* and *solent* and its grand assize? Could right be determined in a writ of trespass? Evidently it could. We saw above that there was a proprietary remedy against a claim to common, the writ *quo jure*, which was in substance a writ of right of freedom from common. But there is reason to think that this did not appear much before 1222, and that in 1234 it was still confined to common of pasture.[75] The first of these two cases, then, looks like a writ of trespass being used to raise the right for want of any other way of doing it.[76] This pair must not be left without referring to a third copied in *Bracton's Note Book* from the same

---

[72] *Ibid.*, pl. 839.
[73] *Ibid.*, II, p. 644, n. 5; *Coll. Papers*, II, p. 153, n. 2. *Cf.* Woodbine, 34 Yale L.J., p. 343, at p. 345.
[74] In the developed scheme *debet* indicates a writ in the mere right, *debet & solet* a writ in the nature of a writ of entry.
[75] No actions *quo jure* can be found from the indices to the first ten volumes of C.R.R. Those in the eleventh and twelfth volumes and all twenty-three (ranging from 1222 to 1233) indexed in *Bracton's Note Book* concern pasture.
[76] The defendants could have brought a writ of right; but the plaintiff could not make them do so.

roll[77]: it is the first writ set out in this article,[78] and was an action by an owner against one asserting a right of way. These three cases, and those of depasturing, show early trespass writs playing a part in the law about easements and profits which does not look like the mere by-product of some basic concept of trespass to land as we conceive it.

Too few fishing cases have been noted to estimate the frequency of *vi et armis*; but the point is of some interest in the entries concerning hunting. An early case was in 1230 [79]—

> *quare furtive & de nocte fregerunt parcum ipsius P de A & parcum illum ingredientes bestias suas in eo ceperunt contra pacem domini Regis;*

and the same roll has an entry in which the defendant's act was said to be *sine licencia*.[80] From 1241 comes another pair: one [81]—

> *quare concurrit in parco ipsius P de A & in eodem venacionem cepit sine licencia ipsius P & contra pacem &c.;*

and the other, in which there were aggravating circumstances including a battery, having *vi et armis* but omitting *sine licencia*.[82] After 1250 the entries are recognisably like the forms in the Register,[83] except that *vi et armis* is more often than not absent, appearing rarely in the Common Pleas,[84] and in perhaps half of the cases in the King's Bench.[85] The following, from 1255, are typical [86]:

> *quare parcum ipsius P in A fregerunt & in eo (or quare liberam warennam ... intraverunt & in ea) bestias ceperunt & asportaverunt sine licencia & voluntate ipsius P & contra pacem &c.*

Thirty years later, the allegation of damage is always added, and *vi et armis* is becoming usual.[87]

One more entry will be quoted, partly to justify the middle term in this heading, and partly to make a point about the nature of the wrong. It is from 1273 [88]:

---

[77] *Bracton's Note Book*, pl. 843.
[78] *Supra*, p. 3, n. 10.
[79] C.R.R., XIII, pl. 2352.
[80] C.R.R., XIII, pl. 2444.
[81] C.R.R., XVI, pl. 1447; cf. pl. 1400.
[82] C.R.R., XVI, pl. 1364.
[83] *Reg.Omn.Brev.*, ff. 109d, 110.
[84] It appears in none of the seven entries in KB. 26/164 (1260), in two of the six in CP. 40/2A (1273), and in five of the nine in CP. 40/49 (1283).
[85] KB. 26/146 (1252); KB. 26/155 (1255); KB. 26/167 & 168 (1260); there are some six cases a term.
[86] KB. 26/155 (1255), mm. 1 (free chase), 3d (two parks and a free warren), 11d (park).
[87] CP. 40/48 (1283), mm. 16d, 24d, 36d, 68d (*vi & armis*); mm. 66d, 68d (no *vi & armis*). See also n. 84, *supra*.
[88] CP. 40/2A, m. 14. Cf. KB. 26/146 (1252), m. 9d (*cum canibus suis*); KB. 26/168 (1260), m. 4 (*cum arcubus & sagittis*).

> *quare cum canibus arcubus & sagittis suis intraverunt in liberam warennam ipsius P in A & in warenna illa lepores ... ceperunt & asportaverunt sine licencia & voluntate ipsius P & contra pacem &c.*

The dogs and bows and arrows, coming in the position soon to be reserved for *vi et armis*, emphasise what is clear from many other entries from the earliest. There was no violence; the defendant had just been poaching. When, therefore, under Edward I *vi et armis* came regularly to be alleged, it was from the beginning a formality, not the vestige of true complaints in rougher times.

These cases raise one last question: Why should the statistical incidence of *vi et armis* seem to place them somewhat apart from other wrongs to land, and towards those which follow? A possible answer is that, since warren and chase at any rate might extend over the lands of others, no wrongful invasion was necessarily involved; the wrong was the taking of game.[89] The anomaly is thus in the writer's classification; a contemporary of Bracton would not perhaps have put these cases here at all.[90]

2. Wrongs to the Person

Assault and battery

This seems to be a late-comer in the royal court. In 1237 an example is found in this form [91]:

> *quare ipsam vulneravit verberavit & maletractavit contra pacem domini Regis.*

That collocation of words, sometimes transposed or with one omitted, and sometimes coupled with a complaint of goods taken [92] or the like, thereafter occurs with increasing frequency; and it was a common form to Bracton.[93] The following example from 1255 shows a new allegation, assault [94]:

> *quare in ipsum insultum fecit & ipsum verberavit & maletractavit contra pacem &c.,*

---

[89] Blackstone, *Comm.* (5th ed.), II, p. 38, says a park extends only over a man's own lands. See also Turner, *Select Pleas of the Forest*, pp. cix et seq., esp. at pp. cxv–cxxii. But the latter's view that the owner of a park had no "property" in the beasts and that the wrong lay in the "trespass" seems too modern. See YB. 3 & 4 Ed. II, Seld. Soc., Vol. 22, pp. 29, 208; see below, p. 28.
[90] Whether there was any class is doubtful; but in 1241 a bunch of essoins are all *de placito quare vi & armis &c.*: C.R.R., XVI, pl. 2556. Cf. Bracton, f. 413.
[91] C.R.R., XVI, pl. 127.
[92] *e.g.*, KB. 26/155, m. 9d.
[93] f. 115.
[94] KB. 26/155, m. 2d.

and this also becomes standard. A compound writ of 1270 has in portmanteau form the further assertions of other enormities and damage [95]:

> *quare in ipsum P insultum dedit & ipsum verberavit & maletractavit & quemdam equum precii 40s. ab eo abstulit & alia dampna enormia ei intulit contra pacem &c.*

The same roll has an entry alleging damage of a stated amount [96]; and an example of the general *ad grave dampnum*, which was to become the commoner,[97] appears in the first year of the new reign.[98]

Vi et armis was not unheard of under Henry III; but it was uncommon, except where, as in the following entry from 1255, an invasion of land was also alleged [99]:

> *quare vi & armis venerunt ad terram ipsius P in A & eidem P insultum fecerunt & homines suos & filias suas verberaverunt & maletractaverunt contra pacem &c.*

Such writs have *vi et armis* perhaps twice as often as not [1]; whereas in cases of pure battery it appears in only about a fifth of the entries in 1260 [2] and 1273,[3] and about a third in 1283 [4]; but it seems to be universal by the end of the century.[5] The common form was then that found in the *Vieux Natura Brevium*.[6] The printed Register [7] and Fitzherbert's *Natura Brevium* [8] embellish the allegation of maltreatment by *ita quod de vita ejus desperabatur*. This was never universal,[9] and is rare under Edward I,[10] and earlier [11]; and it should be added that the appearance of this [12] or other phrases suggestive of serious violence [13] does not necessarily attract *vi et armis*.

---

[95] KB. 26/200A (C.P.), m. 6.   [96] KB. 26/200A, m. 7.
[97] In *Placita Coram Rege, 1297*, there are twelve writs in this form to six naming a figure.
[98] CP. 40/2A, m. 14.
[99] KB. 26/155, m. 3d. *Cf.* Hall, *op. cit.*, at p. 69, writ S6.
[1] They so often allege also the taking of goods that separate figures have not been kept; the combined figures will be found *infra*, **p. 18, n. 56**.
[2] KB. 26/168 (4 cases out of 19); KB. 26/164 (C.P., no cases out of 4).
[3] CP. 40/2A (1 case out of 4); CP. 40/4 (2 cases out of 11).
[4] CP. 40/49 (8 cases out of 24).
[5] *Placita Coram Rege, 1297, passim.*
[6] f. 48.
[7] *Reg.Omn.Brev.*, f. 93.
[8] f. 86I.
[9] See *Liber Intrationum* (1546); both forms appear, at f. 19 and f. 43.
[10] See n. 12, *infra*; CP. 40/49 (1283), mm. 51d, 54; *Placita Coram Rege, 1297*, p. 171.
[11] KB. 26/168 (1260), mm. 2, 5d. *Cf.* KB. 26/201 (1271), m. 7, where it was not the plaintiff whose life was despaired of: X beat Y *ita quod de vita ejus desperabatur*; P's men were taking X to prison *quousque sciretur de convalescentia prefati Y prout moris est in regno*; and DD rescued X. This may explain the phrase.
[12] CP. 40/4 (1273), mm. 2, 52, 53d; *Sel.Cas. in K.B.*, I, p. 30.
[13] KB. 26/167 (1260), m. 22; CP. 40/4, m. 51.

In view of what will be said below it is proper to add that there is no evidence of these writs being used when the harm was indirect, or when it happened during an operation to which the plaintiff had consented. The earliest example noted of indirect harm is the curious writ against a servant for poisoning his mistress. This appears in an entry of 1367 [14] from which the precedent in the Register [15] was evidently taken; the parties were named John, Joan and John, and the Register, with confusing fidelity, uses the initial for all of them. There is, however, one difference: the 1367 entry has *contra pacem*. We shall see that this phrase appears also in the earliest forms of other writs for indirect harm. Of actions arising out of an agreement by the plaintiff, the earliest noted is one against a surgeon in 1364.[16] This will be discussed in a subsequent article.

False imprisonment

The story of this is similar, but it makes an earlier appearance in the rolls. There is in print from 1222 a straightforward action against a constable,[17] and from 1224 [18] and 1225 [19] there are ancestors of the other form in the Register,[20] alleging a holding to ransom. The simplicity of these still prevails in 1241 and 1242 [21]:

> *quare ipsum ceperunt & imprisonaverunt contra pacem domini Regis;*

but by the beginning of the new reign the writ is usually infected by the verbiage of battery [22]:

> *quare ipsum P in campis de A ceperunt & ipsum verberaverunt vulneraverunt & maletractaverunt & imprisonaverunt ad dampnum ipsius P & contra pacem &c.;*

a development which caused trouble with a conscientious jury.[23] From this time also damage is regularly alleged, sometimes with a figure named,[24] more usually by the general *ad grave dampnum*.[25]

---

[14] CP. 40/429, m. 18. There are two entries, one for poisoning the husband himself, the other for poisoning the wife. In form it is a special writ; whether the *cum* clause reciting the service was more than just narrative depends upon whether the wrong was actionable only because of petty treason.
[15] *Reg.Omn.Brev.*, f. 102.   [16] KB. 27/414, m. 37d.
[17] C.R.R., X, p. 324.   [18] C.R.R., XI, pll. 1821, 2383.
[19] *Bracton's Note Book*, pl. 1041.
[20] *Reg.Omn.Brev.*, f. 93.
[21] C.R.R., XVI, pll. 1416, 1457, 1732, 2316.
[22] CP. 40/2A (1273), m. 10. *Cf.* mm. 1, 15. Assault might also be mentioned; CP. 40/48 (1283), m. 45d. The simple form is still sometimes found; *Sel.Cas. in K.B.* II, p. 157 (1293).
[23] YB. 32 & 33 Ed. I, R.S., p. 258.
[24] *Sel.Cas. in K.B.*, II, p. 115 (1292), p. 157 (1293); III, p. 7, (1294), p. 78 (1298).
[25] As in all nine examples in *Placita Coram Rege, 1297*, and *Sel.Cas. in K.B.* III, p. 105 (1301), 147 (1305), 154 (1306).

As with battery, *vi et armis* does not regularly appear until surprisingly late. Except for cases involving an invasion of land and other wrongs,[26] the writer has not actually noted an example earlier than 1283[27]; but by the turn of the century it is almost always present.[28]

These wrongs done to servants

As where the wrong was done to the plaintiff himself, the earliest cases are of imprisonment; examples are in print from 1222 onward.[29] The formulation was often more loquacious[30] than in the ordinary writs for battery and false imprisonment, but with the same key phrases.[31]

Damage is specifically alleged in 1270[32]; and Britton insists that the master may recover only for his own loss of service.[33] This restriction, which no doubt gave rise to the *per quod servitium amisit* form,[34] is not found earlier. Bracton had said that the master could recover for the insult even if he had suffered no loss[35]; and at least one early case seems to contemplate the master's having damages on behalf of his men.[36]

Abduction

If the classification were other than arbitrary this topic, and the one preceding, would perhaps fit better with wrongs to goods. The rolls yield many examples, often of dramatic rather than legal interest; but it may be useful to record the principal varieties.

Ravishment of ward, which will not be discussed now, was the commonest. Abduction of sons, on the other hand, seems rare. *Bracton's Note Book* tells of a house entered *vi et armis* in 1238, and the son taken *a posse Domini Regis* into Wales and there held to ransom[37]; but no other entries have been noted until one of 1352[38]:

[26] KB. 26/168. (1260), m. 16d; CP. 40/4 (1273), m. 35.
[27] CP. 40/49: present on m. 55d, absent on mm. 5d, 11d, 23, 50d. KB. 26/168 (1260), and CP. 40/2A (1273) had six entries each, all without *vi et armis*.
[28] All nine writs in *Placita Coram Rege, 1297*, have it; and so have *Sel.Cas. in K.B.*, II, p. 157 (1293), and III, p. 7 (1294); p. 78 (1298); p. 147 (1305); p. 154 (1306); but not II, p. 115 (1292), or III, p. 105 (1301).
[29] C.R.R., X, p. 350 (1222); XI, pll. 2303, 2837 (1224); *Bracton's Note Book*, pl. 314 (1229).
[30] *e.g.*, C.R.R., XVI, pll. **1204, 1325** ; KB. 26/161 (1260), m. 22.
[31] *e.g.*, C.R.R., XVI, pl. **1234**.
[32] KB. 26/200A (C.P.), m. 6 (*ad grave dampnum*). *Cf.* CP. 40/2A (1273), m. 2 (figure stated); and CP. 40/8 (1275), m. 22 (*in ipsius P dampnum non modicum*).
[33] (ed. Nichols), I, p. 131.
[34] As to which see Mr. Gareth Jones's article (1958) 74 L.Q.R. p. 39.
[35] f. 115.
[36] *Bracton's Note Book*, pl. 1121 (1234–35); *cf.* KB. 26/201 (1271), m. 7 (*ad grave dampnum ipsius P & hominum suorum*).
[37] *Bracton's Note Book*, pl. 1232.
[38] CP. 40/373, m. 17. *Cf. Reg.Omn.Brev.*, ff. 98d, 99; Pollock and Maitland, II, p. 444; YB. 9 Ed. II, Seld. Soc., Vol. 45, p. 28.

quare vi & armis X primogenitum filium ipsius P infra etatem existentem cujus matrimonium ad ipsum P pertinet apud A inventum ceperunt & abduxerunt & bona & catalla sua . . . ceperunt & asportaverunt & alia enormia ei intulerunt ad grave dampnum ipsius P & contra pacem Regis &c.

Many actions were started in the mid-fourteenth century for the abduction of wives, using the standard writ *de uxore abducta cum bonis viri* based upon the Statutes of Westminster.[39] That a remedy existed at common law [40] appears from a curious case of 1241. There is no mention of chattels taken; one William was to answer [41]:

quare domum predicti X in A de nocte nequiter fregit & predictam Matillidem contra voluntatem ipsius P inde abduxit & contra pacem domini Regis.

And in the preceding entry Matilda, the plaintiff's wife, was to answer:

quare prebuit assensum Willelmo . . . ad domum X in A de nocte nequiter frangendam & se ipsam inde abducendam contra voluntatem ipsius P & contra pacem domini Regis.

William made fine for both of them. Curious in the bookseller's sense was a 1255 case of the ravishment of a lady whose relationship to the plaintiff was a matter of dispute.[42]

Prisoners were liable to be snatched from their jailers. Lucky ones were rescued [43]; others were hanged by rival franchise owners [44]; and sometimes the writ does not disclose the defendant's purpose.[45] Into the same category perhaps comes the rescue of a fugitive villein [46]; but the commoner writs for the abduction of villeins [47] or servants [48] are more interesting. In 1359 five defendants were to answer [49]:

quare vi & armis bona & catalla ipsius P ad valenciam £60 apud A inventa ceperunt & asportaverunt & X nativum suum apud B in servicio suo existentem ceperunt & abduxerunt & alia

---

[39] Ibid., f. 97. Stats.Westm.: I, c. 13; II, c. 34. *Cf. Sel.Cas. in K.B.*, III, p. 100 (1300).
[40] See Fitzherbert, *Natura Brevium*, f. 52K; Coke, 2 Inst. 434; Blackstone, Comm. (5th ed.), III, p. 139. *Cf.* Plucknett, *Legislation of Ed. I*, p. 121.
[41] C.R.R., XVI, pll. 1532, 1694, 1756.
[42] KB. 26/155, m. 5.
[43] *e.g.*, KB. 26/201 (1271), m. 7; CP. 40/370 (1352), m. 122.
[44] *Bracton's Note Book*, pl. 821 (1233); KB. 26/146 (1252), m. 1d.
[45] *e.g.*, C.R.R., XVI, pl. 1207.
[46] *Reg.Omn.Brev.*, ff. 100d, 101; KB. 27/405 (1362), m. 41d.
[47] *e.g.*, CP. 40/399 (1359), mm. 28d, 62, 86d, 185d.
[48] *e.g.*, CP. 40/399, m. 112; YB. Mich. 39 Ed. III, m. 37d.
[49] CP. 40/399, m. 144d. There is no mention of the Statute of Labourers.

enormia ei intulerunt ad grave dampnum ipsius P & contra pacem Regis.

Four pleaded not guilty. The fifth *dicit quod quo ad venire vi et armis et de bonis asportatis non est culpabilis. Et quo ad capcionem et abductionem predicti X, dicit quod idem X predictis die et anno fuit communis operarius, videlicet carpentarius, et fecit conventionem cum predicto D ex libera voluntate sua tanquam extra servicium alicujus . . . absque hoc quod ipse predictum X nativum &c. cepit & abduxit sicut predictus P superius versus eum narravit.* The plea sounds like one of mistake as to X's position; and it seems that in such cases, as in those of ravishment of ward or abduction of a wife, the taking could be peaceful. By the sixteenth century, at any rate, the action for procuring a servant to leave his master was regarded as one in case [50]; but an honest writ for enticing away a wife [51] was not invented until our concept of trespass was being formulated in words.

3. Wrongs to Goods

De bonis asportatis

Cases in which a plaintiff's goods have been taken from the plaintiff himself are interesting only for the incidence of *vi et armis*. Two examples are in print from 1220, in both of which there were invasions of land and this phrase appears.[52] In 1241 a similar writ [53] may be contrasted with another in which there was no invasion and no *vi et armis* [54]; and this contrast can be matched in 1255.[55] In 1260 and 1273 entries alleging an invasion have *vi et armis* about twice as often as not [56]; those not alleging an invasion hardly ever have it.[57] By 1283 the phrase is in almost all entries of the former kind, and about a third of the latter.[58] By the turn of the century it seems to be universal in both kinds.[59] Damage is generally, though not invariably, alleged by 1270.[60]

---

[50] Gareth Jones, *op. cit.*, at p. 45. The view now proposed confirms, so far as it goes, Mr. Gareth Jones's suspicions about the early history of the procurement action.
[51] *Winsmore* v. *Greenbank* (1745) Willes 577.
[52] C.R.R., VIII, p. 204, and *Bracton's Note Book*, pl. 85; C.R.R., VIII, p. 394.
[53] *Infra*, p. 19, n. 61.   [54] C.R.R., XVI, pl. 1826.
[55] KB. 26/155, mm. 5d, 10d (invasion and *vi & armis*); m. 9d (neither).
[56] See p. 14, n. 1, *supra*. In KB. 26/168 (1260) it occurs in twenty-five entries out of thirty-six; in CP. 40/2A (1273) in fifteen entries out of twenty-three. A genuinely violent invasion may not attract *vi et armis*; CP. 40/2A, m. 5.
[57] KB. 26/168, no entries out of ten; CP. 40/2A (1273), one entry out of nine.
[58] CP. 40/49, seventeen entries out of nineteen, and seven out of twenty-two, respectively.
[59] *Placita Coram Rege, 1297*, pp. 3, 30, 94, 96 (invasion); pp. 66, 95, 151, 178 (no invasion).
[60] e.g., KB. 26/200A (C.P.), mm. 5, 6 (*ad grave dampnum*); CP. 40/2A m. 19 (*in dampnum ipsius P non modicum & gravamen*); CP. 40/4 (1273), m. 26d (*in grave prejudicium predicti executoris*); CP. 40/8 (1275), m. 39d (no allegation).

Cases in which the goods did not belong to the man from whom they were taken may be interesting in themselves. Either party might take action. In the following, from 1241, the plaintiff sues the defendants for taking his master's goods from his custody, in the house of a third party [61]:

> quare vi & armis ingressi sunt domum X & inde asportaverunt blada domini sui que fuerunt in custodia sua contra pacem domini Regis.

From the following year comes an example of the converse situation [62]:

> quare occasione cujusdam debiti quod X debuit predicto D [principal defendant] res & mercandisas ipsius P ad valenciam 26m. quas idem P dimiserat in custodia predicti X in nundinis sancti Edmundi ceperunt & eas inde contra pacem domini Regis asportaverunt & predictas res & mercandisas suas asportatas injuste detinent &c.

A writ of 1255, for taking animals from a servant on the way to market, is the earliest noted mentioning damage to the plaintiff [63]; this may first have seemed necessary when he himself was not the immediate victim. For broadly similar facts a century later there was a special writ [64]:

> quare cum idem P quandam literam suam absolutionis sigillo officiali episcopi Wyntonie consignatam X servienti suo tradidisset custodiendam predictus D literam illam prefato X apud A vi & armis abstulit & alia enormia ei intulit ad grave dampnum ipsius P £20 & contra pacem Regis.

When the special writs are considered, similar *cum* clauses will be seen playing a more exciting part.

Damage: (a) By fire

There is a quantity of material about damage to goods, and it has therefore been split up according to the way in which the damage was done. The category is in its nature likely to raise questions about mental elements; and it will also raise the question whether the plaintiff's action was barred if the defendant had come to the property with his consent. The first subdivision, that of damage by fire, will include damage to houses as well as goods.

[61] C.R.R., XVI, pl. 1585.
[62] C.R.R., XVI, pl. 1933.
[63] KB. 26/155 (1255), m. 1d.
[64] CP. 40/399 (1359), m. 220d.

It will be best to begin with a curiosity from the Common Pleas in 1260 [65]:

> quare cum ipsi P & P uxor ejus profecti fuerunt Londinium pro negotiis suis eadem D sine voluntate predictorum PP quandam domum suam in A fraudulenter ingressi sunt (sic) & ignem ibidem accendit ita quod per ejus incuriam dicta domus valoris 45s. fuit combusta & catalla sua ad valenciam 30s. devastata fuerunt unde eam appellant &c.

This may chiefly be relevant in considering the relationship, or the meanings, of trespass and appeal; but it should also warn us that the terseness of orthodox trespass writs may be misleading. Take, as examples, a pair from 1273 [66]:

> quare bona & catalla ipsius P apud A inventa ad valenciam 10m. combussit ad ipsius P dispendium & gravamen non modicum;

and [67]:

> quare cartas ipsius P combusserunt ad dampnum ipsius P & contra pacem domini Regis H. patris domini Regis nunc.

The first is an *op. se*,[68] so we do not know the facts. *Contra pacem* may have been left out because of the demise of the crown, actually referred to in the second entry; but it is notable that damage is alleged in the form most common in the viscontiel writs of trespass.[69] In the second case it appears from the count that the burning was deliberate.[70] But nothing about the nature of the wrong can be deduced from the words of the writ or the presence of *contra pacem*. In 1290 a similar writ complains of another fire, and a more serious one both for the parties and for us [71]:

> quare domos ipsius P apud A & bona & catalla sua ibidem existencia ad valenciam £200 conbusserunt & alia enormia &c. ad grave dampnum ipsius P & contra pacem &c.

This was not deliberate. The defendants were guests of the plaintiff, and they went to sleep leaving a candle burning. He said that the fire happened *per eorum insipienciam et malam custodiam*, they

---

[65] KB. 26/164, m. 16d.
[66] CP. 40/2A, m. 12d.
[67] CP. 40/4, m. 30d.
[68] *P optulit se iiijto die versus D . . .* The entry begins like this if the defendant did not appear; it contains nothing but the writ and directions for further process. Such entries make up the bulk of the plea rolls.
[69] *Reg.Omn.Brev.*, ff. 92–93.
[70] The defendants had taken the charters home and burned them there. *Cf.* a case of 1255 in which the writ speaks of coming and burning houses and carrying off goods; KB. 26/155, m. 3d.
[71] *Sel.Cas. in K.B.*, I, p. 181. *Cf. Bracton*, f. 146d: *. . . incendia fortuita, vel per negligentiam facta, et non mala consciencia, non . . . puniuntur quia civiliter agitur contra tales.*

(214)

that it was *per infortunum*; the jury returned a special verdict, and we do not know what was decided. The writ could therefore be had, and had in the same general form, whether the fire was deliberate or not, and whether it was started by an invader or a guest. Seven years later there is an example, also in print,[72] specifically alleging malice; and though no other examples of this have been noted in writs for burning, there are many in writs for other sorts of damage. If its presence means anything, so may its absence.

The 1297 writ had not only malice but also *vi et armis*, which allegation was by then being put into all the writs so far considered. The question is whether it had any effect. The writ for burning in the Register [73] is a colourless *vi et armis* with no mention of malice, and in the plea rolls the writer has noted only *op. ses* which say nothing of the circumstances.[74] But a Year Book case of 1374 seems to show that the writ would avail against a tenant at will who burned the place down by negligence [75]; and if so the insertion of *vi et armis* had not altered the law from what it had been in 1290 when the guests went to sleep with their candle burning. The plaintiff could call it *vi et armis* and *contra pacem* if a defendant, in his house with his consent, burned it down unintentionally.

Damage: (b) By animals

Depasturing is an example which has already been discussed under wrongs to land. The usual early use of that writ was against persons claiming common, when the act would always be deliberate; but it lay for a mere escape, certainly after 1353 and perhaps before.[76]

Other cases noted are all of one kind: animals belonging to the plaintiff have been injured by the defendant's dogs. Dr. Glanville Williams considered that, until the introduction of the *scienter* writ, the defendant was liable only if he had set his dogs on to do the damage.[77] This fits in precisely with the notion of trespass as a direct injury; and, what is more important, it fits in with the words of the writ. The form in the Register says explicitly that the

---

[72] *Placita Coram Rege, 1297*, p. 168.
[73] *Reg.Omn.Brev.*, f. 110.
[74] *e.g.*, CP. 40/370, m. 78; CP. 40/371, mm. 8, 53, 98; CP. 40/373, mm. 1, 42d; KB. 27/380, m. 7d.
[75] YB. Mich. 48 Ed. III, pl. 8, f. 25. The jury found that the burning was not *vi & armis*, and was by negligence not malice; and the question was whether the defendant was tenant at will or for years. The argument is that if she was tenant for years, the writ should be waste. On the negligence aspect, *cf.* the verdict on a bill in 42 *Lib.Ass.*, pl. 9, f. 259d, and (in waste) YB. 21 & 22 Ed. I., R.S., p. 28.
[76] *Supra*, p. 10.
[77] *Liability for Animals*, pp. 277 et seq.

defendant chased the beasts with his dogs, inciting the dogs to bite.[78]

This form is found in 1321,[79] and appears to have been standard for harm done by dogs until *scienter*. It was not common[80]; but the writer has come across only one example in which incitement was not alleged. That case may suggest, however, that the writ did not always mean exactly what it said: it was an action in 1352 for breaking the plaintiff's fold and chasing his sheep,[81] and may be compared with a case twenty years earlier in the Year Books,[82] on similar facts, in which incitement to bite was alleged. The Year Book case was substantially a dispute about the defendant's right to free fold,[83] and the defendant had come to drive the plaintiff's sheep off to his own fold. The dogs were being deliberately used as sheep-dogs, but it is unlikely that they were meant to bite the sheep.[84]

To that extent at least, then, the words of the writ were not in every case to be taken literally; and indeed the wrong actually denoted must have been rare. But still the application of the dogs was deliberate, and the question arises whether the writ was ever available when they were in no sense set on by their master. That it probably was so in 1364 appears from an entry in which the writ consists first of the standard formula for hunting in the plaintiff's free warren, and secondly of the standard formula for chasing his sheep, inciting the dogs to bite; and the count makes it clear that these were not unconnected events.[85] The writer knows of one landowner with a propensity for shooting sheep if no better game presents itself, but this cannot be a common foible; the likely explanation of the entry is that the dogs were taken onto the plaintiff's land to hunt hares and so forth, and worried his sheep as a venture of their own. A case of the following year puts the matter beyond doubt. It is recorded in the *postea* to such a writ that the justices at *nisi prius* asked the jury to supplement their verdict on incitement by saying whether the dogs concerned had previously been in the habit of biting like this, *absque aliqua*

---

[78] *Reg.Omn.Brev.*, f. 97 (two variants).
[79] *Plac.Abb.*, p. 337b. The allegation of incitement has been omitted, but it appears on the roll; KB. 27/244, m. 71.
[80] About four entries a term in 1352: CP. 40/370, mm. 26d, 74d, 100, 155d, 156d; CP. 40/371, mm. 12, 122, 223, 240; CP. 40/373, mm. 75d, 96, 97; and in 1359: CP. 40/399, mm. 55, 120d, 153d, 215.
[81] CP. 40/371, m. 56.
[82] YB. Hil. 3 Ed. III, pl. 7, f. 3.
[83] This will be discussed in connection with special writs.
[84] Indeed they may not have bitten them. *Cf.* entries of 1359 in which the defendant is sued for chasing sheep himself, *verberando*, and causing their deaths; there is no mention of dogs; CP. 40/399, mm. 89, 204d. The real wrong was probably the over-driving.
[85] KB. 27/414, m. 24.

excitatione. The jury said no, and judgment was given for the defendant.[86]

This last case seems to establish that, in 1365 at any rate, the incitement writ was being used to impose a liability like that of *scienter*; and the asking of the question at *nisi prius* perhaps suggests that this was no innovation. But if it was not new, no earlier chinks have yet been found in the screen presented by the standard form. Nor can we learn much from forms used before the standard writ developed, except that they do not mention incitement. An example of 1283 is colourless [87]:

> *quare cyngnos ipsius P in A cum canibus suis occiderunt ad dampnum ipsius P 100s. & contra pacem &c.*

The entries are *op. ses*, and there is no way of telling whether this was a swan-hunt by the defendants or a frolic by their dogs. The case mentioned above of the unintended fire [88] makes it difficult to exclude the latter on *a priori* grounds; and if it was deliberate the writ is reticent in comparison with that provoked by an undoubted swan-hunt, with nets instead of dogs, in the same year [89]:

> *quare septem cyngnos ipsius P apud A existentes cum retibus & aliis ingeniis suis maliciose ceperunt & asportaverunt & alia enormia ei intulerunt ad grave dampnum ipsius P £20 & contra pacem &c.*

We shall see under the next heading that allegations of malice were common in writs for doing damage; and it is at least possible that their presence or absence might mean something. Indeed, *maliciose* appears in the earliest known occurrence of the standard incitement writ itself, in 1321 [90]; the writer has seen no other example of this. Perhaps the formula was worked out for a particular case of truly deliberate harm, and then adopted as standard; and it may from the beginning have been used, as it evidently was in 1365, in situations for which it was not literally appropriate, but in which the defendant was in some fairly obvious sense a wrongdoer. It is even possible that for genuinely malicious harm the writ came to seem inadequate; in 1353 there was an entry [91]:

> *quare vi & armis triginta oves ipsius P precii 100 s. apud A inventas cum quibusdam canibus maliciose interfecit & alia*

[86] KB. 27/418, m. 10; Dyer, 25d; Glanville Williams, *op. cit.*, p. 277, n. 15.
[87] CP. 40/48, m. 28d; CP. 40/50, m. 40d.
[88] *Supra*, p. 20.
[89] CP. 40/49, m. 5. *Cf.* KB. 26/168 (1260), m. 11d.
[90] KB. 27/244, m. 71.
[91] CP. 40/373, m. 153d.

> *enormia ei intulit ad grave dampnum ipsius P & contra pacem &c.*

This, however, seems unique, and may just have been copied from an old precedent.

We pass now to the *scienter* writ, which turns out to appear earlier than has been supposed.[92] This one is from 1367[93]:

> *quare quosdam canes ad mordendum oves consuetos scienter retinuit qui quidem canes centum oves ipsius P apud A inventas tam graviter momorderunt quod quadraginta oves precii 100s. de ovibus predictis interierunt & oves residue intantum deteriorate fuerunt quod idem P proficuum falde sue ibidem de ovibus predictis per magnum tempus amisit & alia enormia ei intulit ad dampnum ipsius P £10 & contra pacem Regis.*

Rastell has been castigated[94] for starting a muddle when he put *scienter* together with the incitement writ under the heading of trespass[95]; but history seems to be on his side. In the first place the writ above has *contra pacem*. These words evidently caused a difficulty: they are taken out in 1373,[96] put back again in 1387,[97] and have finally gone from the forms in the Register.[98] Moreover, if the writ is compared with the incitement writ[99] it will be observed that the resemblance is not confined to *contra pacem*: only the *scienter* opening is different. Finally, we have just seen that in 1365, two years earlier, there was an incitement action in which the justices had found it necessary to ask, not only about incitement, but also *si canes predicti hujusmodi morsus facere ex consuetudine antea exstiterant absque aliqua excitatione.*[1] It seems that the novelty was the writ, not the liability; that the invention of the *scienter* form was a rebellion against inappropriate standard words, and marks a fit of honesty rather than a change in the law.

Damage: (c) By other means

It will be convenient to take first the largest category: damage to the plaintiff's animals done by the defendant himself rather

---

[92] Dr. Glanville Williams knew of one in 1387: *op. cit.*, p. 278; Dr. Kiralfy in 1373: *Action on the Case*, p. 101.
[93] CP. 40/429, m. 357.
[94] By Dr. Glanville Williams, *op. cit.*, p. 280.
[95] *Entrees* (1574), f. 558: *Trespas per misfesans de chien*. He has a cross-reference under *Accion sur le case*, at f. 3.
[96] Kiralfy, *op. cit.*, p. 101.
[97] Glanville Williams, *op. cit.*, p. 278.
[98] *Reg.Omn.Brev.*, ff. 110d, 111.
[99] e.g, *Reg.Omn.Brev.*, f. 97.
[1] *Supra*, pp. 22-3.

than by his dogs. The basic formula may be exemplified by this entry of 1352 [2]:

quare vi & armis quoddam jumentum ipsius P precii 4 m. apud A inventum interfecit & alia enormia ei intulit ad grave dampnum ipsius P & contra pacem Regis.

Apart from the kind and value of the animal, the only important internal variation is that sometimes there is inserted before *interfecit* the word *maliciose;* the same roll furnishes an example.[3] There is, however, an external variation: the writ may or may not also allege other wrongs. Four possibilities are thus opened, and it may be worth recording the writer's impression of their relative frequency.

Malicious killing accompanied by no other wrong seems rare.[4] Coupled with some other wrong such as depasturing,[5] or *de bonis asportatis*,[6] or impounding without cause,[7] it seems slightly commoner. Rather more common again is killing accompanied by other wrongs and not specifically said to be malicious; the accompanying wrongs noted have been depasturing,[8] *de bonis asportatis*,[9] battery of the plaintiff's servant,[10] and an evidently violent invasion.[11] Much the commonest of all, however, are cases of killing with no other wrong and no malice mentioned, the writs being exactly in the basic form printed above. The victims noted include a falcon, two nesting swans, sixteen pigs, twenty goats, three cows and twenty sheep, two foals and two bullocks,[12] and many separate single horses.[13] The problem is to guess at the facts which lay behind these entries. Malicious killing of beasts accompanied by depasturing sounds like an excess committed during some dispute over rights of common; but what of a horse killed

---

[2] CP. 40/371, m. 144; *cf. Reg.Omn.Brev.*, f. 109. This form crystallised about 1300. As early as 1260 an example is found in which damage to the plaintiff is specifically alleged: KB. 26/167, m. 17 (swan).
[3] CP. 40/371, m. 2 (a horse).
[4] Beside the case mentioned above, the writer has noted only two examples: *Placita Coram Rege, 1297*, p. 104 (pigs); CP. 40/370, m. 148 (another horse).
[5] CP. 40/373, m. 119; CP. 40/399, m. 85d. *Cf.* CP. 40/370, m. 12d: *maliciose* is not used, but the defendants killed four of the plaintiff's pigs and *contemptibiliter* cut off the tails of ten others, as well as depasturing with their own beasts.
[6] CP. 40/373, m. 185; CP. 40/399, m. 57.
[7] CP. 40/370, m. 12d.
[8] CP. 40/373, m. 60d; CP. 40/399, m. 161.
[9] CP. 40/373, m. 168d; CP. 40/399, mm. 155d, 189d. *Cf.* CP. 40/371, m. 138: killing pigs, digging, and removing the earth.
[10] CP. 40/371, m. 203; CP. 40/399, m. 19.
[11] CP. 40/399, mm. 80, 103.
[12] CP. 40/373, m. 71; CP. 40/371, m. 13; CP. 40/370, m. 101; CP. 40/312, m. 47; CP. 40/399, m. 63; CP. 40/370, m. 126d, in that order.
[13] CP. 40/370, mm. 35d, 46, 73d; CP. 40/371, m. 144; CP. 40/373, mm. 57d, 94; CP. 40/399, mm. 35, 135d, 155, 210; KB. 27/405, m. 23; KB. 27/414, m. 50d.

with no malice mentioned? Could it, for example, have been an accident? And is there any possibility that, as with *scienter*, the facts of some later and more explicit writ are blanketed under the common form?

Two pairs of explicit writs may throw light on these questions. An entry in 1352 speaks of chasing the plaintiff's horse into a fenland marsh in which it died, and of battery of his servants.[14] It is *contra pacem* but not *vi et armis*, and may be compared with an entry of 1367 curious enough to print [15]:

> *quare magnam quantitatem luti juxta pasturam ipsius P apud A projecerunt ita quod per projectionem hujusmodi & defectum predictorum DD unus equus & duo pullani predicti P precii 10 m. de pastura predicta in lutum predictum incedentes in eodem interierunt & alia enormia &c. ad grave dampnum &c. & contra pacem &c.*

This also, it should be noted, is *contra pacem*. The two cases look to us widely different; but if what really happened in the earlier was that the horse bolted because of some uproar, which seems more likely than that it was deliberately driven into a fen, they may not have looked so different to contemporaries. The use of *contra pacem* suggests that, as with *scienter*, the later writ was not a completely new departure; and it would hardly have seemed worth trying unless there was some background of liability for unintended harm.

Another pair of entries is more important, and displays a clearer parallel with *scienter*. The later member is the writ in the farrier's case.[16] It is an *op. se* of 1371, a year before the report, and shows that the Year Book has the words substantially right [17]:

> *quare quemdam clavem in vivum pedis cujusdam equi ipsius P apud A fixit per quod idem P proficuum equi sui predicti per magnum tempus amisit & alia &c. & ad dampnum ipsius P 40s. &c.*

This general form was later replaced by forms containing special matter,[18] but it is the earlier history which is our present concern. Dr. Kiralfy noted that before 1372 there were *vi et armis* actions against smiths [19]; and of the dozen or so examples noted by the

---

[14] CP. 40/373, m. 78.
[15] CP. 40/429, m. 576.
[16] YB. Trin. 46 Ed. III, pl. 19, f. 19.
[17] CP. 40/443, m. 133.
[18] *Reg.Omn.Brev.*, f. 106; Fitzherbert, *Natura Brevium*, f. 94D.
[19] *Action on the Case*, p. 142. Dr. Kiralfy thought that these were actions for deliberate injury, that a plea denying "trespass against the peace as alleged" may indicate an attempted extension to negligent injury, and that this may have led to the abandonment of the *vi et armis* form. Even for deliberate harm this would not fit with our idea of trespass. But surely few smiths would deliberately injure their customers' animals.

writer of the ordinary writ for killing a horse, two named smiths as defendant, one in 1352 [20] and the other in 1359.[21] The 1352 writ is actually that transcribed first under this heading to exemplify the basic formula.[22] Fate could hardly be so mischievous as to set a lot of smiths throwing stones, or the like, at strangers' horses; and it seems likely that these were actions for professional misdeeds. This is made reasonably certain by a more explicit writ in 1352, an earlier version of that used in the farrier's case [23]:

quare vi & armis duos claves in vivo pedis cujusdam equi ipsius P apud A fixit ita quod per fixuram illorum equus predictus precii 50s. interiit & alia enormia &c. & contra pacem Regis.

The defendant is again said to be a smith; and the only room for doubt is that the entry is an *op. se.* Doubt will be felt: it is shocking to us that a *vi et armis* writ could be used against one who had come to the object with the plaintiff's consent. Other indications to the same effect will, however, be noted when actions against bailees are considered; the writs are mostly in special form, and must therefore be deferred to a later part of this study.

It turns out, then, that we cannot take the straightforward writs for killing animals at their face value; we are not entitled to assume that we know even roughly what happened. This must be true also of writs for damage other than to animals, which, it may be remarked, are less common. One example will be given to illustrate the difficulty. In 1353 a Henley butcher was to answer a plaintiff from Harwell [24]:

quare vi & armis quoddam doleum vini ipsius P precii £10 apud A inventum fregit per quod vinum in eodem doleo contentum totaliter emanavit & alia enormia ei intulit ad grave dampnum ipsius P & contra pacem Regis.

Possible explanations seem to range from a deliberate act to something like *Coggs* v. *Bernard*. Nor is the reticence of a standard form peculiar to writs. The pleadings in this case are typical: to a formal count, adding to the writ only a date, a ficticious array of weapons, and a claim of £20 in damages, the defendant *defendit vim & injuriam quando &c. Et dicit quod non fecit predicto P predictam trangressionem contra pacem Regis sicut idem P versus eum superius narravit. Et de hoc ponit se super patriam . . .* And so to the country, whose verdict, even when it is recorded,

[20] CP. 40/371, m. 144.
[21] CP. 40/399, m. 210.
[22] *Supra*, p. 25.
[23] CP. 40/371, m. 135.
[24] CP. 40/373, m. 15.

which in this case it is not, will normally consist only of another blank door: guilty or not guilty. We are peering through keyholes.

4. SOME CONCLUSIONS

Certain conclusions may at this stage be drawn from the material so far considered. The first is obvious, and is not news. *Vi et armis* did not necessarily mean what it said. In 1304 Bereford disregarded an express finding, in a verdict for the plaintiff, that the wrong had not been done *vi et armis*.[25] In 1310 a doweress brought a *vi et armis* action against the owner for hunting in his own park and taking every third deer. To the defendant's protest that he could not come with force and arms to his own park, counsel for the plaintiff says: *Coment qe nous avoms fait mencioun de venir &c. ceus sount que paroulles &c. Force et armes ne doynent cause de damage, einz le trespas &c.*; and the court agreed with him.[26] The formality of the allegation is exposed also in the counts, where, in the fourteenth century, it was always meticulously elaborated; but the elaborations were as standard as the phrase itself. In the Common Pleas the formula was almost invariable: *vi et armis scilicet gladiis arcubus et sagittis*. In the King's Bench it was commonly *scilicet gladiis &c.*; and if the *&c.* was expanded it was generally with rough things like clubs, hardly ever with bows and arrows.

A second conclusion has not been obvious. At any rate in some writs there never was a time when *vi et armis* did mean what it said. We can no longer suppose the gradual formalisation of words once literally true in all cases. This appears most clearly from the writs for wrongful hunting. The evidence is that the phrase was originally in some sense at home in cases involving an invasion of the plaintiff's land, and that it was imported wholesale into the other forms during the closing years of the thirteenth century. This importation, for which a reason will be suggested below, was followed promptly by the cases just mentioned in which the words were disregarded.

Another conclusion depends upon the cases of damage to property. At any rate in the fourteenth century, *vi et armis* had not even the attenuated effect we give it today, an effect which has long seemed to the writer to suppose an unlikely sort of sophistication so early in the career of trespass. But some disingenuousness is inherent in the material; the impression of peering

---

[25] YB. 32 & 33 Ed. I, R.S., p. 258. *Cf.* the preceding case, in which the jury expressly denied the formal allegations of battery in a writ of false imprisonment (*supra*, p. 15, n. 23).

[26] YB. 3 & 4 Ed. II, Seld.Soc., Vol. 22, pp. 29, 208, xxxv. The writ is special in form. Note the sense of trespass.

through keyholes at something we are not meant to see is too strong to be the result of coincidence. We are up against a kind of fiction. A part of what has been taken as the beginnings of case, in the years around 1367, turns out to be after all not a series of new departures in the law; it was the abandonment of standard forms in certain particularly inappropriate cases, the abandonment of disguises. The farrier's case, for example, was indeed what the Year Book reporter made of it, an argument about the form of a writ [27]; the liability had been enforced under cover of a general writ for many years.

All this can hardly have been to baffle legal historians, so who was to be deceived? Probably nobody. The aim of fictions, even of much more whole-hearted ones than these, is not deception; it is to keep records straight: without the fiction the proceedings would be improperly constituted. What might have been improper about an action started by the writ in the farrier's case, but twenty years earlier? The likely answer is, not that the farrier had committed no wrong, but that it was a wrong over which the court should not take jurisdiction. It would be no surprise to the writer if the 1352 writ, *quare vi et armis claves fixit*,[28] was indeed quashed, not because it disclosed no wrong, but for precisely the quality that makes it useful to us: you can see through it; and what you see is a different kind of wrong.

Upon this basis some synthesis may be attempted of the facts concerning general writs. Whatever else was involved in the origins of trespass, Professor Plucknett has made one thing clear: what was going on in the thirteenth century was not primarily a process of invention by the royal judges; it was a shift in jurisdiction.[29] Wrongs had been dealt with elsewhere, and now they were beginning to flow into the king's courts. It will be common ground that the flow was regulated in general by considerations of the royal interest; and the most comprehensive interest for this purpose was preserving the peace. This was probably the ticket by which all the standard general writs came in, though it might be liberally understood; an entry of 1275, for example, complains of the *contra pacem* breaking of a bridge, to the inconvenience of the plaintiff and the men of the countryside.[30] Again in the writs for depasturing [31] and for hunting,[32] to name two, *contra pacem* cannot have meant much more than unlawfully; and it cannot have meant anything more in the action against the guests who unintentionally burned the house down.[33] Under Henry III, indeed, there was

[27] YB. Trin. 46 Ed. III, pl. 19, f. 19.
[28] *Supra*, p. 27.
[29] *Concise History* (5th ed.), p. 370.
[30] CP. 40/8, m. 20d.
[31] *Supra*, p. 8.
[32] *Supra*, p. 12.
[33] *Supra*, p. 20-21.

probably little theory about the matter: in 1242 an action was entered against a pledgee for what we should call conversion, no breach of the peace being alleged.[34]

In the last years of the thirteenth century, however, the element of breach of the peace was emphasised: within little more than a decade *vi et armis* was put into all the general writs. Why? An answer is suggested by the Statute of Gloucester in 1278, which was intended to reduce the flow of trespass actions into the royal courts: they were not to hear cases in which less than 40s. was in dispute.[35] The same spirit may have demanded a royal interest in trespass actions.[36] If so it met a similar fate. The statute came to be misconstrued as setting a ceiling to other jurisdictions; and *vi et armis*, if its insertion had ever narrowed the scope of any writ, became ineffective; became indeed a cloak under which actions went into the royal court. The flow was not to be arrested. What happened about 1367 was, in part, the acceptance of this fact. Plaintiffs might bring their cases in without wrapping them up in formal lies; though even then there was hesitation about dropping *contra pacem* itself.[37]

The rift between the view proposed and the received notion of early trespass development is, at this point, exceedingly narrow. But it is deep. Even if the preservation of the peace was the only ticket which might admit wrongs to the royal court, it would not follow that the concept of wrong was confined to those so admitted, or that they formed the entity which we call trespass today. There would still, for example, be those viscontiel writs of trespass, put first in the printed Register,[38] which must have been trespasses at common law even if the actions were heard in other courts; and the exclusive factor would still be the external one of jurisdiction, and nothing in the nature of trespass itself. Moreover, as will be shown in the next article, some special writs, equally writs of trespass, came into the royal court for quite other reasons. The preservation of the peace was not the only ground on which the king's judges might concern themselves with wrongs.

---

[34] C.R.R., XVI, pl. 2241.   A remarkable entry: the executor of X brings a writ *quare vendidit de averiis que fuerunt X qui ei tenebatur in 25 m. ultra valorem predictarum 25 m. ut dicitur*. X was presumably dead before the sale.
[35] 6 Edw. I, c. 8.
[36] *Cf.* the adoption of the rule requiring a seal in covenant.
[37] See the writ for poisoning, *supra*, p. 15; the *scienter* writ, *supra*, p. 24; and the curious writ for leaving mud, *supra*, p. 26. We shall find *contra pacem* making improbable appearances at about the same time in certain special writs.
[38] *Reg.Omn.Brev.*, ff. 92–93.

PART II: SPECIAL WRITS

THIS is the second of three articles tracing the development of early trespass writs. The proposition is that in the thirteenth and fourteenth centuries there was no entity equivalent to our tort of trespass, and that the only concept denoted by the word trespass was the elementary one of wrong. It was a generic term; had there been a medieval *Salmond* or *Winfield*, trespass would have been the title, not of a chapter, but of the book.

The first article dealt with general writs [1]; and it was suggested that their common element, the allegation of breach of the peace, was due not to some property of trespass but to the external factor of jurisdiction. The king's courts were meant to hear only those trespasses in which the king had an interest, and the commonest interest for this purpose was preservation of the peace. It was suggested also that general writs making such allegations might be used, as it were, fictitiously, and that part of what we have taken as the beginnings of the action on the case was the unmasking of liabilities so established. More will be said of this in the third article.

Special writs, with which this article is concerned, are those in which the main clause saying what the defendant did is amplified by some account of the circumstances. This could be done, and in the earliest days it usually was done, by means of adjectival clauses; but in the decade beginning about 1260 the device of the preamble came into common use, the circumstances being set out in an introductory *cum* clause. This was later normal in actions on the case.

The possible functions of the special matter are various. Sometimes it seems to be an unnecessary rehearsal of details, or to be inserted in anticipation of a defence; sometimes it aggravates what would any way be wrongful, or shows that the substantive complaint is not of the defendant's act in itself but of the consequences; and sometimes it is the sole foundation of the action, without which the operative part of the writ would disclose no wrong at all. An arbitrary classification, adopted for ease of exposition, arranges the kinds of special matter under four headings. The first, for want of a better label, is called " Narrative matter," and consists

[1] (1958) 74 L.Q.R., p. 195, here pp. 1-30.

of cases in which the *cum* clause seems either to be unnecessary or to play a small part. The second group consists of writs in which the *cum* clause sets out a special right of the plaintiff, and the third of those in which it sets out a special duty of the defendant. These are all considered below. The remaining group, writs in which the *cum* clause tells of some transaction between the parties, will be postponed to the third article.

Two matters must be mentioned by way of preface, and first a caution. Some of the material below is unfamiliar; and the writer is not sure that his explanations of free boar and free fold, to name two examples, are correct. This is a difficulty for the investigator. The second point troubled contemporaries. Even apart from the distortions to which our law has been subjected, the boundary between property and wrong is not always obvious.

This point was touched upon in the discussion of general writs. It obtruded itself in two early cases concerning fishing,[2] and was implicit in what was said about *ejectio firme*.[3] *Ejectio custodie* is another example which may be noticed here, because the writs protecting wardship form too large a group for inclusion in the material. This started as a trespass writ, and its early history followed the pattern of those below; the earliest example noted, in 1255, set out the plaintiff's title in relative clauses,[4] but in 1273 the *cum* construction was employed.[5] At first it was normally *contra pacem*,[6] and sometimes *vi et armis*, even the earliest entry noted of the form in the Register[7] being embellished, after *violenter ejecit*, with *alia enormia* and *contra pacem*[8]; but in the same year, 1283, these embellishments might be dropped.[9] In 1329 the writ still *soune en trespas fait enconter le peas*[10]; but in 1337 the two things are said to be of different natures,[11] and the addition of other trespasses, formerly common,[12] was fatal. Property had got the upper hand.

[2] (1958) 74 L.Q.R., at p. 204, here pp. 10-11.
[3] *Ibid.*, at p. 198, here pp. 4-7.
[4] KB. 26/155, m. 6.
[5] CP. 40/2A, m. 6d; CP. 40/4, m. 41d.
[6] Not CP. 40/4, m. 41d, a remarkable case: the writ says PP are executors, who had recovered the wardship in the former reign, and DD *vi & armis ejecerunt & ipsos executores impediverunt quominus seisinam ipsius custodie uti potuerunt ad grave dampnum ipsorum executorum non modicum & gravamen in contemptum curie prefati domini H. regis patris domini Regis nunc, etc.* Cf. CP. 40/2A, m. 10d.
[7] *Reg.Omn.Brev.* (1634), f. 162.
[8] CP. 40/48, m. 51.
[9] CP. 40/50, m. 24. The writ is called trespass in Stat.West. II, 1285, c. 35.
[10] YB. Mich. 3 Ed. III, pl. 17, f. 30. *Cf.* the argument in YB. 5 Ed. II, Seld. Soc., Vol. 31, p. 49.
[11] YB. 11 & 12 Ed. III, R.S., p. 51. Process then came to be by summons, not attachment; *Reg.Omn.Brev.*, f. 162d. The wrong is called trespass in 38 *Lib.Ass.*, pl. 9, f. 223d.
[12] CP. 40/2A, m. 6d; CP. 40/48, m. 57d.

A source of trouble is that only in the course of the fourteenth century was it settled that specific relief could not be had in trespass writs. No more precise date is suggested; trespass was not necessarily such an entity that a general rule could be adopted, and the practice may have been settled in different writs at different times. For wrongs like battery specific relief is any way impossible. In *de bonis asportatis* a judgment for the return of the goods as well as damages was reversed in 1324; *in hujusmodi brevi de transgressione secundum legem &c. dampna tantum adjudicari & recuperari debeant &c.*[13] Interference with continuing rights is more difficult; even if you are limited to compensation for the past you may want an order about the future. In 1315 a defendant, who had suffered judgment for disturbing the plaintiff's collection of tithes, did it again after the next harvest; here the court could only recommend another similar action.[14] But in certain special writs we shall see specific orders being made many years later.

Another aspect of the same point had among the general writs a solitary harbinger; a writ concerning a right of way was cast in the present tense.[15] So are many of those which follow. If specific relief is available, there is no important difference between the past infringement of a continuing right and a continuing infringement. The high-water mark is a formula *quare, cum* the plaintiff has a right, the defendant *non permittit* him to exercise it. This is for a time found in trespass writs; but its very words are reminiscent of *quod permittat*.

The rights for which *quod permittat* evidently seemed appropriate were those which, like easements, avail specifically against the proprietary right of another; he may disturb your enjoyment and raise a proprietary question between you and him. Apart from free fold, which was in the nature of a profit but involved a structure on the plaintiff's land, it will be seen that only two entries have been found of trespass writs reciting what may be easements or profits as special matter. Disturbance by anyone else would lead to a trespass writ, and one in which special matter was unnecessary; though probably it would do no harm. With such rights, there was danger of framing a writ of ambiguous nature. An example will be found under free fold. Another has adventitious fame as one of the earliest actions to be called trespass *sur le case*; it was a writ in 1367 against a miller demanding why, whereas the plaintiff had a prescriptive right to mill free of multure, the defendant *predictum P sine multura molere vi & armis impedi-*

---

[13] *Plac.Abb.*, p. 346b. Cf. *Sel.Cas.Proc. without Writ*, p. 122, at p. 124.
[14] YB. 9 Ed. II, Seld. Soc., Vol. 45, p. 69.
[15] (1958) 74 L.Q.R., p. 195, at p. 197 , here p. 3.

vit. This was quashed; the plaintiff was told he should bring *quod permittat* against the lord or general trespass against the miller.[16] That it was not just the special matter which gave it this hybrid nature, but also the *quare impedivit* formulation, seems possible from a case in 1370; a writ with similar special matter, but alleging actual takings of multure, was upheld.[17]

Most of the special writs, however, are concerned with rights such as franchises, which do not avail against anybody in particular unless it be the king. No matter who disturbs your enjoyment, you treat him as a wrongdoer and sue him in trespass. You may, however, want specific relief. So long as this is available, the writ may well be in the present tense, in some such form as *quare non permittit*; and when it ceases to be available *quare impedivit* is an appropriate formula. There is here no danger of confusion with a proprietary remedy. In some of these situations, however, the need for specific relief was such that special processes came to provide it. These were prohibitions, to be followed in the event of disobedience by attachments; but since the attachments were essentially trespass actions for damages, though no doubt with the possibility of added penalties for contempt, the plaintiff gained little. This must equally have been the case with the specific orders made in early trespass writs themselves, and was probably a reason why they ceased to be made.

1. NARRATIVE MATTER

Title recited

The propriety of special matter, at any rate in the thirteenth century, was partly a matter of taste. In trespass to land, for example, a plaintiff could state his title; and this was not uncommon when he had come to the land recently, or there was something unusual about his position. An entry from 1228 has a *cum* clause asserting that the plaintiff was his brother's heir and had entered after his death.[18] A pair from 1259 recite a lease to the plaintiff: in one this may have been only to avoid describing the property as his [19]; but in the other the defendants included the lessor himself [20]:

quare cum predictus D dimisisset eidem P quandam terram in A ad terminum qui nondum preteriit iidem DD vi & armis

---

[16] YB. Mich. 41 Ed. III, pl. 17, f. 24. Brooke *Abridgment* (1576), *Quod Permittat*, pl. 5. The *quod permittat* is at *Reg.Omn.Brev.*, f. 153d; examples are CP. 40/7 (1275), m. 9d and CP. 40/236 (1320), m. 100.
[17] YB. Trin. 44 Ed. III, pl. 16, f. 20. *Cf. Reg.Omn.Brev.*, f. 154d.
[18] *Bracton's Note Book*, pl. 287.
[19] KB. 26/161, m. 22; the lease is stated in a relative clause.
[20] KB. 26/161, m. 22d.

> *noctanter venerunt ad predictam terram & blada ejusdem P in terra illa crescencia messuerunt & asportaverunt contra pacem &c.*

Again in 1270 a *cum* clause asserted that the plaintiff after the battle of Evesham had primer seisin of a manor *quod fuit X inimici Regis*.[21] All these would have made sense without their *cum* clauses. They would indeed have been ordinary general writs[22]; and it became uncommon for such special matter to be put in. But putting it in did no harm: as late as 1371 a writ for fishing began by reciting a grant of King Stephen, and, though *il ad plus en son briefe que il ne deveroit*, it was not quashed.[23]

A story told

Circumstances may be explained, either because it would be difficult to frame a writ otherwise, or because they caused consequential damage. An example of the former is a writ of 1332 for taking the plaintiff's coal and damaging the fixtures of his mine; it was grammatically convenient to explain the construction of the mine in a *cum* clause.[24] Other examples are writs for taking and detaining the plaintiff's ship, which may begin with a *cum* clause specifying the voyage.[25] Another writ concerning a ship will introduce those in which the special matter is to explain consequential damage; it is of 1335, and is intelligible only if the ship was not the plaintiff's[26]:

> *quare cum idem P turbas & aliq bona & catalla sua in quadam navi apud A poni fecisset ad ea exinde usque B pro sustentacione sua ducenda predicti DD navem illam ... apud C vi & armis arestaverunt & velum & ancoram necnon alia attilia navis predicti ceperunt & asportaverunt & navem illam sic absque regimine exire permiserunt per quod bona & catalla predicta in eadem navi existencia ad valenciam £10 pro defectu regiminis totaliter perierunt & alia enormia &c. ad grave dampnum &c. & contra pacem &c.*

Economic damage is illustrated by loss of trading profits; what is basically a simple writ for damaging goods in 1292 has a *cum* clause

---

[21] KB. 26/200A (CP.), m. 33d. Cf. KB 26/161, m. 3d.
[22] This is not always so. In 1283 a writ ran: *quare cum solum sabuli in A sit proprium solum ipsius P ita quod non liceat alicui alii in sabulo illo sine licencia & voluntate ipsius P domum aut cayam levare iidem DD ... quasdam cayas levaverunt ad grave dampnum ipsius P &c.*; CP. 40/49, m. 45d.
[23] YB. Mich. 46 Ed. III, pl. 21, f. 28d. An entry of the writ shows it was Stephen, not John; CP. 40/443, m. 237d.
[24] CP. 40/291, m. 229d.
[25] CP. 40/2A (1273), m. 21d and CP. 40/5, m. 98; CP. 40/350 (1347), m. 80d.
[26] KB. 27/300, m. 95d.

explaining that the goods were merchandise which the plaintiff had ready for a fair, so that beyond the physical damage he had lost his profit.[27] The writer has seen also two writs complaining of damage immediately done by a third party. One, of 1352, is not even *contra pacem*: the defendant as archdeacon's commissary had put a sequestration on the plaintiff's goods, which he thus lost *ad grave dampnum ipsius P & contra legem & consuetudinem regni Regis Anglie*.[28] The other, of 1357, is neat enough to print [29]:

> *quare cum idem P decem pannos laneos sigillis Regis pro custumis pannorum venalium juxta formam statuti inde editi ordinatis consignatos usque ad A . . . duxisset predicti DD sigilla Regis predicta sic eisdem pannis nomine custume apposita de pannis predictis vi & armis abstraxerunt per quod panni illi tanquam non custumati Regi forisfacti fuerunt ad dampnum ipsius P £20 & contra pacem Regis.*

These are both *op. ses.*

Rescue and pound-breach

These are essentially writs *de bonis asportatis*, with special matter added to explain why the defendant is being sued for taking his own property. The importance of the law of distress made them the source of a substantial body of rules [30]; and they have a section to themselves in the Register, among the trespassory writs but not under *De Transgressione*. This section *De Rescussu* [31] is quite long, not because the operative parts of the writs vary much —they are sometimes left out altogether—but because precedents are given of a wide variety of *cum* clauses to justify the distress.[32]

That these are writs of trespass needs no arguing. They are called by that name in the Year Books [33] and *transgressio* in the plea rolls [34]; they are *vi et armis* and *contra pacem*; and they could include counts for other trespasses.[35] This last apparently seemed odd to Fitzherbert,[36] but in the thirteenth century it was common.[37] Their formal development, moreover, is parallel with that of other

---

[27] Sayles, *Sel.Cas. in K.B.*, II, p. 113.
[28] CP. 40/370, m. 22d.
[29] CP. 40/391, m. 213.
[30] Prohibition would issue to stop a plea of rescue without writ; CP. 40/350 (1347), m. 16.
[31] *Reg.Omn.Brev.*, ff. 116d *et seq.*
[32] If it was to enforce a payment due under a franchise, the *cum* clause might be very long, *e.g.*, CP. 40/399 (1359), m. 158.
[33] YB. 9 Ed. II, Seld. Soc., Vol. 45, p. 52; Pasch. 4 Ed. III, pl. 5, f. 15; Pasch. 7 Ed. III, pl. 23, f. 19.
[34] CP. 40/2A (1273), m. 22d; CP. 40/429 (1367), m. 295.
[35] *Reg.Omn.Brev.*, f. 117d; Fitzherbert, *Natura Brevium* (1588), f. 101D.
[36] *Ibid.*
[37] KB. 26/161 (1259), mm. 19, 19d; CP. 40/2A (1273), m. 22d.

trespass writs, the *cum* formulation beginning to be common about 1260,[38] and the allegation of damage a little later.[39]

Whether genuine violence was necessary is doubtful; two cases may be mentioned. In 1309 a jury found that while the defendant was away his servants had rescued two cows, and that he had ratified this, neither paying his arrears nor handing over the cows; the plaintiff recovered and the defendant was committed to the marshal.[40] In 1329 beasts being distrained wandered from the road along which they were being driven and entered their owners' property; the owners were liable in rescue for not giving them up.[41]

Pillory; free boar; free fold

There is no warrant for putting these together, but they are all actions for damage to an object of the plaintiff's, which object, however, he enjoys only by some special title. His writ is basically an ordinary writ for taking or damaging property; but it has a *cum* clause setting out his right, as it were in anticipation of the defence.

The right to a pillory might exist either by franchise or as an incident of lordship.[42] In 1294 a defendant was sued for having come with force and arms and by night and torn down the plaintiff's pillory; and the writ, which can be deduced from the report, set out the grant to the plaintiff of a franchise of fair and market with the usual incidents. The defendant was grantee of the hundred; and he claimed that even in fair and market time he had used the right of pillory in his leet jurisdiction, and that the plaintiff's pillory was new. The court seemed to favour the defendant, but no decision is recorded.[43] In a similar writ in 1331 the plaintiff apparently asserted his right to have a pillory as incidental to his lordship of the manor; and the defendant, failing to defeat the writ on the ground that this right could exist only by franchise, conducted his pleadings on the footing that you could have a pillory on your own land as incident to the lordship, but to have it on another's land you needed a prescriptive title; and he justified his act on the ground that this pillory had been newly erected on his

---

[38] KB. 26/155 (1255), m. 10d (a pound-breach with no *cum* clause); KB. 26/161 (1259), m. 19 (the same with), m. 19d (a rescue without); and references in next note.

[39] Rescue: CP. 40/2A (1273), m. 21d; CP. 40/48 (1283), m. 61. Pound-breach: KB. 26/201 (1271), m. 19d; CP. 40/49 (1283), m. 13.

[40] *Plac.Abb.*, p. 306b. *Cf.* C.P. 40/4, m. 17d: taking from pound *sine licencia*.

[41] Fitzherbert, *Abridgment, Rescous*, pl. 12; *Vieux Natura Brevium* (1584), f. 53. The case was presumably heard in the eyre of Northampton, 3 Ed. III.

[42] It might be incident to a franchise such as market, see *e.g.*, YB. 2 & 3 Ed. II, Seld.Soc., Vol. 19, p. 71, at p. 74. For its relation to lordship, see Pollock & Maitland, *History of English Law*, 2nd ed., Vol. I, p. 582.

[43] YB. 21 & 22 Ed. I, R.S., p. 482.

land.⁴⁴ The form in the Register conceals the plaintiff's title under an " etc."; but that it was for such situations appears from the statement that the pillory was *nuper erectum*.⁴⁵

Pillory might involve other people's land; free boar and free bull necessarily did. Their essence apparently was that you might have your boar or bull wandering at large within the area concerned, and were not liable for any damage it did. If it ate your neighbour's crops, he might no doubt drive it out; but he could not sue you or distrain it damage feasant.⁴⁶ The right seems to be one which a lord could acquire by prescription,⁴⁷ or, doubtless a later stage of the same thing, to be annexed to certain lands.⁴⁸ It came up in the courts rarely, and then generally in replevin to answer an avowry of distress damage feasant.⁴⁹ The following is a trespass writ from 1275 ⁵⁰:

> *quare cum prefatus P habere debeat & ipse & antecessores sui temporibus retroactis habere consueverunt liberum aprum suum in A prefati DD aprum ipsius P ibidem inventum vi & armis interfecerunt & alia enormia ei intulerunt ad dampnum ipsius P 100 s. & contra pacem &c.*

This is the only example noticed in the rolls; but the Register has a writ *de libero tauro abducto*.⁵¹ This recites a right to free bull throughout the hundred *occasione cujusdam tenementi*, and cryptically says that the defendant *cepit et abduxit* the bull *et ipsum &c.*, thus concealing its fate. The question is what purpose such writs served. If the defendant wantonly made off with the animal, or killed it, one would expect a general writ; if he took it damage feasant one would expect replevin. To the latter point the likely answer is that the plaintiff sought damages for taking something which his *cum* clause showed to be immune from distress. The writ for killing is more difficult. If the *cum* clause had any function, it follows that the killing would have been lawful were it not for the special right. Perhaps animals damage feasant might be

---

⁴⁴ YB. Mich. 5 Ed. III, pl. 49, f. 46. If it was on the plaintiff's land, he would probably use a general writ; *cf.* CP. 40/373 (1352), m. 189d, a general writ for maliciously breaking *furcas ipsius P in solo suo apud A nuper erectas*.
⁴⁵ *Reg.Omn.Brev.*, f. 109.
⁴⁶ This seems to meet the difficulty felt in *Brevia Placitata*, Seld.Soc., Vol. 66, p. cxxvi. For a harrowing vision of life in a vill where two persons each claimed both free bull and free boar, see YB. 5 Ed. II, Seld.Soc., Vol. 33, p. xxxii.
⁴⁷ YB. 6 Ed. II, Seld.Soc., Vol. 34, p. 99.
⁴⁸ *Reg.Omn.Brev.*, f. 109.
⁴⁹ *Bracton's Note Book*, pl. 881; YBB 32 & 33 Ed. I., R.S., p. 270; 5 Ed. II, Seld.Soc., Vol. 33, p. 141; 5 Ed. II, Seld.Soc., Vol. 63, p. 208.
⁵⁰ CP. 40/7, m. 47; CP. 40/8, m. 48.
⁵¹ *Reg.Omn.Brev.*, f. 109.

killed if they were too fierce to be impounded[52]; the owner of a bull or boar so destroyed would then have a remedy if it were " free " but not otherwise. It may be added that the Register has a *quod permittat* for free bull.[53]

Little Domesday refers often to fold-soke, an obligation to fold sheep on the lord's land to manure it[54]; and the benefit of this seems to become the right known as free fold. Originally a possible incident of lordship, it came to be annexed to the demesne lands, and may have been capable of existing in gross.[55] The right was most common in East Anglia,[56] and it might operate only at certain seasons.[57] The Register has a *quod permittat*,[58] and also a trespass writ[59]; and the relation between them caused trouble. Take first an entry of 1283[60]:

quare cum prefata P occasione terrarum & tenementorum que fuerunt quondam X viri sui in A in manibus ipsius P existencium liberam faldam suam in eisdem terris & tenementis habere debeat & prefatus X & antecessores sui terras & tenementa predicta tenentes liberam faldam suam in eisdem terris & tenementis habere consueverunt temporibus retroactis predictus D simul cum Y nuper ad faldam ipsius P in predictis terris & tenementis existentem vi & armis veniens cleyas ejusdem falde asportavit & oves ab eadem terra fugavit non permittens predictam P liberam faldam in eisdem terris & tenementis habere sicut predictus X & antecessores predicti liberam faldam suam habere consueverunt ad dampnum ipsius P £10 & contra pacem &c.

This may be compared with a writ of 1292 which begins with a similar *cum* clause but ends differently. It omits the *non permittens* passage and speaks simply of breaking *contra pacem*, but then it adds *et ipsum P faldam suam ibidem sicut eam habere debeat habere non permittunt*. This writ was quashed: *istud breve fundatum est in parte super jure falde predicte habende et similiter super quadam transgressione contra pacem regis facta*.[61]

---

[52] There seems once to have been a general right to kill; Glanville Williams, *Liability for Animals*, pp. 9 et seq.
[53] *Reg.Omn.Brev.*, f. 155. A *justicies* form is in *Brevia Placitata*, Seld.Soc., Vol. 66, p. 149.
[54] Maitland, *Domesday Book and Beyond*, pp 76, 91.
[55] YBB. Hil. 1 Ed. III, pl. 4, f. 1; Hil. 3 Ed. III, pl. 7, f. 3; Pasch. 8 Ed. III, pl. 48, f. 37. *Cf.* YB.Pasch. 1 Hy. VII, pl. 17, f. 24d.
[56] YB. Hil. 1 Ed. III, pl. 4, f. 1; and references below.
[57] *Plac.Abb.*, p. 223b (1290, Norfolk).
[58] *Reg.Omn.Brev.*, f. 155.
[59] *Ibid.*, f. 103. *Cf.* the 1371 example given at the end of this heading.
[60] CP. 40/49, m. 17d (Cambridgeshire).
[61] *Sel.Cas. in K.B.*, II, p. 135 (Cambridgeshire).

The facts behind such an action must be that the defendant had come and removed his own sheep from the plaintiff's fold; and the *cum* clause was partly to anticipate the justification that the sheep belonged to the defendant, and partly to get damages not only for the breaking of the fold but also for the loss of manure. It may be that a general writ would serve; pleas so started were not uncommon.[62] It would be tidy if these were all, as some certainly were, actions the other way round, the claimant to free fold having sent his men to remove the plaintiff's sheep from the plaintiff's to his own fold.[63] But this cannot be so; some general writs specify that the fold broken was "free."[64] We must conclude that either a general or a special writ would do, perhaps depending upon whether there were any sheep in the fold other than the plaintiff's own. Special writs did not go out of use. One is found as late as 1371[65]:

> quare cum idem P . . . ratione tenementorum illorum quandam faldam ibidem habere debeat . . . DD faldam predicti P ibidem nuper erectam prostraverunt & claias & palos . . . vi & armis fregerunt & ipsum P quo minus faldam ipsam prout ad ipsum pertineat erigere vel aliquod commodum de falda illa percipere potuit per magnum tempus impediverunt & alia enormia. . . .

Rights of way, etc.

Two entries have been found reciting what look like easements or profits as special matter. In 1314 a *cum* clause asserted a prescriptive right to take sand from a certain stretch of shore for the plaintiff's manor; and

> predictus D nuper batellum prefati P sabulone in litore predicto apud A oneratum . . . vi & armis cepit & abduxit & ipsum P & servientes suos quominus sabulonem ibidem capere & usque manerium suum predictum ducere potuerunt ut solebant multipliciter impedivit & alia enormia. . . .

To this the defendant *dicit quod nichil [fecit] contra pacem domini Regis*.[66] The other, from 1357, is only an *op. se*[67]:

> quare cum idem P habeat . . . & omnes predecessores sui . . . habere consueverunt liberum chiminum ad cariandum fenum

---

[62] CP. 40/7 (1275), m. 23; KB. 27/215 (1314), m. 92; CP. 40/291 (1332), m. 52; CP. 40/340 (1344), m. 16; CP. 40/391 (1357), mm. 72d, 127d.
[63] CP. 40/9 (1275), m. 6; YBB. Hil. 3 Ed. III, pl. 7, f. 3; Pasch. 8 Ed. III, pl. 48, f. 37; Rastell, *Entrees* (1574), f. 581.
[64] KB. 27/215 (1314), m. 83d; CP. 40/235 (1320), m. 117; KB. 27/405 (1362), m. 64.
[65] CP. 40/443, m. 250d.
[66] KB. 27/215, m. 69d; the plaintiff also had a protection.
[67] CP. 40/391 (1357), m. 120. *Cf*. CP. 40/17 (1276), m. 13.

suum . . . prefati DD homines & servientes dicti P quominus ipsi fenum . . . per dictam viam cariare potuerunt vi & armis . . . impediverunt & in dictos homines . . . insultum fecerunt . . . per quod idem P servicium . . . per magnum tempus & proficuum feni sui predicti totaliter amisit & alia enormia ei intulerunt ad dampnum ipsius P £20 & contra pacem Regis.

Perhaps general writs were more often used in such cases.

2. Franchises and Other Special Rights

Waifs, strays, wrecks, etc.

The class is of objects to which the plaintiff has a title by franchise.[68] The right is not, as with free bull, to enjoy what in an obvious sense is his, but to take something which in that obvious sense is not his. Wreck of the sea is washed ashore, a straying animal appears within the manor; the lord, if he has the franchise, is entitled to it; and for another to take it is an obvious wrong. The remedy in each case is a writ appearing in the Register under *De Transgressione*: it is *vi et armis* and *contra pacem*; and it has a *cum* clause setting out the right.[69]

One example will be given, a case of estray in 1339 [70]:

quare cum idem P & predecessores sui . . . a tempore quo memoria non existit semper hactenus habere consueverunt infra libertatem manerii sui de A animalia que dicuntur stray iidem DD duos pullanos precii 40s. ad predictum P tanquam stray pertinentes apud A inventos vi & armis ceperunt & abduxerunt & alia enormia ei intulerunt ad grave dampnum ipsius P & contra pacem &c.

This case is in the Year Books, and the report is instructive about the role of the special matter. To an objection that the title was not properly set out, Shareshulle said, according to one version, that the plaintiff needed to say no more than that he was seised of the franchise, and according to another, that the plaintiff could equally well have brought a common writ.[71] From a case about

---

[68] One example noted was not a franchise. In 1347 a writ said that P was entitled to heriots, and DD had taken the best beast of a dead tenant *contra consuetudinem predictam & pacem Regis*. The best beast was a charger worth £50; CP 40/350, m. 104.

[69] Wreck: *Reg.Omn.Brev.*, f. 102d; YBB. 9 Ed. II, Seld.Soc., Vol. 45, p. 49; Mich. 5 Ed. III, pl. 91, f. 59; CP. 40/312, m. 247; CP. 40/340, m. 62; CP. 40/399, m. 58d. Estray: *Reg.Omn.Brev.*, f. 100d; CP. 40/312, m. 64; CP. 40/429, mm. 79, 511d; KB. 27/430, m. 39. Waif: *Reg.Omn.Brev.*, f. 100d; YB. Hil. 40 Ed. III, pl. 19, f. 10; CP. 40/399, mm. 11, 76d; CP. 40/408, m. 76; CP. 40/429, m. 92. *Catalla felonum*: *Reg.Omn.Brev.*, f. 101; CP. 40/443, m. 124d. Deodands: YB. Hil. 45 Ed. III, pl. 5, f. 2d.

[70] CP. 40/320, m. 334.

[71] YB. 13 & 14 Ed. III, R.S., p. 134.

waifs in 1366 it appears conversely that, though a plaintiff who had taken possession of the object could have a common writ, it would not matter if he got a special one.[72]

Fitzherbert in his *Natura Brevium* calls the special writs trespass, but noting with a tinge of surprise that they lie even though the plaintiff never had possession of the thing [73]; and in his *Abridgment* he actually calls the 1339 example trespass *sur son cas*.[74] Rastell puts a precedent for estray under *Trespas*, but puts also a cross-reference to it under *Accion sur le case*.[75] We are coming to a boundary.

Market and Fair

In the cases just considered, the plaintiff became entitled by his franchise to specific objects. Other franchises created obligations: the franchise owner might suffer a loss and a wrong just as obvious, but not to be put in terms of an object being taken. Most prominent is the franchise of market, the value of which lay partly in the dues such as stallage paid by those who sold in the market, and partly in the toll payable on each transaction. The owner might be wronged in many ways, divisible into two principal groups: wrongs done by traders in the market or those who should trade there, and wrongs done by outsiders.

Outsiders might try either to get for themselves the profits of the plaintiff's market, or just to prevent him from holding it.[76] A simple writ for taking the profits comes from 1270 [77]:

> quare cum predictus P & antecessores sui dudum habuerunt mercatum & liberam feriam in A & B cum omnibus libertatibus & liberis consuetudinibus ad mercatum & feriam pertinentibus ex concessione domini Regis predicti DD die ferie predicte attachiamenta transgressionum panis & cervicie & aliarum transgressionum in predicta [feria] fecerunt & emendaciones illarum transgressionum & tholnetum & stallagium in eadem feria que ad predictum P pertinent vi & armis ceperunt & ea adhuc detinent ad grave dampnum predicti P non permittentes eundem P libertatibus & liberis consuetudinibus ad predictum

---

[72] YB. Hil. 40 Ed. III, pl. 19, f. 10.
[73] f. 91B, D. *Cf.* YB. Mich. 5 Ed. III, pl. 91, f. 59.
[74] *Briefe*, pl. 674.
[75] *Entrees*, ff. 577 and 7 respectively.
[76] The latter might be by way of abating what was said to be a nuisance to D's market. For nuisance actions see *Bracton's Note Book*, pll. 494, 578, 786, 1037; KB. 27/215, m. 100.
[77] KB. 26/200A (CP.), m. 9d. *Cf.* a remarkable writ in 1367 for *vi et armis* erecting a fold in the fair and so taking profits which should have gone to the franchise owner; CP. 40/429, m. 374d.

> *mercatum & feriam pertinentibus ibidem pacifice uti quibus ipse & antecessores sui hactenus usi sunt &c.*

More recondite is a case of 1337 in which the plaintiff says he and the defendant are each entitled to a moiety, and the defendant has beaten the plaintiff's collector and taken all the profits for himself; the defendant unsuccessfully objects that the plaintiff does not specify what was taken, as in *de bonis asportatis*.[78] These are analogous to the wreck and stray cases, with the difference foreshadowed: the wrong cannot be expressed as the taking of specific objects.

Attempts to prevent the plaintiff from holding his market are common in the rolls. The defendant could go about it either by a direct attack on the market, or by besetting it and driving away those who would do business there—picketing. Direct attacks led to actions of the kind described in connection with pillory.[79] The writ would demand *quare, cum* the plaintiff had his franchise, the defendant had come *vi et armis* and torn down his toll-booth or the like, or, as in the precedent in the Register,[80] had impeded the men responsible for collecting the profits,[81] or had done both.[82] Such a writ might be very long[83]; and it would normally include, after describing the attack, some such phrase as *et ipsum P quominus mercatum habere et tenere potuit impediverunt per quod idem P . . . proficuum . . . amisit.*[84]

Picketing raises a subsidiary point, and it will be well to begin with a straightforward example; it is from 1347[85]:

> *quare cum eadem P habeat & habere debeat ipsaque & ejus antecessores a tempore cujus contrarii memoria non existit habere consueverunt quoddam mercatum singulis septimanis . . . iidem DD in mercatores ad mercatum predictum cum mercandisis suis venientes & in eodem mercato existentes vi & armis insultum fecerunt & ipsos verberaverunt vulneraverunt & maletractaverunt ita quod iidem mercatores mercandisas suas predictas ibidem exercere non sunt ausi per quod eadem P proficuum mercati sui predicti ad valenciam 20m. amisit &*

---

[78] YB. 11 & 12 Ed. III, R.S., p. 38. *Cf.* the precedent for free fold, *Reg.Omn Brev.*, p. 103.
[79] In YB. 21 & 22 Ed. I, R.S., p. 482, *supra*, p. 37, the pillory was incident to a fair.
[80] *Reg.Omn.Brev.*, f. 103.
[81] CP. 40/291 (1332), m. 42; CP. 40/340 (1344), m. 286; *cf.* CP. 40/370 (1352), m. 94, formulated as a general writ.
[82] KB. 27/279 (1330), m. 51; KB. 27/300 (1335), m. 8.
[83] It might be further swollen by a reference to the Statute of Northampton, 1328, c. 3; *e.g.*, KB. 27/358 (1350), m. 42.
[84] Abbreviated from KB. 27/279, m. 51.
[85] CP. 40/350, m. 56d.

alia enormia &c ad grave dampnum &c & contra pacem Regis &c.

Cases are found in 1259–60. One will be mentioned below. In another the defendants had also knocked down fixtures,[86] and the combination with a direct attack occurs again in a comprehensive writ of 1335.[87] A writ just for picketing was expressly upheld in 1304,[88] but doubts may later have arisen. In 1329 it is said that *si un home soit en chivachant vers mon marche, vient un auter & luy arrest, issint qe il ne vient pas, pur qe jeo parde mon tolle, per ce qe il nest pas tenus de droit de vener, jeo navera jammes action.*[89] This may, however, have depended upon the supposed event being isolated, and not directed at the franchise. Contrast this from 1340: *si jeo porte bref de trespas devers vous de ceo qe vous avez destourbe certeins gens de venir a mon marche ove lour marchandise dont jeo suy destourbe de tenir mon marche ou ma faire, le bref est assetz boun.*[90] Here the situation was offered as the type of those in which one might complain of a wrong *prima facie* done to others; and we may note how delusive is the likeness to modern trespass. The writ is a *bref de trespas*,[91] and it has *vi et armis*; but the force and arms were not taken to the plaintiff, and his loss was as indirect as it could be.

A picketing case in 1259–60 illustrates what was mentioned at the beginning of this article, a trespass writ in the present tense [92]:

quare cum dominus Rex concesserit per cartam suam predicto P & burgensibus suis de A quasdam libertates quibus hucusque usi sunt predicti DD burgenses predictos contra tenorem carte domini Regis predicte in grave dampnum & dispendium ipsius P & burgensium suorum predictorum molestare non cessant homines de partibus illis quo minus ad liberam feriam sive mercatum ipsius P de A que habet ex concessione domini Regis cum mercandisis suis venire possint impediendo quosdam ipsorum verberando . . . & plures alias injurias eis inferendo contra pacem &c.

A plaintiff adopting this formulation probably wanted specific relief, and writs are found demanding *quare non permittit.* This example is from 1273 [93]:

[86] KB. 26/161, m. 18d.
[87] KB. 27/300, m. 8, *supra*, n. 82.
[88] YB. 32 & 33 Ed. I, R.S., p. 50.
[89] YB. Hil. 2 Ed. III, pl. 20, f. 7 at f. 8.
[90] Y.B. 14 & 15 Ed. III, R.S., p. 88 at p. 97. *Cf.* YBB. Hil. 29 Ed. III, f. 21 at f. 22; Mich. 41 Ed. III, pl. 17, f. 24 at f. 24d.
[91] YBB. 32 & 33 Ed. I, R.S., p. 51; Mich. 2 Ed. III, pl. 9, f. 15; Pasch. 29 Ed. III, f. 18d; and references in last note.
[92] KB. 26/161, m. 6. *Cf.* KB. 26/167 (1260), m. 19 (past tense).
[93] CP. 40/2A, m. 10d; CP. 40/4, m. 31; CP. 40/5, m. 89.

> quare . . . certos homines ad mercatum illud cum rebus & mercandisis suis venientes verberaverunt vulneraverunt & maletractaverunt & ipsos PP mercatum suum predictum habere non permittunt ad dampnum eorundem PP £100 & ad exheredacionem manifestam & contra pacem &c.

Two do not even specify what means the defendant used, and apparently have not *contra pacem*. One is from 1283 [94]; the other is as late as 1320 [95]:

> quare cum idem P habere debeat . . . unam feriam . . . idem D ipsum P quominus feriam predictam . . . habere possit prout antecessores sui predicti & tempore predicto habere consueverunt impedit minus juste ad grave dampnum ipsius P &c.

Such forms disappeared as specific relief ceased to be available, leaving only those referring to past events.

From the wrongs of outsiders we pass to wrongs done by those who do or should trade in the market. They might refuse to pay their dues, or they might evade them. It seems unlikely that refusal to pay could be called a trespass [96]; but an entry of 1371 complains that the defendants had refused to pay shoppage themselves and had *vi et armis* impeded collection from others,[97] and in 1362 somebody even thought a writ could be framed like this [98]:

> quare cum idem P dominus manerii de A existat ipseque in eodem manerio unum mercatum . . . & duas ferias . . . habere debeat . . . predictusque D theolonium ad valenciam £60 ad ipsum P ratione mercati & feriarum predictarum pro mercandisis per ipsum D ibidem emptas & venditas pertinens asportavit ad dampnum ipsius P £60.

Forms concerning other tolls will be found below.

Evasion of dues is the most interesting of all the wrongs to a market. You were not bound to trade at all; but if you did trade, you had to do it in the market; and if you conducted a black market, selling privately elsewhere, this was an obvious wrong to the franchise owner. His protection was an action of trespass, and the Register has a precedent, though an unusually elaborate one, under *De Transgressione*; it is, of course, neither *vi et armis* nor *contra pacem*.[99] There is an excellent example in the Year

---

[94] CP. 40/49, m. 45.
[95] CP. 40/235, m. 160d.
[96] An entry of 1359 complains that the defendants rescued chattels distrained for toll, and *solvere recusarunt & adhuc recusant*; CP. 40/399, m. 188d.
[97] CP. 40/443, m. 375d. *Cf.* CP. 40/429, m. 592, *infra.*, p. 47.
[98] CP. 40/408, m. 30.
[99] Reg.Omn.Brev., f. 107.

Books of 1309.¹ The writ is called a writ of trespass; the wrong is called a trespass; and there is reference to the defendants being found guilty, *coupable trove*. The writ ran ²:

> *quare cum predictus P habere debeat & ipse & predecessores sui . . . a tempore quo non extat memoria semper hactenus habere consueverint liberum mercatum suum singulis septimanis per diem Veneris in quodam loco qui vocatur Priorshalfe in villa de Coventre ita quod mercimonia & alia bona quecunque venalia alibi in eadem villa quam in loco predicto per diem predictum vendicioni exponi seu vendi non debent nec hactenus consueverunt predicti DD mercimonia & alia bona sua venalia in domibus & in seldis suis in villa predicta extra dictum locum constructis jam de novo ad diem predictum vendicioni exponunt & vendunt ad grave dampnum ipsius P &c.*

A feature which does not appear from the Selden Society's note is that the main verbs are in the present tense. The plaintiff wanted a remedy, not just for a past event, but for a state of affairs; and he got it. As well as his damages he was granted what looks like an injunction. Maitland wondered whether this could have much effect,³ and probably it had not.

More important is the nature of the wrong. Objection was taken to the writ, but only because it did not mention the dues lost; and this drew from Bereford the retort: " The sum and substance of his action is that you have been selling outside his market, whereby he lost profit, etc. So the marketing is the main cause whence his action arises." Of all the trespasses in the fourteenth-century sense this is the most unlike ours, and it may be important that such an action was no novelty in 1309. Here is an entry from 1241⁴:

> *quare in domibus suis in A vendiderunt res & mercandisas suas durantibus nundinis ipsius P in eadem villa contra libertates eidem P concessas de predictis nundinis per cartas predecessorum domini Regis regum Anglie & cartam ipsius domini Regis.*

This was before special matter came regularly to be put in a *cum* clause, and shows what an improvement that was: if you are going to ask why the defendant sold his own goods in his own house, it is elegant to explain yourself first. The pleadings are interesting. The defendants admitted the plaintiff's right, but said that they

---

¹ YB. 2 & 3 Ed. II, Seld.Soc. Vol. 19, p. 71.
² CP. 40/174, m. 151d.
³ YB. 2 & 3 Ed. II, Seld.Soc., Vol. 19, p. 74, n. 1.
⁴ C.R.R., XVI, pll. 1727, 1764.

had always been entitled to sell in their own houses and that the plaintiff should send his bailiff to collect the dues so arising. The plaintiff reasonably replied that he would have no check; but issue was taken on his further incautious assertion that the defendants *minati fuerunt ballivos suos quod ipsos verberarent si domos suas intrarent,* and all the defendants waged their law that they had not threatened the bailiffs.

Tolls and other dues

The defendant might have taken the dues for himself, or prevented the plaintiff from collecting them. In the former case it could be argued that it was a wrong to the victim who had been made to pay, but no wrong to the plaintiff who could make him pay again [5]; this will be mentioned in connection with jurisdictional franchises. Actions for preventing the plaintiff from collecting his dues are not uncommon. There is a good example in print from 1260: the burgesses of Huntingdon claim toll in St. Ives *tam tempore nundinarum quam extra,* and they sue the Abbot of Ramsey, who owned the fair, for preventing collection; the writ is in the present tense.[6] Writs from a century later look similar, but they have *vi et armis* and *contra pacem* and speak of past events.[7] As with the precedent in the Register,[8] it is not always clear whether the defendant is a rival, as was the Abbot of Ramsey, or one from whom toll is due. An example of the former from 1371 concerns the profits of an office; the defendants *vi et armis multipliciter impediverunt* the plaintiff from collecting them, and took them *ad opus suum proprium.*[9] An example of the latter comes from 1367 [10]:

> *quare cum . . . DD theolonium hujusmodi eisdem ballivis solvere recusarunt & ipsos ballivos quominus dictum theolonium ab eis levare potuissent vi et armis impediverunt & alia enormia. . . .*

These were actions brought by the party claiming toll. More interesting are those brought against him by persons claiming to be free of toll. There are several examples, mostly without writ, in *Bracton's Note Book,* typical forms being *quare non permittunt eos habere libertates,* and *quare contra libertates . . . capit ab eis*

---

[5] YB. Trin. 2 Ed. III (additional cases), pl. 11, f. 24 at end of f. 25. Note also the formulation of the writ.
[6] *Plac.Abb.,* p. 151b; KB. 26/161, mm. 9d, 17d.
[7] e.g., CP. 40/429 (1367), m. 193d.
[8] *Reg.Omn.Brev.,* f. 103. *Cf.* Fitzherbert, *Natura Brevium,* f. 91G, where the writ, though with the *cum* clause, is called a general writ.
[9] CP. 40/443, m. 416.
[10] CP. 40/429, m. 592. *Cf.* the writs concerning market tolls, *supra,* p. 45.

thelonium.[11] These early complaints are often cast in the present tense; but there is no reason to think that the second example above was different in nature from this of 1241 [12]:

> *quare cepit theolonium de hominibus ipsius P de A contra libertates quas habet per cartas predecessorum domini Regis regum Anglie quibus libertatibus hucusque usus est &c.*;

or that there was any distinction between a pair in 1259, one *quare distringit eosdem PP ad dandum ei theolonium* and the other *quare prefatos PP compulerunt ad dandum theolonium*.[13] That there was no important difference between a past event and a continuing wrong is made very clear in a writ printed by Mr. Hall from a Register of about 1272.[14] It is captioned *De Transgressione*, and is generally like those above except that the special matter is put in a *cum* clause [15]; it is *contra libertates*, not *contra pacem*, and is in the present tense. An unusual feature is that the toll was demanded, not from the plaintiff, but from his suppliers; this may be more striking to us, with our notions about directness, than it was to contemporaries. The gist of the trespass was that the plaintiff could not get his goods without paying the amount of the toll; and he probably wanted specific relief.

Specific relief came to be supplied in the writs *De essendo quietum de theolonio*, which were prohibitions against the taking of toll, and if disobeyed were followed by attachments.[16] Except that they refer to the prohibitions, these attachments look like the trespass writs; they are called trespass,[17] and the Register has a specimen under *De Transgressione* [18] as well as under *De essendo quietum*. The relationship between this machinery, of which there are traces from the last years of Henry III,[19] and the trespass writs is not clear. The former looked primarily to the future, while the latter came to seek only compensation for past wrongs; but since the only sanction of the former was essentially another trespass action the distinction cannot have been sharp. An entry of 1371 which looks like a pure trespass action, and makes no mention of

---

[11] pll. 145 (1222) and 1720 (1226) respectively. Others are pll. 16, 1123, 1188, 1250; *Curia Regis Rolls*, xi, pl. 891; xii, pl. 2577. Most are in the present tense.
[12] C.R.R., XVI, pl. 1547.
[13] KB. 26/161, mm. 4 and 3d respectively. *Cf. Plac.Abb.*, p. 151a.
[14] (1957) 73 L.Q.R., p. 65 at p. 72, writ B.9.
[15] *Cf. Plac.Abb.*, p. 160b (1267).
[16] *Reg.Omn.Brev.*, ff. 258d *et seq.*
[17] YB. Trin. 39 Ed. III, f. 13d.
[18] *Reg.Omn.Brev.*, f. 101.
[19] A record from 1267 speaks of D's act being in *contemptum mandatorum domini Regis*; *Plac.Abb.*, pp. 160b, 174 a & b. Two entries of 1283 say it was *contra prohibicionem*; CP. 40/48, m. 25d; CP. 40/49, m. 25.

any earlier order, may in fact be an attachment, because the plaintiff sues *tam pro domino Rege quam pro se ipso*[20]; and an " injunction " was apparently granted as well as damages on a trespass writ in 1308,[21] and also, if the report is to be believed, as late as 1369.[22]

This last case is placed by Fitzherbert in his *Abridgment* under *Accion sur le case*[23]; and in his *Natura Brevium* he gives case or a general writ or *De essendo quietum* as the remedies in this situation.[24] Rastell puts it under *Trespass concernant toll*; but as usual he guards himself by a cross-reference under *Action sur le case*.[25] In 1375 it is said that plaintiffs, from whom the toll had been taken, could have had a general writ; but the special matter made some difference to the pleading.[26]

Jurisdictional franchises

With market there were two main kinds of wrong: those which outsiders might commit, and those which traders might commit. There is here no analogy to the latter: the suitors would not conduct a " black market " court; and though, unlike traders, they were under an obligation to come, this was enforced only by distraint.[27] Outsiders might seek either to prevent the plaintiff from holding his court, or to compel his men to attend another court. An early example of the latter is this from 1221 [28]:

> *quare distrinxit eum & homines suos ad faciendum sectam & ad habendum visum franci plegii contra libertatem suam quam habet per cartas regis & quas* (sic) *predecessores sui . . . semper habuerunt & quibus semper usi sunt usque in hodiernum diem.*

For such cases a specific remedy like the writs *De essendo quietum de theolonio* was evolved, prohibitions with the sanction of attachment. This machinery, which perhaps started about the end of Henry III's reign,[29] is described by Fitzherbert for the case in which tenants of one having the view of frankpledge are distrained by the bailiffs of the honour[30]; and the Register has under *De*

---

[20] C.P. 40/443, m. 416.   [21] *Plac.Abb.*, p. 305b.
[22] YB. Mich. 43 Ed. III, pl.14, f. 29d; adjudged that P is to recover *son fraunchise et ses damages*. The writ is called trespass. The toll had been taken from one of P's tenants.
[23] pl. 32.
[24] f. 94F.
[25] *Entrees*, ff. 605 and 13d respectively.
[26] YB. Hil. 49 Ed. III, pl. 10, f. 6.
[27] Fitzherbert, *Natura Brevium*, f. 158D: no *secta ad curiam*, as *ad molendinum*, because no loss. Suitors might obstruct the holding of the court, but this would not differ from an outsider's doing so.
[28] C.R.R., x, p. 165.
[29] KB. 26/201 (1271), m. 9; royal orders were issued, but apparently only the plaintiff himself was being distrained.
[30] *Natura Brevium*, f. 94G.

Transgressione a prohibitory writ to the bailiffs in the same circumstances.[31] If the wrongdoer was the sheriff, as he was in the 1221 case, there was similar machinery, the details of which can be deduced from Year Book cases of 1340 and 1343.[32]

The earlier of these is informative about the purely trespassory aspect. There had been a prohibition to the defendant sheriff, but instead of pursuing this by an attachment in the King's Bench, the plaintiff chose to start afresh in the Common Pleas. His writ recited the prohibition; but when the defendant objected that he should answer to that in the King's Bench, the plaintiff said it was mentioned only in aggravation. The defendant then argued that there was no cause of action apart from the contempt: the distraint might be a wrong to those distrained; but it was no wrong to the plaintiff, who could still hold his court and compel his suitors to come.[33] The plaintiff sought to counter this, in a passage previously quoted, by the analogy of picketing a market.[34] This was not a good analogy: as the defendant pointed out, these people had not been kept away from plaintiff's court and he had suffered no loss. But though the defendant had the best of the argument, the plaintiff was held to have a cause of action: it was as much a wrong for the sheriff to distrain against such a franchise as it would be for him to execute writs within a liberty whose lord had the return.[35]

Less difficult were cases in which the plaintiff was prevented from holding his court. Under Edward I entries are found in the present tense, *quare non permittit*; for example in 1283 the Bishop of Ely brought this writ against the Abbot of Ramsey who owned St. Ives Fair[36]:

> *quare cum idem P singulis annis in nundinis predicti D de sancto Ivone . . . curiam suam de hominibus suis de placitis & querelis inter eos ibidem motis & eciam amerciamenta hominum suorum in curia predicti D nundinarum predictarum amerciatorum pro transgressionibus aliis quam hominibus ejusdem P per ipsos ibidem illatis & eadem amerciamenta per servientem suum proprium virgam deferentem . . . habere*

[31] *Reg.Omn.Brev.*, f. 103d.
[32] YBB. 14 & 15 Ed. III, R.S., p. 88; 17 & 18 Ed. III, R.S., p. 212; Mich. 17 Ed. III, pl. 37, f. 56; and, for formulation of issue in the latter case, CP. 40/340, m. 257. Both are called trespass in the reports. In the latter, it is only from the writ and other extracts from the record printed in the Rolls Series that we learn about the prohibition.
[33] *Cf.* YB. Trin. 2 Ed. III (additional cases) pl. 11, f. 24 at end of f. 25, a similar argument in connection with tolls.
[34] *Supra*, p. 44.
[35] *Cf. Reg.Omn.Brev.*, f. 103d.
[36] CP. 40/49, m. 31. *Cf. ibid.*, m. 6, a similar writ for amercements only.

> *debeat & ipse & predecessores sui . . . habere hactenus pacifice consueverint predictus D servientem predicti P virgam deferentem ad officium suum faciendum & ipsum P curiam suam de hominibus suis & amerciamenta predicta . . . habere ibidem jam de novo non permittit sicut . . . habere debeat & solet temporibus retroactis ad dampnum ipsius P £100 & prejudicium libertatis sue & ecclesie Eliensis non modicum &c.*

Under Edward III the usual form is *quare vi et armis impedivit*, alleging specifically that the plaintiff's servants were prevented from holding the court.[37] But the means used are not necessarily mentioned and the present tense may still creep in. An entry of 1355 simply says that the defendants *vi et armis impediverunt & impediunt* the plaintiffs[38]; and the following, from 1357, has neither *vi et armis* nor, apparently, *contra pacem*[39]:

> *quare cum idem P in manerio suo de A habere debeat . . . visum franciplegii cum omnibus ad visum illum spectantibus de quibusdam residentibus infra manerium predictum predictus D ratione quorundam tenencium suorum infra idem manerium residencium hujusmodi visum franciplegii ibidem tenere noviter incepit & predictum P quominus ipse proficuum visus sui predicti percipere & habere potuit a diu impedivit & adhuc impedire non desistit ad dampnum ipsius P £40 &c.*

In this last case the defendant had apparently used no other means to prevent the plaintiff from holding his court than holding it himself. If so, it is an example of the two possible wrongs being combined, the defendant exercising the plaintiff's jurisdiction and taking the profits. This situation seems to have caused difficulty. There is in print from 1262–63 a *quod permittat* for view of frankpledge, followed by trespass for having erected gallows and hanged a thief contrary to the plaintiff's liberty.[40] But, as suggested at the beginning of this article, *quod permittat* was not appropriate for franchises; and the only protection came to be in trespass. In a well-known case of 1350 the writ recited that the parties were lords of the two manors in Chesham, and the sheriff's tourn was held in the plaintiff's at Easter each year and in the defendant's at Michaelmas; each had had a prescriptive right to pay the sheriff one mark when the tourn was held in his manor, and thereupon to take all but certain of the profits arising from his own tenants;

---

[37] CP. 40/391 (1357), m. 155; CP. 40/429 (1367), m. 417; CP 40/443 (1371), m. 196d. The main clause of the last is typical: *ballivum ipsius P . . . quominus predictum visum tenere potuit vi et armis impedivit.*
[38] KB. 27/380, m. 49d.
[39] CP. 40/391, m. 242.
[40] *Plac.Abb.*, p. 154b; the trespass writ is formulated with a *cum* clause.

the king then granted the tourn to the defendant; after which, though the plaintiff tendered his mark at each Easter tourn:

> *idem D dictam summam a prefato P recipere non curavit set ipsum quominus hujusmodi proficua de leta predicta percipere potuit voluntarie impedivit ad dampnum ipsius P £100 ut dicit.*

Like the writ, last set out, this is neither *vi et armis* nor *contra pacem*; and it is called trespass in the report.[41]

3. SPECIAL DUTIES

Statutes

The plea rolls contain many entries of trespass writs beginning *cum de communi consilio regni regis provisum sit* or *cum ad communem utilitatem regni regis statutum sit*, and ending *contra formam provisionis* or the like. If the statute provided special penalties for what was anyway wrongful, then it was recited to secure those penalties[42]; but it might be the sole foundation of the action. Such writs sometimes have *vi et armis* and more often have *contra pacem*; but they may have neither. The formulae are standard, and a selection is found in the Register under *De Transgressione*[43] including two writs on the Statutes of Labourers for refusal to work.[44] In the Year Books, writs based on these statutes are called trespass, not only when they are against third persons,[45] but also when they are against the servant himself for leaving or refusing employment[46]; and it may have been difficulties with the trespass rules about the joinder of defendants which brought about a distinction.[47]

Royal commands

These also might be recited either as the basis of the action or as aggravating what would anyway be wrongful. The most common example of the latter is the writ reciting a protection. The form is in the Register; it consists of an ordinary writ *de bonis asportatis*

---

[41] YBB. Trin. 24 Ed. III, pl. 12, f. 28; Trin. 24 Ed. III, pl. 44, f. 56d. The record is printed in Kiralfy, *The Action on the Case*, p. 206. The reports seem to be variant versions; and there was only an *op. se* in Easter term; CP 40/360, m. 4d.

[42] *e.g.* YB. Mich. 47 Ed. III, pl. 7, f. 10d.

[43] *Reg.Omn.Brev.*, esp. at ff. 97d, 98.

[44] *Reg.Omn.Brev.*, f. 101 r & d. Most of the writs under these statutes are among the *Brevia de Statuto* at ff. 189 *et seq.*

[45] YB. Hil. 38 Ed. III, f. 5d.

[46] Leaving employment: YBB. Mich. 40 Ed. III, pl. 2, f. 35; Mich. 47 Ed. III, pl. 15, f. 14. This writ might be general, *quare a servicio . . . recessit in Regis contemptum & ipsius P grave dampnum & contra ordinacionem*; KB. 27/414 (1364), m. 17d. Refusing employment: YB. Trin. 38 Ed. III, f. 12d.

[47] YBB. Pasch. 39 Ed. III, f. 6d; Mich. 40 Ed. III, pl. 2, f. 35; Mich. 47 Ed. III, pl. 23, f. 16.

or the like, with a standard *cum* clause inserted at the beginning and *contra protectionem* before *contra pacem* at the end.[48] Not dissimilar, except that the plaintiff sues *tam pro domino Rege quam pro seipso*, are entries consisting again of ordinary general writs, but with special matter inserted alleging that the plaintiff was in the king's service; for example he was sent by the sheriff to make summonses and attachments and was beaten,[49] or he was the contractor to provide stone for work on the palace of Westminster and the stone was taken from him *in Regis contemptum & prejudicium & expedicionis operacionum suarum predictarum retardacionem manifestam & grave dampnum ipsius P & contra pacem Regis*.[50] Of commands specifically directed to the defendant we have already noted examples in the writs *De essendo quietum de theolonio* and the analogous writs against jurisdictional poaching. The attachments on these were like the ordinary writs for taking toll or wrongfully distraining, and the command was recited in aggravation.[51]

The most obvious example of a royal command forming the basis of the action is prohibition itself; the attachments are called trespass in early Year Books,[52] and in an unusual case the defendant pleaded *quod ipse in nullo est culpabilis de transgressione predicta*.[53] This soon became a distinct entity, and only certain orders concerning lay litigation will here be considered.[54] First are cases in which those responsible for an inferior court have continued to act after a *recordari facias*. The writ would require the defendants to answer the king and the plaintiff *quare, cum* a *recordari facias* was issued, they proceeded further in contempt of the king and to the damage of the plaintiff. There are two examples in the Year Books of 1338 and 1340, one of them the subject of three reports; and the action, which was for damages, is called trespass each time.[55] A precedent, evidently taken from another action against

[48] *Reg.Omn.Brev.*, f. 121. Examples: CP. 40/235 (1320), m. 155d; CP. 40/350 (1347), m. 66; CP. 40/370 (1352), m. 137. If the writ needed other special matter, the protection would be worked into the operative part; KB. 27/215 (1314), m. 69d, *supra*, p. 40 (protection omitted for sake of brevity and clarity).
[49] CP. 40/370 (1352), m. 159d.
[50] CP. 40/360 (1350), m. 56d; the plaintiff was Martin de Ixnyng, and he had bought the stone at Abbotsbury in Dorset. *Cf. Cal.Pat.Rolls*, 1348-50, pp. 450, 474. In CP. 40/350 (1347), m. 1d, the contempt was just in the wrong, knocking down a length of the Oxford city wall.
[51] *Supra*, pp. 48, 49.
[52] YBB. 21 & 22 Ed. I, R.S., p. 74; 11 Ed. II, Seld.Soc., Vol. 61, p. 220.
[53] K.B. 27/300 (1335), m. 131. *Cf.* Y.B. 30 & 31 Ed. I, R.S., p. 454.
[54] Deceit is too large a topic for consideration here.
[55] YBB. 11 & 12 Ed. III, R.S., pp. 500, 516; 14 Ed. III, R.S., pp. 230, 232. The argument that the plaintiff, who substantially complains of losing his land, should use novel disseisin might suggest that the action was new: but

the same defendants as in one of these cases, is found in the Register not under *De Transgressione* but as an attachment under *Recordari*.[56] A converse wrong was refusing to hear a case, and the Register similarly has attachments under the writs of right for use against lords maliciously suppressing such writs.[57] Two examples are in print, curiously between the same parties, a defendant who paid damages in 1292 [58] being at it again in 1297 [59]; the earlier of these writs even has *contra pacem*. Lastly there are writs against sheriffs for various misdeeds: in 1241 an elaborate action was brought for neglecting to protect the plaintiff against evil-doers as the sheriff had been ordered to do [60]; and the Register has, under *De Transgressione*, writs for letting prisoners go and for wrongly returning *non est inventus*.[61] Fitzherbert puts these last two with actions on the case.[62]

Duties to repair

Duties of keeping dykes repaired or ditches cleaned out might rest upon the terre-tenants. How they arose is obscure, though the writs which follow may throw some light. They were enforced in various ways: *reparari facias*; presentment; special commission; and private enterprise. The last appears from an action *de bonis asportatis* in 1347: the defendant avowed as servant of one who claimed to be lord of the manor of Woolwich, and to have *supervisionem & custodiam walliarum . . . contra aquam Thamisie*; this, he said, consisted of a right to warn the responsible tenant to do necessary repairs, and in default to do them himself, recovering from the tenant double the cost by distraint.[63]

If the repairs were not done and floods resulted, the responsible tenant might be sued in trespass by his neighbours. The earliest example seen was in 1273–6 [64]:

there was a not dissimilar *op. se* in 1320; KB. 27/242, m. 100, where the writ was the *attachiamentum super ballivos* at *Reg.Omn.Brev.*, f. 13.
[56] *Reg.Omn.Brev.*, f. 11.
[57] *Reg.Omn.Brev.*, ff. 6d, 9d; Fitzherbert, *Natura Brevium*, ff. 3E, 12D. This is for not letting the court be seised of the plea; inactivity thereafter would be remedied by tolt.
[58] *Sel.Cas. in K.B.*, II, p. 117.
[59] *Placita Coram Rege*, 1297, p. 224.
[60] C.R.R., XVI, pl. 1879.
[61] *Reg.Omn.Brev.*, f. 98d. The plaintiff in the latter is he of whom the sheriff made the return, who was thereupon imprisoned under a *capias*. Sheriffs might be sued by bill in the Exchequer; see *e.g.* 38 *Lib.Ass.*, pl. 13, f. 224d.
[62] *Natura Brevium*, f. 93 A, B, C.
[63] CP. 40/350, m. 135. For the more usual methods of enforcement, see *Reg. Omn.Brev.*, ff. 127, 153d; Fitzherbert, *Natura Brevium*, f. 126.
[64] CP. 40/2A, m. 23d; CP. 40/4, m. 48d; CP. 40/13, m. 35.

> *quare cum predictus D ratione tenementi sui in A in marisco de B reparare debuisset & consueverit quasdam wallias contra mare per certas portiones in eodem marisco ad defensionem ejusdem marisci predictus D predictas wallias ipsum contingentes reparare recusavit sicut eas reparare debuit & solebat per quod wallie predicte dirute sunt & blada ejusdem P in tenementis suis infra mariscum predictum seminata submersa fuerunt & consumpta ad dampnum ipsius P £40 &c.*

The defendant *bene concedit quod reparare debet predictas wallias set bene defendit quod predicta P nunquam per defectum reparacionis . . . aliquod dampnum habuit. Et quod ita sit ponit se super patriam.* An elegant writ of 1320 attributes the duty to local custom [65]:

> *quare cum secundum legem & consuetudinem in partibus de A hactenus optentatam quilibet homo cujus terra super aquam de Ouse se extendit ripas ejusdem aque per tantum spatium quantum terra sua durat defendere debet & quociens opus fuerit reparare ita quod per defectum suum aut negligentiam vicini sui dampnum non incurrant predictus D ripas . . . quas juxta consuetudinem predictam defendere debet & reparare ut predictum est tempore debito non defendit nec reparavit set eas reparare recusavit per quod terra pratum pastura & mora predicti P . . . submersa sunt & sewere & fossata sua ad moras & terram suam assewerandum facta sabulone wasea penitus obstructa & blada sua in grangiis suis & turbe sue superundata & putrefacta in ipsius D defectum existunt ad dampnum ipsius P £100 & contra consuetudinem predictam &c.*

The entries of this are *op. ses*; but when attornies are appointed the roll says it is *de placito transgressionis*.[66] Later entries make the duty prescriptive [67]; but in the most famous case, and the earliest hitherto known, its origin may possibly have been ascribed, as was that of the wall itself, to some legislative decision.

This case occupied the courts between 1340 and 1344.[68] It

---

[65] CP. 40/235, m. 156; CP. 40/236, m. 117d; CP. 40/237, m. 161d. The day last given was in a term of which the roll is not at present open to inspection.
[66] CP. 40/238, roll of attornies, m. 10. Such entries are known as *po. los.*: *P ponit loco suo X versus D de placito transgressionis.*
[67] e.g., CP. 40/370 (1352), m. 49d; CP. 40/429 (1367), m. 422; KB. 27/430 (1368), m. 26.
[68] YBB. 14 & 15 Ed. III, R.S., p. 246; 15 Ed. III, R.S., p. 86; 16 Ed. III (vol. i), R.S., p. 256; 18 Ed. III, R.S., p. 234; Trin. 18 Ed. III, pl. 6, f. 23. The record of the count and subsequent proceedings, but not the writ, are printed in the third of these at p. 259, and partly reproduced in condensed form in Kiralfy, *op. cit.*, p. 208. The relevant assignments of error are set out in *Public Works in Medieval Law*, vol. i, Seld.Soc., Vol. 32, p. 309, and the answers thereto are printed by Kiralfy, *op. cit.*, p. 209.

started in the Common Pleas with a writ called *bref de Trespas* in the reports and *breve de transgressione* in the record [69]:

> quare cum idem D ratione terrarum & tenementorum que tenet in A reparare & emendare debeat ipseque & omnes alii terras & tenementa predicta tenentes a tempore quo non extat memoria semper hactenus reparare & emendare consueverint quatuor particatas cujusdam wallie in eadem villa pro salvacione terrarum & tenementorum ibidem contra fluxus aque de Humbre ab antiquo facte & ordinate predictus D quatuor particatas predictas reparare & emendare non curavit per quod ducente acre prati ipsius P ob defectum reparacionis & emendacionis hujusmodi per fluxus aque predicte superundate fuerunt idemque P proficuum predicti prati amisit ad dampnum ipsius P £60.

Issue was taken on a denial that the terre-tenants had been accustomed to repair, and, though the verdict left room for argument, it was adjudged that the plaintiff should have damages.[70] This moved a reporter to query how the defendant was to be made to do the repairs; and next day the court was asked to add an order for their doing, which, after hesitation, it did. The defendant thereupon got a writ of error, assigning one error turning on the terms of the verdict, and three more which were variations on a single theme: the writ was *de transgressione*, and the count, being in the right, called for *reparari facias*; issue had been taken on the right, when the writ called for one *de injuria*; and the order to repair was in the right and so not warranted by the writ *de transgressione*. No decision is recorded.[71]

In view of the earlier entries, the difficulty cannot have been that this was the first appearance of trespass in a field regarded as the preserve of *reparari facias*.[72] It may have been that the latter only became clearly distinct as specific remedies ceased to be given in trespass; and that such proceedings, once perfectly regular, now seemed to confuse two separate things.[73] In 1355 the same point was raised in another way. To a similar writ the defendant objected that it sounded in the right rather than in trespass, since it would oblige him to repair what would last for ever; and therefore process

---

[69] CP. 40/330, m. 304; KB. 27/338, m. 41. Note that both the earlier writs had alleged a refusal to repair. This and subsequent ones have a simple *non curavit*; *e.g.* CP. 40/370, m. 49d; KB. 27/430, m. 26. But requests to repair might still be alleged in the count; YB. Pasch. 29 Ed. III, f. 32d.

[70] Fixed by the jury at 20s. instead of the £60 claimed, a point upon which the record confirms the report; YB. 18 Ed. III, R.S., p. 234.

[71] The original plaintiff joined an expedition to Brittany and produced letters of protection.

[72] As Dr. Kiralfy seems to infer from the assignments of error; *op. cit.*, p. 60.

[73] *Cf.* the argument in YB. Trin. 2 Ed. III (additional cases), pl. 13, f. 26.

should be by summons and not by attachment. This objection was overruled, issue being taken on the defendant's assertion that the damage had been caused, not by any fault of his, but by an exceptional flood [74]; but it is noteworthy that in 1273 and in 1340 process was by summons.[75] A ghost of this difficulty still haunts the action in 1372: the defendant demanded a view, and *le view fuit ouster pur ceo qe il fuit trespas en nature*.[76] This case, it may be added, is the earliest of the kind in which the writ is said in the report to be *foundu sur le cas*, though Dr. Kiralfy has shown that a similar phrase was used in the proceedings in error in 1344.[77] That there was in this period no antithesis between trespass and case will be suggested in the last of these articles; but it is to be noted here that, besides those so far mentioned, there are examples of 1371 and 1372 called trespass in the reports, and classified as case in Fitzherbert's *Abridgment*,[78] and that the writ is put with those *De Transgressione* in the Register, and with those on the case in the *Natura Brevium*.[79]

A curious part of the story, and one difficult to interpret, is a false step taken in 1371: *contra pacem* was put into the writ. It had not happened in 1367 or 1368 [80]: but the words appear in two of three entries noted in Trinity term, 1371,[81] and the Year Books tell us that in the same term a writ was abated for this reason [82]; the Register has a warning note referring to the case.[83] This was no doubt a muddle, but it may indicate how lawyers were thinking. In the first article it was suggested that certain early writs on the case were sawn-off *vi et armis* writs, and that in these a difficulty was felt about dropping *contra pacem*. This development, whereby the formal dress of *vi et armis* could be discarded when it was too uncomfortable, must have been the outstanding fact in the field of trespass at that time; and if in such cases *contra pacem* was at first retained as a concession to the proprieties, it may have seemed

---

[74] YB. Pasch. 29 Ed. III, f. 32d. Record in Kiralfy, *op. cit.*, p. 210.
[75] CP. 40/13, m. 35; CP. 40/330, m. 304.
[76] YB. Mich. 46 Ed. III, pl. 16, f. 27. The same objection had also been made in the 1355 case, n. 74 on this page.
[77] *The Action on the Case*, pp. 23, 36, 209. Dr. Kiralfy regards this as an early action on the case, having no connection with direct trespass; *ibid.*, pp. 36, 60.
[78] YB. Trin. 45 Ed. III, pl. 6, f. 17d is *Accion sur le case*, pl. 34; YB. Pasch. 46 Ed. III, pl. 2, f. 8d is *Briefe*, pl. 597.
[79] *Reg.Omn.Brev.*, f. 100; Fitzherbert, *Natura Brevium*, f. 93G. *Cf. Reg.Omn. Brev.*, f. 104d.
[80] Respectively CP. 40/429, m. 422 and KB. 27/430, m. 26.
[81] CP. 40/443, mm. 106, 232. The former is worded without a *cum*, the duty being asserted in a relative clause. For the third entry, see *infra*, n. 85.
[82] YB. Trin. 45 Ed. III, pl. 6, f. 17d.
[83] *Reg.Omn.Brev.*, f. 100.

necessary in all trespass actions coming into the royal court, and been zealously put into a writ which had no use for it.

There remains a class of case which may differ from the foregoing in an important way. With river walls the duty was public, not owed particularly to the plaintiff; but it might be otherwise with gutters. In 1352 there was a *reparari facias* for a gutter *que diruta est & confracta ad nocumentum liberi tenementi ipsius P* [84]; and the following is a trespass writ from Trinity term, 1371 [85]:

> *quare cum idem D quandam gutteram inter domum suam & domum predicti P apud A reparare & sustentare debeat ipseque & omnes alii domum ipsius D ibidem tenentes a tempore cujus contrarii memoria non existit gutteram illam reparare & sustentare consueverunt predictus D gutteram illam per magnum tempus reparare & sustentare non curavit per quod maeremium & parietes dicte domus ipsius P per pluviam descendentem putride devenerunt.*

This apparently omits some words at the end, so we can not tell whether, like the other two from the same roll, it would have had *contra pacem*.[86]

Innkeepers

The writer has only a small contribution. The plaintiff in the famous case of 1368 was a royal official,[87] and the writ, of which one of the two precedents in the Register is a transcript,[88] makes a good deal of this: the defendant was to answer the king as well as the plaintiff; some of the money taken was the king's; and the wrong was said to be in contempt of the king. This element is absent from the other precedent in the Register,[89] and also from the other report of 1368 to which the Register refers[90]; but the two reports end in so similar a way that they may be two versions of the same case. It is therefore worth recording that a writ was entered substantially in the second form, the plaintiff being an ordinary citizen, in 1371.[91]

The official's writ had *contra pacem*. So did the other 1368 report, if it is of a different case; but the precedent said by the

---

[84] CP. 40/370, m. 67d.
[85] CP. 40/443, m. 124d.
[86] So far as it goes this form is identical with *Reg.Omn.Brev.*, f. 104d. The latter ends normally, alleging damage but not *contra pacem*, but in turn omits words in the middle. *Cf.* Rastell, *Entrees*, f. 10d, *Action sur le case pur nient faire Reparations*.
[87] 42 *Lib.Ass.*, pl. 17, f. 260d. Record in Kiralfy, *op. cit.*, plate V, at p. 152.
[88] *Reg.Omn.Brev.*, f. 105. There are insignificant differences.
[89] *Reg.Omn.Brev.*, f. 104.
[90] YB. Pasch. 42 Ed. III, pl. 13, f. 11.
[91] CP. 40/443, m. 308.

Register to be based on that report has instead *contra legem et consuetudinem supradictas*.[92] The appearance of *contra pacem* is reminiscent of the writs last discussed. No evidence is known of earlier actions against innkeepers at common law, but Dr. Kiralfy has remarked that there were not dissimilar actions in the City of London[93]; and it may again be that these words were at first thought necessary to give jurisdiction. Their insertion may have been responsible for the further mistaken idea that process could be by *capias*[94]; but of this more will be said in the last of these articles. It should be noted, yet again, that the precedents are under *De Transgressione* in the Register, and that both 1368 reports call the action trespass.

4. SOME CONCLUSIONS

These were writs of trespass; and trespass was therefore not an entity characterised by direct forcible injury. Consider three of the wrongs to a market: a direct attack is trespass in our sense; driving away merchants who would do business there might be a trespass in that sense to the merchants, but not to the franchise owner; and conducting a black market is not a trespass in our sense to anybody. The cases of failure to repair and of the innkeeper's liability are nonfeasances: one can, of course, disregard what they were called and say that these were actions on the case and therefore different; but then they must be among the earliest offshoots of trespass in our sense, and this is not easy to square with other aspects of the traditional view. There are also the objections made to special writs: it was sometimes argued that the question was not one of trespass, but only to assert that it was one of property; there is no trace of our concept.

It is important to add that whereas rescue, for example, is common, most of the writs above are not. This must mainly reflect the relative frequency of events; though everyone has a body to be beaten or goods to be taken, few have markets or free bulls. But, although the common law of wrongs was richer than we have generally thought, it was not meant to be comprehensive. Even special writs speak of *vi et armis* and *contra pacem* whenever they can, and about 1370 the latter made its way briefly into forms where it was quite inappropriate. This brings us back to the point of jurisdiction. Breach of the peace was so much the normal ticket

---

[92] *Reg.Omn.Brev.*, f. 104. The entire end of the writ, in this case as well as in the others, grammatically refers to the unknown malefactors rather than the defendant; but, in this case at least, that makes nonsense. The 1371 entry unhelpfully ends *& alia enormia &c.*
[93] *Op. cit.*, p. 151.
[94] 42 *Lib.Ass.*, pl. 17, f. 260d; YB. Pasch. 42 Ed. III, pl. 13, f. 11.

by which wrongs came into the royal courts, that even when the need for tickets was abandoned some thought it suitable to put in a formal *contra pacem*. While tickets were still necessary, any breach of the peace could be alleged, battery of others being as good as battery of the plaintiff, and hence the formulation of many of these writs. Whether the violence was always genuine is doubtful; issue is commonly taken on the special matter rather than on the main clause of the writ. Whether even the allegation was always essential is also doubtful: we have seen some entries where it could have been made but was not; and in some it could not decently be made at all. The writ for selling outside a market was presumably acceptable because the protection of franchises as such was proper matter for the royal court; and if so the other wrongs to a market could perhaps have come in on the same ticket. Injury from failure to repair river walls was probably cognisable because of the public nature of the duty; and it may be relevant that no trespass action for failing to repair a gutter has been noted before 1371. The barrier was then going down; private wrongs could come in as such, and needed no other credentials.

PART III: MORE SPECIAL WRITS AND CONCLUSIONS

THIS is the last of three articles tracing the development of early trespass writs.[1] General writs were considered in the first article, and most kinds of special writ in the second; but space required the holding over of special writs reciting a transaction between the parties, and these form the first section below. The remaining sections discuss, under self-explanatory headings, various aspects of the subject as a whole.

1. WRITS RECITING TRANSACTIONS

Bailment: (a) Actions against third parties

In 1241 a plaintiff sued one for taking *blada domini sui que fuerunt in custodia sua*,[2] and this is the nearest approach found to an action by the bailee against a third party. Probably bailees would use ordinary general writs so that the bailment would never be mentioned. A general writ was certainly used in a case of 1374, and the defendant, who had some justification as against the bailor, objected: *vous averes accion de trespas per auter bref, fesant mencion dicelle qe ils fueront en vostre garde, et nemy per general bref*. It is answered that *il nad nul auter briefe en la Chauncery en le case.*[3]

This report is more famous for another passage: *Et jeo die en cest case, cestuy qe ad la propertie poit aver bref de Trespas, & cestuy qe ad la garde un auter bref de Trespas.* This is the earliest clear evidence that the bailor could sue a third party. In the first article three relevant entries were mentioned: but in two the writ described the immediate victim as the plaintiff's servant[4]; and in the third, though the writ said only that the plaintiff *dimiserat in custodia predicti X* the goods, the count explained that he *retinuisset predictum X in servicio suo ad vendendum pannos suos* and that the taking was from the plaintiff's shop.[5] The only other entry

---

[1] The first two were: "Trespass from Henry III to Edward III, Part I: General Writs," (1958) 74 L.Q.R., p. 195; "Part II: Special Writs," (1958) 74 L.Q.R., p. 407: here pp. 1, 31.
[2] 74 L.Q.R., p. 195, at p. 213, here p. 19.
[3] YB. Mich. 48 Edw. III, pl.8, f. 20d; what looks like an intrusive note refers to writs for executors, which have some phrase like *sub custodia ipsorum executorum inventa*; Reg.Omn.Brev., ff. 92d, 94, 102d. *Cf.* YB. Mich. 47 Edw. III, pl. 10, f. 12.
[4] 74 L.Q.R., p. 195, at p. 213, here p. 19, nn. 63, 64.
[5] *Ibid.*, n. 62; C.R.R., XVI, pl. 1933.

noted as relevant was printed in the second article: the plaintiff had his goods embarked in a ship; the defendants arrested the ship, took away its sail and other equipment, and *navem illam sic absque regimine exire permiserunt per quod bona & catalla predicta in eadem navi existencia . . . pro defectu regiminis totaliter perierunt.* The action concerns the goods only, and we infer that the ship was somebody else's; but the *cum* clause is curiously reticent, saying only that the goods were put *in quadam navi.*[6] This reticence suggests the possibility—it is no more—that in less unusual circumstances the bailor might use an ordinary general writ; but probably it was normally for the bailee to sue.

Bailment: (b) Bailee against bailor

The entries found all concern the retaking of animals delivered by way of agistment or the like, as in an example of 1359[7]:

> *quare vi & armis clausum ipsius P apud A fregit & quendam bovem quem idem D cum prefato P agistavit non soluto agistamento illo ibidem inventum cepit & abduxit . . . & alia enormia ei intulit ad grave dampnum ipsius P & contra pacem &c.*

Here the plaintiff's interest is a sort of lien for the hire of his pasture. Conversely the animals might be hired, and the Register has among its viscontiel writs of trespass one for the retaking, *clam* and *sine licencia & voluntate,* of a bull delivered *certis conditionibus usque ad certum terminum.*[8] This may be compared with an entry of 1367[9]:

> *quare cum idem D 60 oves suas predicto P certis conditionibus usque ad certum terminum tradidisset in falda ipsius P apud A pro terra sua ibidem cum animalibus predictis compostanda idem D faldam illam vi & armis fregit & oves predictas infra terminum illum cepit & abduxit & alia enormia &c.*

Another writ on the same roll is substantially identical with another viscontiel precedent and is without *vi & armis*; but, unlike the precedent, it has *contra pacem.* It is for retaking sheep delivered to the plaintiff *super terram & pasturam suam apud A per unum annum moraturas & custodiendas.*[10]

Bailment: (c) Bailor against bailee

It will be convenient to begin with what for the present purposes is the end of the story. After about 1367 the bailee is liable in tort

---

[6] 74 L.Q.R., p. 407, at p. 411, here p. 35.
[7] C.P. 40/399, m. 27. *Cf.* YB. Mich. 30 Edw. III, f. 11, 11d.
[8] *Reg.Omn.Brev.,* f 92d.
[9] CP. 40/429, m. 600.
[10] CP. 40/429, mm. 282d, 552; *Reg.Omn.Brev.,* f. 92 (*moraturas vel custodiendas*).

not only for his own misdeeds but also for negligence in letting harm come to the goods. The Register has two precedents, both concerning sheep, one with an *assumpsit* and the other without,[11] and Dr. Kiralfy has shown how persistent these were.[12] The earliest example noted of the latter form is from 1367 [13]:

> *quare cum idem P 300 oves suas eidem D apud A tradidisset custodiendas idem D oves predictas minus sufficienter custodivit per quod 160 oves precii £20 de ovibus predictis interierunt ad dampnum ipsius P £100 &c.*

The defendant *dicit quod ipse bene & sufficienter custodivit oves predictas ita quod nulle earum pro defectu custodie ipsius D perierunt prout predictus P superius versus eum narravit.* Three years later a jury gave its verdict: *predictus D culpabilis est de transgressione infracontenta prout idem P queritur ad dampnum ipsius P 35s.* The same roll contains an *op. se* even closer to the Register's form; it says that the sheep were delivered *debite custodiendas*, and that the defendant *tam negligenter & indebite custodivit* that some died and the rest *multipliciter deteriorate fuerunt.*[14] Similar is a curiosity from 1371 [15]:

> *quare cum eadem P prefato D quoddam molendinum suum apud A ad certum terminum debite custodiendum dimisisset predictus D molendinum illud tam negligenter custodivit quod per ipsius defectum molendinum predictum totaliter dirrutum fuit & confractum & alia enormia ei intulit ad dampnum ipsius P £20 & contra pacem Regis.*

The ending may be due to clerical hypnosis, but this was the time at which *contra pacem* was making other unexpected appearances.

The *assumpsit* form was found by Dr. Kiralfy in 1373 in an action against a shipmaster, matched by a precedent in the Register.[16] But the Register has also an *assumpsit* not to carry but just to look after [17]; it again concerns sheep, and may be compared with an *op. se* of 1371 in which the defendant is described as a shepherd [18]:

> *quare cum idem D ad 200 oves ipsius P super pasturam suam apud A bene & fideliter custodiendas assumpsisset predictus D oves illas ita negligenter custodivit quod 100 oves precii £20 de ovibus predictis interierunt & alia &c.*

[11] *Reg.Omn.Brev.*, ff. 110d, 107 respectively.
[12] *The Action on the Case*, p. 159.
[13] CP. 40/429, m. 471.
[14] CP. 40/429, m. 86d.; *Reg.Omn.Brev.*, f. 107.
[15] CP. 40/443, m. 20d.
[16] *Op. cit.*, p. 159; *Reg.Omn.Brev.*, f. 108.
[17] *Reg.Omn.Brev.*, f. 110d.
[18] CP. 40/443, m. 235.

The pasture was presumably the plaintiff's; and it would be reasonable, as a matter of language rather than of law, to use this form where the defendant was mainly to perform a service rather than to receive goods.[19]

These writs appearing about 1367 prompt two remarks. One is that the actions are called trespass: the Register has its precedents under *De Transgressione*, and the jury's verdict in the first 1367 case was *culpabilis est de transgressione*.[20] The second is that according to the traditional view this liability for careless custody sprang up out of nothing, there being no earlier liability even for active and wilful harm. Even if this were so, the jump is too large for a conceptual development, and is explicable only as the collapse of a jurisdictional barrier.

We turn now to the beginning of the story. In the first article a case of 1242 was mentioned, in which executors sued one who must have been their testator's pledgee for selling goods beyond the amount of the debt.[21] A *querela* of 1259 was similarly for destruction and waste in selling goods pledged, but the plaintiff sought recovery *secundum consuetudinem mercatorum*.[22] Even in the thirteenth century such cases were rare in royal courts; and, detinue apart, the normal protection of the bailor no doubt lay elsewhere. The Register has, among its viscontiel writs of trespass, one for use against a pledgee who refuses redemption[23]; and there must have been remedies for, say, malicious damage. The question is whether, before about 1367, there was any remedy in a royal court.

Under Edward II remedies were sought and sometimes granted. The Year Books report at least three actions by bailors against bailees and at least one, to be considered under the next heading, by a purchaser against his vendor in possession. Two of these succeeded and two failed; three were by special writs, and one by a special bill. The bill, in an eyre of 1321, said that the plaintiff had bailed a locked chest containing £40 for safe-keeping, and that the bailee and another *a force e armes lavantdit cofre pristrunt e embriserunt e les deners pristrunt e emporterunt &c.* The plaintiff was not answered, *pur ceo quil ne poet estre entendu qe home poet a force e armes en contre la pees emporterunt chose qest en sa garde de*

---

[19] In view of later arguments, another entry of 1367 may be mentioned; the plaintiff is a former sheriff: *quare cum idem D in faciendo execucionem de X . . . certis de causis morti adjudicato a prefato nuper vicecomiti sub pena £100 manucepisset predictus D execucionem illam prout tenebatur non fecit set ipsum X evadere permisit pro quaquidem evasione idem nuper vicecomes in quadam summa pecunie erga Regem oneratus fuit ad dampnum ipsius nuper vicecomitis £40*; CP. 40/429, m. 592. Cf. *Reg.Omn.Brev.*, f. 110.
[20] *Supra*, nn. 11, 13.
[21] 74 L.Q.R., p. 195, at p. 224, here p. 30, n. 34.
[22] KB. 26/161, mm. 1d, 17d.
[23] *Reg.Omn.Brev.*, f. 92d.

demeyne, and because *bille de detenue &c. luy ust servy proprement en ceo cas*.²⁴ In a note apparently based on this case, the reporter distinguishes between a deposit, where the plaintiff is allowed to put a chest at his own risk in the defendant's house, and a delivery *en garde*: in the former case the plaintiff may, and in the latter he may not, have a writ saying that the defendant broke the chest *vi & armis*.²⁵ In each of the other two actions the writ complained of injury to a writing which the plaintiff, as the *cum* clause said, *bona fide tradidisset inspiciendum*.²⁶ In 1312 it was quashed; in 1318, although challenged *pur ceo qil poeit mye ceo qil avoit en sa garde demesne a force et armes debruser*, the writ was upheld by Bereford.

After Edward II such actions vanish; and bailors appear to have no remedy in tort against their bailees until about 1367. But we may be deceived in this, as may best be explained in terms of the action for injuring a writing delivered for inspection. Bereford gave no reason for upholding the writ in 1318 ²⁷; but the reason for quashing it in 1312 is stated clearly. It is not that this was not trespass, but that, with the allegations of delivery and of taking by force and arms, *issint est le conte repugnant*, or, in the words of the roll, *que quidem contrariantur*. What we should call the headnote also makes repugnancy the point of the case.²⁸ Supposing that it is a formal point, a cure would be to cut out the allegations of *vi et armis* and *contra pacem*. What remains after this excision is a good writ, and is actually in the Register ²⁹; but it is a viscontiel writ of trespass, and would not have been made returnable in a royal court. There may have been attempts to get such writs made returnable; an *op. se* from 1310 appears to lack even *contra pacem* ³⁰:

> *quare cum predicta P 18 marcas sigillo suo signatas prefato D apud A in deposito custodiendas tradidisset predictus D sigillum predictum maliciose fregit & predictas 18 marcas cepit & asportavit & alia enormia &c. ad grave dampnum &c.*

But at that date the Chancery would not normally be induced to make such writs other than viscontiel. Our hypothetical excision

---

²⁴ R. V. Rogers, *Eyre of London, 14 Edw. II*, p. 74; *Eyre of Kent*, II, Seld.Soc. Vol. 27, p. xxvii, n. 3.
²⁵ Rogers, *op. cit.*, p. 44.
²⁶ YBB. 5 Edw. II, Seld.Soc. Vol. 31, p. 215; 11 Edw. II, Seld.Soc. Vol. 61, p. 290.
²⁷ YB. 11 Edw. II, Seld.Soc. Vol. 61, p. 290. For explanations see Plucknett, *Concise History* (5th ed.), p. 469, n. 5 (momentary delivery would not count), Holdsworth, Seld.Soc. Vol. 61, p. xxviii (*vi et armis* a formal allegation). The precedent (n. 29 below) has *inspiciendam vel custodiendam*, and the 1312 reporter speaks of custody although the roll says the delivery was for inspection.
²⁸ YB. 5 Edw. II, Seld.Soc. Vol. 31, p. 215. Another objection was tried first.
²⁹ *Reg.Omn.Brev.*, f. 92d. *Cf.* f 106d, a special writ for use by the heir.
³⁰ KB. 27/201, m. 22d.

thus looks like the reverse of what happened. The writ was basically viscontiel, and was embellished with *vi et armis* and *contra pacem* to get it into the royal court. This made it vulnerable for repugnancy, and the only cure was to cut out the recital of delivery. If this operation is performed, what remains is an ordinary general writ.

The conclusion that bailors might use general writs was reached, for the particular case of smiths, in the first article.[31] For other situations there is no direct evidence; but, if general writs came consistently to be used, there would not be. Consider writs in this form [32]:

> *quare vi & armis quandam cistam ipsius P apud A inventam fregerunt & bona & catalla sua ad valenciam 100s. in eadem cista inventa ceperunt & asportaverunt & alia enormia ei intulerunt ad grave dampnum ipsius P & contra pacem &c.*

These are not uncommon and there is a precedent in the Register.[33] Since they can be matched by forms alleging the breaking of the plaintiff's room or house as well as his chest,[34] they must have been for use against persons having lawful access to the place where the chest was; and though there are many possibilities, the defendants include parsons, priors and other likely bailees.[35] But the pleadings give no hint of the facts: to the writ printed above the defendants *bene defendunt quod ipsi non fecerunt predicte P transgressionem predictam contra pacem Regis sicut eadem P superius queritur* [36]; and that is all we know. The only conclusive evidence for which we can hope is the chance discovery of explicit special verdicts.[37]

There is, however, one piece of direct evidence that narrative matter might be removed to avoid a formal difficulty of the kind contemplated. A bill in the King's Bench in 1353 complained that the defendant had taken the plaintiff's horse to such a place and had there killed it *encontre le peace &c.* The defendant said that he had taken it damage feasant and put it in the common pound, had tied it up because it was savage, and that it had strangled itself. Upon this admission the plaintiff demanded judgment. The defendant, however, demanded judgment of the bill: *per la pris*

---

[31] 74 L.Q.R., p. 220, here p. 26; Kiralfy, *op. cit.*, p. 142.
[32] CP. 40/373 (1353), m. 39.
[33] *Reg.Omn.Brev.*, ff. 94d, 95; examples are: CP. 40/236, m. 103; CP. 40/240, m. 51; KB. 27/300, m. 60; CP. 40/340, mm. 191, 375; CP. 40/350, mm. 19, 118d, 251d; CP. 40/360, m. 56d; CP. 40/373, mm. 137d, 172.
[34] *Reg.Omn.Brev.*, ff. 108, 110d, 111; CP. 40/235, m. 208 (house); C.P. 40/236, m. 31 (room); CP. 40/391, mm. 20d, 236 (houses).
[35] *e.g.*, KB. 27/300, m. 93 (vicar); CP. 40/360, m. 101d. (prioress); CP. 40/360, m. 72d (man and wife).
[36] CP. 40/373, m. 39. *Cf.* K.B. 27/300, m. 60, *in nullo est culpabilis*.
[37] One such in print at least shows a general writ used for appropriating goods on the defendant's own land; YB. 6 & 7 Edw. II, Seld.Soc. Vol. 36, p. 16.

a tort &c. fuit la propertie devestu de vous, et vestu en nous, & per consequens nous ne poiomus occire nostre chival demesne encontre le peace. On this ground the court was prepared to abate the bill; but the plaintiff produced another bill, *per quel ne fuit suppose forsque le defendant avoit occis son chival encontre le peace &c.*, and he won.[38]

Sale of goods

The Year Books of Edward II report two actions of trespass by buyers against sellers. Bereford would not swallow the form, or probably the substance, of a writ in 1313: the plaintiff said that the defendant had agreed under law merchant to sell him four sacks of good flax, and had treacherously put in some hemp. The defendant demanded judgment of the writ, because the plaintiff *ad counte de un covenant qe se prist etc. et il ad counte encountre la pes.* The plaintiff sought to justify his *contra pacem* by showing that the writ alleged *alia enormia*; but Bereford would not have it: *Rens ne put estre encountre la pes sil ne seit a force et pur ceo git enprisonement et vous naves rienz moustre qe fut fet a force par quei avisez vous.*[39] The report ends with the plaintiff asking leave to seek a better writ, and we can only speculate what better writ he might have had; presumably there were at the time of the agreement no specific sacks, so that the defendant had just delivered adulterated goods.

> The other case was an action in 1317 against a man and wife[40]: *quare cum idem P quoddam doleum vini de prefato D apud A pro 6m. 6s. & 8d. nuper emisset et doleum illud ibidem dimisisset quousque illud querere demandasset predicti DD magnam partem vini illius a doleo predicto vi & armis extraxerunt & loco illius vini sic extracti doleum illud aqua salsa impleverunt per quod totum vinum predictum putrefactum devenit & omnino periit ad grave dampnum ipsius P & contra pacem &c.*

The count adds nothing but a date, a claim for £10 in damages, and news that the defendants cleverly got the wine out of its cask *vi et armis scilicet gladiis arcubus et sagittis etc.*[41] The expected objection was taken: *vous avez dit qe nous fumes seisi et qe nous venismes a force et armis qe ne put estre entendu*; but it sounds perfunctory, and counsel at once took another point, that the place

---

[38] 27 *Lib.Ass.*, pl. 64, f. 143. *Cf.* the distinction between replevin, affirming property in the plaintiff, and trespass, affirming it in the defendant; YB. 6 Edw. II, Seld. Soc. Vol. 34, p. 142.
[39] YB. 7 Edw. II, Seld.Soc. Vol. 39, p. 14.
[40] YB. 10 Edw. II, Seld.Soc. Vol. 54, p. 140.
[41] See 74 L.Q.R., p. 195, at p. 222, here, p. 28.

of the trespass was not named. This also failed, and issue was taken on the defendants' denial *quod ipsi numquam predictis die et anno vinum predictum a predicto doleo vi et armis extraxerunt seu loco illius vini aquam salsam imposuerunt nec aliquam transgressionem ei fecerunt prout predictus P superius queritur*. Such cases are not found after Edward II and there is the same possibility as with bailors' actions, namely that instead of a retrenchment of the law and a later dramatic expansion there was steady litigation under the cover of general writs.

Carriage of goods

A precedent in the Register provides evidence of this. It is a general writ for *vi et armis* taking wine from its cask and substituting sea water; but the cask is described as embarked in a ship for carriage, and the ship is the defendant's.[42]

Another general writ of 1355 may not advance the matter much, but is instructive:[43]

> *quare vi & armis quinque sarplaria lanarum & quingentas pelles lanutas ipsius P in navi ipsius D apud A abinde usque ad partes Flandrie ducenda cariata propter inundacionem aque maritime bene & sufficienter ibidem cooperta discooperuit ita quod major pars lanarum & pellium predictarum putrida devenit & totaliter deperiit & in X servientem suum ibidem insultum fecit & ipsum verberavit vulneravit & maletractavit per quod idem P servicium servientis sui per magnum tempus amisit ad dampnum ipsius P £20 & contra pacem &c.*

The pleadings tell us no more of the facts: to a count virtually repeating the writ, the defendant *dicit quod ipse in nullo est inde culpabilis de transgressione predicta*. With the battery the case is consistent with our idea of trespass; but the goods were on the defendant's ship, and, whether or not the plaintiff's servant was to travel with them, it may be that a carrier like this would anyway fall under the 1321 reporter's category of depositee rather than transferee *en garde*.[44]

These were general writs, and they were for harm caused by the defendant actively interfering with goods committed to him. We turn now to harm which the carrier did not himself do, but for which he was to blame. An *op. se* of 1352 lacks even *contra pacem*[45]:

---

[42] *Reg.Omn.Brev.*, f. 95d. The cask was put *in navi predicti J*. J. could only have been *predictus* as one of the parties, and the plaintiff is W.
[43] KB. 27/380, m. 79.
[44] *Supra*, pp. 64-65.
[45] CP. 40/370, m. 165. Since the ship itself was the plaintiff's, this case could have been put with those on bailment.

> *quare cum idem P quandam navem suam precii £100 cum bonis & catallis suis ad valenciam £40 in eadem navi existentibus apud A prefato D suo periculo custodiendam & regendam tradidisset idem D navem predictam ibidem absque custodia & regimine dimisit per quod idem P navem & bona & catalla predicta totaliter amisit & alia enormia ei intulit in ipsius P dampnum non modicum & gravamen.*

The interesting thing is that there is another *op. se* of this case in the following term; but the writ then has a new ending. Instead of *in ipsius P dampnum non modicum & gravamen*, which will be noted below as normal in viscontiel writs, it has *ad grave dampnum ipsius P & contra pacem Regis*.[46] The writ has been embellished as already inferred in the case of the writing handed over for inspection, presumably to increase its chance of being acceptable in a royal court. One would imagine that again this would make it vulnerable for repugnancy; the addition is particularly incongruous where the harm was immediately done by the elements. Unfortunately no further entries of the case have been found.

Contra pacem appears again in the next entry noted, which, being in 1368, is in every other respect clearly what we should call an action on the case [47]:

> *quare cum idem P diversa bona & mercimonia prefatis DD apud A abinde in quadam navi usque B ducenda tradidisset predicti DD bona & mercimonia predicta ita negligenter custodierunt quod bona & mercimonia illa totaliter amissa fuerunt ad dampnum ipsius P £60 ut dicit & contra pacem &c.*

The count adds only a list of the goods, and to it the defendants *veniunt & defendunt vim & injuriam quando &c.*; but the case goes no further because jurisdiction is claimed by the Bishop of Norwich. There is, however, compensation for this abrupt ending. The Bishop is allowed his liberty on the basis of a precedent of 1365: *hujusmodi libertas* was allowed in a plea *de quadam transgressione* between certain named parties. A precise reference is given, and it turns out to be an ordinary action for battery.[48] The liberty thus included jurisdiction over pleas of trespass, and this carrier's carelessness was as much a trespass as the battery was.

Needless to say the Register's precedent for the loss of goods carried by water has no *contra pacem*; it is formulated with an *assumpsit*, and there was an example in 1373.[49] The other particularly hazardous kind of carriage was evidently the carriage of liquids

---

[46] CP. 40/371, m. 138.
[47] KB. 27/430, m. 33.
[48] KB. 27/419, m. 24.
[49] *Reg.Omn.Brev.*, f. 108; Kiralfy, *op. cit.*, pp. 159, 160.

by land. The Register has two precedents, one for wine and one for oil, and each has an *assumpsit*.⁵⁰ An example without comes from 1371⁵¹:

> *quare cum idem P prefatum D ad quoddam doleum vini ipsius P cum quadam carecta sua a villa de A usque villam de B salvo & secure cariandum pro certa summa pecunie conduxisset prefatus D carectam illam prefato doleo cariato ita maliciose & negligenter fugavit quod doleum illud confractum extitit & predictus P vinum in eodem doleo existentem precii £10 totaliter amisit.*

No earlier entries have been found patently on such facts, but in the first article suspicion was directed at a general writ for *vi et armis* breaking a cask of wine so that it all ran out.⁵² If a ship is wrecked and the cargo lost, it is not easy to say, or to ask a jury to say, that the shipmaster destroyed the cargo; but it is quite easy to say that the driver broke a cask if he had run his cart into a ditch. The two writs mentioned first under this heading are both for harm done in an obvious sense by the defendant, and both general; and in simpler circumstances they might have been in common form, with no adjectival phrases to betray the facts, as seems to have been the case with smiths.

The distinction suggested is between harm which the carrier could be said to have done, and harm for which he might be to blame but which a jury would not say he had done. In the former situation the only difficulty might be the insubstantial one of repugnancy, and it seems that ordinary general writs came to be used. In the latter the same formal difficulty perhaps appeared, and the entries of 1352 and 1368 seem to tell of a viscontiel writ being rigged out with *contra pacem* to get it into the royal court, and the *contra pacem* eventually being dropped to leave what we should identify as a pure writ on the case.⁵³ But in this latter situation there was also a difficulty of principle, the argument that it sounded in contract rather than in tort.

Only with trepidation is anything added to all that has been written about the *Humber Ferry Case*,⁵⁴ but it loses its mystery if

---

⁵⁰ *Reg.Omn.Brev.*, ff. 110, 111d.
⁵¹ CP. 40/443, m. 188. *Maliciose & negligenter* presumably translates as recklessly.
⁵² 74 L.Q.R., p. 221, here p. 27. A mistake was made over the date; it should be 1353.
⁵³ *Supra*, nn. 45, 46, 47.
⁵⁴ 22 *Lib.Ass.*, pl. 41, f. 94; Plucknett, *Concise History* (5th ed.), p. 470. Kiralfy (1953) 11 C.L.J., p. 421; Hastings, XIII, *Bulletin of Inst. of Hist. Research*, p. 36; Holdsworth, H.E.L., Vol. III, p. 430. Fifoot, *History and Sources of the Common Law*, at p. 331, dismisses the case as "not a precedent but a freak."

there was nothing unusual about suing bailees or carriers; and actions may by 1348 have been common under the cover of general writs. These would not serve if the harm had been permitted rather than done, and overloading a ferry comes near the border-line; hence the litigation, and the argument that this was not trespass but covenant, or, in our language, not tort but contract.[55] The decision that it was trespass, or tort, may have been made easier by the public nature of the ferryman's duty: ferries at this date might be in some sense " common "; and for a ferryman to take excessive charges or to keep travellers waiting unreasonably were offences which a jury might present.[56] As to the question whether this was trespass or case, there was at this date no antithesis: when the judge said it was trespass he did not have our concept in mind; it did not exist. He just meant it was tort. As to the process, which was by *capias*, later a hall-mark of trespass in our sense, it will be suggested below that it normally accompanied *contra pacem*. Whether this bill had *contra pacem* is doubtful[57]; but, on the state of the law postulated, actions against bailees or carriers would ordinarily be by general writs, so that a *capias* would be the usual thing. What makes the case remarkable to us is that for once we are told about the delivery. What made it important for contemporaries was not that this was an action against some sort of bailee or carrier, but that it was an action against him for harm which was his fault but which he had not in the most obvious sense done.

Surgeons

The earliest Year Book report is of 1374; Dr. Kiralfy has printed the record of that case,[58] and also a very interesting record of 1369.[59] Less informative than these about the terms in which argument might be conducted, but more informative in another way, is an entry of 1364; husband and wife sue for harm to the wife[60]:

> *quare cum brachium & manus sinistra ipsius P casualiter lesa fuissent idem D prefatis PP fideliter promisisset quod ipse brachium & manum predicta adeo bene & salvo sanaret sicut aliquis surgicus in Londinio cujus promissionis pretextu iidem*

---

[55] The new readings seem preferable to the vulgate text. Plucknett, *op. cit.*, p. 470, n. 1; Kiralfy (1953) 11 C.L.J., p. 424.
[56] *Public Works in Medieval Law*, Vol. II, Seld.Soc. Vol. 40, pp. 306 (1362), 309 (1328).
[57] No mention in report or record; the latter gives only the terms of the verdict.
[58] YB. Hil. 48 Edw. III, pl. 11, f. 6; *The Action on the Case*, p. 225.
[59] *Ibid.*, p. 224 (not mentioned in the text at p. 139).
[60] KB. 27/414, m. 37d.

> PP de fidelitate & industria ipsius D in hac parte confidentes curam brachii & manus predictorum juxta promissionem predictam fideliter faciendam prefato D pro competenti salario suo commisissent idem D admissa cura predicta & parte salarii sui predicti prae manibus percepta curam illam ita indiscrete negligenter aut maliciose apud Londinium fecit quod eadem P manum suam predictam per defectum ipsius D totaliter amisit ad dampnum ipsorum PP £100 ut dicunt.

To a count adding only a date and place, the defendant *dicit quod ipse in nullo est culpabilis de transgressione predicta sicut predicti PP per breve & narracionem suam supponunt.* Nearly two years later the verdict is given: *in nullo est culpabilis de transgressionibus predictis.* This is the language one might expect on any general writ. Since the Register also puts all its three precedents against surgeons under *De Transgressione*,[61] we must conclude that the surgeon's carelessness, like the carrier's, was as fully a trespass as any wrong could be.

It is not impossible that surgeons had previously been exposed to writs of battery. The earliest report expressly says that the writ was not *vi et armis* or *contra pacem*, a point which became important when the defendant sought to wage his law [62]; but no other evidence has been noted, and on *a priori* grounds such a usage is less likely than with the smith. The doubt here is about the earlier existence of any remedy in a royal court [63]; that there were remedies elsewhere is likely. The 1364 case, like those of 1369 and 1374, arose in London, where the surgical profession was regulated by the City [64]; and litigation of some sort was apparently possible in the City courts as early as 1300,[65] though there is no clear record before 1377.[66]

2. Some Features of Trespass Actions

Process

For the present purpose only two matters demand notice, the use of summons and the use of *capias*. In the fourteenth century the normal first step towards getting the defendant into court to answer any kind of trespass action was attachment by gage and pledge; but sometimes the original writ would instead tell the sheriff to summon the defendant. This made the procedure "more dilatory

---

[61] *Reg.Omn.Brev.*, ff. 105d, 112.
[62] YB. Hil. 48 Edw. III, pl. 11, f. 6.
[63] *Cf.* Kiralfy, *op.cit.*, p. 138.
[64] *Cal. of Early Mayor's Court Rolls, 1298–1307*, p. 81; *Cal. Letter Books, G*, p. 236; *Cal. of Plea and Memoranda Rolls, 1364–1381*, p. 236.
[65] *Cal. of Early Mayor's Court Rolls, 1298–1307*, p. 81; Kiralfy, *op. cit.*, p. 139.
[66] *Cal. of Plea and Memoranda Rolls, 1364–1381*, p. 236.

by a day," starting the action one stage further back in Bracton's scheme of process.[67] The applicability of the possible stages in this scheme to the various kinds of action depended originally upon the royal interest. *Fet Asaver* allots the most stringent process to offences against the king's peace, the next to offences against his command, and the least stringent to personal actions in which the king has no interest at all.[68]

In the light of this it may be of interest to list the trespass actions noted as starting by summons. They are: the early actions for taking toll from those who should be quit[69]; certain cases about jurisdictional franchises,[70] including that of 1350 in which the defendant refused to accept the payment which the plaintiff claimed would entitle him to exercise the jurisdiction[71]; the black market cases[72]; and the earlier cases of failure to repair.[73] None of these had *contra pacem*; and, though perhaps not a rule to begin with,[74] it was soon settled that writs making that allegation ordered an immediate attachment. In the fourteenth century, however, there was a sophistication: process by summons became associated with questions of property. In a case of failure to repair in 1355 the defendant objected that there should have been summons and not attachment since the action would oblige him to repair what would last forever.[75] Another example is *ejectio custodie*, whose change in nature from trespass to property was signalised by summons driving *contra pacem* out of the writ.[76] The same idea presumably explains the curious rule governing an action by executors against their testator's lessor who entered after the death but before expiry of the term: if he took any chattels, the writ and process were normal; if not, there was no *contra pacem* and process was by

---

[67] Britton (ed. Nichols), Vol. 1, p. 132; Bracton, ff. 439 *et seq.*; Pollock and Maitland, H.E.L. (2nd ed.), Vol. II, p. 593.
[68] Woodbine, *Four Thirteenth Century Law Tracts*, p. 112; *cf.* Britton (ed. Nichols), Vol. I, pp. 125 *et seq.* The *Fet Asaver* passage makes "trespass" cover things like debt, a usage perhaps explicable by disobedience of the *praecipe* form; *cf. Modus Componendi Brevia*, Woodbine, *op. cit.*, p. 143.
[69] *Bracton's Note Book*, pll. 145, 1250, 1720; C.R.R. XI, pl. 891; C.R.R., XVI, pl. 1547; Hall, "Some Early Writs of 'Trespass'," (1957) 73 L.Q.R., p. 65, at p. 72, writ B.9.
[70] C.R.R., X, p. 165, 74 L.Q.R., p. 425, here p. 49; C.P. 40/49, m. 31, *ibid.*, at p. 426, here p. 50.
[71] YB. Trin. 24 Edw. III, pl. 12, f. 28 (mistakenly attributed to Easter term in 74 L.Q.R., p. 428, here p. 52, n. 41); Trin. 24 Edw. III, pl. 44, f. 56d; Kiralfy, *op. cit.*, p. 206.
[72] C.R.R., XVI, pll. 1727, 1764; YB. 2 & 3 Edw. II, Seld.Soc. Vol. 19, p. 71, and CP. 40/174, m. 151d.
[73] CP. 40/13, m. 35; CP. 40/330, m. 304.
[74] C.R.R., XVI, pl 36 (1237), really trespass but called waste. *Cf. Fet Asaver*, Woodbine, *op. cit.*, p. 112.
[75] YB. Pasch. 29 Edw. III, f. 32d, 74 L.Q.R., p. 432, here p. 56. The association with property may be much older; *cf. Bracton's Note Book*, pl. 843.
[76] 74 L.Q.R., p. 408, here p. 32. The two might for a time appear in the same writ; CP. 40/48, m. 51.

summons.⁷⁷ In the end summons, being associated with property, disappeared altogether from the field of wrongs: the objection in the non-repair case of 1355 was overruled; and all trespass actions came to be started by attachment.

The use of *capias* was of lasting importance: when trespass and case became distinct, the availability of *capias* was a hall-mark of the former.⁷⁸ This seems, however, to be not a rule about a form of action but the result of a principle appropriating *capias* to breach of the peace; and it applied to novel disseisin as well as to trespass. If the assize found that a disseisin was done *vi et armis*, the disseisor and his associates were imprisoned, and would not be let out until they had made fine with the king and satisfied the plaintiff; for the latter this meant that he had execution by *capias ad satisfaciendum*.⁷⁹ The point is underlined by the difficulty caused, in novel disseisin as well as in trespass, by a demise of the crown.⁸⁰ More will be said below about the effects of Henry III's death, but a writ of battery in 1273 expressly said that the wrong was done *post pacem domini Regis in regno suo publice proclamatam*.⁸¹ On the death of Edward I it was clearly settled that nobody would be sent to prison for a trespass done in the previous reign⁸²; and on the death of Edward II this caused trouble. In the first year of Edward III a tale was told in court of a successful action for a trespass done in the former reign: the defendant was adjudged to prison, but released on error although he had not paid the damages. This caused a stir: *ceo fuist un graunde mischiefe, coment aviendra ore Sir John a ses damages?* ⁸³ What had been the king's interest was now regarded primarily as giving process by *capias* to the party,⁸⁴ and the effect of the demise was a surprising anachronism. It was removed by statute in the following year: *autiel proces soit fait des trespas fait en temps le Roi Edward piere le Roi qore est come de trespas fait*

---

⁷⁷ *Reg.Omn.Brev.*, ff. 97, 102d. Fitzherbert calls it an action on the case, *Natura Brevium*, f. 92G. An example is CP. 40/443, m. 122.

⁷⁸ Plucknett, *Concise History* (5th ed.), pp. 373, 470.

⁷⁹ The clearest statement is *Fleta*, Lib. IV, c. 4, s. 6. *Cf. Bracton*, ff. 162 *et seq.*; *Britton* (ed. Nichols), Vol. I, pp. 354–355. Examples are YBB. 21 & 22 Edw. I, R.S., p. 272, at p. 276; 2 & 3 Edw. II, Seld.Soc. Vol. 19, p. 36. *Cf.* YB. Mich. 17 Edw. III, pl. 105, f. 73; 8 Co.Rep. 59 b.

⁸⁰ KB. 27/236 (1319–1327), m. 89; held that no fine is payable to the king for breach of his predecessor's peace in novel disseisin.

⁸¹ CP. 40/2A, m. 22d.

⁸² YB. 3 Edw. II, Seld.Soc. Vol. 20, p. 104: defendants imprisoned because case pleaded to issue in time of late king.

⁸³ YB. Hil. 1 Edw. III, pl. 10, f. 2, conceivably an old story from the death of Edward I. *Cf.* YB. Pasch. 1 Edw. III, pl. 19, f. 9d, at f. 10: in ravishment of ward the defendant denies anything against the peace of the king's father, and the reporter wonders about the process.

⁸⁴ *Cf. Vieux Natura Brevium*, f. 123 on process in *ejectio firme*; YB. Hil. 14 Hen. VII, pl. 5, f. 15.

en temps le Roi qore est.[85] The plaintiff would thereafter be unaffected, except that he should perhaps leave *contra pacem* out of his writ.[86]

The appropriation of *capias* to breach of the peace, the usual ticket letting trespass actions into the royal court, might have had the same result as with attachment; and *capias* might have spread to all kinds of trespass. In 1310 a defendant in replevin protested that he had come by the *capias*, and Bereford said *Pur qei noun? N'est ceo un bref de trespas?* [87] But this did not happen, and it may have been stopped by statute in 1344 [88]: *Item qe nul exigende isse deformes en cas ou homme est enditez de trespas qe ne soit encontre la pees....* Probably this did not apply only to criminal proceedings; and the prohibition of outlawry would prohibit also *capias*.[89] Be this as it may, *capias* and outlawry, though extended seven years later to debt and detinue,[90] were not available for non-forcible trespasses until very much later. This may partly explain some of the events around 1370. The "fictitious" use of general writs would entail unjustifiably stringent process, thus creating a demand for honest formulae. The same result would follow from the insertion of *contra pacem* into an otherwise honest writ; and since the insertion evidently seemed to some necessary to give jurisdiction, the touchiness of the courts about that phrase becomes fully intelligible. It has already been suggested that the mistake in the innkeeper's case arose from the *contra pacem* in the writ.[91]

The significance of certain phrases

First come *vi et armis* and *contra pacem*. Once within the royal court their main effect was on process [92]; but more important was their prior function of bringing cases into the jurisdiction.

---

[85] Stat.Northampton, 2 Edw. III, c. 13 (1328).
[86] YB. 16 Edw. III, R.S. (ii), p. 246.
[87] YB. 3 & 4 Edw. II, Seld.Soc. Vol. 22, p. 195.
[88] 18 Edw. III, Stat. 2, c. 5. *Cf.* Plucknett, *op. cit.*, p. 471, n. 1.
[89] Exigent went with *capias*, whether *ad respondendum* or *ad satisfaciendum*. At one time it was also doubted whether you could make an attorney if *capias* lay; Stat.Gloucester, 6 Edw. 1, c. 8.
[90] 25 Edw. III, Stat. 5, c. 17. *Cf.* Plucknett, *op. cit.*, p. 389.
[91] 74 L.Q.R., p. 435, here p. 59. Conversely the dogma that you must not have a *vi et armis* writ for anything the defendant did within his fee (see next note, and 74 L.Q.R., p. 200, here p. 6) apparently grows out of Stat. Marlborough, c. 3, which was taken in effect to prohibit *capias* for a distraint within the fee: *non ideo puniatur dominus per redemptionem*.
[92] There are others. The interest in the peace might make an act done by night unlawful which would have been lawful by day; CP. 40/2A, m. 11; YBB. 20 & 21 Edw. I, R.S., p. 462; Mich. 5 Edw. III, pl. 31, f. 41; Pasch. 10 Ed. III, pl. 37, f. 21d. The argument, mentioned under *ejectio firme*, that nothing a man does within his fee can be *vi et armis*, *e.g.*, YBB. 6 Edw. II, Seld.Soc. Vol. 34, p. 142; Pasch. 44, Edw. III, pl. 28, f. 13d;

The rule is always expressed as limiting not royal but lower courts. An early statement dates from before the spread of *vi et armis*: *omnia brevia transgressionis cujuscunque generis fuerint possunt placitari in comitatu . . . exceptis illis brevibus in quibus fit mencio de vulneribus et imprisonamento et de vi et armis.*⁹³ The Register has a *regula* to its viscontiel writs: *non debet dici vi & armis . . . neque contra pacem nostram: quia vicecomes non potest terminare ea.*⁹⁴ It has also a *supersedeas* to stop such a plea, *cum placita de transgressionibus . . . vi & armis & contra pacem nostram factis in minori curia quam coram nobis vel alibi coram justiciariis nostris . . . plactitari non debeant.*⁹⁵ The original position thus seems clear⁹⁶: trespasses, wrongs, were normally to be settled in the county, but breach of the king's peace must come to the king's courts. Other trespasses could come there, but there was from the beginning a reluctance to hear private wrongs with no royal interest. This reluctance was embodied in the Statute of Gloucester in 1278: sheriffs were to hear pleas of trespass in their counties as the custom was.⁹⁷ Such are the opening words of the chapter, and they were surely meant to affirm a principle which was not being observed.

In the rolls of the central courts there seem to be two traces of this mischief. Some trespass writs are entered which do not allege *contra pacem*⁹⁸; and some use another phrase betraying them as aliens. The usual formula alleging damage in returnable writs is *ad grave dampnum*, but in viscontiel writs it is *ad dampnum ipsius P non modicum & gravamen.*⁹⁹ In the early years of

Trin. 44 Edw. III, pl. 16, f. 20; Hil. 48 Edw. III, pl. 10, f. 5d, is commonly referred to Stat.Marlborough, c. 3 (see last note); but it may be connected with the point about novel disseisin and with the early association of *vi et armis* with wrongs to land; see *infra*, p. 78.

⁹³ *Harleian MS.* 748, f. 53; *Brevia Placitata*, p. lxiv, n. 1.
⁹⁴ *Reg.Omn.Brev.*, f. 92.
⁹⁵ *Ibid.*, f. 111d.
⁹⁶ It did not remain so. Consider the plight of Fitzherbert, who discusses viscontiel and returnable writs of trespass at length, *Natura Brevium*, ff. 85–86H, but is obliged to fit case in. Viscontiel writs are divided into trespass and case, f. 86B; and returnable writs are said to abate if they lack *vi et armis*, unless they are case which abate if they have it.
⁹⁷ Stat. 6 Edw. I, c. 8; *cf. Fleta*, Lib. II, c. 1 (Seld.Soc. Vol. 72, at p. 108).
⁹⁸ *e.g.*, CP. 40/2A, m. 28; CP. 40/13, mm. 1, 19; and references in nn. 1, 3, 4 below.
⁹⁹ *Reg.Omn.Brev.*, f. 92 *et seq.*; Richardson & Sayles, *Sel.Cas. of Proc. without Writ*, p. cxv. The formula is found in some returnable writs, as follows. In the Register under *De Transgressione*: against sheriff wrongly returning *non est inventus* or releasing prisoner, ff. 98d, 99; against bailiff wrongly ordering return of beasts, f. 99d; attachment *de essendo quietum de theolonio*, f. 101, KB. 27/430, m. 36; CP. 40/443, m. 416; one of the two against innkeeper, f. 105, Kiralfy, *op. cit.*, Plate V; against borrower over-riding horse, f. 106d; and against one not abiding by award, f. 111. Outside *De Transgressione*: most writs *De Deceptione*, ff. 112–116d; various attachments for disobedience of writs, *e.g.*, ff. 18, 81. From plea rolls, excluding those of early Edward I: writs about jurisdictional franchises, KB. 26/201, m. 9;

Edward I, however, there are many entries with this latter formula. They fall into three classes. The first, and probably the largest, consists of ordinary writs *de bonis asportatis* or the like, only in viscontiel form: they end with the phrase under discussion instead of *ad grave dampnum ipsius P & contra pacem Regis*.[1] The second group consists similarly of ordinary formulae, but ending with *ad dampnum ipsius P non modicum & gravamen & contra pacem*,[2] a curious hybrid. The third group is more curious still: *contra pacem* is not alleged, and could not decently be, the writs being special and the wrongs peaceful in character. Three from the Common Pleas have a proprietary element.[3] In 1273 a plaintiff claims the right to all wine-casks emptied during a certain fair, and says that the defendant *predicta dolea sicut ea habere debet & solet habere non permittit ad dampnum ipsius P non modicum & gravamen &c*. In 1276 an abbot and prior are sued because, by charter of a former abbot, the plaintiff claims certain periodical allowances of food and clothing, which the defendants *subtraxerunt in ipsius P dispendium non modicum & gravamen*. In the same roll plaintiffs claim a right to have the standard measure delivered to them by the clerk of a market and to take the amends arising therefrom, and they say that the defendants maliciously procured its delivery to themselves and do not permit them to take the amends *in ipsorum PP dispendium non modicum & gravamen*. Professor Sayles has printed two examples from the King's Bench with no proprietary element.[4] In 1275 a plaintiff, reciting his good reputation in a *cum* clause, sued the mayor of his town and another defendant for having it proclaimed that he should be ostracised *in ipsius P prejudicium non modicum dedecus et gravamen*. And in 1276 a merchant, reciting that he was sent to collect customs, complained that the defendant had put it about that he was a forger of money, so procuring his imprisonment *in ipsius mercatoris dampnum non modicum et gravamen ac scandalum ipsius et totius societatis predicte manifestum*.

The omission of *contra pacem* from entries which might have had it can be explained by the demise of the crown, and the use

---

CP. 40/49, m. 31 (74 L.Q.R., p. 426, here p. 50); YB. 17 & 18 Edw. III, R.S. p. 212, at p. 215; earliest, but not later, writs for picketing market, KB. 26/161, m. 6 (74 L.Q.R., p. 420, here p. 44), m. 18d; KB, 26/167, m. 19. These last, and the innkeeper, alone have *contra pacem*. The formula thus seems proper, but not necessary, when that phrase was absent, as it necessarily was from viscontiel writs.

[1] CP. 40/2A, mm. 12d (see 74 L.Q.R., p. 214, here p. 20), 19, 19d; CP. 40/4, mm. 8, 29, 40; CP. 40/5, m. 101d; CP. 40/13, mm. 7, 25, 49, 61.

[2] CP. 40/2A, m. 21d; CP. 40/8, m. 22; CP. 40/9, m. 38d; CP. 40/13, mm. 27, 31, 38.

[3] Respectively CP. 40/2A, m. 2d (two entries, one with *ad grave dampnum*); CP. 40/13, m. 71; *ibid.*, m. 24.

[4] *Sel.Cas. in K.B.*, I, pp. 15, 29.

of the viscontiel formula by the novelty of alleging damage in any form. But these entries seem more likely to mark the shift of trespass litigation into royal courts at which the Statute of Gloucester was aimed. The demise of the crown may have accelerated this shift. Henry III's long reign had seen the blossoming of trespass in royal courts; and if the breach of his peace had been the main ticket by which it came in, there would, for wrongs done before his death and sued upon after, be no criterion determining whether to make writs viscontiel or returnable.[5] The appearance of viscontiel writs in the royal court would be a natural consequence.

Whatever the cause, the statute establishes the fact; and the spread of *vi et armis* to all general writs looks like a result.[6] The phrase was previously commonest when invasions of land were alleged; and this must be connected with the effect, explained in discussing process, of a finding of force in novel disseisin: it gave the king a special interest.[7] No such interest was needed to give jurisdiction over a disseisin, but it was for a trespass; and perhaps a mere wrongful entry could not normally be called *contra pacem* unless *vi et armis* were alleged. A traditional function of emphasis for jurisdictional purposes would fully explain why, during the decade or so after the jurisdictional principle had been reaffirmed, the words were put into all general writs. The job was done thoroughly; and in 1312 it could be urged that any writ having *contra pacem* must also have *vi et armis*.[8] The answer to a like argument in 1343 shows an attempt to rationalise the admission of some special writs: *Asquns gentz dient qe ceo qest fait countre la defense le Roi et son estatut est countre la pees*.[9]

Defences to an action of trespass

A proper account of pleading in special writs would have to consider the varying functions of *cum* clauses. The outline may be seen from the case in which a special right or duty is recited as the foundation of the plaintiff's action: the defendant can take issue on the special matter.[10] A similar thing could happen in

---

[5] Some writs referred to the peace of the late king, *e.g.*, 74 L.Q.R., p. 195, at p. 214, here p. 20.
[6] *Supra*, p. 30. Mr. M. J. Prichard, to whom as always the writer is indebted, suggests that the phrase may have helped to exclude wager of law, referring to *Sel.Cas. of Proc. without Writ*, pl. 123, p. 122. *Cf.* YB. Hil. 48 Edw. III, pl. 11, f. 6. Wager is found in a few early cases, *e.g.*, C.R.R., XVI, pl. 1195 (1240); and later any taint of breach of the peace may exclude it even where it is in principle appropriate; YB. 17 & 18 Edw. III, R.S., p. 466.
[7] *Supra*, p. 74.
[8] YB. 5 Edw. II, Seld.Soc. Vol. 33, p. 94
[9] YB. 17 Edw. III, R.S., p. 2, at p. 5. *Cf.* 9 Co.Rep., 50b; Godbolt, pl. 492, p. 426.
[10] *e.g.*, 74 L.Q.R., p. 407, at p. 432, here p. 56.

certain general writs: to a writ for poaching quoted in the first article, the defendant *petit quod sibi ostendi si quid habeat de predicta warenna. Et quia predictus P nichil inde habet . . . nisi simplex dictum suum*, the defendant won.[11] Otherwise the pleading in special writs was much as in general writs: if the plaintiff recited, for example, a franchise of estray, the defendant could deny his right, or justify the taking as damage feasant, or plead the general issue.[12]

With general writs we need consider only pleas in justification and the general issue. Justifications are of many kinds, and include rights which might, if the position of the parties were reversed, be set out in special writs: to a general writ for breaking the plaintiff's close and taking casks of wine, it was pleaded that they were wreck of the sea and the defendants' master had the franchise; and to a general writ for breaking a fold and taking sheep, the defendant pleaded his right of free fold.[13] Easements and profits are often set up, for example: a right of estovers to a writ for cutting wood [14]; common of pasture to a writ for depasturing,[15] or for knocking down some erection on the land concerned[16]; and rights of way to writs for knocking down embankments and the like.[17] Other common justifications are by jailers and peace officers,[18] or by persons claiming to have made a lawful distress.[19] All these normally have *sicut ei bene licuit*, and may be met by an assertion that the defendant acted *de injuria sua propria absque aliqua causa*. A special plea without the former phrase is *son assault demesne: D dicit quod idem P predictis die anno & loco in ipsum D insultum fecit & ipsum verberasse & vulnerasse voluit per quod idem D se defendebat & sic dicit quod si aliquod malum idem P habuit hoc fuit de insultu suo proprio & in defensione ipsius D.*[20] Similar is *son default demesne*, available in an action for depasturing if the plaintiff

---

[11] 74 L.Q.R., p. 206, here pp. 12-13.; CP. 40/2A, m. 14; CP. 40/9, m. 13. *Cf.* Plac. Abb., p. 194a. The plea underlines the meaninglessness of *vi et armis* in later writs for poaching.
[12] Examples are, respectively: YB. 13 & 14 Edw. III, R.S., p. 134; KB. 27/430, m. 39; YB. 9 Edw. II, Seld.Soc. Vol. 45, p. 49 (actually franchise of wreck).
[13] Respectively: CP. 40/360 (1350), m. 48; CP. 40/9 (1275), m. 6.
[14] CP. 40/391, m. 244.
[15] CP. 40/291, m. 226; CP. 40/312, m. 189; CP. 40/391, m. 47; 74 L.Q.R., p. 195, at p. 202., here p. 8.
[16] CP. 40/50, m. 52d; CP. 40/235, m. 91.
[17] YBB. 5 Edw. II, Seld.Soc. Vol. 33, p. 125; 6 & 7 Edw. II, Seld.Soc. Vol. 36, p. 1; Trin. 25 Edw. III, pl. 4, f. 80d.
[18] *Sel.Cas. in K.B.*, IV, p. 24; KB. 27/215, m. 66d; KB. 27/380, mm. 17, 45d; CP. 40/399, m. 51. *Cf.* CP. 40/370, m. 159 (provisor).
[19] KB. 27/300, m. 96d; CP. 40/340, m. 82; CP. 40/350, mm. 79, 135 (74 L.Q.R., p. 407, at p. 430 , here, p. 54).
[20] From CP. 40/391, m. 57. *Cf.* CP. 40/350, m. 302d; KB. 27/380, m. 71; CP. 40/399, m. 115; KB. 27/405, mm. 2, 3d; YB. Mich. 24 Edw. III, pl. 72, f. 66d.

should have fenced and had not.²¹ Neither of these had *bene licuit*, but both might be met by the replication *de injuria*.²²

The general issue might be pleaded in three ways; and in case anything should hereafter seem to turn on them, the formulae will be set out. The first specifically denies each allegation of the count, for example in *de bonis asportatis*: *bene defendit quod ipse nunquam predictis die & anno aliqua bona seu catalla ipsius P cepit seu asportavit nec aliquam transgressionem ei fecit contra pacem &c. sicut idem P superius queritur*.²³ The other two are general denials: the defendant says either *quod ipse non fecit predicto P predictam transgressionem contra pacem domini Regis prout idem P superius versus eum queritur*,²⁴ or *quod in nullo est culpabilis de transgressione predicta*.²⁵ The first was cumbersome ²⁶; and it went out of use. The relationship between the second and third forms is less clear; probably they represent progressive simplifications, the second being a condensed version of the first, and the third a more condensed version of the second. In the King's Bench the first two seem rare in 1314; and by 1335 the third has a monopoly.²⁷ In the Common Pleas most entries are still in the first form in 1320, and all the others in the second; in 1332 the first form is rare, and the second two occur in roughly equal numbers; and in 1357 the first has disappeared and the others share the field.²⁸ A plea in the first form may be followed by a verdict in either of the other two, a plea in the second form by a verdict in the third, and a plea in the third form by a verdict in the second.²⁹ The persistence of the second form in the Common Pleas was thus probably due to conservatism; and it is unlikely, but not quite impossible, that it meant something different from the simple Not Guilty.³⁰

---

²¹ 22 *Lib.Ass.*, pl. 42, f. 94d (as to the garden); CP. 40/399, m. 168. *Cf.* Glanville Williams, *Liability for Animals*, p. 218.

²² *e.g.*, CP. 40/391, mm. 11, 117, 130 (*son assault demesne*); CP. 40/399, m. 168 (*son default demesne*).

²³ From CP. 40/235, m. 126. *Cf. supra*, p. 68.

²⁴ From CP. 40/391, m. 125. *Cf.* 74 L.Q.R., p. 195, at p. 221, here p. 27; see also *supra* p. 66.

²⁵ From KB. 27/215, m. 4 and *passim*. *Cf. supra*, p. 68; *infra*, nn. 31, 35.

²⁶ *e.g.*, YB. 9 Edw. II, Seld.Soc. Vol. 45, p. 49, at p. 51.

²⁷ Respectively KB. 27/215 (about six pleas in the first form and one in the second, out of about 60); KB. 27/300 (all in the third form).

²⁸ Respectively CP. 40/235 (8 cases out of 12 in the first form); CP. 40/291 (one case out of 8 in the first form); CP. 40/391 (none in the first form). In CP. 40/350 (1347), the second form seems commoner than the third.

²⁹ YB. 9 Edw. II, Seld.Soc. Vol. 45, p. 49, at p. 51 (plea in first, verdict in second); KB. 27/215, m. 60d (plea in first form, verdict against some defendants in second, for others in third); CP. 40/350, m. 184 (plea in second, verdict in third); KB. 27/300, m. 13 (plea in third, verdict in second).

³⁰ Dr. Kiralfy evidently suspected this form of a special significance; *op. cit.*, p. 142 (on smiths). *Cf.* 74 L.Q.R., p. 195, at p. 220, here p. 26, n. 19.

The point has been examined because the general issue is the door which keeps us from the proceedings before the jury, and so from the facts. One aspect of this was discussed in connection with the "fictitious" use of general writs; here it is enough to mention that to the incitement writ of 1365 in which the court was prepared to impose *scienter* liability, the defendant pleaded *quod ipse in nullo est inde culpabilis*, and only the enrolment of a special verdict tells us what was going on.[31] Another aspect brings the writer onto dangerous ground: we would do wrong to suppose that we know, or are likely to know, much about medieval principles of liability. What could be specially pleaded is in the Year Books and plea rolls; but what could be put to a jury on the general issue may be irretrievably lost.

The compulsion of circumstances might be a defence whether specially pleaded or not. In 1271 the defendant to a *vi et armis* writ for knocking down the plaintiff's house pleaded specially: nearby houses were on fire, and *ad impediendam predictam combustionem & pro communi utilitate*, he with the neighbours *prostravit predictam domum in pace domini Regis sicut ei bene licuit ne ignis ulterius transiret*.[32] To an action for battery and false imprisonment in 1348 the defendant pleaded that the plaintiff was having a fit, and he and others tied him up and beat him by way of treatment.[33] In two other cases we learn the facts only from a special verdict upon the general issue. Several defendants to an action *de bonis asportatis* in 1270 had been *vi & metu ducti & compulsi* by a third party; but, though none took any of the goods for himself, they were imprisoned.[34] A problem in 1317 was more difficult. To a *vi et armis* writ for entering the plaintiff's house in Durham, breaking his chest, and taking his money, the defendant *dicit quod ipse in nullo est culpabilis de transgressione predicta*. The verdict is less reticent. A Scottish force threatened the city, and all swore to stand by any decision. The Scots were bought off for a sum to be paid immediately; and it was ordained that the defendant and other searchers should go from house to house taking money *in deposito*, which would be repaid by the commonalty. The plaintiff had sworn the oath, but did not consent to the taking. Judgment was given for him, chiefly on the ground that he could have no other redress. This was reversed in error in 1320: the defendant had done nothing against the peace, especially

---

[31] 74 L.Q.R., p. 216, here pp. 22-23; KB. 27/418, m. 10.
[32] KB. 26/201, m. 7d. *Cf.* Dyer, 36 b; 12 Co.Rep., 63.
[33] 22 *Lib.Ass.*, pl. 56, f. 98. The plaintiff replied *de injuria*.
[34] KB. 26/200A (C.P.), m. 5.

since the plaintiff had freely taken the oath; and the latter could recover from the commonalty.[35]

These were excuses for deliberate acts; and it is notable that even commonplace justifications like abating a nuisance, at any rate early in the fourteenth century, may appear only in a verdict on the general issue.[36] Between excuse and accident comes mistake, and what looks like an example in 1359 was pleaded in an intermediate manner, by special traverse. The action, for abducting a servant, was mentioned in the first article as indicating the "fictitious" use of a *vi et armis* writ; the defendant pleaded that the man entered his employment *ex libera voluntate sua tanquam extra servicium alicujus . . . absque hoc quod . . . cepit & abduxit*.[37]

The problem of accident is discussed, though not in connection with trespass *vi et armis*, in a law book of early Edward I. The Harvard *Brevia Placitata* propounds a *Cas marvellous sur vee de naam*, in which two horses are independently taken damage feasant and put together in a pound, and one kills the other. The distrainor must not plead specially because if he admits the taking he will have to restore or pay. He should therefore plead the general issue, *e mettre sey en la grace du pays*.[38] Glimpses of fault being raised by the general issue are the plea of Not Guilty in the 1364 surgeon's case and the question about *scienter* in the 1365 incitement action.[39] But it is only the cases concerning fire which tell a connected story, the tone being set by a writ of 1260 which says it happened *per ejus incuriam*.[40] In 1290, to a colourless general writ, accident was specially pleaded: issue was taken on the defendants' assertion that the fire started *per infortunum et*

[35] KB. 27/242, m. 60. A subsidiary ground of the judgment below was that this was the plaintiff's own money *in propria custodia*, and not *in deposito*. On the main point, the King's Bench said that the defendant had acted *ut nuncius & serviens* of the plaintiff and others of the commonalty, and *pro communi utilitate*. For some discussion of superior orders see YB. Trin. 7 Edw. III, pl. 1, f. 23.
[36] CP. 40/50 (1283), m. 29d (process by bailiffs); KB. 27/215 (1314), m. 72 (abating nuisance). Doubts about the proper scope of the general issue and justification could arise much later; YB. Mich. 41 Edw. III, pl. 30, f. 29d. *Cf.* the efforts to make all sorts of pleas "tantamount to the general issue"; YBB. Pasch. 46 Edw. III, pl. 9, f. 11d; Mich. 46 Edw. III, pl. 40, f. 32d.
[37] 74 L.Q.R., p. 212, here pp. 17-18, where the plea is set out in full. *Cf.*, for the relevance of mistake in the action on the statute, Fitzherbert, *Natura Brevium*, f. 168C.
[38] *Brevia Placitata*, p. 207; Plucknett, *op. cit.*, p. 478. Professor Plucknett takes the words to mean that the jury may be kind over damages; but it seems likely that the hope was for a verdict in his favour. *Cf.* the concluding words of *Gibbons* v. *Pepper* (1695) 1 Ld.Raym., p. 38. In 1353 a defendant, on not dissimilar facts, ignored this advice and tried pleading specially; 27 *Lib.Ass.*, pl. 64, f. 143, *supra*, pp. 66-67.
[39] Respectively KB. 27/414, m. 37d, *supra*, pp. 71-72; KB. 27/418, m. 10; 74 L.Q.R., p. 195, at pp. 216-217, here pp. 22-23.
[40] *Ibid.*, at p. 214, here p. 20.

non per aliquam malam custodiam seu nequiciam ipsorum.[41] No such pleas are found later; but it is hard to believe that the light of reason just went out, and hard also to imagine a better way of putting the plea than *In nullo est culpabilis* or the like. A Year Book of 1293 advises on the pleading in waste if the tenement is burned down, and its teaching is that of *Brevia Placitata*: the tenant should plead the general issue without mentioning the fire; the sheriff will then have to find out by inquest whether it was intended or not, and if not, whether it was the tenant's fault; *e sy yl returne ke par defaute de tenant, yl recovera ces damages.*[42] Lastly there are actions of trespass *vi et armis* in 1368 and 1374, in each of which, though the circumstances were different, the defendant pleaded Not Guilty. In 1368 the verdict was that a fire started suddenly in the defendant's house, *il nient sachant*, and burned his goods and the plaintiff's house; judgment was thereupon given for the defendant.[43] In 1374 the jury found that the fire happened through the defendant's fault, *per male garde*; and the very words are those of 1290, *mala custodia*.[44]

As with *scienter*, these *vi et armis* actions for burning were to divide and produce an action on the case with an element of fault mentioned in the writ; and the entire process whereby the "fictitious" use of general writs was replaced by honest writs on the case was to reduce the number of *vi et armis* actions in which questions of fault would as a matter of fact arise. But that is another story. The present point is that we have been misled by finding no special pleas of accident; it was not specially pleaded but raised upon the general issue, and so out of our sight. Neither Year Books nor plea rolls are concerned with the jury's proceedings, and we may never know what they did. We should, however, be unwise to imagine any unified principle; trespass was not a tort but a category, and what made a defendant guilty would vary from wrong to wrong.

3. ORIGINS

The origins of trespass: a footnote to the theories

Most inquiries have sought a pedigree for trespass imagined as an entity, a definite tort: but there was no such entity. No narrower concept was involved than that of wrong; and in the

---

[41] 74 L.Q.R., p. 214, here pp. 20-21; *Sel. Cas. in K.B.*, I, p. 181.
[42] YB. 21 & 22 Edw. I, R.S., p. 28. It looks like another teacher's problem.
[43] 42 *Lib.Ass.*, pl. 9, f. 259d.
[44] YB. Mich. 48 Edw. III, pl. 8, f. 25. Argument followed about the form of action; *supra*, p. 21, esp. n. 75; *infra*, p. 87, n. 70.

thirteenth century wrongs were primarily redressed in local courts. The appearance of trespass in royal courts, as Professor Plucknett has made clear,[45] was an extension of their purview rather than the making of a new thing. But its relationships with other ways of dealing with wrongs are a part of the story, and some isolated points follow.

As to novel disseisin, a link has been suggested above between this and the original role of *vi et armis*.[46] As to appeals, though some cases seem to confuse the language,[47] Britton makes it clear that, for many wrongs, trespass and appeal were alternative remedies; and for him the main reason for using trespass would be that the defendant could not choose to fight.[48] This may explain entries in which some of several defendants are appealed and the others sued in trespass. Both examples noted involve an abduction. One, of 1238, is in print.[49] The other is a series of entries in 1241, all about an incident in which the plaintiff's house was broken into, and his goods and two girls, heiresses in his wardship, were taken away: some defendants are appealed, with words of felony; and others are sued in trespass.[50]

The relationship with indictment also needs investigation. The king's suit was distinct from his interest in a breach of the peace convicted at the suit of another,[51] and a pardon of the former did not pardon the latter.[52] In an action at the party's suit it was irrelevant that the king might take the verdict for an indictment[53]; and, unless statute provided otherwise,[54] the defendant was liable to no punishment except to redeem himself for the breach of the peace. By the time of Edward III the chief importance of this was in giving execution by *capias*[55]; and the recession of the king's interest, and the increasingly civil character even of trespass

---

[45] *Op. cit.*, p. 370.
[46] *Supra*, pp. 4, 14, 18, 74, 78.
[47] *Supra*, p. 20.   *Cf.* 42 *Lib.Ass.*, pl. 8, f. 259d; Hall, 73 L.Q.R., p. 65.
[48] *Britton* (ed. Nichols), I, esp. at p. 123. He also purports to command that the consequences of an appeal of mayhem shall be approximated to those of a trespass action; one is found, resulting in damages, in 1362, K.B. 27/405, m. 16d. *Cf.* Plucknett, *op. cit.*, p. 428, n. 1; Keilwey, p. 95; 1 Leon., p. 318; 4 Co.Rep., 43a.
[49] *Bracton's Note Book*, pl. 1232; 74 L.Q.R., p. 195, at p. 210, here p. 16.
[50] C.R.R., XVI, pll. 1744, 1834, 2775.   The goods in each case come before the girls; *cf.* Plucknett, *Legislation of Edward I*, p. 115. The four appealed all put themselves on the country; perhaps the plaintiff knew they would.
[51] *Cf.* Britton (ed. Nichols), I, p. 97.
[52] *Sel.Cas. in K.B.*, IV, pp. 86–88.
[53] YB. 18 & 19 Edw. III, R.S., p. 14.
[54] As Stat.Westm. I, 3 Edw. I, c. 20.   *Cf.* YBB. Mich. 30 Edw. III, f. 11; Mich. 47 Edw. III, pl. 7, f. 10d.
[55] *Supra*, p. 74.

vi et armis, appeared when process was considered. Other symptoms are the sorting out of difficulties over principal and accessory,[56] and the statute of 1327 permitting attaint upon the main question as well as upon the damages.[57] Forty years later the royal court accepted the logic of this, and would hear wrongs where there was not even the pretence of a royal interest. But the royal interest was what first brought trespass actions into the royal court; and the criminal aspect, ignored in these articles, must be in a sense the key to the " origins of trespass."

The origins of trespass on the case

Trespasses, wrongs, were redressed in local courts. In the thirteenth century royal courts would hear cases in which there was a royal interest, generally breach of the peace; hence that odd assortment which the common law finally managed to make into the entity called trespass. In the fourteenth century the requirement of a royal interest was dropped, and private wrongs were admitted as such; hence that other assortment called case. There were conceptual developments, in local as well as royal courts; but they are overshadowed by the jurisdictional shift.

This basic story is complicated by two sub-plots; and these are what have chiefly been relied upon as inconsistent with the older views. One is that breach of the peace was not the only ticket which would admit wrongs; and we saw among the special writs certain actions which we should identify as actions on the case, notably that for failure to repair, appearing surprisingly early and under the name of trespass. These were just trespasses, wrongs, admitted for other than the usual reasons.

The other sub-plot is the " fictitious " use of general writs to bring in wrongs which in truth contained no element of breach of the peace. It may be useful to collect together the apparent examples; but the evidence is in its nature accidental, and a usage may be older than the chance which lets us see it. Of wrongs to land, cattle-trespass has been an anomaly ever since the writ for depasturing became available for an escape. This is clear in 1353, probable in 1348; an honest writ on the case was never invented.[58] Of personal wrongs, *vi et armis* writs for abduction were used fictitiously. The case of a wife was complicated by statute, and

[56] 74 L.Q.R., p. 198, here p. 4, n. 15; CP. 40/13, m. 50; *Sel.Cas. in K.B.*, IV, p. 4; YBB. Mich. 6 Edw. III, pl. 10, f. 38; Mich. 9 Edw. III, pl. 17, f. 29; 22 *Lib.Ass.*, pl. 59, f. 98d; 38 *Lib.Ass.*, pl. 9, f. 223d. *Cf.* KB. 26/155, m. 5d (benefit of clergy).
[57] 1 Edw. III, Stat. 1, c. 6.
[58] 74 L.Q.R., p. 204, here p. 10; 22 *Lib.Ass.*, pl. 51, f. 96; inference from 22 *Lib.Ass.*, pl. 42, f. 94d, with which *cf.* CP. 40/399, m. 168, *supra*, pp. 79, 80.

by the husband's ownership of chattels; there was no action on the case until 1745.[59] Enticing away servants or apprentices was actionable in local courts early in the fourteenth century.[60] There are traces of a *vi et armis* writ being used in 1359, and again in 1365 [61]; and the Register gives what seems to be a *vi et armis* writ for taking away an apprentice *quia in isto casu non datur breve de ordinatione, eo quod apprenticius non est retentus in servitio per formam ordinationis*.[62] Of wrongs to goods, the incitement writ could enforce a *scienter* liability in 1365, and it may be no innovation; the *scienter* writ itself is found in 1367.[63] Actions against bailees and the like are found undisguised under Edward II, and it looks as if they continued under the cover of general writs.[64] The only undisguised action against a smith was the *op. se* of 1352,[65] but since the first article went to press more general writs for killing horses have been noted with smiths as defendants: in 1321 and 1347 the horse was said to have been killed maliciously, but no such allegation was made in 1335 or 1367.[66] Early actions started by honest writs are the *Farrier's Case* and *Walden* v. *Marshal*; and both reports become clearer when set against this background.[67] The plaintiff in the former could apparently have succeeded with a general writ, but probably no jury would have said in the latter that the defendant killed the horse; with bailees generally, the new honest writs brought more cases into the royal court than could previously be smuggled in under a *vi et armis* guise. Lastly comes fire. It seems that the liability for negligent keeping, later enforced by an action on the case, could be imposed by general writs. A *vi et armis* action was so used in 1368, and apparently failed because the defendant was not at fault [68]; and in 1371 a version of the writ on the case has *contra pacem*.[69] There is also the situation analogous to that of the bailee; a guest or tenant burns the place down. Examples are found in 1290 and 1374; and from the latter

---

[59] 74 L.Q.R., p. 195, at p. 212, here p. 18.
[60] Gareth Jones, 74 L.Q.R., p. 39, at p. 41, n. 18 (1301); *Cal. Early Mayor's Court Rolls of City of London, 1298–1307*, p. 168 (apprentice, 1305).
[61] Respectively 74 L.Q.R., p. 211, here pp. 17-18; YB. Mich. 39 Edw. III, f. 37d (alternative to action on the statute).
[62] *Reg.Omn.Brev.*, f. 109.
[63] 74 L.Q.R., p. 195, at pp. 216–218, here pp. 22-24.
[64] *Supra*, pp. 162 *et seq*.
[65] 74 L.Q.R., p. 195, at p. 221, here p. 27.
[66] Respectively, CP. 40/238, m. 30d; CP. 40/350, m. 185d; KB. 27/300, m. 17; CP. 40/429, m. 232d. It is conceivable that cases of malice were the first to come to the royal court; but see 74 L.Q.R., p. 220, here p. 26, n. 19.
[67] Respectively, YBB. Trin. 46 Edw. III, pl. 19, f. 19; Mich. 43 Edw. III, pl. 38, f. 33. Note the fuss over *contra pacem* in the latter, and the reversed repugnancy argument in the former: there is no mention of a bailment, and so the writ should have *contra pacem*.
[68] 42 *Lib.Ass.*, pl. 9, f. 259d.
[69] Kiralfy, *op. cit.*, p. 214.

it appears that a *vi et armis* writ could be had whenever, from the nature of the tenancy, waste was not available.[70] Similarly it was held in 1347 that one tenant in common could have trespass *vi et armis* against another for reaping crops, but that for cutting trees he could, and therefore must, use the writ of waste *pro indiviso*.[71] The idea of trespass *vi et armis* as a residuary remedy appears also in the Register's note about abducting an apprentice[72]; this position was later, and more effectively, occupied by the action on the case.

There remain the related points of form and nomenclature. Most actions on the case adopted the *quare cum* formulation of special writs, and the reason is not far to seek: no standard wrong was involved such as breach of the peace, and the wrongfulness of the act had to be explained. Each action depended upon its facts; and that is also the short explanation of the name. Phrases like " on the case " are first used to make the obvious point that writs must be appropriate; the *Modus Componendi Brevia* speaks of a writ of entry *juxta casum suum formatum prout patet in registro*.[73] This point is most to the fore when a writ has to be made up, and it is natural that such phrases should be associated with special writs and contrasted with common writs. In 1294 a writ complained of various conspiracies and of the abduction of a woman, and the defendant objected: for the abduction there is *breve ad communem legem de cancellaria regis formatum*, and this writ of conspiracy *est breve de judicio vel quasi in speciali casu concessum*.[74] In 1312 another defendant said *Son bref est commun bref de ravissement et il ad counte en cas especiel . . . ou il pout aver eu bon bref acordaunt a son cas*.[75] In 1344 a writ of account against a guardian in socage, which has special matter in a *cum* clause, is said to be *fourme sur le cas*.[76] In 1348 a plaintiff in replevin answered an avowry by saying that the distress was made in pursuance of a plaint against him maliciously procured by the defendant; *sur tiel matter monstre*, says the defendant, *il averoit briefe de trespas sur son case, in quel briefe le deverance se serra auxy come in briefe de pris faites in haute estrete, et in auters briefes*

---

[70] 74 L.Q.R., p. 214, here pp. 20-21; YB. Mich. 48 Edw. III, pl. 8, f. 25. Waste was particularly inelastic; *cf.* YB. Mich. 46 Edw. III, pl. 32, f. 31. In 1587 a *vi et armis* writ was used against a tenant at will who felled trees; Gouldsborough, p. 72 (pl. 17); 4 Leon., pl. 271, p. 167. *Cf.* 5 Co.Rep., 13b.
[71] YBB. Hil. 21 Edw. III, pl. 26, f. 9; Mich. 21 Edw. III, pl. 8, f. 29. *Cf.* Reg.Omn.Brev., f. 76; YB. Mich. 47 Edw. III, pl. 54, f. 22d.
[72] *Supra*, p. 86.
[73] Woodbine, *Four Thirteenth Century Law Tracts*, p. 146. *Cf. Casus Placitorum*, p. 141.
[74] *Sel.Cas. in K.B.*, III, p. 22, at p. 23.
[75] YB. 5 Edw. II, Seld.Soc. Vol. 33, p. 94, at p. 95.
[76] YB. 18 & 19 Edw. III, R.S., p. 325; *Reg.Omn.Brev.*, f. 136.

de trespasse dones per estatut.⁷⁷ It would be hard to find a clearer description, or a better example, of a special writ; in 1369, the *especial bref sur le statute* for taking in the high street is actually called *especial bref sur le cas*.⁷⁸ Again in 1365 it is said *Sil ust monstre tout celle al chancellor il naveroit pas tiel bref generall, eins un bref sur son cas*.⁷⁹ Dr. Kiralfy has other examples which, in this writer's view, point the same way.⁸⁰

Writs on the case were therefore special writs, and writs of trespass on the case were special writs for wrongs. The language was not new in 1367, but it was particularly apt to describe the writs then beginning to come to the royal court with no other credentials than the wrongfulness of the conduct complained of.

4. A General View

Conceptual developments in the law of wrongs during this period are less important than jurisdictional developments. Instead of supposing a growing body of remediable wrongs, we come nearer the truth if we suppose a fixed body: what increased was the proportion remediable in royal courts. In this process there were three crises. The first is one of the things we mean by the origins of trespass, namely the original entry of royal judges into the field of delict. It was settled that breach of the king's peace could not be determined in lesser courts; and this was far the commonest reason for taking cases in the royal court. But it was not the only reason, as appears from some of the special writs: a royal interest in franchises or in the performance of public duties, or perhaps just a proprietary element, might suffice. Under Henry III, indeed, a few cases are found which would be at home in local courts, but which can only have reached the king's judges by the exercise of persuasive arts.⁸¹ It was not that they could not hear cases with no royal interest, but that normally they would not.

The second critical stage culminated in the Statute of Gloucester. Actions in which the king had no interest appeared in his courts in objectionable numbers, and confusion after the death of Henry III may have played a part in this.⁸² Whatever the reason, bad habits were formed; and the statute sought to stop them by reaffirming that wrongs should normally be tried in the county. The intention was no doubt to insist upon a genuine royal interest

---

⁷⁷ YB. Mich. 22 Edw. III, pl. 48, f. 15. *Cf.* YB. Hil. 44 Edw. III, pl. 16, f. 4: *Par que ales en la Chauncery et purchace bref a vous sur vostre cas.*
⁷⁸ YB. Mich. 43 Edw. III, pl. 16, f. 30.
⁷⁹ YB. Trin. 39 Edw. III, f. 18d; the case may have involved bailees.
⁸⁰ *Op. cit.*, pp. 23 et seq., 49 et seq.
⁸¹ *e.g., supra*, p. 64, at nn. 21, 22.
⁸² *Supra*, p. 78.

in cases coming to the royal court, and the effect in general writs was apparently to emphasise the element of breach of the peace by the regular insertion of *vi et armis*.[83] What mattered, however, was not the embellishment of standard forms, but the adoption of a firmer principle of exclusion. A parallel is the rule, then emerging, that actions of covenant would not be entertained without a seal. Private wrongs and private agreements, trespasses and covenants, were still primarily for lesser courts.

The third crisis was the development about 1370 which has been taken as the beginnings of case. What had been stopped under Edward I was allowed to happen: the requirement of a royal interest was abandoned; and private trespasses came to the royal court in their own right. That this change could be made with so little ado may be explained by two factors. One is the existence of some of the special writs: not only was machinery established; but also the admissibility of actions for reasons other than breach of the peace had prevented any clear formulation of the exclusive principle.[84] The second is that the principle had become unreal, and the change was more momentous in theory than in fact. Even genuine breaches of the peace had come to be seen primarily as private wrongs, with the king's interest important mainly for the process it gave; and sometimes breach of the peace was alleged untruthfully. This may have been so with some special writs, where the allegation has the air of being tacked onto an essentially economic complaint; and general writs were being used " fictitiously " to remedy wrongs later redressed by actions on the case.

The absence of conceptual development is the essential difference between this and the received view. The latter, by effectively ignoring special writs and supposing breach of the peace to have been the only ticket to the royal court, makes the common law of wrongs unduly poor; but that is a detail. The fundamental objection is to assuming that the miscellany admitted by that ticket became a conceptual entity.[85] Around this entity further conceptual development is imagined; and the mischief of the *In*

---

[83] 74 L.Q.R., p. 195, esp. at pp. 198, 224, here pp. 4, 30; also *supra* p. 78.
[84] See, *e.g.*, *supra*, p. 78, at n. 9.
[85] When it became such an entity is a question. A distinction between trespass *vi et armis* and case soon became clear, *cf.* n. 96, *supra*, but both were categories rather than entities. It is doubtful whether trespass was thought of as " a " tort before the 18th century, if then; the tests so laboriously proposed cannot have been obvious for 500 years. Blackstone's account in Bk. III, c. 12, deserves study: for him the broad meaning of the word " trespass " is wrong, and the narrow meaning is " layman's trespass " to land. The significance of this was pointed out to me by Professor Hollond; it is the least of my debts to him.

consimili casu tale has been, not the particular theory of how case grew out of trespass *vi et armis*,[86] but the belief that it grew out of it at all. That belief in turn has haunted our understanding of how case developed, and of how it ousted the older forms of action to make the modern common law. Some consequences of laying this ghost were briefly adumbrated some years ago [87]; and to these the writer hopes now to return.

---

[86] See Plucknett, 31 Columbia L.R., p. 778.
[87] [1954] Camb.L.J., p. 105 , here pp. 91-103.

2

NOT DOING IS NO TRESPASS:

A VIEW OF THE BOUNDARIES OF CASE

THIS article will tell some elementary stories about the history of contract and tort. Its purpose is primarily pedagogic: although the stories are largely old, they are not very clearly explained in the books, and in particular they are done something less than justice in the standard work, Mr. Fifoot's invaluable *History and Sources of the Common Law*. Since the present aim is to explain what the stories are, rather than to prove that they are true,[1] their telling will be as little encumbered as possible with old cases and their technicalities. A secondary purpose is to set the stories together, and show how far they turn out to be the same story. It is doubtful whether even Ames, who first stated the most important of them,[2] fully realised how far the point was the same in each; and since in one guise or another it is the point of much legal history it deserves more emphasis than it has had. Finally, since Professor Plucknett freed us from the sterile delusion that case was somehow " like " trespass,[3] there has grown up a new background of ideas in which the old stories must be set afresh.

A foundation may be laid by considering the nature of trespass and case. The old theory was roughly this: that trespass always meant what it means today, that wrongs involving no direct force therefore once went without remedy, and that trespass on the case was developed under the powers of the *In Consimili Casu* clause[4] to fill the gap. The newer idea[5] began with Professor Plucknett's

---

[1] They may not be capable of strict proof, but only of being made more or less credible. It is, however, hoped that this article may remove some difficulties. The stories told by Ames in his *Lectures on Legal History* seem to the writer to have been there established in principle. For the others fuller references will be given.

[2] Ames, Lectures XIII and XIV (*assumpsit* and *indebitatus assumpsit*) and VII (trover).

[3] 31 Col.L.R. 778; 52 L.Q.R. 220.

[4] Stat. Westm. II, c. 24.

[5] In one form or another this has been bandied about for some time: the first published indication was in Professor Plucknett's *Concise History of the Common Law*, 4th ed., pp. 352–3. The version here outlined was formed, largely in discussions with Professor Hollond, when the writer was preparing lectures in 1949. He has not altered it since the publication of Dr. Kiralfy's book on *The Action on the Case*, and thinks that Dr. Kiralfy may agree with it as far as it goes.

perception that the statute played no part in the matter [6]; but it goes further and denies that case grew out of trespass *vi et armis* at all. The suggestion is that trespass at first meant no more than wrong or tort,[7] and that the royal courts would remedy trespasses which were not forcible as well as those which were: the only difference was that standard writs soon evolved for the wrongs which came up most often, the obvious forcible wrongs; whereas for other wrongs a writ had to be concocted on each occasion. This was reflected in the nomenclature; the standard writs for forcible wrongs were known as general trespass or common trespass, the others as special trespass. Examination of the writs will suggest that the real distinction was between acts which were obviously wrongful and those which were not [8]: it was sensible to require a defendant to answer *quare clausum fregit* without more ado; but a writ asking why he had sold his own goods in his own house needed an introduction explaining that the plaintiff had a franchise of market and had lost his market dues.[9] There was, however, no difference in nature; the one was as much a trespass as the other; and if a special writ was used when a common one would have served, nobody minded.[10] This was the position until the second half of the fourteenth century, and it is a question of words whether special trespass is or is not to be called case. The name case appeared about 1370, when the introductory part of special writs [11] began to be put to a new use; whereas before it had recited known rights like franchises, whose existence could be established by other legal processes, it might now assert new rights and duties which had no independent existence in the common law. Special trespass had protected existing rights, but case created new ones. The distinction between case and the old routine trespass now mattered; and

---

[6] Except, perhaps, as one more expression of the feeling that wrongs should not go unremedied.

[7] See *e.g.*, Y.B. 2 & 3 Ed. II (S.S.), 71; note 9 below. Professor Hamson drew attention to this instructive case in lectures in 1947.

[8] Historically, Lord Raymond's suggestion in *Reynolds* v. *Clarke*, 1 Str. 634, may have been nearer the mark than has been thought.

[9] Y.B. 2 & 3 Ed. II (S.S.), 71. See especially the beginning of the Note from the Record at p. 74. The record itself (C.P.40, no. 174, m.151d) shows that *vi et armis*, etc., were not, of course, alleged.

[10] Y.B. 13 & 14 Ed. III (R.S.), 134. The plaintiff claimed a franchise of estray in the manor of M., and brought his action of trespass because the defendant had taken straying foals. Shareshull J., at p. 136, said: ". . . And I tell you that, if the [plaintiff] had brought a common writ of Trespass in respect of the taking of the foals, you would have had to answer to that." It appears from the other report at p. 138 that Shareshull J. thought it might be sufficient for the plaintiff to rely on his seisin. The record (C.P.40, no. 320, m.334) shows that the writ both set out the special matter of the franchise and alleged *vi et armis* and *contra pacem*. Contrast the case in the preceding note.

[11] The *cum* clause, which might be very long.

it became fatal to use a special writ where a general one would have been appropriate.

For the present purpose, the important difference between the two theories is this. The old theory supposed, overlooking special trespass, that direct forcible injury was from the beginning the gist of trespass, which was thus always synonymous with trespass *vi et armis*; and that from trespass in that sense there was descended trespass on the case. Further, it contemplated the existence of other things on the case, for example deceit on the case as a descendant of deceit, all of which would be species of the genus case. The new theory regards trespass *vi et armis* not as the ancestor of trespass on the case but as a distinguished member of the same generation; they were all just actions in tort, and there was no special magic about those redressing direct forcible injuries. Trespass meant wrong, and trespass on the case meant an action on the case for a wrong. Trespass on the case was therefore not merely a species of case, but identical with it; and there could not be anything else on the case in the sense contemplated by the old theory.

To believers in the old theory it was clear that for a wrong to be " like " the direct force of trespass, the defendant must at least have done something. Slogans such as that used as a title for this article were thus themselves sufficiently explained, and in turn provided a sufficient explanation of the objection to using trespass on the case to remedy a nonfeasance. Mr. Fifoot's treatment [12] of the extension of *assumpsit* to cover nonfeasance is a good example. Mr. Fifoot agrees with Professor Plucknett that the statute had nothing to do with case, but substantially he accepts the old theory; while agreeing that the statute did not act as midwife, he does not doubt that case was born of trespass (meaning trespass *vi et armis*), or that there might be other things on the case such as deceit on the case. On this footing he logically represents what happened as follows. Attempts to use trespass on the case for the mere non-performance of a promise at first failed, because trespass on the case, being descended from trespass *vi et armis*, had inherited as a vestige of direct force the requirement that the defendant should have done something. These failures prompted experiments with deceit on the case, whose heredity was not similarly embarrassed. Mr. Fifoot thinks, however, that while deceit on the case played a part, Ames overstressed its claim to be the ancestor of *assumpsit*.[13] He observes that much of the later

---

[12] *History and Sources of the Common Law*, Chaps. 14 and 16.
[13] *Ibid.*, p. 333 and n. 12. In the historical introduction to Cheshire and Fifoot, *Law of Contract*, deceit is dismissed in a footnote; 3rd ed., p. 10, n. 4.

litigation was called trespass on the case, and explains the final step to remedying nonfeasance, prompted by commercial necessity and competition from the chancellor, by saying that "Case . . . had now become a generic form of action and the basic analogy of trespass had lost its power of attraction." [14]

None of this can be accepted by a follower of the new theory, who believes neither that there was any inheritance from trespass *vi et armis* which could have caused a difficulty, nor that deceit on the case was a separate entity which might have been looked to for a solution. What, then, was the difficulty of nonfeasance? Was it ever true that "not doing is no trespass," and if so why? Part of the answer is that this never was wholly true. The innkeeper who did not keep thieves out of his inn, so that his guest's goods were stolen, had been guilty of a nonfeasance [15]; so, even earlier, had the defendant who, being under a duty to do so, failed to repair a river wall on the Humber so that the plaintiff's land was flooded.[16] These were both liable; why was not one who made a promise and broke it? The reason surely is that in any system of law "not doing is no trespass" (meaning wrong or tort) unless there was a duty to act. A duty was imposed on the innkeeper by a mysterious custom of the realm, on the dweller near Humber by his tenure; and these duties were recited in the introductions to the writs. But one aggrieved by a broken promise could not set out any duty in trespass, and the reason is found in the cases over and over again: "This sounds in covenant." The objection is commonly regarded as a formal one, namely, that the action of covenant should have been brought; and this conveys the essential point. In fact, however, it seems that the word covenant has been overtaken by a fate similar to that of trespass. There is no reason to think that covenant meant anything except what we mean by contract, or that the action of covenant should be expressed in modern English otherwise than as the action on a contract.[17] If, then, a plaintiff brings an action of trespass on the case for failure to keep a promise, and the defendant says "Not doing is no trespass; this sounds in covenant," he is simply making the clear-sighted objection that this is not tort but contract. It does not much matter whether the unexpressed major premise is thought of as one of substantive law, "Contracts need seals," or as purely formal, "The right action here is that on a contract, in which the plaintiff would have to produce a seal": a contemporary,

---

[14] *History and Sources of the Common Law*, p. 337.
[15] Y.B.Pasch. 42 Ed. III, f. 11, pl. 13; 42 Lib.Ass., f. 260b, pl. 17.
[16] Y.B. 15 Ed. III (R.S.), 86.
[17] The trouble may have been caused by headings and side notes in Year Books, Abridgments, the Register, etc.

thinking in terms of the forms of action, would have seen no difference. For him the point would have been that here was a man who in making a contract had omitted, no doubt by mistake,[18] to observe the formalities, and was now unjustifiably trying to call the breach a tort and gain his remedy that way.

If that was the difficulty of nonfeasance, then the problem confronting a plaintiff who had failed to contract in the right way was formidable but rational: how plausibly to express a breach of contract as a tort? This is where the notion of deceit, already made familiar in cases of misfeasance, played its great part. The plaintiff put the matter this way: "The defendant made me a promise, in return for which I gave him something; he has failed to keep his promise, and this makes the whole transaction a deceitful wrong by means of which he has got the something from me." Nothing turns on any supposed distinction between trespass on the case and deceit on the case. Deceit on the case, written out in full, reads like this: an action of trespass (meaning tort) on the case for a wrong deceitful in nature.[19] Ames probably supposed that the two things were different, but this does not affect the validity of his conclusion about the way in which the plaintiff put his complaint. It is not a vague assertion that to break a promise is deceitful, but a definite complaint of a tort; the defendant has got something from the plaintiff by a deceitful course of conduct. Nobody can suppose that the judges were taken in by so blatant a dodge, or blame them for hesitating to accept it. They saw that if they allowed it in one hard case, they would have to redress in tort every breach of agreement in England, and subvert the law of contract as they knew it. This happened.

The proposition that consideration in contract sprang from damage in tort has been denied by Mr. Fifoot[20] and others; and there is an evident breach of continuity if it is supposed that deceit on the case was something different from trespass on the case, and that *assumpsit* for nonfeasance came into being through the agency of both. An affiliation order for consideration could not be had against every kind of tortious damage; but if it is agreed that deceit on the case was merely a kind of trespass (meaning tort) on the case, and that the importance of deceit was as a way of putting the matter, then it seems clear that what the plaintiff has been tricked out of when the transaction is expressed as a tort will be the consideration when it is viewed as a contract. The only breach

---

[18] Professor Thorne, in his recent lectures in Cambridge, emphasised that the early cases should be regarded as oddities, hard cases in which the normal contractual device of the conditioned bond had been omitted.
[19] See *e.g.*, Kiralfy, *The Action on the Case*, p. 94ff.
[20] *History and Sources of the Common Law*, Chap. 16.

of continuity is in the quantum of damages; and it was a circumstance essential to the working of the dodge that damages in trespass (meaning tort) were at large, so that the plaintiff was not restricted to getting back what he had parted with. Two modern rules of consideration are illuminated by this story. The case generally cited for "Past consideration is no consideration" is *Roscorla* v. *Thomas*,[21] where a warranty given after the conclusion of a sale was held invalid for want of consideration. That was in 1842. In 1490 the point was put like this [22]: "Note . . . that if a man sells something and afterwards at another place he warrants it, this warranty is void because not made on the bargain, and [the other] shall not have an action of deceit on it." In neither case had the plaintiff done anything or parted with anything on the faith of the warranty. There might be another explanation of that rule, but it is hard to imagine one for "Consideration must move from the plaintiff." [23] If Tom was suing Dick substantially in contract, but expressing the case as a tortious deceit, it was evidently no use for him to allege that Harry had been tricked out of something; if he had been, it was for Harry to sue. Consideration soon began to be discussed as a thing in itself, as the sixteenth-century reports abundantly show; but there seems no doubt that it first appeared as the vital part of the disguise when contract was dressed up as tort.

This was the most spectacular exploit of case; and it is the easiest to understand because it turns upon the familiar idea of contract. That contracts need seals is today a more intelligible proposition than its equivalent, that case ought not to be used where covenant is appropriate. The concepts of debt and detinue are less familiar, but the point of their relations with case is the same. To speak in terms of "due process" is not a bad approximation, so that the use of case where debt was appropriate would be objectionable as depriving the plaintiff of a constitutional right to wage his law. The real objection, however, was more radical; debt and tort were different kinds of thing, and confusion of the forms was unthinkable. Professor Plucknett warns us [24] against attaching too much significance to the wording of old writs, but it may help to illustrate the point. The *praecipe* writs, which include covenant, debt, and detinue, seek in terms to enforce the defendant's primary duty: he is to be told to keep his promise, pay what he owes, or hand over what he detains; and only if he does not do it is

---

[21] 3 Q.B. 234.
[22] Y.B.Trin. 5 Hy. VII, f. 41b, pl. 7.
[23] Ames noted the relevance of this rule; *Lectures on Legal History*, p. 145.
[24] *Concise History of the Common Law*, 4th ed., p. 344. But *cf.* p. 352.

he to be brought to court. In the *quare* writs, on the other hand, which include [25] trespass in all its forms and senses, it is assumed that the defendant's primary duty has been irrevocably broken, that there has been a wrong which can only be compensated for by damages. The problem before a plaintiff who wishes to use a *quare* writ, where on the face of it a *praecipe* would be appropriate, is thus always the same: to express what has happened as a tort, an irrevocable wrong, instead of as the mere non-performance of the positive duty which the *praecipe* writ exists to enforce.

That this was the problem in *indebitatus assumpsit*, by which case became available in place of debt, seems not to have been fully appreciated. The outline of events is well known. It was established that if one was indebted (*indebitatus*), so that the action of debt could have been used against him, and he subsequently promised (*assumpsit*) to pay, then he could be sued in *assumpsit* instead of debt. The King's Bench [26] exploited this by presuming the subsequent promise alleged by the plaintiff; whereas in the Common Pleas the truth of that allegation could be made the issue in the action.[27] *Slade's Case* [28] finally upheld the King's Bench practice, and thereafter the subsequent promise was always alleged but could never be denied; the *assumpsit* thus being presumed, the sole issue was whether the defendant was *indebitatus*, and the action of debt was overthrown.

This is a story with two points, the later of which is clear enough: it is evident that the subsequent promise was for some reason necessary to take the matter out of the sphere of debt, and that *Slade's Case* did not so much dispense with this requirement, as keep all future records straight by hallowing the lie that it was satisfied. What is not so clear is the original point. Why was the subsequent promise necessary? And why was it sufficient? Suppose that Tom had sold goods to Dick, and Dick had genuinely made a subsequent promise to pay the price, and Tom wished to sue him in *assumpsit*. The first question that arises is why Tom needed to rely on the subsequent promise at all. At the time of the sale Dick must have agreed to pay the price, so why did Tom not rely on that promise? Why did he not put the matter this way: " I parted with my goods on the faith of Dick's promise to pay, and his failure makes the transaction a deceitful wrong by which I have been tricked out of

---

[25] There is a sense in which the forms of trespass may almost be said to comprise the *quare* writs.

[26] The court was so called in the reign of Elizabeth I. See *e.g.*, Stat. 27 Eliz. I, c. 8: " An Act for Redresse of erronious Judgementes in the Courte commonly called The Kinges Benche."

[27] Dalison 104, pl. 45.

[28] 4 Co.Rep. 91.

my goods "? If he had supplied the goods to Harry on the faith of Dick's promise to pay, that is substantially how he would have put his case [29]; why not here? Ames explored this question,[30] and the answer is that the same objection applied as in the case of covenant. The transaction between Tom and Dick had raised a debt; Dick had got the goods as *quid pro quo*; and Tom should seek his debt by the action of debt. Here, indeed, the objection applied with greater force because debt actually was available; whereas in the covenant situation, while covenant was the proper action, in practice it could not be used for want of a seal.

That sufficiently explains why some new element was necessary to take the matter out of the sphere of debt, but there remains a question not considered by Ames. Why was the subsequent promise sufficient for that purpose? In the litigation between Tom and Dick, how was Tom's case notionally put? To say that by the middle of the sixteenth century *assumpsit* had become a purely contractual action, and that a debt precedent was accepted as a sufficient consideration, is an unsatisfying restatement; it also supposes that *assumpsit* had forgotten its parentage with unfilial alacrity. The likely answer is that here was another and more recondite application of the deceit ploy, and that Tom put his case like this: " I had sold Dick goods and could have got my money from him by an action of debt; but because of his promise I did not do so, and have been kept out of my money for a time by his deceit." [31] Put in modern terms, the suggestion is that the subsequent promise really worked because made in consideration of forbearance of the debt. Expressed in terms of tortious deceit, it will be noticed that Tom was formally complaining of damage in being kept out of his money for a time rather than of the loss of the amount of the debt; and this explains the opening words of the fourth resolution in *Slade's Case*: " that the Plaintiff in this Action on the Case in *Assumpsit* should not recover only Damages for the special Loss (if any be) which he had, but also for the whole Debt. . . ." [32] If this is right, the allegations of deceit found in every *indebitatus* count were not mere abuse of the defendant for breaking his promise but, in principle, the assertion of a definite wrong causing definite harm; and their original purpose was to express the matter as something other than mere

---

[29] See *Baxter and Read's Case*, Dyer 272n. *Cf.* Y.B.Mich. 12 Hy. VIII, f. 11, pl. 3.

[30] *Lectures on Legal History*, pp. 150–1. The observations about grants should be accepted with some reserve. *Cf.* n. 24 above. See also Dalison 84, pl. 35.

[31] *Cf.* Rastell's *Entrees*, 1574 ed., f. 4, *sub. tit.* Action sur le case in lieu de action de dett; also Coke's *Entries*, f. 1, Action sur le case 1 (*Pinchon's Case*).

[32] 4 Co.Rep. 91 at 94b.

non-payment of the debt for which the action of debt properly lay.[33]

The circumvention of detinue by case was a process of which some details, especially of chronology, are in doubt[34]; but it is evident that Ames was right[35] in identifying as the original point a peculiarity of detinue itself. Detinue had developed[36] so as to enforce two distinct kinds of liability. There was first detinue on a bailment, in which the plaintiff's case was founded upon the transaction by which he had let the defendant have the thing; it was because the defendant came by it as bailee that he was bound to restore it. Secondly there was detinue otherwise than on a bailment, in which the plaintiff relied not at all upon the manner in which the defendant had come by the thing, but solely upon the fact that he was entitled[37] to it and the defendant refused to hand it over.[38] In the former the duty to restore, although only made immediate by a demand, commenced with the bailment: in the latter the duty inhered in the defendant, not when he got the thing, but when the plaintiff demanded it.[39] In the first kind the plaintiff always recited the bailment. In the second he took to counting that he had lost the thing and the defendant had found it; and a brief outline of how that probably came about must suffice for the present purpose. At first the plaintiff would really explain how the thing came into the possession (*devenit ad manus*) of the defendant, who could deny the story. Then it became evident that nothing turned on the means by which the defendant had come to have it,[40] and to prevent the case going off on an immaterial point it was settled that the defendant could not deny whatever story the plaintiff told[41]; this

---

[33] Mr. Prichard and the present writer were each fortified by learning that the other had asked the same question and supplied the same answer. As always, the writer is indebted to Mr. Prichard for discussions.

[34] It is hoped that these doubts may be cleared up by the use of record evidence; a difficulty will be to discover what happened in cases where part of the story is blanketed by a fiction.

[35] *Lectures on Legal History*, Lecture VII, esp. at p. 84.

[36] The development was intricate and important; what was in question was the the idea of property in chattels. The writer hopes at a later date to give some account of it.

[37] Until the development was complete, one must beware of supposing the plaintiff to claim " my property." Title deeds seem to have played an important part in the story.

[38] The distinction between the two kinds of liability is not confined to detinue, but appears also in debt; see *e.g.*, Y.B.Hil. 21 Hy. VI, f. 23, pl. 5 (debt against abbot for the price of goods sold to his predecessor; can the defendant wage his law?). There is a distinction between *debet* and *detinet*, which cuts across the distinction between debt for fungibles and detinue for specific goods.

[39] Y.B.Pasch. 27 Hy. VIII, f. 13, pl. 35.

[40] This may mark the point at which the plaintiff can speak without more ado of " my property."

[41] See Y.B.Trin. 29 Ed. III, f. 38b. The defendant was one Alice Halyday, and it is a wild but not impossible conjecture that Littleton was referring to this case when he spoke of the " new found haliday "; *Malpas's* case, see next note.

confined the issue to the substantial question, did the defendant detain something the plaintiff was entitled to have? Finally, plaintiffs took to telling the standard lie of loss and finding.[42] Why? A circumstance which appears to provide a sufficient explanation is this: although the defendant could not deny the truth of the plaintiff's story, he could object to it in point of law; for example, if it ended by saying that the defendant got the thing as executor, there might be a question whether he was charged as such and should be so named in the writ.[43] The count in trover may have been attractive just because it was a simple story with no moving parts and nothing to go wrong in law; and it effectively conveyed the necessary information, that the defendant was in possession lawfully but not as bailee.

There were, then, detinue *sur bailment*, based on a duty binding the defendant because he had got the thing as he did, and detinue *sur trover*, based on a duty arising from detention after a demand. It follows that in principle, while detinue was always available against a bailee whether he still had the thing or not, there was a difficulty about using it against one who had had the thing otherwise than by bailment, but had disposed of it before the demand was made.[44] Here was a gap which the action on the case could properly fill, and this was the origin of the action for conversion.[45] To anticipate the objection that he should be using detinue, the plaintiff would explain how the defendant had come to have the thing otherwise than as his bailee. He would then make his substantive complaint, that the defendant had converted it to his own use; the word conversion, it should be noted, was used more or less literally; the goods had been consumed or disposed of. Later, instead of explaining how the thing had really come into the possession of the defendant, the plaintiff would borrow the count in trover from detinue and use that[46]; it aptly said what was necessary about the nature of the possession.

---

[42] See Y.B.Trin. 33 Hy. VI, f. 26b, pl. 12 (*Malpas's Case*). There is some doubt when and how long it was true that the plaintiff could allege a *devenit ad manus* generally, without saying how. See Y.B.Trin. 16 Ed. II, f. 490. In Y.B.Hil. 9 Hy. VI, f. 58, pl. 4, Paston said that the plaintiff need not say how the defendant had got the deed *because* he might have found it. This may have suggested the count in trover. Shortly after *Malpas's Case* it seems that the plaintiff again had to say how the defendant had got the thing, but to allege a trover would do; Y.B.Mich. 35 Hy. VI, f. 25b, pl. 33, at f. 27.

[43] *Cf.* Y.B.Trin. 29 Ed. III, f. 38b.

[44] Y.B.Pasch. 27 Hy. VIII, f. 13, pl. 35.

[45] Ames, *Lectures in Legal History*, Chap. 7, esp. at p. 84.

[46] The chronology of the matter is not clear. The count in trover was in use in the mid-sixteenth century; Bro.Ab., Action sur le Case 113; Dyer 121 and Benloe p. 41, pl. 73. A precedent is given in Rastell's *Entrees*, 1574 ed., (also 1566) f. 4b, 5, *sub tit.* Action sur le case in lieu de action de detinewe; the same title contains a precedent for use against a bailee of title deeds, but by

If the foregoing is right, there is no deception about this use of the action; it filled a genuine gap in the law, if a queer one. Reflection will suggest, however, that while there was no harm to a defendant in detinue if the plaintiff counted on a trover instead of on a bailment, there was clear harm if he did so in conversion, because it would mask his resort to the wrong form of action.[47] And the principal difficulty, both for contemporaries and for modern investigators, arose out of the use of the action for conversion against bailees. Ames explained why this use was inevitable.[48] Case had long been the proper action against any possessor, bailee or other, who damaged the goods without destroying them; detinue was irrelevant here, because the wrongdoer might already have restored them in their impaired state, and if not he could meet the action by doing so. It would therefore appear not altogether reasonable to deny the use of case against the bailee who destroyed or disposed of the goods, when it was available if he merely damaged them, and was also available against any other possessor who destroyed or disposed of them. Perhaps more important, the use of case to remedy damage would emphasise the difference between misdealing with the goods, which could be regarded as a tort whether it resulted in their destruction or not, and the mere failure to surrender them which was the gist of detinue.

Here was a problem which seems to have caused much difficulty, and it is by no means clear when it was solved.[49] It is, however, clear what the final solution was: principle and expediency triumphed together. It was agreed that no action but detinue

---

the purchaser of the land and not the bailor himself. The doubt arises over how and when the bailee could at this time be made liable in case. See further note 49 below.

[47] *Contra*, Kiralfy, *The Action on the Case*, p. 113.
[48] *Lectures on Legal History*, p. 84.
[49] In Y.B.Hil. 18 Ed. IV, f. 23, pl. 5, Brian was against allowing the action against a bailee, but already there is talk of the property being altered. In Keilwey, 160 (2 Hy. VIII) the discussion was opened by Moore putting in terms the point made in the text above; Dr. Kiralfy (*The Action on the Case*, p. 111) says the Common Pleas held that case would lie against a bailee who sold the goods, but that was only the opinion of " divers des Justices." There are other similar dicta, *e.g.*, in *Core's Case* (28 Hy. VIII), Dyer 20 at 22b. In Bro.Ab., Action sur le Case 113 (4 Ed. VI) the count in trover was used fictitiously, and it was apparently a good plea that the plaintiff had pledged the thing to the defendant; the writer has found no evidence that the count was used when in fact there had been a bailment for some time after that, but it may have been. Rastell's only precedent which seems relevant is for use against a bailee who has been negligent, and it is based on an *assumpsit*; *Entrees*, 1574 ed., f. 9. As late as 1600, when a plaintiff actually counted a bailment and then a conversion, the defendant thought it worth while to take the point; it was overruled " for the conversion takes away the property from him," but it is interesting that it was made; *Gumbleton* v. *Grafton*, Cro.Eliz. 781. Thereafter plaintiffs seem to have been generally careful to count in trover or on a *devenit*, so avoiding what was by then a formal difficulty.

would lie against a bailee; but it was further agreed that a conversion altered the property and ended the bailment. By converting the goods the bailee ceased to be bailee, and he could properly be charged in case as if he had come to them otherwise than by delivery.[50] The effect was that, as in detinue, there would henceforward be no harm to the defendant in conversion if the plaintiff counted on a trover when in fact there had been a bailment.

So far this story is like that of *indebitatus assumpsit*, and what has happened is as innocuous [51]; there has been little change in substantive rights, but the plaintiff has gained a better remedy. There remains, however, a further step, which has had pernicious consequences. The conversion of the goods has so far been more or less literal; they have generally been consumed or sold. If a bailee or any other possessor had still got the goods, and did no more than refuse to give them up, then detinue was unquestionably the proper action; but here too a plaintiff would wish to use case, and he could cogently argue that the harm to him was the same whether the defendant had got rid of his goods or still had them. This variant of the old problem was solved by a move as ingenious as it was unfortunate. Conversion became metaphysical; it might consist in a denial of the plaintiff's title. The first step was to hold that while a mere refusal to deliver could not in itself be a conversion, it might be evidence of one [52]; and it soon appeared that a jury might find the refusal itself in the circumstances to be a conversion, as a denial of title.[53] In the situation which gave rise to it, this idea of conversion was harmless and even beneficent. Applied elsewhere, as it necessarily was, it has done mischief. A muddle over what kind of title was in question was eventually cleared up.[54] Doubts about the real nature of the wrong are with us yet, as was strikingly shown in *Oakley* v. *Lyster*.[55] Denial of title, introduced to take a detention out of the field of detinue, has grown into an unnatural tort.

The story of each of these achievements of case has turned out to have the same point. The old actions of covenant, debt, and detinue enforced positive duties, and a plaintiff who wished to use

---

[50] See *Gumbleton* v. *Grafton*, Cro.Eliz. 781; *Isaack* v. *Clark*, 2 Bulstrode 306, esp. per Dodderidge J. at p. 309.

[51] Critics of *Hollins* v. *Fowler*, L.R. 7 H.L. 757 may think that there was something to be said for the law as ordered by detinue.

[52] *Chancellor of Oxford's Case*, 10 Co.Rep. 53b at 56b, 57a; *Isaack* v. *Clark*, 2 Bulstrode 306.

[53] See Croke J. in *Isaack* v. *Clark*, 2 Bulstrode 306, at 311; *Agar* v. *Lisle*, Hobart 187, Hutton 10.

[54] See Mr. Fifoot's account of the matter, *History and Sources of the Common Law*, p. 110ff, and especially *Ward* v. *Macauley*, 4 T.R. 489 and *Gordon* v. *Harper*, 7 T.R. 9.

[55] [1931] 1 K.B. 148.

case instead had so to put the matter that he was formally complaining, not of the non-performance of the duty in question, but of a definite and irrevocable wrong: he had to find, or invent, a difference. Since, apart from their archaic procedure, the old actions were sensible, this introduction of differences was a process not without peril. Upon the whole we have been lucky. The doctrine of consideration is a small price for a law of contract better than anything covenant and debt could have given us; *indebitatus assumpsit* has been almost wholly beneficent; and conversion, though artificial, mostly works well enough.

Finally, these stories are old-fashioned enough to have a moral. The incoherence of legal history has lately been emphasised; Mr. Fifoot, for example, speaks of "the mirage of continuity." [56] Nobody believes more strongly than the present writer in the importance of misunderstanding as a means by which the law is kept related to social needs. But however much the lawyer may mistake and distort his authorities, he rarely ignores them; and if he does, his opponent is always there to bring them up. Every time a change is made, the judge who makes it must be persuaded that what he is doing is intellectually defensible; there must be a way of putting the matter which, on the existing authorities, is at least plausible. This necessity tends to perpetuate patterns in the law, which may long outlast its content. Case was poured into a mould of which the old personal actions formed part, and their traces survive in the cast. The process goes on. Today new torts, based on principles of liability and resulting mainly from the disappearance of the forms of action, are being poured into a mould made up of the old torts created by the forms; and if negligent misstatement is not a tort,[57] that is because the new tort of negligence is flowing round the older tort of deceit.

---

[56] *History and Sources of the Common Law*, at p. 398.
[57] *Candler* v. *Crane Christmas & Co.* [1951] 1 All E.R. 426.

SALE OF GOODS IN THE FIFTEENTH CENTURY

THIS is a descriptive article, without a point, begun with two aims. The narrower was to survey the vicinity of certain landmarks: the "real" nature of contracts enforced by debt and detinue, and the passing of property. Dejectedly looking at the result, little can be said except that the landmarks are gone; but some facts have emerged which seem worth recording. The wider aim was selfish: the writer is preparing a study, in more detail than those existing, of the personal actions down to 1600; and the difficulty, as always, is in asking the questions. Some of the material has therefore been rearranged round an elementary transaction, in the hope of seeing what kind of thing might worry the lawyers on each side.

SELLER'S ACTION FOR THE PRICE

The writ should claim a total sum, leaving the count to specify how it was arrived at: *e.g.*, a horse was sold for so much, of which the buyer paid so much; so much more was borrowed and so much again is due on an obligation. Separate demands would be made in the writ only if one of the claims were for chattels other than money. A claim in detinue could be joined with debt for money; and so, *a fortiori*, could a claim in debt for fungible goods; but claims could not be framed in the alternative,[1] and transactions of the part-exchange or sale-or-return varieties might raise difficulties of analysis. A sale of cloth for £500, the seller to take jewels for £300, was a sale not for £500 but for £200 and the jewels; but it would be otherwise if the arrangement about the jewels were later.[2] In sale-or-return the seller would presumably sue for the money after the arranged date; though in the unlikely case of the option being his, we are told that he could choose whether to sue for the money or the thing.[3]

An ordinary exchange, a horse for an ox, is called a sale; and what is more the "seller's" action for the ox is called debt.[4] This introduces a difficulty which will defeat us when the buyer sues for the goods: a writ for chattels, even debt for fungibles, must never say *debet* and so will look like detinue. If, therefore, the price was

---

[1] Joinder: *Reg.Omn.Brev.* (1634), ff. 139d. 140; YB. T. 11 Hy. VI, pl. 6, f. 48d; CP. 40/1140 (1549), m. 306d Alternative: YB. M. 9 Ed. IV, pl. 14, f. 36d.
[2] YB. M. 39 Hy. VI, pl. 46, f. 34d.
[3] YB. M. 7 Hy. VI, pl. 9, f. 5 at f. 7, *per* Cheine. Fitzh., *Natura Brevium*, f. 121B speaks of the writ for the horse as debt in the *detinet*.
[4] YB. M. 39 Hy. VI, pl. 46, f. 34d. Fitzh., *op. cit.*, f. 119, G, H.

in corn, the seller's writ should be in the *detinet* only. Even for money, *debet* was appropriate only between the original parties, so that if it is the seller's executors who sue, the writ should again be in the *detinet*.⁵ Sales and purchases by agents will be considered later.

A problem confronted the seller if the amount due to him was less than 40s. The Statute of Gloucester forbade his suing in the king's courts, and the writs of debt placed first in the Register are those *De debito in comitatu*.⁶ What hardship this caused, in denying justice and discouraging credit, depends mainly on the extent to which local civil jurisdictions had become ineffective before the value of money fell in the sixteenth century; but it was being evaded in the fifteenth. The rule was neither about the value of the transaction nor about the amount recoverable, but about the amount claimed.⁷ If, therefore, a plaintiff had sold his horse for 30s. he could get his action into the royal court by claiming forty; and what he did about the extra ten will throw some light upon the misunderstood " strictness " of the action of debt. The principle was that the plaintiff must at no stage give the lie to his own writ. If he did, the writ abated; but if he fought for the whole of his claim and lost in part, he could have judgment for the rest.⁸ His count in our hypothetical case must therefore support his writ by showing 40s. as due, either by misstating the price of the horse or by alleging that 10s. was owed on another transaction.

As to the first possibility, a suspiciously high proportion of counts do allege sales for just 40s.; and a Year Book of 1425 shows the defendant in such a case asserting that the sale was for a smaller sum, which he tendered, and taking the general issue on

---

⁵ For the use of *debet* generally see Fitzh., *op. cit.*, f. 119 G, M. It was also said that even if the executors had themselves sold, their writ for the price should be in the *detinet*; *Reg.Omn.Brev.* f. 140; *Vieux Natura Brevium* (1584), f. 61; YB. 30 & 31 Ed. I, R.S., p. 391; but this was not always obeyed; C.P. 40/957 (1501), m. 310. Otherwise if they themselves took an obligation; *Reg.Omn.Brev.*, f. 140. *Cf.* YBB. 17 & 18 Ed. III, R.S., p. 355; M. 20 Hy. VI, pl. 14, ff. 4d, 5 at f. 6.

⁶ Stat. 6 Ed. I, c. 8; *Reg.Omn.Brev.*, f. 139. The statute was never taken as confined to "trespasses"; we are not here concerned with its interpretation as placing a maximum on lower courts, for which see YBB. 20 Ed. III, R.S. Vol. ii, p. 146; H. 19 Hy. VI, pl. 17, f. 54. See the statute misquoted in *Vieux Natura Brevium*, f. 61. In 1601 an attempt was made to stop evasions and keep small cases out; Stat. 43 Eliz., c. 6. It was, however, ineffective; Holdsworth, H.E.L., Vol. 1, p. 74, n. 7.

⁷ Though loose statements to the contrary can be found, *e.g.* YB. H. 14 Hy. IV, pl. 33, f. 25 at f. 26–26d. *Cf.* YBB. P. 1 Hy. V, pl. 5, f. 4d; T. 3 Hy. VI, pl. 12, f. 49d; M. 19 Hy. VI, pl. 19, f. 8d.

⁸ YBB.: M. 3 Hy. IV, pl. 8, f. 2; H. 11 Hy. IV, pl. 38, f. 55; M. 13 Hy. IV, pl. 38, f. 11d; T. 1 Hy. V, pl. 1, f. 6 at f. 7d; T. 3 Hy. VI, pl. 6, f. 48; M. 10 Hy. VI, pl. 17, f. 5; M. 11 Hy. VI, pl. 9, f. 5; T. 2 Ed. IV, pl. 1, f. 10 at f. 10d.; M. 4 Ed. IV, pl. 15, f. 32d at f. 33–33d; T. 9 Hy. VII, pl. 4, f. 3 at f. 3d. But *cf.* YB. M. 42 Ed. III, pl. 10, f. 25d.

the rest.⁹ This was the normal way to plead if the defendant admitted the purchase but contested the price, though later the tender would not be explained.¹⁰ Usually, however, he would admit nothing; and the common event in the rolls, with 40s. cases as with others, is that he takes the general issue on the whole amount and so shuts us off from the facts: even if he has a jury its verdict is rarely recorded; and the few examples of a recorded verdict being for less than the 40s. may be because of a payment.¹¹ It seems likely on statistical grounds that some of the 40s. prices were disingenuous, and, on *a priori* grounds, that some claims for smaller sums would be brought in this way if it was safe. A possibility that it was not safe will be considered below: briefly it is that misstating the contract might enable the defendant to treat the count as a fabrication having nothing to do with his actual purchase, with the result, on principle, that the plaintiff would lose this action but could try again.¹²

Though again statistical, there is stronger evidence that the 40s. was sometimes made up by counting of a separate and fictitious transaction, usually a loan alleged to have been made at the same time as the sale; there are too many incredible counts. In Easter term 1437, for example, 25s. for malt and 15s. lent, 12s. for cloth and 28s. lent, and 6s. 8d. for corn and 33s. 4d. lent, might be acceptable separately, though hardly together; and 25s. 11d. for torches and 14s. 1d. lent looks contrived even in isolation.¹³ Coincidence might get the sum right: a sale of skins for 13s. 4d. and a furrier's fee of 26s. 8d. looks genuine; a sale of hoods for 26s. 8d., a furrier's fee of 4s., and a loan of 9s. 4d. does not.¹⁴ Such counts are not uncommon after the early years of the fifteenth century; and examples are found, conceivably honest, in the fourteenth.¹⁵ An interesting variant occurs when the price was more than 40s., but a payment had brought the debt below that figure; for example: sale for 46s. 8d., 26s. 8d. paid, 20s. lent; and sale for

---

[9] YB. T. 3 Hy. VI, pl. 12, f. 49d. YB. H. 46 Ed. III, pl. 16, f. 6 may be a similar case, though the nature of the 40s. contract is not stated. *Cf.* CP. 40/1064 (1530), m. 307, where P counted on a sale of malt for 40s., and D tendered 26s. 8d. and took the general issue on the balance. *Liber Intrationum* (1546), f. 126d, second entry, looks like a precedent; it is repeated in Rastell, *Entrees* (ed. 1574), f. 158.

[10] YB. H. 22 Hy. VI, pl. 28, f. 43d at f. 44. *Cf.* CP. 40/521 (1391), m. 185d; CP. 40/574 (1404), mm. 244, 477d; CP. 40/957 (1501), m. 110; CP. 40/1064 (1530), m. 355d.

[11] The writer has noted only two: CP. 40/521 (1391), m. 28; CP. 40/1064 (1530), m. 421. *Cf.* CP. 40/521, m. 435d, verdict for £17 of £24 claimed.

[12] Below, p. 116.

[13] CP. 40/705, mm. 261d, 441, 431d, 298d respectively.

[14] CP. 40/957 (1501), m. 285d, CP. 40/915 (1491), m. 124. This sort of combination was naturally not uncommon; YB. H. 16 Ed. IV, pl. 3, f. 10d.

[15] CP. 40/488 (1383), m. 437; CP. 40/521 (1391). m. 300.

£4 4s. 6d., £3 paid, 15s. 6d. lent.[16] It would have been simpler to misstate the amount paid, and this suggests that there was an advantage in truthfulness about the real transaction. The defendant could, of course, give separate answers on each claim,[17] and he might be led into an answering fit of truthfulness; thus in 1501 to a count for 12s. on a sale, 28s. on loan, he took the general issue on the loan and tendered the 12s.[18] Usually, however, the general issue is pleaded to the whole demand, and we learn no more of the facts.[19]

The plaintiff might thus count untruthfully to bring his case within the jurisdiction. At the beginning of the fifteenth century he might also do it for another purpose. In debt on sale, and indeed in almost all actions of debt except when the plaintiff relied upon an obligation, the defendant could wage his law; but he could not do this if the plaintiff was claiming arrears of rent on a lease, or arrears on an account before two auditors.[20] Suppose then that a seller, fearing that his buyer would perjure himself, declared upon a fictitious account instead of the sale: the natural plea would be the general issue, *non debet*; there would have to be a jury; and the jury, seeing that the defendant did indeed owe, might be persuaded to find against him.[21] Such a situation always modified the judges' enthusiasm for the general issue, namely that it would have to go to a jury who might misunderstand or abuse its generality: the cure was to allow a special plea; and the result in this case was the plea *nul tiel accompt*.[22] In 1403 statute provided another remedy: the court could examine the plaintiff or his

---

[16] CP. 40/875 (1481), m. 133d; CP. 40/1140 (1549), m. 102. Cases are found in which the payment alleged just leaves 40s. outstanding, *e.g.*, CP. 40/705 (1437), mm. 115d (price 7m. payment 4m.), 151 (price 48s. payment 8s.).

[17] YB. P. 9 Ed. IV, pl. 1, f. 1, *per* Choke. For 40s. examples, though not sale, see YB. T. 9 Hy. VI, pl. 7, f. 16; CP. 40/957 (1501), m. 150d. For an example with larger sums, see YB. H. 3 Hy. VI, pl. 38, f. 37d.

[18] YB. T. 16 Hy. VII, pl. 8, f. 14 (reported on the implications of *tout temps prist*); *Liber Intrationum* (1546), f. 126d, first entry. In 1437, however, when the sale was counted at 25s. 11d. with the rest ascribed to loan, the defendant tendered 6s. 8d. and took the general issue for the rest; CP. 40/705, m. 298d. above, p. 107, n. 13.

[19] No example of a 40s. sale and loan has been noted where the verdict matched the count. But in 1549 a plaintiff counted on an obligation for 26s. 8d. and a loan for 13s. 4d., and the jury found for him on the first and against on the second; CP. 40/1140, m. 248d.

[20] For an attempt to use the rule about lease to oust wager on a contract see YB. P. 9 Ed. IV, pl. 1, f. 1. *Cf*. Rastell, *Entrees* (ed. 1574), f. 175. The rule did not apply to hiring of chattels; YB. M. 1 Hy. VI, pl. 3, f. 1; Seld.Soc., Vol. 50, p. 12. For account see *e.g.*, YB. T. 11 Hy. IV, pl. 21, f. 79d.

[21] The statute of 1403 (below) envisaged that the plaintiff's apprentices, etc., might play the part of auditors; but it is not clear that there was necessarily much in the way of deception of the jury.

[22] YB. H. 11 Hy. IV, pl. 27, f. 50, *per* Hankford. It could later be argued, though unsuccessfully, that to take the general issue was to admit the account; YB. P. 20 Hy. VI, pl. 6, f. 24.

attorney on the truthfulness of the count.[23] When in an early case this disclosed that the debt was really the price of wool sold, the proper result was apparently thought to be judgment for the defendant, though as a matter of grace the plaintiff was allowed to count afresh.[24] Later the result was to allow wager against the original count, presumably leaving it open to the plaintiff to start a new and more truthful action; and the impossibility of his counting again on this writ is noted at the end of a case in which he could affirm some sort of account, perhaps as the statute envisaged before his own apprentices or the like, but in respect of the price of goods sold, which *ne gist en accompt*.[25]

The best-known device for ousting wager was in the action of account: if the defendant was charged with a receipt by the hand of someone other than the plaintiff, he could not wage his law. Analogies were inevitably explored in debt on contracts and detinue on bailments, and the process tells us something about sales through third persons. To begin with the answer, it seems that wager could never be ousted by counting of a third hand; though if a simple contract debtor died his executors could not wage, and here the result was to oust also the plaintiff's action. Two principles were involved, and that governing account had no application to debt or detinue.[26] In account the usual pleas were that you were not receiver (or not bailiff), or that you had accounted: whereas in debt on a sale you could never plead that you had not bought, or had paid, because both were subsumed under *non debet*. The third-hand rule in account applied when issue was taken on the receipt, and its main justification seems to have been that if a third person was involved the country could know about it.[27] But in debt on a sale issue could not be taken on the sale, of which the country's knowledge was irrelevant; there might have been, for example, a payment to justify the *non debet*. This does not explain the effect of a debtor dying, which depends not upon what the country can, but upon what the defendant cannot know about: the executor could not know whether his testator had bought or had paid. Wager, in short, was available only to one who necessarily

[23] Stat. 5 Hy. IV, c. 8. *Cf.* Hastings, *The Court of Common Pleas*, p. 199.
[24] YB. H. 14 Hy. IV, pl. 21, f. 19. D admitted a small part of the debt as to which he pleaded *tout temps prist*, and for the rest he took the general issue and waged his law.
[25] YB. M. 8 Hy. VI, pl. 25, f. 10d.; and pl. 36, f. 15d.
[26] YB. M. 18 Hy. VIII, pl. 15, f. 3. The case was detinue on a bailment.
[27] For the invention of the rule see YB. 16 Ed. III, R.S. Vol. ii, p. 25 and p. xvi. For early statements see YBB. 7 Ed. II, Seld.Soc. Vol. 39, p. 104; 10 Ed. II, Seld.Soc. Vol. 54, p. 109; 12 Ed. II, Seld.Soc. Vol. 65, p. 7; 12 Ed. II, Seld.Soc. Vol. 70, p. 146. More will be said elsewhere of its origin and reason. *Cf.* Plucknett, *The Medieval Bailiff*, p. 24.

knew the facts involved in the issue [28]; and even he might be barred from it (though the rule in account, early established, is the only one consistently applied) if the issue was upon an event involving a third person of which therefore the country could also know. But these two principles were not always distinguished; nor was the result reached all at once by logic.

Let us first suppose that the " agency " was on the seller's side. In 1356 a plaintiff counting of a sale by his servant was held to be in this dilemma: if the servant had indeed sold, the plaintiff had no remedy against the buyer, but only account against his servant: if he himself had sold, even through his servant, it was still his own sale, so that the analogy of account did not help him and wager was available.[29] This was reaffirmed in 1443 which may explain why the writer has noted no such count in the rolls, though Rastell has a precedent.[30] The reasoning seems formalistic: the real point of difference between debt and account is not noticed, and the reason of the account rule is scarcely avoided by the point taken; the courts were probably out to protect wager. After early argument wager seems to have been regularly allowed in actions by executors on sales by their testators [31]; this case would carry with it the abbot suing on a sale by his predecessor [32]; and there was probably never any doubt about a married couple suing on a sale by the wife *dum sola*,[33] when the wife would be party to the action.

The converse situations, where the " agency " was on the buyer's side, raised also questions of liability. If a woman purchased *dum sola* and then married, the seller should sue husband and wife jointly with a writ in the *debet*, the husband having charged himself with the duty by his marriage.[34] They could wage,

---

[28] YB. P. 1 Hy. VII, pl. 18, f. 25, *per* Brian.
[29] YB. M. 30 Ed. III, f. 18d. *Cf.* YB. T. 29 Ed. III, ff. 36d, 37; Fitzh., *Abridgment*, Ley 63 (H. 24 Ed. III).
[30] YB. H. 21 Hy. VI, pl. 3, f. 23, *per* Ascue (but he or his reporter seems to mistake the 1356 case in another respect); Rastell, *Entrees* (1574), f. 201. *Cf.* YB. M. 9 Hy. VI, pl. 37, f. 53d. Similarly if a wife or servant sold without authority, and the husband or master subsequently assented, it was said that this assent supplied the necessary will and made the sale " perfect "; but it was the sale of the husband or master, and he should express it as such in his action of debt; YB. M. 27 Hy. VIII, pl. 3, f. 24, *per* Spilman at f. 25 and FitzJames at f. 25d.
[31] CP. 40/574 (1404), mm. 244d, 494; CP. 40/1064 (1530), m. 255. *Cf.* YBB. 2 & 3 Ed. II, Seld.Soc. Vol. 19, p. 15; 3 & 4 Ed. II, Seld.Soc. Vol. 22, p. 21; 6 Ed. II, Seld.Soc. Vol. 34, p. 153, *per* Tiltoun at p. 154; Fitzh. *Abridgment*, Ley, 70 (M. 14 Ed. II); 14 & 15 Ed. III, R.S., p. 195; 17 Ed. III, R.S., p. 7; T. 29 Ed. III, ff. 36d, 37.
[32] CP. 40/574 (1404), m. 382.
[33] CP. 40/574 (1404), m. 386d.
[34] YBB. 32 & 33 Ed. I, R.S., p. 15; 4 Ed. II, Seld.Soc., Vol. 26, p. 13; 10 Ed. II, Seld.Soc., Vol. 52, p. 102; M. 47 Ed. III, pl. 56, f. 23d; T. 9 Ed. IV, note between pl. 32 & 33, f. 24d; M. 15 Ed. IV, pl. 4, f. 2d. For an example see CP. 40/574 (1404), m. 89d.

but must make their law jointly; she could not confess the action, but she could lose it for her husband by defaulting on the law; and her death ended his liability.[35] If a married woman bought, the writ should be against the husband alone not naming the wife, and the plaintiff must not count of a contract made by her [36]; indeed, though in the fourteenth century it may have been proper to mention her in the count, the writer has noted no examples of this in the fifteenth, when the purchase was seen as that of the husband.[37] This was also the theory when a master was sued on a purchase by his servant, and the conditions for liability of husband and master are usually discussed together. It seems that they would be liable on a contract they had ordered, whether or not they knew the order was carried out or ever got the benefit.[38] At the other extreme, they were not liable on a contract they neither authorised nor ratified, even for necessaries consumed in the household; there could be a general authority to buy necessaries, but it is doubtful whether these played any larger part.[39] Express order aside, there was no liability unless the goods came to the use of the husband or master, but it is not clear what more was necessary: difficult discussions suggest that prior authorisation was sufficient, but subsequent ratification was not unless the purchase had been expressly made for their use.[40] These rules are discussed in cases usually about something else; neither in the Year Books nor in the plea rolls do we find husbands or masters pleading that some ingredient of liability is missing. Perhaps they took the general issue: the requirements would then be matters to be explained to a jury, or to be argued between the defendant and his conscience when he waged his law. That wager was available seems clear,[41] and on principle proper: the account reasoning was inappropriate, and if

---

[35] YB. M. 33 Hy. VI, pl. 23, f. 43; Fitzh., *Natura Brevium*, f. 120F.

[36] YBB. T. 2 Hy. IV, pl. 1, f. 21, *per* Markham; 6 Ed. II, Seld.Soc., Vol. 34, p. 153; *Eyre of Kent*, Seld.Soc., Vol. 27, p. 46. For an example of a plea of coverture see CP. 40/957 (1501), m. 318d.

[37] YBB. 6 Ed. II, Seld.Soc., Vol. 34, p. 153; P. 46 Ed. III, pl. 7, f. 10 at f. 10d, *per* Finchden; *Long Quinto*, f. 70d at f. 73d, *per* Danby; M. 27 Hy. VIII, pl. 3, f. 24 at f. 25d, *per* FitzJames.

[38] Fitzh., *Natura Brevium*, f. 120G. YB. M. 8 Ed. IV, pl. 9, f. 9 at f. 11d, *per* Pigot.

[39] YB. M. 21 Hy. VII, pl. 64, f. 40d; *Vieux Natura Brevium* (1584), ff. 61d & 62; Brooke, *Abridgment*, Contract bargen & achate, 41. *Cf.* YB. P. 11 Hy. VI, pl. 16, f. 30 at f. 30d.

[40] YBB. H. 20 Hy. VI, pl. 19, f. 21 at f. 21d, *per* Markham, at f. 22, *per* Newton; M. 21 Hy. VII, pl. 64, f. 40d, *per* Fineux. *Vieux Natura Brevium*, ff. 61d–62.

[41] YB. M. 13 Hy. VII, pl. 2, f. 2d, *per* Mordaunt at f. 3d. It is denied by Ascue in YB. H. 21 Hy. VI, pl. 3, f. 23; but he or the reporter refers to YB. M. 30 Ed. III, f. 18d, which does not support this point. Rolfe, at the end of YB. M. 9 Hy. VI, pl. 37, f. 53d, suggests it would be wrong to allow a question of law about the master's liability to be raised on the general issue; but there the master was seller.

the conditions of liability were as stated the defendant would, unlike executors, have the necessary knowledge. The difficult case was that of an abbot sued on a purchase made in the time of his predecessor. If it had been a question of simple contract, there would have been no action on the analogy of executors: but there was an *in rem verso* element, and the house, through its head, was liable if the goods had come to its use; indeed it was liable in the *debet*. There was a special plea denying that they had come to the use of the house, and this was triable by jury [42]; but whether wager should be allowed on the general issue was an insoluble problem. At the end of the fifteenth century Brian held out for logic: the contract was relevant and this defendant could not know about it. But opinion was then against him [43]: a practical reason was that since unlike executors he could be sued, he should not be worse off than his predecessor; and a justification suggested was that liability was in the *debet* and the house privy throughout.

Before leaving *auter contract* more should be said of executors, whose immunity was of great practical importance. Some thought that they could waive it, and that if they pleaded to an issue they could not raise it in arrest of judgment or on error; but in 1475 Littleton of his own motion stopped such an action.[44] Their immunity was deduced strictly from their inability to wage, and if their testator could not have waged they could be sued.[45] They were thus liable on an obligation, for arrears of rent on a lease, and for the arrears on an account. The fictitious use of this last to avoid wager, and the statutory remedy of examination, have already been mentioned. Since the consequence of examination was to permit wager, it could not be demanded by executors [46]; and though *nul tiel accompt* would usually protect them, it may be that an unpaid seller who hatched up a colourable account might have some chance of recovery.[47] There was one kind of simple contract in which wager was not available, and in which therefore executors could be sued, namely, when the plaintiff's performance was compellable. The important case was that of servants or

---

[42] YBB. T. 22 Ed. III, pl. 16, f. 8; M. 25 Ed. III, pl. 2, f. 48; M. 12 Ed. IV. pl. 2, f. 11d; M. 13 Hy. VII, pl. 2, f. 2d. at f. 3, *per* Kingsmill; *Liber Intrationum* (1546), f. 41.
[43] YBB. P. 1 Hy. VII, pl. 18, f. 25; M. 13 Hy. VII, pl. 2, f. 2d. *Cf.* YBB. H. 21 Hy. VI, pl. 3, f. 23; M. 12 Ed. IV, pl. 2, f. 11d, *per* Littleton. Brian's view seems finally to have prevailed; Keilwey, T. 7 Hy. VIII, pl. 3, f. 180.
[44] YBB. M. 10 Hy. VI, pl. 84, f. 24d at f. 25 *per* Cottesmore; P. 15 Ed. IV, pl. 7, f. 25. YB. T. 41 Ed. III, pl. 3, f. 13d, does not say whether the action was stopped *ex officio*. *Cf. Norwood* v. *Read*, Plowden, p. 180 at p. 182.
[45] See, *e.g.*, YBB. M. 34 Hy. VI, pl. 42, f. 22d at f. 23; M. 13 Hy. VII, pl. 2, f. 2d at ff. 3, 3d.
[46] YBB. P. 11 Hy. IV, pl. 17, f. 64; T. 11 Hy. IV, pl. 48, f. 91d; P. 20 Ed. IV, pl. 14, f. 3; M. 13 Hy. VII, pl. 2, f. 2d at f. 3d.
[47] See above, p. 108.

labourers within the statute suing for their pay [48]; but another may have been proposed relevant to sale, namely, the victualler. Two passages, neither clear, hint at this [49]; and it is the likely background to a series of attempts by suppliers of food and drink to recover from executors or to avoid wager. None were victuallers, and the only one to succeed was a gaoler who had fed his prisoner.[50] In 1494 it was said that victuallers could be compelled to sell only for cash,[51] which would destroy their case. The only chance of which we are told for simple contract creditors in general was to sue by *quominus* in the Exchequer, when the king's interest would prevent wager.[52] It is asserted in 1496 and again in 1535 that it was common practice to sue executors in this way, but on the latter occasion Fitzherbert denies it; and in 1504 we are told that for executors to pay a simple contract debt, unless presumably there was a specific direction in the will, was a *devastaverunt*.[53] Most of us die with bills unpaid, and this must have been a motive for experimenting with the action on the case: in 1520 Fitzherbert as counsel actually got a judgment against executors; but in 1535, on the occasion when he denied that there was any course for recovery in the Exchequer, he advised that the report should be taken out of the books *car il nest ley sans dout*.[54]

We will now suppose that the plaintiff has made a straightforward count on a sale and that it is the defendant's move. There was a time when he could try to undo the plaintiff's case by demanding examination of his suit; but he could have no other answer, a feature which remained even when it was settled in the fourteenth century that there could be no examination.[55] He must therefore plead; and nearly always he would take the general issue, which could be tried by wager of law or by jury. Early in the fourteenth century there had been a tendency to exclude wager in situations of which the country might have knowledge; the third-hand rule in account was largely a result of this, and we have seen that its reasoning did not apply to debt in which liability was not established by proving the transaction. There was also a

---

[48] YBB. H. 2 Hy. IV, pl. 12, f. 14d; H. 3 Hy. VI, pl. 26, f. 33d; P. 3 Hy. VI, pl. 13, f. 42; P. 4 Hy. VI, pl. 5, f. 19d; T. 11 Hy. VI, pl. 5, f. 48; M. 38 Hy. VI, pl. 30, f. 13d; H. 38 Hy. VI, pl. 4, f. 22; H. 16 Ed. IV, pl. 3, f. 10d.
[49] Y.B. M. 19 Hy. VI, pl. 25, f. 10 *per* Yelverton; Brooke, *Abridgment*, Ley Gager, 55 (a version of YB. H. 15 Ed. IV, pl. 3, f. 16).
[50] *Ibid.*; YBB. M. 22 Hy. VI, pl. 18, f. 13d (an attempt to base it on *notice del paies*); M. 28 Hy. VI, pl. 21, f. 4d (Brooke, *op. cit.* Ley Gager, 8).
[51] YB. M. 10 Hy. VII, pl. 14, f. 7 at f. 8.
[52] YB. 20 Ed. III, R.S., Vol. i, p. 17.
[53] YBB. T. 11 Hy. VII, pl. 9, f. 26d; T. 27 Hy. VIII, pl. 21, f. 23; YB. M. 20 Hy. VII, pl. 5, f. 2d.
[54] YB. T. 27 Hy. VIII, pl. 21, f. 23. The 40s. rule would provide another motive for experiment.
[55] YBB. 2 & 3 Ed. II, Seld.Soc., Vol. 19, p. 195; 17 & 18 Ed. III, R.S., p. 73.

tendency to exclude wager when land was involved: it was not available in detinue of charters or in debt for rent on a lease; and that it was available on a sale of land was something which needed saying.[56] Though traces of these feelings are found in the fifteenth century,[57] it was settled that in debt on a sale the defendant could always choose. From the rolls it appears that his choice steadily swung toward jury trial. The figures below are for pleas of the general issue when the plaintiff had counted simply on a sale [58]:

Term		Wager	Jury
Trinity	1358	3	3
Mich.	1370	5	9
Hilary	1383	12	6
Easter	1391	6	6
Trinity	1404	13	11
Hilary	1419	10	10
Easter	1437	5	10
Trinity	1460	2	2
Hilary	1481	5	12
Trinity	1501	9	13
Hilary	1530	4	18
Easter	1549	3	7

For the dishonest defendant wager seems preferable, and there were advantages for the honest: it was quicker, and by offering to make his law at once the defendant could prevent a nonsuit.[59] It is true that a court once went to extraordinary lengths to frustrate a defendant who thus turned up with his squad of oath-helpers, and allowed a nonsuit quite improperly [60]; but such hostility to wager rarely appears; and confidence in juries was far from general.[61] The shift toward jury trial is therefore probably due to something outside the court-room, either social pressures or the chance of interference by equity if wager was used.[62]

The formula of the general issue varies little: *D dicit quod ipse non debet* (*detinet* if the writ is so; in the fourteenth century *non tenetur* was used, covering both) *prefato P predictos 40s. nec aliquem denarium inde in forma qua* (*prout* is common at the

---

[56] YB. H. 22 Hy. VI, pl. 28, f. 43d at f. 44. *Cf.* YB. 21 & 22 Ed. I, R.S., p. 3.
[57] *e.g.*, YB. M. 22 Hy. VI, pl. 18, f. 13d.
[58] The relevant references are: CP. 40/395; CP. 40/440; CP. 40/488; CP. 40/521; CP. 40/574; CP. 40/632; CP. 40/705; CP. 40/798; CP. 40/875; CP. 40/957; CP. 40/1064; CP. 40/1140.
[59] YBB. H. 8 Hy. V, pl. 14, f. 3d; P. 9 Hy. V, pl. 14, f. 5; M. 3 Hy. VI, pl. 16, f. 13d; T. 3 Hy. VI, pl. 12, f. 49d; Brooke, *Abridgment*, Nonsuite, 52, 55.
[60] YB. H. 2 Hy. IV, pl. 15, f. 15.
[61] See, *e.g.*, YB. M. 7 Hy. VI, pl. 9, f. 5, esp. at ff. 6–6d.
[62] See Barbour, *History of Contract in Early English Equity*, p. 99.

beginning of the fifteenth century; *in forma qua* appears under Henry V, and is usual after the middle of the century) *idem P superius versus eum narravit* (sometimes *supponit*); then follows the offer of wager or the request for a jury. The formula meant the same thing whichever the mode of trial, and you could wage your law without peril to your soul only when a jury should find for you [63]; but exactly what it did mean needs discussion.

First you could honestly take the general issue if what you denied was the contract, and could not plead specially that there had been no contract. This had not always been quite so: under Edward I defendants *bene defendunt quod nullum equum de predicto P emerunt nec in aliquo denario ei tenentur*, and in 1344 it is asserted that in debt on a sale the defendant should always answer to the sale.[64] In the fifteenth century, however, the contract could not normally be denied: *il nest pas plee a vous adire que vous ne achatastes ascun chivall de moy, mes respondes al Dette & nemy al contract.*[65] This rule has to do with the availability of wager. In debt on a lease and on an account before auditors, where there could be no wager, the lease or the account could be specifically denied; as we have seen in the latter case, this was to prevent plaintiffs counting falsely so as to oust wager in the hope that a jury could be beguiled on the general issue.[66] In debt on a simple contract, however, there was no mischief for the defendant in the generality of the general issue because, if he feared what a jury would make of it, he could always wage his law.[67] It is thus no surprise to find it said that in debt against an abbot on the contract of his predecessor, where it was doubtful whether the defendant could wage, issue could be taken on the contract[68]; and echoes of the general *auter contract* argument can be heard in this context also.[69]

This is simple if there had been no contract, but not if there had been one and the plaintiff misstated it in his count. Suppose he had sold the defendant a horse, and counted of the sale of an ox or of two horses; or suppose, to take up a point postponed

[63] See, *e.g.*, YB. P. 21 Hy. VI, pl. 2, f. 35 at f. 35d; Brooke, *op. cit.*, Ley Gager, 93.
[64] CP. 40/50 (1283), m. 16d (*cf.* m. 23, where the general issue is similarly framed on a loan); YB. 17 & 18 Ed. III, R.S., p. 511 at p. 515 *per* R. Thorpe (otherwise, he says, with loan).
[65] YB. H. 8 Hy. VI, pl. 23, f. 29. *Cf.* YB. M. 33 Hy. VI, pl. 17, f. 38d at f. 40 *per* Littleton.
[66] Above, p. 108. *Cf.* YB. H. 38 Hy. VI pl. 4, f. 22, contract traversable in debt on retainer of a labourer, where there was no wager.
[67] YBB. M. 8 Hy. VI, pl. 13, f. 5d; H. 8 Hy. VI, pl. 23, f. 29; M. 33 Hy. VI, pl. 23, f. 43 at f. 44; M. 12 Ed. IV, pl. 2, f. 11d, & pl. 14, f. 14; P. 21 Ed. IV, pl. 24, f. 28d; M. 22 Ed. IV, pl. 10. f. 29d *per* Vavasour.
[68] Above, p. 112; YB. M. 13 Ed. IV, pl. 9, f. 4.
[69] *e.g., Long Quinto*, f. 70d at ff. 73, 73d.

earlier, he had sold a horse for 30s. and counted of a sale for 40s.: could the defendant plead the general issue and wage his law safely, and would a jury be safe from attaint if they found for him? If the misstatement was of the thing sold, the answer seems to be yes. The defendant would mark the particularity of his denial by a small variation in the words of the general issue: instead of *in forma qua* (or *prout*) *idem P. superius versus eum narravit*, he would say *non debet . . . modo & forma prout idem P . . . narravit*; and the words *modo & forma* would, we are told, be part of the jury's charge and would compel them to find for him (from which it follows that he could equally wage his law), on the ground that this action had nothing to do with the true contract.[70] Whether this would work if the misstatement was of the price is doubtful. That the words *nec aliquem denarium* remain in the *modo & forma* plea is inconclusive, since it is the identity of the contract that is denied. In detinue for a chain we are told that you could wage your law if the count misstated its weight but not if it misstated the value[71]; even if this is so the analogy is imperfect, but the writer's guess is that a misstatement of the price on a sale would similarly not be taken as going to the identity of the contract. It could, however, have made a likely talking point; and it may be significant that the only *modo & forma* plea noted by the writer in debt on a sale was to a count of wine sold for 40s.[72] Any successful use of this plea presumably left it open to the plaintiff to sue again, since the true contract had not been in issue; and it was at least possible for a defendant, when the plaintiff had overstated the price, to admit the true amount, tender it, and take the general issue for the excess.[73]

Besides the thing sold and the price, the count would specify the date and place of the contract and the time fixed for payment (usually *cum inde requisitus fuisset*); and the defendant might wish to say that these had been materially misstated, or that there was an unsatisfied condition. As to place, it is once asserted that a misstatement would enable him to take the general issue *modo & forma*[74]; but the matter is usually discussed in connection with conditions. If the plaintiff counted of a simple sale in county

[70] YB. P. 21 Ed. IV, pl. 2, f. 21d at f. 22; Brooke, *Abridgment*, Ley Gager, 93; YB. M. 21 Hy. VII, pl. 45, f. 36 at f. 36d.
[71] YB. P. 22 Ed. IV, pl. 8, f. 2. *Cf.* YB. P. 21 Hy. VI, pl. 2, f. 35 at f. 35d, where the misstatement considered is of the county in which the contract took place.
[72] CP. 40/957 (1501), m. 341.
[73] Above, pp. 106-07, nn. 9, 10; YB. H. 22 Hy. VI, pl. 28, f. 43d at f. 44 *per* Moile.
[74] YB. P. 21 Hy. VI, pl. 2, f. 35 at f. 35d *per* Newton. This would presumably make the action local. *Cf.* YB. P. 21 Ed. IV, pl. 24, f. 28d at f. 29 *per* Littleton.

(268)

A, the defendant could take a special traverse saying that it was made in county B and subject to an unsatisfied condition, *absque hoc* that it was made simply in A in the manner counted. The place was made part of the issue to prevent a jury from inquiring into matters outside their county, and it was not traversable if the defendant alleged that the contract was made conditionally at another place in the same county.[75] If there was no question of venue, a condition would not contradict any of the facts in the count, and the proper plea was not special traverse but confession and avoidance.[76] In 1370 the buyer of a house admitted his purchase, but said that the seller was to dismantle and transport it at his own expense and had not done so [77]; and in the middle of the fifteenth century this was the way to plead a condition in the sale of a horse that the animal was sound,[78] or a condition in a sale of land for livery before payment.[79] In 1454, however, a defendant, having pleaded a condition that goods bought should be delivered before payment, repented and took the general issue; and he would have waged his law in the first place had he not feared a malicious default by his wife, who, as the actual purchaser *dum sola*, would have had to make it with him.[80] It may therefore be that wager was in fact, perhaps improperly, used in such cases; but it seems that if the general issue was taken to a jury, who found the condition in a special verdict, judgment would be given for the plaintiff.[81]

Now let us suppose that the defendant's case rested, not upon the terms of the contract, but upon events since. If he had paid, he should take the general issue [82]; a special plea would confess

---

[75] YBB. M. 8 Hy. VI, pl. 24, f. 10; P. 34 Hy. VI, pl. 13, f. 42; M. 9 Ed. IV, pl. 32, f. 45; P. 21 Ed. IV, pl. 24, f. 28d.

[76] In 1486 a special traverse was demurred to even though the condition (for the date of payment to depend upon a resale) went to contradict a statement in the count that payment was due at a date past; YB. H. 1 Hy. VII, pl. 29, f. 13d. *Cf.* YB. P. 34 Hy. VI, pl. 13, f. 42; Dyer, ff. 29d, 30. But see YB. H. 22 Hy. VI, pl. 28, f. 43d at f. 44 *per* Newton.

[77] YB. M. 44 Ed. III, pl. 6, f. 27d. The seller denied that the contract was conditional.

[78] YB. M. 33 Hy. VI, pl. 17, f. 38d at f. 40 *per* Littleton; Rastell, *Entrees* (ed. 1574), f. 202.

[79] YB. H. 22 Hy. VI, pl. 28, f. 43d at f. 44 *per* Newton. *Cf.* YBB. T. 9 Ed. IV, pl. 34, f. 25 at f. 25d *per* Catesby (payment not to be made until pledge restored); M. 9 Ed. IV, pl. 14, f. 36d.

[80] YB. M. 33 Hy. VI, pl. 23, f. 43; to the first plea the seller was going to say that he had delivered; to the general issue the buyer added a protestation about the condition, presumably to prevent an estoppel in subsequent proceedings. *Cf.* YB. H. 22 Hy. VI, pl. 28, f. 43d at f. 44, where Newton thought wager possible.

[81] YB. M. 22 Hy. VI, pl. 50, f. 33; below, p. 123.

[82] YBB. H. 46 Ed. III, pl. 16, f. 6; P. 9 Hy. VI, pl. 24, f. 9; M. 20 Hy. VI, pl. 9, f. 3, *per* Paston; M. 9 Ed. IV, pl. 14, f. 36d.

the original duty, and without an acquittance this would be fatal.[83] If he had an acquittance, he should say so, but still conclude " *& issint rien luy doit* "[84]; and if he had paid in another county, his plea should take the same form. Payment in a foreign county could be pleaded, without concluding to the *debet*, only when wager was not available; only then was it unfair to make a defendant answer the *debet* and so put foreign matter to a jury of the county in which the action was laid.[85] If the buyer had given an obligation for the price, the contract duty was equally consumed and the seller was left with only his rights on the deed.[86] If he nonetheless declared on the contract, it was said that the buyer could wage his law [87]; but there was a special plea,[88] and certainly a jury left with the general issue might regard the deed as a quibble, not realising that the plaintiff could win another action with it, and so find for him. If wager was indeed available one would expect this to be a sufficient safeguard; but perhaps it was thought wrong to compel the buyer to swear to a conclusion of law.[89] The seller's acceptance of something else in satisfaction would apparently have the same effect as his taking an obligation [90]; but the giving of a pledge, unless it were taken in satisfaction, had no effect: the buyer must pay up and bring detinue for the pledge.[91] It was disputed whether the seller's acceptance of a smaller sum in satisfaction would bar him if he sued for the excess.[92] His acceptance of an obligation from a third party would leave the buyer's liability unaffected.[93]

The last question about the buyer's liability, and the hardest to get a grip on, is how it might be affected by a failure on the

---

[83] YB. T. 1 Hy. V, pl. 1, f. 6 at f. 6d *per* Loddington and f. 7 *per* Hals. *Cf.* YBB. P. 40 Ed. III, pl. 27, f. 24d; H. 14 Hy. IV, pl. 35, f. 27. But *cf.* YB. 33–35 Ed. I, R.S., p. 151.

[84] YBB. M. 32 Hy. VI, pl. 21, f. 14; M. 33 Hy. VI, pl. 23, f. 43.

[85] YBB. H. 11 Hy. IV, pl. 27, f. 50; H. 22 Hy. VI, pl. 1, f. 36; M. 10 Hy. VII, pl. 4, f. 4; M. 11 Hy. VII, pl. 16, f. 4d.

[86] YBB. P. 3 Hy. IV, pl. 14, f. 17d; T. 11 Hy. IV, pl. 21, f. 79d; and references below. This could greatly complicate an action against an abbot on the purchase of his predecessor, if the predecessor had made an obligation which was the deed of himself but not his house; YB. H. 20 Hy. VI, pl. 19, f. 21. If the buyer gave an obligation for part only, the seller would no doubt declare on the contract as though that part had been paid.

[87] YB. P. 3 Hy. IV, pl. 14, f. 17d.

[88] *Ibid.*; YBB. M. 1 Hy. VI, pl. 31, f. 7d at f. 8 *per* Babington; P. 22 Hy. VI, pl. 32, f. 55d at f. 56 *per* Newton; M. 28 Hy. VI, pl. 21, f. 4d; M. 39 Hy. VI, pl. 46, f. 34d; H. 9 Ed. IV, pl. 10, f. 50d *per* Choke. *Cf.* Rastell, *Entrees* (ed. 1574), f. 202.

[89] *Cf.* YB. M. 12 Ed. IV, pl. 2, f. 11d; and pl. 14, f. 14 at f. 14d.

[90] YBB. T. 9 Ed. IV, pl. 34, f. 25, esp. at f. 25d *per* Jenney; M. 9 Ed. IV, pl. 14, f. 36d. *Cf.* YB. H. 41 Ed. III, pl. 15, f. 7.

[91] YB. T. 9 Ed. IV, pl. 34, f. 25.

[92] YB. M. 10 Hy. VII, pl. 4, f. 4.

[93] YB. M. 28 Hy. VI, pl. 21, f. 4d; Brooke, *Abridgment*, Contract bargen achate, 29. The liability of guarantors will not be discussed.

seller's part. The central case is that of non-delivery, but we will start from the periphery. First, and beyond doubt, we are told it was no plea that the seller had retaken the goods; the buyer must pay and sue in tort.[94] Secondly, we are twice told it was no plea that the goods belonged to a third party who had taken them from the buyer.[95] The earlier statement was made in passing by Newton, whose views were unorthodox; but the latter was made by Vavasour in a case which raised the topic and in which he was concerned to argue the other way, and it was accepted by Littleton. The action was for the balance of the price of growing timber sold for a lump sum by a limited owner, whose interest ended when the purchaser had cut half and paid half; its result is not reported. In the ordinary case of *res aliena* it seems likely that the buyer could plead a condition for title by way of confession and avoidance if there was one, and that if not he had no defence in debt but might have a delictual remedy.[96] Thirdly, *res sua* is discussed briefly. A note of 1467 just asks whether the buyer has any defence in debt, but Perkins, whose book was first published in 1530, answers glibly: the sale is void *car ne poet este bon si non que le propertie soyt per ceo alter*.[97] If this result is right, the buyer should presumably take the general issue; and even apart from the sophistication of property passing, the simplest analysis is that he has not bought anything. Fourthly, there are contradictory statements about the sale of a non-existent thing.[98] In 1458 Prisot said that the buyer would have no plea because *caveat emptor*; but his views were unorthodox in the same way as Newton's. Twenty years later it was said that the sale is void for want of *quid pro quo*; this was by Vavasour in the timber case, and he seemed to think his conclusion irreconcilable with his view on *res aliena*.

A contemporary view of the effect of non-delivery was indicated when the pleading of conditions was discussed.[99] We saw that a buyer of land was recommended to plead specially a condition that delivery should precede payment, that a buyer of cloth actually pleaded a similar condition (though he later abandoned it for the general issue), and that as early as 1370 the buyer of a house

---

[94] YB. M. 15 Ed. IV, pl. 5, f. 2d at f. 3 *per* Nele.
[95] YBB. M. 20 Hy. VI, pl. 14, ff. 4d, 5 at f. 6; P. 18 Ed. IV, pl. 30, f. 5d; H. 18 Ed. IV, pl. 1, f. 21d. But *cf.* YB. P. 21 Ed. III, pl. 2, f. 11d at f. 12 *per* Belknap. The case would not arise in market overt.
[96] See below, p. 130.
[97] YB. M. 7 Ed. IV, pl. 2, f. 15; Perkins, *Profitable Booke* (ed. 1586), para. 93, f. 20. Both suppose the sale to be in market overt.
[98] YBB. M. 37 Hy. VI, pl. 18, f. 8d; P. 18 Ed. IV, pl. 30, f. 5d; H. 18 Ed. IV, pl. 1, f. 21d.
[99] Above, p. 117, notes 76–80. The 1370 case of the house is in a different category; but it remains significant that the buyer did not take the general issue on the ground that he had had no *quid pro quo*.

likewise pleaded an admittedly onerous condition for delivery. The inference is that if there was no condition non-delivery was no defence, which is repeatedly stated. Of land it was said by Newton in the case mentioned, in *Doige's* case, and on a third occasion, and said again some fifteen years later by Prisot.[1] Of goods it was said by Fortescue and probably Paston in *Doige's* case, by Prisot, and by Littleton.[2] These statements are generally agreed to be partly right of goods and wrong of land, the difference lying in the passing of property; but we should not assume that the case of goods was first established, and followed by an attempted extension to land. Mr. Fifoot tellingly speaks of a transition from the real to the consensual character of sale[3]; and if the passages of Newton and Prisot about land are read, they seem to represent the idea that " contract " is a consensual thing. The transaction itself generates the liability; and *quid pro quo*, if required at all, is supplied by a remedy the other way (the seller of land being thought liable in deceit). Thus Prisot, discussing the sale of a non-existent thing, thinks in terms of a special plea, which assumes a prima facie liability; the more orthodox Vavasour says there is no *quid pro quo* and the sale is void, and he would presumably take the general issue. Perhaps following upon the rejection of consensual contract, counts on the sale of land came to allege a conveyance as part of the seller's case[4]; and analogous assertions were made in debt on a lease, or against a boarder, and debt on a retainer.[5] The count on a loan, however, never recited delivery of the money; no doubt it was implied in *mutuatus fuisset*. Similarly on a sale of goods the count would not normally allege delivery,[6] which at one time was probably implied in *emisset*; had it not been for this ambiguity, the transition from real to consensual would not have been easy. As it was, no more would be involved than that non-delivery should have been pleaded specially as a breach of condition instead of being automatically covered by the general issue.

---

[1] YBB. M. 19 Hy. VI, pl. 47, f. 23d at f. 24d; T. 20 Hy. VI, pl. 4, f. 34 at ff. 34d–35; H. 22 Hy. VI, pl. 28, f. 43d at f. 44; M. 37 Hy. VI, pl. 18, f. 8d. All these cases were noted by Ames, *Lectures*, p. 140, n. 3.

[2] YBB. T. 20 Hy. VI, pl. 4, f. 34 at f. 35d; M. 37 Hy. VI, pl. 18, f. 8d; P. 18 Ed. IV, pl. 30, f. 5d (of *res aliena* not delivered).

[3] Fifoot, *History and Sources of the Common Law*, p. 227.

[4] Rastell, *Entrees* (ed. 1574), ff. 201, 86d. *Cf.*, *e.g.*, CP. 40/875 (1481), m. 163d; but not CP. 40/632 (1419), mm. 200, 334d.

[5] This did not stop Callow following in the steps of Newton and Prisot and asserting that one retained to build a house for a fixed sum could recover even though he did not build; YB. P. 20 Ed. IV, pl. 17, f. 3d.

[6] It might do so if delivery involved a distinct duty of carriage, *e.g.*, YB. M. 9 Ed. IV, pl. 14, f. 36d *per* Jenney; or in a case such as CP. 40/1064 (1530), m. 139d, where 20 qtrs. of malt were sold for £8, payable *pro rata* on each delivery.

Buyer's Action for the Goods

There is a pervasive difficulty: the writer will often not know whether he is talking about detinue or debt. Specific goods should *a priori* be claimed in detinue, unascertained goods (and presumably fungible goods from stock) in debt. But if Holdsworth is right this cannot at first have been true: detinue supposes a property in the plaintiff, and until the passing of property idea was established all actions by buyers, even for specific goods, must have been debt in the *detinet*.[7] The premiss can be neither proved nor disproved and may be unreal: in 1356 it was said that *accion de Detinue suppose possession precedent*[8]; but this was in an action *de rationabili parte bonorum*, a kind of detinue which would contradict the statement were it not so exceptional that it could be argued it was really debt itself.[9] The plea rolls do not label actions, which will normally be given a name only when one of the parties makes an attorney, often many years earlier; here even this resource fails because the Year Books tell us that for a surprisingly long time actions of detinue might still be entered as *de placito debiti*.[10] If internal evidence provides a test, the writer has not spotted it. Since money is not claimed, the word *debet* should any way be absent. Most of the actions found are for grain; but even if it is clear that the goods are specific our problem is *ex hypothesi* unsolved. What looks like a test, whether the goods are specified in the writ or claimed as *catalla* to such a value, is about fungibles and leaves it open how a specific lot of fungibles may be demanded.[11] Indeed, once one departs from the specific goods test, the question may have little meaning; it arose over the writs *de rationabili parte* only because they necessarily lay against executors, and a procedural statute about actions against executors was in terms confined to debt.[12] A passing reference of 1347 calls the buyer's action detinue,[13] but this may have been just because the goods were specific; and the problem may have obtruded itself only as the property point acquired independent substance. If so,

---

[7] H.E.L., Vol. III, p. 355.
[8] YB. M. 30 Ed. III, f. 25 at f. 25d *per* Gower.
[9] YB. 17 Ed. III, R.S., p. 141. It had its own *ostensurus* writ, and use of the common form caused trouble; YB. 1 & 2 Ed. II, Seld.Soc., Vol. 17, p. 39. *Cf.* the analogous difficulties in YBB. H. 30 Ed. III, f. 2d; H. 39 Ed. III, f. 6; P. 39 Ed. III, f. 9d.
[10] YBB. 17 Ed. III, R.S., p. 141; H. 14 Hy. IV, pl. 37, f. 27d at f. 28d. Under Henry III entries are found *de placito debiti catallorum* and *de placito quod reddat ei catalla ad valenciam . . . que ei debet*; C.R.R., XVI, pll. 1927, 2136. For a late writ in the latter form see YB. H. 30 Ed. III, f. 2d.
[11] YB. 3 & 4 Ed. II, Seld. Soc., Vol. 22, p. 26.
[12] Stat. 9 Ed. III, c. 3.
[13] YB. P. 21 Ed. III, pl. 2, f. 11d at f. 12 *per* R. Thorpe. The reference in YB. 1 & 2 Ed. II, Seld. Soc., Vol. 17, p. 39 at p. 40 is ambiguous.

the earlier casual naming of the action may have been partly responsible for the passing of property idea.

From the plea rolls, however, it appears that this idea was helped into existence by resorting to constructive delivery. Nearly all the actions found are for corn, and may thus be debt; but on any footing the facts are curious. Under Richard II actions by buyers are found, two looking very like detinue: one is for oxen; in the other the writ claims chattels of such a value and the count is for corn, some bailed, the rest purchased.[14] Then there seems to be a gap: negative evidence means little, but in six rolls of the Common Pleas between 1404 and 1468, the writer has found no actions by buyers claiming their goods. In Hilary 1481 there is one,[15] and with the turn of the century numbers pick up again.[16] But in the 1481 example, and in many of those under Henry VII, the count does not allege only the purchase: it expressly says the goods were left with the seller *salvo custodienda* [17]; and sometimes it even says that the goods were to be *re*delivered to the buyer. Both these phrases were standard in counts on bailment; they disappear from buyer's counts under Henry VIII.[18] A word of caution must be added: while common sense suggests the *salvo custodienda* cases were for specific goods, there is no other evidence that this was so; and we shall see that in 1505 a plaintiff, seeking to set up his case in tort as a wrong to goods, used the phrase where the goods were not specific.[19]

The apparent gap in the fifteenth century may well turn out to be a trick chance has played on the writer, or it may reflect economic circumstances; but it may be because buyers were counting not on sale but on bailment. In 1429 to a count on a bailment in detinue for wool, the defendant pleaded that the plaintiff had bought the wool from him on condition that he was to have it if he paid by a certain day, and had not paid. The plaintiff objected that this plea did not confess any delivery by him, to which it was said *Il ad dit que le plaintif ad achate de le defendant les toddes, et les lessa demourrer ove le defendant, le quel countrevail un*

---

[14] CP. 40/488 (1383), m. 456d; CP. 40/521 (1391), m. 156d. Others in the latter roll are mm. 474, 217.
[15] CP. 40/875, m. 420d.
[16] CP. 40/915 (1491)—5; CP. 40/932 (1495)—none; CP. 40/957 (1501)—11.
[17] CP. 40/915, m. 411d; CP. 40/957, mm. 106d, 114d, 173d, 248, 297, 297d (bis), 342d, 361.
[18] It is not found in K.B. bills in KB. 27/999 (1511), m. 20d; KB. 27/1006 (1513), m. 28d, or in any of 14 cases in CP. 40/1064 (1530).
[19] YB. M. 20 Hy. VII, pl. 18, f. 8d; Keilwey, ff. 69, 77; below, pp. 125-6. Some *salvo custodienda* cases have writs demanding *catalla* to such a value; CP. 40/875, m. 420d (20 burdens of steel); CP. 40/957, mm. 173d, 361 (both corn). But this phrase is not conclusive, and writs demanding commodities on bills obligatory may be so worded; CP. 40/1064, m. 310.

livere. . . .[20] This is the only case noted from which it appears that a buyer was counting on a bailment; but there is other Year Book evidence that the seller in possession was treated as a bailee.[21] These facts cannot be explained, but they are consistent with some hypothesis such as this: buyers in the fourteenth century used an action which was innocently called detinue; the property point raised an embarrassment which they eluded by counting on a bailment; and when the passing of property idea had thus been painlessly injected—clear statements are found in 1442–43 [22]—counts on sale reappeared, but at first often referring to a bailment. A possible reason for a return to honest counting is the problem raised by non-payment, clear appreciation of which is shown under Edward IV.[23]

Non-payment must always have been a defence in some circumstances; and when the liability was real one would expect it to be ground for the general issue. But in 1391 a seller pleaded specially that the sale was conditional upon payment at the day fixed for delivery, and the plaintiff buyer replied that he had tendered on that day.[24] A special plea was similarly used in 1428 in the case in which the buyer counted on a bailment[25]; and a case of 1443 suggests that if a seller took the general issue he would lose, even if the jury found such an express condition.[26] The inference is that if there was no condition, non-payment was irrelevant; and the inference from that is that " contract " (in the debt-detinue sense) was seen as to this extent consensual before any idea of property passing and independently of it. The views of Newton and Prisot about sale of land may thus not have been a faulty deduction from the case of goods, but part of a more general view which was retrenched [27]; and what happened in the case of goods did not happen because of the passing of property idea, but was only rationalised by it in real terms.

The solution of this conceptual difficulty intensified the practical one of non-payment; and it is noteworthy that counts on sale,

---

[20] YB. M. 8 Hy. VI, pl. 24, f. 10. It is reported partly on the problem of traversing the place, above, p.117, n. 75.
[21] YBB. H. 39 Hy. VI, pl. 1, f. 36 at f. 36d *per* Moile; M. 16 Hy. VII, pl. 7, f. 2d. *Cf.* YB. 10 Ed. II, Seld. Soc., Vol. 54, p 140; *Sel. Cases on Law Merchant*, Vol. ii, Seld. Soc., Vol. 46, p. 28 at p. 30.
[22] YBB. T. 20 Hy. VI, pl. 4, f. 34; P. 21 Hy. VI, pl. 26, f. 43; T. 21 Hy. VI, pl. 12, f. 55d.
[23] YBB. P. 5 Ed. IV, pl. 20, f. 2d; M. 49 Hy. VI, pl. 23, f. 18d; P. 17 Ed. IV, pl. 2, f. 1; H. 18 Ed. IV, pl. 1, f. 21d.
[24] CP. 40/521, m. 474. The sale was of barley, said to be *solvendum* on the day, suggesting that it was not specific.
[25] YB. M. 8 Hy. VI, pl. 24, f. 10; above, n. 20.
[26] YB. M. 22 Hy. VI, pl. 50, f. 33.
[27] Above, p. 120.

when first they re-emerge at the end of the fifteenth century, commonly allege that cash was paid at the time of the contract.[28] There was then no difficulty in saying that property had passed. Equally no difficulty was felt if a future date had been given for payment,[29] but the Year Books show an understandable confusion about the case where no payment had been made and no definite credit given. Statements of 1465 and 1470 indicate the basic idea of the lien,[30] and its mechanics were expressly stated by Brian in 1477: property passes on the contract, but the unpaid seller can counter detinue by saying *il fuist prist de ceo rendre si lautre ust le paye*. But he did not convince his audience: Littleton thought that the sale must be *sur condition en ley, cestassavoir, si il luy paye que il serra bone, & sinon il serra voyde*, and that property could not pass unless this condition was satisfied; and Choke referred to the other great difficulty raised by the passing of property, the effect of a second sale by the seller.[31] In the following year Brian restated his own position; but he or his reporter gave it as the opinion of some that if after a bargain was struck the buyer went away without paying, and later returned with the money, the seller could choose whether to go on or not because *son entent fuit sur le bargaine daver le money maintenant*.[32] Analyses leading to this result were favoured well on in Henry VIII's reign. Thus in 1523 it was said that the bargain in such a case would not be " perfect " (with special reference to the effect of a second sale), or would be only a " communication," or was conditional upon present payment [33]; and in 1537 it was said that if the price was not paid, and no day given for payment, the contract was void.[34] In pleading, these ideas would presumably reflect themselves in the general issue, and the superficial resemblance to a new real contract is striking. Brian's suggestion, making payment a condition not of there being a contract but of the buyer's right to possession, absorbed the passing of property idea into the existing framework; and non-payment would be pleaded specially as it had been at

[28] This is alleged in the case in CP. 40/875, four of the five in CP. 40/915, eight of the eleven in CP. 40/957, that in KB 27/999, and that in KB. 27/1006; but only one of the twelve in CP. 40/1064. There is thus a correlation in time, but not case by case, with the *salvo custodienda* form.
[29] See the references in the following five notes. The difficulty would of course arise if credit had been given but had expired before the buyer got the goods.
[30] YBB. P. 5 Ed. IV, pl. 20, f. 2d; M. 49 Hy. VI, pl. 23, f. 18d.
[31] YB. P. 17 Ed. IV, pl. 2, f. 1.
[32] YB. H. 18 Ed. IV, pl. 1, f. 21d.
[33] YB. H. 14 Hy. VIII, pl. 1, f. 15d and pl. 7, f. 18d, esp. at f. 19 *per* Carel, f. 21d *per* Brooke, ff. 19d–20 *per* Fitzherbert. For the " communication " idea *cf*. YB. H. 21 Hy. VII, pl. 4, f. 6 at f. 6d *per* Tremaile. For a view that the contract was good, and the payment would relate back to it, see YB. M. 10 Hy. VII, pl. 14, f. 7.
[34] Dyer, ff. 29d, 30.

Sale of Goods in the Fifteenth Century 125

least since the late fourteenth century.[35] When it was accepted is not known. In 1537 the seller pleaded a condition for payment by way of confession and avoidance, and it was said that he could have taken the general issue; but the circumstances make this inconclusive.[36] In the rolls of Henry VII and Henry VIII the writer has come across no special pleas but only the general issue.[37]

Before leaving the buyer's remedies for non-delivery, a word must be said of actions on the case. There is no trace before the sixteenth century of their use by sellers to get their money; but it is well known that buyers of land were experimenting,[38] and buyers of goods made an attempt. Actions against craftsmen, carpenters and the like, are irrelevant here, but of course they covered part of the field occupied for us by the sale of goods; and after the clear answer of the Year Books the steady trickle of writs in the plea rolls alleging nonfeasances as well as misfeasances is surprising. The earliest writs noted alleging simple non-delivery were two in 1437, against a coal merchant and a fishmonger, and seven years later was one concerning corn [39]; all were large transactions, and would normally have been done by conditioned bond. In 1443 an action for non-delivery of wine was reported in the Year Books.[40] The argument was all about whether the plaintiff should have been using debt, detinue or covenant; and though the parties agreed, the impropriety of case seems to have become clear. No similar writs have been seen in the rolls until the turn of the century, when they reappear,[41] this time with a future ahead of them. In this period of renewed experiment attempts were not confined to pure *assumpsit* and a case of 1505 shows a claim formulated in conversion. It forms an interesting pendant to the passing of property development; the buyer, following recent successes against bailees, counted that he had bought corn from the defendant and (according to one report) had left it with him for

---

[35] Above, p. 123, n. 24. The formulation of Brian's plea, though in a seller's action for the price, is found in the 1370 case of the house, above, p. 117, n. 77: the buyer pleaded that the seller was to dismantle and remove the house, and that he had been always ready to pay if the seller had done so.
[36] Above, p. 124, n. 34.
[37] Once *modo and forma*; detinue for a bullock bought for 14s. The action was by bill, the defendant being *in custodia marescalli*, and presumably the Statute of Gloucester did not apply. The count alleged payment; KB. 27/999 (1511), m. 20d. If in such a case the defendant wished to deny the payment, he may have been able to do so by special traverse; YB. M. 16 Ed. IV, pl. 7, f. 9d.
[38] YBB. T. 20 Hy. VI, pl. 4, f. 34; M. 16 Ed. IV, pl. 7, f. 9d. *Cf.* references in YBB. H. 22 Hy. VI, pl. 28, f. 43d at f. 44 *per* Danby; M. 21 Hy. VII, pl. 66, f. 41.
[39] CP. 40/705, mm. 50d, 52d; KB. 27/731, m. 63d. Only the buyer of fish (200 tench) alleged that he had paid. All are *op. ses.*
[40] YB. T. 21 Hy. VI, pl. 12, f. 55d.
[41] *e.g.* CP. 40/957 (1501), m. 475d; KB. 27/1006 (1513), m. 47 and roll of attorneys, dorse. Both allege payment.

safe keeping (the standard *salvo custodienda* allegation in detinue on bailment, and for a time used in counting on a sale), and that the seller had converted it to his own use; but the corn was not specific, and the general opinion was that he should be using debt.[42]

Buyer's Action for Defects

Glanvill mentions a sort of *actio redhibitoria*, and this remedy for breach of warranty was available in some local courts under Edward I and perhaps later.[43] More usually such courts gave damages; and sometimes the promise is emphasised and the action called covenant, sometimes fraud is emphasised and the action called trespass or deceit.[44] The royal courts, because of their exclusive policy, did not enter the field until late in the fourteenth century,[45] when their actions had so hardened that there was no approach in contract; the subject was thus dealt with under delictual forms. Conditions of quality (and possibly title) were at home in the seller's action for the price, and served the buyer as a defence against his contractual liability to pay.[46] Warranties, upon which the buyer could attack the seller, sounded in tort; and precedents are placed in the Register among the writs *De transgressione*.[47]

The ambiguous nature of the action explains most of its difficulties. First, could the seller be liable without an express warranty?

[42] YB. M. 20 Hy. VII, pl. 18, f. 8d; Keilwey, ff. 69, 77. For the early cases of conversion against bailees see the very interesting discussion by Mr. Simpson, 75 L.Q.R., p. 364. The term "conversion" however (*ibid.*, p. 379) is older than its use in tort and seems to have meant no more than appropriation, sometimes proper; YB. H. 20 Hy. VI, pl. 19, f. 21 at f. 21d. It was most commonly used of misappropriation by personal representatives of their testator's goods, exposing their own to execution; YBB. M. 11 Hy. VI, pl. 12, f. 7d; H. 11 Hy. VI, pl. 9, f. 16; P. 11 Hy. VI, pl. 30, f. 35d; M. 34 Hy. VI, pl. 42, f. 22d at f. 23d; and its original home may have been in returns to writs of *fieri facias* in such cases; Rastell, *Entrees* (1574), ff. 306–306d.

[43] Glanvill, X, 14; the goods had to be sold as sound, and to have been unsound at the time of the contract. *Borough Customs*, Vol. ii, Seld.Soc. Vol. 21, p. 182 (denial of warranty; Exeter, c. 1282) *Cal. Early Mayor's Court Rolls, 1298–1307*, p. 68 (seller of horse denies warranty, fails to make his law, made to repay price and a sum for keep; London, 1300). *Cf., Cal. Plea & Memoranda Rolls, 1364–81*, pp. 34, 126.

[44] *Sel. Cases on Law Merchant*, vol. i, Seld.Soc. Vol. 23, pp. 102, 105–106 (both called covenant); but *cf.* p. 91. *Cal. Early Mayor's Court Rolls, 1298–1307*, pp. 154, 216 (both called trespass). *Cf. Sel. Cases on Law Merchant*, vol. ii, Seld.Soc. Vol. 46, p. 28 (law merchant case tried before royal judges in 1278, called *transgressio* at p. 29); *Sel. Cas. in KB.*, vol. i, Seld.Soc. Vol. 55, p. 33, at p. 34 (*deceptio*). There would often, especially with food, be a "criminal" aspect as well.

[45] A case slipped in as early as 1307, but there was a royal interest; *Sel. Cas. in K.B.*, vol. III, Seld.Soc. Vol. 58, p. 179 (called trespass and deceit). YB. 7 Ed. II, Seld.Soc. Vol. 39, p. 14 may be an attempt to get such a case in as *contra pacem*.

[46] Above, p. 117. *Cf. Sel. Cases on Law Merchant*, vol. i, Seld.Soc. Vol. 23, p. 50.

[47] *Reg.Omn.Brev.*, ff. 108 (three writs concerning horses), 111 (malt).

A curious report of 1406 suggests that the action was simply for selling wine knowing it to be bad; in 1430, arguing on the mistaken belief that the writ (also about wine) similarly alleged no warranty, it is said that in the case of food this would not matter; and this is repeated in 1471.[48] Of goods other than food it was also said in 1430, and said again by Paston in *Doige's Case*, that the seller would be liable without a warranty if he knew of the defect; and in 1507 Frowyk combined these propositions: for food the seller would be liable warranty or no warranty and, apparently, knowledge or no knowledge; for other things he would be liable without a warranty only if he knew.[49] In the rolls the writs noted, whether for wool or wine, woad or malt, horses or herring, all allege a warranty. The one exception concerned food sold for immediate consumption; it is an *op. se* of 1419 against an " osteler " of Basingstoke, and illustrates the universality of human suspicions [50]:

> quare cum idem P cum prefato D ad quendam cuniculum assatum ab eo emendum apud B barganizasset predictus D machinans prefatum P callide decipere quendam murelegum assatum loco unius cuniculi prefato P ibidem falso & fraudulenter vendidit & liberavit sicque idem P . . . infectus fuit & de vita ejus desperabatur ad dampnum ipsius P 100s. ut dicit.

No later action on similar facts has been found; Brian in 1471 can be understood as saying either that no warranty need be alleged, or that it would be alleged but could not be traversed.[51] For defects in quality (as opposed to title) of goods other than food, the writer has found nothing to confirm that the seller could be liable without a warranty if he knew; and a traverse of the warranty was perhaps the commonest plea. It was made in 1387, and is found in substantially the same form throughout the fifteenth century: *protestando* that the goods were sound, the defendant pleads that he sold them *simpliciter, absque hoc* that he gave any warranty.[52]

[48] YBB. P. 7 Hy. IV, pl. 19, f. 14d (Brooke, *Abridgment*, Accion sur le case, 35); M. 9 Hy. VI, pl. 37, f. 53d *per* Martin and Babington; T. 11 Ed. IV, pl. 10, f. 6 at f. 6d *per* Brian and Nele.
[49] YBB. M. 9 Hy. VI, pl. 37, f. 53d *per* Godred purporting to rely on a K.B. precedent; T. 20 Hy. VI, pl. 4, f. 34 at f. 35, where Paston purports to rely on a precedent which his reporter contradicts; Keilwey, H. 22 Hy. VII, pl. 16, f. 91.
[50] CP. 40/632, m. 476d. *Cf.* YB. M. 9 Hy. VI, pl. 37, f. 53d *per* Babington; *Cal. Plea & Memoranda Rolls, 1323-64*, p. 251.
[51] YB. T. 11 Ed. IV, pl. 10, f. 6 at f. 6d. The latter would amount to an implied warranty by victuallers; the former would fit in with an implied condition. Benjamin doubts whether the common law ever implied a warranty; *Sale*, 8th ed., p. 681. For sale without title, see below, p. 130.
[52] YB. 11 Rich. II, Ames Found., p. 4; CP. 40/632 (1419), m. 342, white herring; CP. 40/798 (1460), m. 167, horse, issue formulated in jury respite; CP. 40/915 (1491), m. 166, red herring. *Cf.* YB. H. 19 Hy. VI, pl. 5, f. 49 at f. 49d *per* Ascough. The protestation might be omitted; CP. 40/705 (1437), m. 210d, size of cloths; Rastell, *Entrees* (1574), f. 9.

Whether or not knowledge could fix liability on a seller who had not warranted, it was always alleged against those who had. No special plea denying it has been found, and the question is whether ignorance could be raised on the general issue which, in a 1468 action about a horse, was pleaded as: *in nullo est culpabilis de deceptione predicta*.[53] The Year Books do not answer this question, though they do stress the seller's opportunity for knowing; and Frowyk in 1507 clearly thought that liability on a warranty was independent of knowledge.[54] The London system seems to have been directed at passing the loss back to the party originally at fault,[55] and the common law would most nearly achieve such an aim by ignoring innocence at each step. Notwithstanding the words of the writ, attributable to its delictual form, it may therefore be that the seller's state of mind was irrelevant. The buyer's, on the other hand, was not: he had to be deceived, and we find the sort of discussion you would expect about obvious defects, defects which are not apparent to the senses but require a test such as measurement, and buyers who are blind or have not the goods before them.[56] These matters would be raised perhaps by the general issue, perhaps by a special plea of acceptance.[57]

The basis of liability was also raised by sales through servants. In 1430 a buyer sued master and servant: if the report is right, the writ alleged that only the master knew of the defect, but nothing is made of this and the servant pleaded that the goods were sound; the master wished to plead that he had not sold otherwise than through his servant, but was told that if he had authorised the sale, so that it was indeed his, he would be liable.[58] In 1471 the servant was sued alone, and pleaded conversely that he had not sold otherwise than for his master, and a verbal objection underlines that this meant the sale was the master's and not the servant's at all. Littleton remarked that the plaintiff might not have bought but for the servant's warranty and so was deceived, but even he tried to imagine the servant into contractual privity; everybody else assumed that only the seller could be liable, and the plaintiff sought to evade the result by saying the sale was in

---

[53] CP. 40/828, m. 154d.
[54] YB. T. 11 Ed. IV, pl. 10, f. 6, esp. at f. 6d *per* Brian; Keilwey, H. 22 Hy. VII, pl. 16, f. 91. If YB. M. 9 Hy. VI pl. 37, f. 53d is accurately reported, the writ alleged knowledge in only one of two defendants; the other pleaded that the goods were sound.
[55] *Cal. Early Mayor's Court Rolls, 1298–1307*, p. 216; *Cal. Plea & Memoranda Rolls, 1364–81*, p. 34 (in which the ultimate liability was in a fuller for a misfeasance).
[56] YBB. M. 13 Hy. IV, pl. 4, f. 1; T. 11 Ed. IV, pl. 10, f. 6. *Cf.* YB. M. 9 Hy. VI, pl. 37, f. 53d *per* Rolfe *ridendo*.
[57] YBB. 7 Hy. IV, pl. 19, f. 14d; M. 13 Hy. IV, pl. 4, f. 1.
[58] YB. M. 9 Hy. VI, pl. 37, f. 53d.

market overt and the property irrelevant.[59] In the same case warranty by a stranger is considered; it would not be actionable unless under seal because not part of the contract. That a warranty must not have been given after the contract would follow equally in tort; but we are told also that it must not be in any way separate, for example at another place.[60]

Despite the form of the writ, then, contract seems to have had the upper hand in its working. But it retained some features which we should associate with deceit rather than with warranty. For example writs sometimes alleged payment; and as late as 1494 it needed saying that the buyer could sue although he had not paid, because the seller had debt.[61] More important, the warranty had to be about present facts and not future performance: you could warrant the nature of seed, and that it was good, but not that it would grow.[62] There was a special plea that the goods accorded with the warranty,[63] and we do not know whether this (or indeed anything except a denial that the defendant had sold at all) could be raised on the plea of not guilty, last reminder of delict.

A note may be added about the different kinds of warranty found. The transaction is nearly always an ordinary sale of existing goods: but an early entry concerns an exchange of horses; and in a late one the plaintiff had bespoken an organ from organ-makers who had undertaken to deliver with a warranty that it should be *benesonans & concordans ac boni metalli*, and who *falso & fraudulenter* sold it knowing it to be *discordans & mali metalli ac non benesonans*.[64] The latter is an attempt to combine warranty with a misfeasance writ; these cannot be discussed here, but their ambivalence between contract and tort is particularly clear in their use against manufacturers. By far the commonest are ordinary warranties of quality by ordinary sellers: *bonus, sanus* and *sufficiens* are the adjectives most often used of commodities, and wool is said to be clean, and animals healthy. Sometimes the action is about the nature of the goods: the nearest we can get in the rolls to *aes pro auro* is a mazer warranted *ex auro & argento puro ligatum*, and actually bound with copper.[65] More important commercially, though buyers were probably expected to know,

---

[59] YB. T. 11 Ed. IV, pl. 10, f. 6.
[60] YBB. T. 5 Hy. VII, pl. 7, f. 41d; H. 5 Hy. VII, pl. 10, f. 17d at f. 18.
[61] CP. 40/574 (1404), m. 195; K.B. 27/639 (1421) m. 69; Rastell, *Entrees* (1574) f. 9; YB. H. 9 Hy. VII, pl. 21, f. 21d.
[62] YB. T. 11 Ed. IV, pl. 10, f. 6 at f. 6d *per* Brian and Choke.
[63] YBB. M. 9 Hy. VI, pl. 37, f. 53d, B's plea; P. 11 Hy. VI, pl. 1, f. 24 at f. 24d *per* Martin; 14 Hy. VI, pl. 66, f. 22d, where it may have been necessitated by the point of venue.
[64] CP. 40/521 (1391), m. 174; CP. 40/957 (1501), m. 181. Both are *op. ses.*
[65] CP. 40/744 (1447), m. 31.

would be the golden fleece; and wool sold as of Leominster turned out to be Welsh.[66] Size might be warranted: the parties in the wool case were also litigating about cloths proving to be smaller than was said; two other examples of this have been found, and one about the size of oak trees; and the Year Books have another about the size of cloths and one about the weight of wool.[67] Value is something one would think could not be warranted, but a writ has been found about the annual value of land, and a London action alleges deceit in this among other things.[68] London also provides some of the evidence about warranties of title, though again it concerns land.[69] At common law the earliest of all actions for this sort of deceit was a bill brought in 1368 against a seller of chattels without title [70]; but the writer has found only one other example, a jury respite of 1444 [71]:

> *quare cum idem P cum prefato D ad 20 pelles bovinas ab eo emendas apud A barganizasset predictus D sciens ipsum aliquam proprietatem seu interesse in pellibus illis non habere nec potestatem illas aliqualiter vendere seu liberare pelles predictas prefato P pro magna pecunie summa falso & fraudulenter vendidit & liveravit quorum quidem vendicionis & liberacionis pretextu idem P variis laboribus & expensis diversimodis fatigatus extitit & depressus ad dampnum ipsius P £20 ut dicit.*

The claim must have been accepted as good in law; and it will be noticed that, like the man who ordered rabbit and was served with cat, the plaintiff alleges no warranty and complains of consequential damage. It would be interesting to know how later claims were formulated.

Some Conclusions

No more will be said of the facts which have emerged except in relation to the difficulties that remain. The passing of property on the contract, extraordinary as it is, was not a happy invention

---

[66] CP. 40/744, m. 276. The plaintiff, John Salman, also bought cloth (see next note) and the defendant was a chapman, John Wroth; it may therefore not have been a transaction in the regular wool trade. For the " Lemster ore " see Power, *Medieval English Wool Trade*, p. 20 et seq. Cf. CP. 40/828 (1468), m. 22d (growth of wine); YB. T. 11 Ed. IV, pl. 10, f. 6, at f. 6d *per* Brian (seed). For correspondence with sample, see YB. 14 Hy. VI, pl. 66, f. 22d.
[67] CP. 40/744 (1447), mm. 111d, 358d; CP. 40/705 (1437), m. 210d (plea, no warranty); CP. 40/632 (1419), m. 492; YBB. T. 11 Ed. IV, pl. 10, f. 6; M. 13 Hy. IV, pl. 4, f. 1.
[68] CP. 40/744 (1447), m. 283d; *Cal. Select Pleas & Memoranda, 1381–1412*, pp. 153–154.
[69] *Cal. Plea & Memoranda Rolls, 1323–64*, p. 260; ibid., *1364–81*, p. 126.
[70] 42 *Lib.Ass.*, pl. 8, f. 259d.
[71] KB. 27/731, m. 82.

making sale the unique consensual contract under the old forms. In the sense that the transaction might be sued upon with no performance on either side, except perhaps for conventional formalities, sale seems to have become consensual before our period opens, and long before we find any talk of property passing. Nor is this on reflection surprising: the path from real to consensual, through part payment, earnest and the like, would be neither long nor difficult; and there were, apparently by chance, no obstacles embedded in the standard pleadings.

How and why then did the passing of property come about? As to how, it must be connected with the practice of buyers in counting wholly or partly on a bailment; and why would probably be answered if we knew why they did this. It may have been precisely because a difficulty was suddenly felt about executory contracts. It may have been due to some development in detinue prima facie irrelevant, such as the differentiation of the bailment and the *devenit* liabilities. Or, perhaps more likely, it may have been a way of evading the difficulty that detinue asserts a property in the plaintiff: a choice had now to be made between debt and detinue, or a choice made when it did not matter had now to be justified. This supposes that the separation of detinue from debt was not finally settled by the specific goods test, which indeed cuts across any distinction between obligation and property: *de rationabili parte bonorum* was in a sense a claim to property in unascertained goods; the buyer's claim to specific goods lay first in obligation; and it was the obligation element which divided bailees from *devenit* possessors. The recurrent difficulty of identifying the action must represent a failure by the writer; but it may reflect also an inherent ambivalence which names would not altogether resolve.

Only partly explicable in such a way is the related difficulty, again pervading the investigation, of being sure when the goods were specific; even in *salvo custodienda* cases there is room for doubt. It is just possible that this is no accident. Although the consensual nature of sale was not a consequence of the passing of property, it was rationalised in those terms; and this rationalisation would not cover an executory contract for unascertained goods. The buyer of some of a stock might therefore have a motive for supposing a delivery and redelivery. Outside the field of sale, an immediate effect of the rationalisation may have been actually to arrest the development of contract. The *quid pro quo* was under fire in the fifteenth century, and some thought that the sale of land and perhaps other contracts might be enforceable although executory; by explaining sale in real terms, the passing of property knocked away their central argument.

Lasting consequences of property passing were the problems of a second sale by the seller and of the buyer suing before he has paid. These were fully apprehended before 1500 and the final solution of the latter proposed. The first reaction however, which seems to have obtained in the early decades of the sixteenth century, was to solve difficulties by denying that there was a contract; if no day had been fixed, payment was seen as a condition of its existence. This illustrates in little a process of which the entire story is itself an illustration, the building up of the abstract substantive law. It had become a question whether the condition was of the existence of the contract, now seen as an entity in its own right, or was a term of it; originally it was a condition of the defendant's liability in this action, and no more.

The story may be taken also as a new text for two old sermons. First, it was not only the rules of law that were being shaped but its elementary concepts. The buyer's action for the goods did something to define (and much to obscure) the borderline between property and obligation; within obligation, his action for defects did the same for the line between contract and tort; and in both the causes seem to have been accidental. Secondly, though we are compelled by our sources to study the common law in isolation, we misunderstand its development as well as mistaking social facts if we imagine it as existing in isolation. With actions like that on a warranty, the jurisdictional frontier affected the development of the law. With debt and detinue it is our picture that may be affected. The 30s. creditor who bluffed his way into the royal court got more effective justice, but probably did not remove himself and his transaction into a wholly different system of ideas; and if he did not, it is a question how far these ideas took shape below rather than above.

ACCOUNT STATED IN THE ACTION OF DEBT

AN article by Mr. Derek Hall [1] has brought to light the forgotten *concessit solvere*, a customary form of pleading in London and elsewhere which enabled a creditor, particularly one with multiple claims, to declare in debt without specifying the underlying transactions. Details would be given in evidence when the unhappy defendant took the general issue; but so far as the pleadings were concerned the claim rested, not on the transactions themselves, but on a subsequent admission of the amount or " grant " or promise to pay it. Similarities to *indebitatus assumpsit* and account stated are obvious; and Mr. Lücke's articles [2] have illuminated the obstacles which the former had to get round. Since local customs may often be regarded as the discards of the common law, some fragments are here brought together about the early use of *concessit solvere* in London and the fate of similar ideas in Westminster Hall. [3]

Matters came to revolve around the classical action of debt on account, which was distinguished from most other actions of debt not based upon a sealed obligation in that the defendant could not wage his law. Two conditions were necessary: that there had been an accounting before auditors, who had found the balance now claimed; and that this accounting had been of matters which lay in account and could have been compelled by action of account. Not until the last years of Edward III are actions of debt found which satisfy these conditions, and the reason is simple. In 1285 the Statute of Westminster II, c. 11, had provided that auditors finding an accountant in arrear should commit him to the nearest royal prison; and there he would stay, subject to a possible appeal to the Exchequer by *ex parte talis*, until he paid up. There was no need to bring debt; and the appearance of the classical form of debt on account marks some breakdown of the statutory machine. Since there had never been an *album* of accredited auditors, [4] the proliferation of accountability in the fourteenth century may have introduced so much uncertainty that royal jailers would not take custody of alleged accountants, except from auditors appointed by some court

[1] (1963) 7 *American Journal of Legal History* 228 at 236–238.
[2] (1965) 81 L.Q.R. 422, 539; (1966) 82 L.Q.R. 81.
[3] A short description of the early account stated was given by Dr. Jackson in *The History of Quasi Contract*, pp. 27–28. *Cf. ibid.* pp. 105–111.
[4] *Cf.* Denholm-Young, *Seignorial Administration in England*, Chap. IV; Plucknett, *Legislation of Edward I*, pp. 153–156. The statute may never have worked as smoothly as has been made out; see the very early case in *Sel. Cas. in Exchequer of Pleas*, Seld. Soc. Vol. 48, p. 121.

after an action of account. Be that as it may, the earliest plaintiffs in this action of debt were in no better position than one relying on a simple contract such as a sale. In at least three cases between 1369 and 1391 the defendant waged his law.[5] And although objections were always made to this,[6] there was some fumbling before a plaintiff hit upon the one which succeeded, namely, that the auditors were judges of record. This has seemed implausible enough to be fathered on Coke.[7] But it was the basis of a demurrer in 1389,[8] and as early as 1405 it was expressly linked with the power of committal.[9] Twenty years later, indeed, it was possible to argue that auditors were judges of record only if they did in fact commit, a suggestion which would have brought the action back to its starting-point by making wager available in nearly every case in which the plaintiff had to sue.[10]

It would, however, have confined the ouster of wager to accounts before auditors whose credentials were acceptable to somebody, namely to royal jailers. As things were, even supposing that an accountant could always be identified, it seems that any Tom and Dick could be auditors, and any Harry appoint them. If this was so in the real world, almost anything could happen in the wonderland of pleaders. So it did, as appears from a statute of 1403.[11]

> " To eschew divers mischiefs . . . as well within the City of London, as within other Cities, and other places . . . for that divers fained suits of debt have [been] taken . . . against divers people, surmising . . . that they had made accompt before Auditors assigned of divers receipts, duties and contracts had betwixt them, . . . suggesting by the same suits sometime their Apprentices, and sometime other of their servants to be Auditors, where there was never receit nor duty betwixt such parties, and where the said Apprentices nor servants did any thing know of such accompt, to the intent to cause them against whom such Suits were taken, to put them in Inquest . . . and to put them from the waging of their Law . . .; By reason

---

[5] Y.BB. H. 43 Edw. III, pl. 3, f. 1d; H. 49 Edw. III, pl. 6, f. 2d; C.P. 40/521, m. 249.
[6] The earliest was knowledge of the countryside; Y.BB. H. 43 Edw. III, pl. 3, f. 1d; H. 49 Edw. III, pl. 6, f. 2d. This never ousted wager in debt, because however notoriously the debt was created it could have been secretly discharged.
[7] Plucknett, *Legislation of Edward I*, p. 154, referring to 2 Inst. 380.
[8] Y.B. 13 Ric. II, Ames Found., p. 95, foreshadowed in Y.B. 49 Edw. III, pl. 6, f. 2d. The result of the 1389 action is not known, because the record printed is not that of the case reported. Wager was accepted some 18 months later; C.P. 40/521, m. 249. But the possibility must have been dead by 1403, the date of the statute below.
[9] Y.B. H. 6 Hen. IV, pl. 28, f. 6, *per* Horton. *Cf.* below, p. 140, n. 36.
[10] Y.B. P. 4 Hen. VI, pl. 3, f. 17d at f. 18, *per* Paston. There would still have been effects in actions against executors, too large a subject to be opened here.
[11] Stat. 5 Hen. 4, c. 8, as rendered in *Statutes at Large*, ed. 1695.

whereof, by such favourable Inquests taken thereupon of the neighbors of those which have prosecuted such Suits, divers have been condemned in great sums ... It is ordained ... that the Justices in the King's Courts, and other Judges ... in Cities and Boroughs ... shall have power to examine the Attornies, and other whom please them, and thereupon to receive the defendants to their Law ... after the discretion of the Justices and Judges aforesaid."

Exceptional solidarity among the neighbours would be needed before a plaintiff making up his story from whole cloth could rely on a favourable inquest. And why should such a one be treated so mildly? Too much may have turned on fictions to allow punishment for deceit; but if he failed the statutory examination, why not at least dismiss his case? Why should the defendant still be put to his law? A partial answer is suggested by the working of the statute. Examinations generally disclosed, not that the plaintiff had no cause of action, but that he was not within the scope of this one.[12] Either the alleged account was defective in form, being, for example, before a single auditor, whereas Westminster II used the plural [13]; or, more commonly and for our purposes more relevantly, the matters supposed to have been accounted for did not lie in account.[14] But dealings between the parties had given rise to a genuine claim.

If this was the size of the mischief, we have gone some way to explaining how the statute came to be passed within a decade of the ouster of wager from the classical action of debt on account. The interval is short for abuse on the grand scale to have grown from nothing. But if, to come abruptly to the point, there was an established practice of reckoning liabilities so that the debtor could be sued on his promise to pay the balance agreed, it would not be a large step for creditors to call in, or for pleaders to conjure up, persons who could be called auditors. Such a practice would be a ready vehicle for the mischief, which arose, as the opening words of the statute proclaim, " as well within the City of London, as within other Cities, and other places."

[12] Here we must rely on year book evidence. The fact of examination was enrolled, *e.g.*, C.P. 40/632, mm. 102d, 304d, but not the questions and answers; Y.BB. M. 35 Hen. VI, pl. 5, f. 5, *per* Laicon; *Long Quinto*, f. 140d at f. 141, the prothonotary's answer to Littleton. For this reason it was important for a defendant whose examination had been successful to make his law at once. Otherwise the plaintiff could be non-suited, and his claim lived to fight another day.
[13] Y.BB. T. 4 Hen. VI, pl. 3, f. 25d; H. 20 Hen. VI, pl. 4, f. 16d; T. 20 Hen. VI (additional cases), pl. 17, f. 41d.
[14] Examples which look more or less like accounting situations are: Y.BB. H. 20 Hen. VI, pl. 2, f. 16; H. 22 Hen. VI, pl. 13, f. 41; *Long Quinto*, ff. 140d–141.

The earliest discussion of *concessit solvere* is in a year book case of 1460, when it arose indirectly: the point, repeated some eighteen months later,[15] was that an action based on the *concessit solvere* would lie only in the London courts.[16] But the custom appears from the argument, and so do the facts. The custom was to declare upon a *concessit solvere* in respect of various things sold, without setting them out in detail; and, since the defendant could wage his law, it seems that this sufficiency of a general reference to the underlying transactions was the only advantage the creditor normally gained. But more was at stake on the facts before the court, because the sales had been in Flanders. The creditor could not therefore sue in England on the transactions themselves [17]; and for that very reason, he says, he had made *un rekening* with his debtor, and *pur touts choses entre nous il concessit solvere le summe*. On this he now wanted to sue in London.

That was more than half a century after the statute. But a century before it a case in the City courts seems to rest on a similar custom.[18] The plaintiff declares that he and the defendant *temporibus retroactis de diversis mercandisis ad invicem mercandizassent*, and that on a date specified they met *et de mercimoniis suis inter ipsos prehabitis computaverunt, super quo compoto* the defendant *indebitatus remansit* to the plaintiff in the sum claimed, which *satisfacere concessit* on a specified day. Another custom enabled the plaintiff to repel the defendant from the general issue by producing two witnesses to the accounting [19]; and it is likely that had all this happened in 1402 instead of 1302, these would have figured in his declaration as auditors.

The matters accounted for in that case, profits of trading in partnership, probably did at that date lie in account.[20] But there is no indication that this was relevant; and it was not true in a case of 1320. The one surviving sheriff's court roll, no doubt preserved by reason of the 1321 eyre,[21] has an action of debt against executors: the plaintiff declares that the testator had bought fish from him on various occasions (*per vices*) between specified dates, no more details being given; and that, on a date also specified, testator and plaintiff

---

[15] Y.B. M. 1 Edw. IV, pl. 13, f. 5d at f. 6d. This must be the sense.
[16] YB. P. 38 Hen. VI, pl. 12, f. 29d. Brooke, *Abridgment*: *Ley Gager* 69; *London* 15.
[17] *Cf. Liber Albus*, Rolls Ser. Vol. I, pp. 215–216.
[18] The quotations are from Mayor's Court Roll G, m. 6. The case is abstracted in *Calendar of Early Mayor's Court Rolls of the City of London, 1298–1307*, pp. 181–184.
[19] *Cf. ibid.* p. xxxviii.
[20] On the facts of the case, though the declaration is ambiguous, the plea is explicit. For the scope of account at this time, see *Novae Narrationes*, Seld. Soc. Vol. 80, p. clxxx *et seq.*
[21] It is in the Guildhall Record Office. References are by the modern numbering of the membranes.

adinvicem computaverunt ubi predictus testator *remansit in debito* to the amount claimed, which *infra quindenam proxime sequentem solvere concessit.*[22] The London rule allowing simple contract debts to be enforced against executors, which later led to the provision of a special formula for wager,[23] would be particularly hard in such a case; and it is unfortunate that the entry breaks off leaving the plea unfinished. But it stands as a clear example of *concessit solvere*, using those words and according with the custom described in 1460 and still used in the seventeenth century and later.

A Londoner of the time, however, would probably not have seen anything out of the way in the enforcement of a promise to pay the sum agreed at an informal accounting, and certainly not in the phrase *concessit solvere*. The same sheriff's court roll shows that this was common form in actions of debt. Even a declaration on a single sale often recites the transaction and price, and goes on to say that the defendant *concessit solvere* the amount within a specified time, usually a fortnight. This fixing of the time for payment was apparently without particular consequence: it does not seem, for example, to have taken such cases out of the London rule that no damages were awarded in debt.[24] The significance of the formulation is that it rests the claim on the defendant's promise rather than on the transaction. Consider, for example, another case in the sheriff's court roll, in which there had been two transactions. The declaration begins with the later (not using the *concessit solvere* formulation), and then says that at the time of that later transaction the defendant also *concessit solvere* within a specified period the amount outstanding on the earlier.[25] The earlier transaction comes in only as the reason for the promise, and the promise is the basis of the claim. In the common pleas the promise would not even have been mentioned, and the claim would have rested directly on the two transactions.

What survived in London as a pleading custom therefore looks like the fossil remains of a rather different conception of debt from that of the classical common law, one which perhaps derived from mercantile custom, and which would have been more readily expressible in terms of promises for cause than liabilities contracted *re*. But probably nobody did express it, and in most cases it would make no practical difference. Even the difference in theory would often be obscured by the generality of the general issue: the sheriff's court roll shows a husband waging his law on behalf of himself and his wife *super eo quod* the wife *non emit* from the plaintiff four quarters

---

[22] Sheriff's Court Roll, m. 15d.
[23] *Borough Customs*, Vol. I, Seld. Soc. Vol. 18, pp. 210–211.
[24] *Ibid.* p. 208.
[25] Sheriff's Court Roll, m. 7d.

of barley for twenty shillings, *nec eos ei infra quindenam proximo sequentem solvere concessit nec in aliquo denario ei ratione emptionis predicte tenentur.*[26] But it would matter, and hence the appropriation of a common form to be the name of a special custom, in any case in which there might be dispute about the enforceability or extent of the underlying claim.

Returning to the common pleas, we find indications that the custom of London in this respect had not always been clearly distinct. There is first a matter too fundamental for more than a mention here, namely, the use of the phrase *concessit se teneri*. This was a common form which has been supposed, wrongly, to denote a deed.[27] It may be used for simple contracts, generally in a manner consonant with the accepted notions of debt at common law. For example, a plaintiff in 1358 declares that the defendant *concessit se teneri* in four shillings for every week that his wife and daughter should be at board with the plaintiff, and that they were at his board for so many weeks; the defendant takes the general issue and wages his law.[28] This use of the phrase to introduce the transaction, to record the making of the contract and the fixing of the price, contrasts with the use of *concessit solvere* in the City to express something subsequent to the transaction and separate from it. But there are other appearances of *concessit se teneri* in the fourteenth century, not numerous but striking, which do not square with accepted notions. Claims are based on a promise or " grant " which is neither under seal nor for *quid pro quo* in the sense of a present or future return. One example will be given later because it happens to be combined with a *concessit solvere* claim.[29] The wider implications must be left with the suggestion that the requirement of a seal in covenant may have been followed by a parallel retrenchment in debt, establishing the dichotomy between obligation and *quid pro quo* and excluding some claims in between.

The phrase *concessit solvere* itself has been found only three times in the common pleas; and though other examples may have been passed over as unappreciated variants of *concessit se teneri*, it was certainly rare. One of the three concerns a single pre-existing obligation. In 1370 a plaintiff declares that in an action before the bailiffs of Norwich he was awarded damages against the defendant, who on that same day *concessit se solvere* the amount at Easter following. The defendant takes the general issue, *non tenetur*, without reference either to the bailiff's judgment or to his promise,

---

[26] *Ibid.* m. 7.
[27] G. J. Turner evidently assumed this in Y.B. 4 Edw. II, Seld. Soc. Y.B. Series, Vol. VI, p. 11, n. 2; but it does not affect his reading of the case.
[28] C.P. 40/395, m. 226d.
[29] Y.B. P. 29 Edw. III, ff. 25d–26; below, pp. 139–40.

and wages his law.³⁰ At this date an action in the common pleas based directly on the bailiffs' judgment would have been vulnerable on several scores.³¹ The formulation may not therefore be a matter of chance.

It can hardly be chance that the other two examples of *concessit solvere* both concern accounting situations, though good fortune did arrange that they should respectively illustrate the two earliest kinds of debt on account to appear in the common pleas. We have seen that the classical action, based upon an account before auditors of matters lying in account, was unnecessary when auditors and accountant were recognisable and the power of committal effective. But the year books themselves show one situation in which, even then, resort had to be made to the action of debt, namely, when the balance found was in favour of the accountant. Auditors could not commit the master, and if he would not pay willingly the accountant had to sue. Questions of great interest were thereby raised.³² Some receivers might have no authority to pay out anything.³³ Even a manorial bailiff had authority to pay out only his master's money; and if he was in credit he must have paid out his own. The common law had no *actio negotiorum gestorum*; and an unauthorised payment on another's behalf could not easily be represented as a loan made to him. Such considerations prompted, in the earliest of these cases of the accountant found in credit, a famous and misleading remark: *Acount veot estre amene per equite & nemy per reddour de ley come allower ceo qe est allowable & disalower ceo qe est desallowable*.³⁴ It was the auditors who were governed by equity. Their function was not to decide, according to the rigour of the law, questions which could have been raised in a series of actions of debt between the parties, and then to reckon the balance. The underlying transactions lay in account, and gave rise to no claim except to an account; and when the auditors found a balance, they created for the first time a cause of action in debt.

But the one-way character of accounting relationships, which treated payments as diminishing the obligations created by receipts but not as creating positive claims, may still have left a difficulty for the accountant in credit. If so, sense prevailed over logic. But the doubt may explain why such a plaintiff in 1355 resorted to the

---

30 C.P. 40/440, m. 61.
31 The use of debt to recover the fruits of earlier litigation will be discussed elsewhere.
32 Plucknett, *The Medieval Bailiff*, p. 29, n. 2.
33 *e.g.*, Y.BB. P. 7 Edw. III, pl. 2, f. 12; M. 38 Hen. VI, pl. 14, f. 5d; Fitzh., *Natura Brevium*, f. 121 I.
34 Y.B. 19 Edw. II (1326), pp. 655–656, *per* Stonor. *Cf.* Y.B. 12 Edw. II, Seld. Soc. Y.B. Series, Vol. XXIV, p. 146 at p. 147; Plucknett, *The Medieval Bailiff*, p. 28.

concessit solvere formula. A separate claim makes striking use, already mentioned, of *concessit se teneri*; and the whole case might have been made up as an examination problem to raise fundamental questions. The plaintiff sues for fifteen pounds. As to ten, he declares that he was the defendant's bailiff, and on an account before auditors assigned by the defendant he was found that much in credit, *on a fine daccompt le defendant graunta quil luy paieroit mesme les x.li.* And as to the five pounds he declares that after his period as bailiff was over (and the order of events is reaffirmed in the argument), *pur son service quil luy auoit fait . . . il luy graunta este tenus en C.s.* The defendant by protestation refuses to admit the service, the account or any grant; but he actually pleads the general issue.[35]

All other claims by the accountant in credit rest directly on the account and not on an undertaking to pay. But though the account was as much a cause of action for him as it became for his master, it did not acquire the property of excluding wager. Since the master could not be committed to prison, it was decided that the account could not be of record against him.[36] In this respect it was like an account before a single auditor. And suppose there were no auditors?

The last of the three examples of *concessit solvere* found in the common pleas is indeed in an action based upon an informal accounting without auditors. The entry is of 1358, a decade before the earliest known example of the classical debt on account. The plaintiff declares that he and the defendant *insimul computaverunt de diversis pecuniarum summis* delivered by the plaintiff to the defendant's wife at the defendant's order, *et similiter de diversis rebus & contractibus* between the parties, whereby the defendant *adtunc remansit in debito* to the amount now demanded, *quod quidem debitum* the defendant *concessit se solvere* on a specified date. The defendant pleads the general issue, *non tenetur*, and goes to a jury.[37]

Unless an obscure precedent in *Novae Narrationes* was for use in the common pleas,[38] this is the earliest example found of liability there based on an informal accounting. The phrase *concessit solvere* does not appear again; but *insimul computaverunt* became common form. By chance the same roll has an example of its use when the

---

[35] Y.B. P. 29 Edw. III, ff. 25d–26. On *concessit se teneri*, see above, p. 138.
[36] Y.BB. 14 Hen. VI, pl. 71, f. 24d; M. 38 Hen. VI, pl. 14, f. 5d. The same point is discussed in connection with the liability of an executor in Y.B. M. 10 Hen. VI, pl. 84, f. 24d.
[37] C.P. 40/395, m. 133.
[38] *Novae Narrationes*, Seld. Soc. Vol. 80, p. 112, B. 216.

account had been before auditors; but the case concerns an accountant in credit.[39] In the report of 1389 in which the argument about auditors being judges of record first appears, the phrase is again used of an account before auditors, but again not a compellable account: the declaration is *qe le pleintif et defendant accompterent ensemble de lour assent devant certein auditours*.[40] Otherwise the phrase is not used when there had been auditors. And although an accounting just between the parties is at first more commonly denoted by saying that the defendant *computavit cum* the plaintiff,[41] *insimul computaverunt* or *insimul computassent* slowly gains in favour until a prothonotary in 1464 describes it as a standard form to distinguish the case from that of the account before auditors: *lentre de cel count sera insimul computaverunt, issint que ceo nest en maner forsque reckening*.[42]

What did he mean by a reckoning? The creditor of 1460, just four years earlier, who had made a series of sales in Flanders and wished to sue on a *concessit solvere* in London, had made *un rekening* with his debtor, and he used the word to mean just an addition of debts.[43] But the point of his case was that he had no remedy at common law: and he could have used *insimul computaverunt*, and there would have been nothing special about the London custom, if that was what the prothonotary meant. The reckoning of *insimul computaverunt* must have been a true account, made without auditors but dealing with matters that lay in account. The question arose, though not quite squarely, in a case of 1462, and the answer is stated by Moile: *si jeo porte dette sur arrerages daccompt de v.li. supposant que le defendant & jeo ensemble accomptames de petit det queux il devoit a moy s. parcel sur achate dun chival, parcel sur un apprompt, & parcel sur arrerages de rent sur lesse a terme, tout le quel summe fuit trove enter nous que il avenoit a v.li. sur que accion accruist a moy a demander les v.li., sur ma conusance demesne, ma accion ne vaut, en tant que il apparust que ceux choses ne gisont my en accompt*.[44]

But the informal account had not always been so restricted. In the earliest known example, the 1358 entry using both *insimul computaverunt* and *concessit solvere*, the accounting had been of

[39] C.P. 40/395, m. 86d.
[40] Y.B. 13 Ric. II, Ames Found., p. 95. The record printed does not belong to the case.
[41] *e.g.*, C.P. 40/440 (1370), m. 530d; C.P. 40/574 (1404), mm. 290, 367.
[42] Y.B. P. 4 Edw. IV, pl. 6, f. 6 at f. 6d.
[43] Y.B. P. 38 Hen. VI, pl. 12, f. 29d; above, p. 136. *Cf. Long Quinto*, f. 140d at f. 141, where the word is used of an accounting before auditors of matters which, as statutory examination disclosed, did not lie in account.
[44] Y.B. M. 2 Edw. IV, pl. 2, f. 14 at f. 14d.

money delivered to the defendant's wife at his order and *de diversis rebus & contractibus* [45]; and both seem to lie in debt and not in account. In 1367 a plaintiff *counta que le defendaunt devoit a luy certeins petits dets, des queux ils accompterent entre eux, issint que tout amount a xl. li. & auxi que il luy apresta xx. li*; and the case goes off on another point without any objection being reported.[46] Entries of 1370 and 1404 speak of money paid out on the defendant's behalf in circumstances which might just be said to lie in account by stretching the idea of the accountant in credit.[47] But another case of 1404 says that the parties *insimul computassent de diversis summis* owed (*debitis*), to wit, the arrears of an annuity [48]; and that can have nothing to do with a true account.

To return to the statute of 1403, we therefore have evidence from the rolls that a mere addition of debts was at that date still a possible cause of action at common law as well as in London; and there is some corroboration in its own wording which makes the surmised account " of divers receipts, duties and contracts had betwixt them." But such an action was answerable by wager; and the statutory remedy of examination, reducing claims to the same potency, fits neatly into this background. An account could not be of record without auditors, nor could auditors set the stamp of record on matters which did not lie in account. But in either case there was still a cause of action. That based on an addition of debts, moreover, being older than the action against the true accountant (though probably not as old as the action by the accountant in credit), may have been of independent origin, springing from the London *concessit solvere* or from the ideas behind it. But these ideas were becoming unacceptable in the common law,[49] and *insimul computaverunt* gravitated into the ambit of the newly arisen debt on a formal account, and therefore of accountability, the pull of which was no doubt increased by the statute itself.

The working of the statute was indirectly affected by this. If, as seems likely, the draftsman had intended only to cancel out the fictitious record element, leaving the true claims to proceed on their merits, the symmetry of his work was now spoiled. If examination disclosed a want of auditors, there was still a genuine claim to which the resulting wager could be supposed to be directed. But if it disclosed a want of accountability, the wager had become otiose:

[45] C.P. 40/395, m. 133; above, p. 140.
[46] Y.B. H. 41 Edw. III, pl. 15, f. 7.
[47] C.P. 40/440, m. 530d (possibly a mercantile agent); C.P. 40/574, m. 188 (the household bills of *senescallus hospicii*).
[48] C.P. 40/574, m. 233d.
[49] *Cf.* the discussion of *concessit se teneri* above.

the underlying claims could not now be in issue at all,[50] and the claim on the account had already been exposed as baseless. There was, however, a feeling that the examination should not be conclusive,[51] which no doubt explained or rationalised the anomaly which seems to have overtaken this case.[52]

Insimul computaverunt declarations themselves were of course outside the scope of the statute and outside its mischief; there could be no question of ousting wager. But they were not beyond the reach of fiction, and for this reason we cannot be sure how—or how long—the restriction to accountable relationships worked in practice. What was certainly fatal, as appears from Moile's statement in 1462,[53] was for the plaintiff to declare upon an accounting of specified matters which on his own showing did not lie in account. But by that time the declaration had become standard: the accounting was said to have been of various receipts of the plaintiff's money.[54] The cover of a common form may therefore have enabled plaintiffs to cheat; but if so it equally prevents us from catching them at it. Reflection will suggest, however, that any widening of the action was more likely due to confusion or to changing ideas of accountability than to fiction, because the defendant himself would be the judge of propriety. If, for example, the creditor who had made a reckoning in England of sales in Flanders had sued at common law and declared in this way, his debtor could no doubt have waged his law with a clear conscience. It was series of transactions such as this which seem to have made *concessit solvere* specially important as a local custom; and in the common pleas the tradesman's bill, wearily reciting individual sales across foot after foot of parchment, occurs more and more often.[55]

However the system worked in practice, the conceptual pattern was clear and coherent. If a relationship of accountability existed

---

[50] *Cf.* Y.B. H. 20 Hen. VI, pl. 2, f. 16, where one of the underlying claims was for rent. To the argument that no harm was done by the present action, since wager would equally be excluded on that claim, Newton replies that the plaintiff could recover in this action and then sue again on the lease.

[51] It may not have been conclusive *against* the defendant, even to settle that the matters did lie in account; Y.B. M. 10 Hen. VI, pl. 67, f. 20d.

[52] It also leaves open a possibility, whatever the draftsman had intended, that the wager was always and in all cases to this extent otiose, being understood as going to the exact terms of the declaration which had *ex hypothesi* already been negatived. But this seems improbable, particularly in the case in which there really had been a reckoning before " auditors " but no accountability. *Cf.* Y.B. M. 8 Hen. VI, pl. 25, f. 10d, continued in pl. 36, f. 15d, where on such facts a plaintiff refused to amend his count. Since examination could only be demanded by a defendant tendering his law, we cannot hope for light either from further pleadings or from a special verdict.

[53] Y.B. M. 2 Edw. IV, pl. 2, f. 14 at f. 14d; above, p. 141.

[54] This form occurs as early as 1404; C.P. 40/574, mm. 290, 367.

[55] Retail sales must also have come increasingly into the common pleas as the 40 shilling barrier was lowered by inflation.

between the parties, it should be ended by an account; and this could be formal or private. A private accounting was as much a cause of action in debt as a formal account before auditors, though it lacked the property of excluding wager. It was also as effective a plea if an action of account was brought on the original relationship.[56] The duty to account had been extinguished and replaced by a fresh duty in debt. But if the relationship between the parties was already that of debtor and creditor, even on multiple causes, private arithmetic was without effect and " auditors " would make no difference. It could not form a fresh unitary cause of action. Nor could it extinguish the old; and the rule associated with *Pinnel's Case*, if not inevitable, was at least a likely corollary.[57] The common law had come to rest simple contract debts rigorously on transactions, and the point at which it had turned away from the custom of London was not just about particularity in pleading: expressed in modern terms,[58] it was about the role allowed to promises.

---

[56] Y.B. M. 45 Edw. III, pl. 13, f. 14d.
[57] *Pinnel's Case*, 5 Co.Rep. 117a was actually about payment of a sum smaller than that required by the condition of a conditioned bond. This point is elaborated by Mr. Simpson in " The Penal Bond with Conditional Defeasance," (1966) 82 L.Q.R. 392 at 405 *et seq*. Under the rules of pleading in debt, the question in its simplest form was unlikely to come into the open.
[58] The qualification is necessitated by the insistent language of grant. The significance of this will be discussed elsewhere.

5

RICHARD HUNNE'S 'PRAEMUNIRE'

To the authorities for Hunne's Case collected by Miss Jeffries Davis [1] there may be added the record of his *praemunire* action. It is in the King's Bench roll [2] for Hilary term, 4 Henry VIII (1513), and its date is perhaps the most notable thing about it. More [3] thought that Hunne ' was detected of heresye before the premunire sued or thought upon ', and that the action was a manoeuvre to delay the heresy proceedings ; this may be so, but the beginnings of the latter must then be sought earlier than has been supposed. Gairdner and Mr. Ogle,[4] for example, assumed that the entire tragedy happened in the few months before Hunne was found dead on 4 December 1514.

The facts stated in the pleadings are as follows. The infant Stephen Hunne was put to nurse in the parish of St. Mary Matfelon (Whitechapel), and died there on 29 March a.r. 2 (1511). Thomas Dryffeld, the rector, demanded his bearing-sheet as a mortuary, which Hunne refused on the ground that it belonged to him and not to the infant. Some thirteen months after the death, on 26 April a.r. 4 (1512), Dryffeld sent Henry Marshall, his chaplain and parish priest at Whitechapel, to start suit for its recovery at Lambeth. Hunne was summoned on 28 April ; and on 13 May he appeared before Cuthbert Tunstall and denied the truth of Dryffeld's libel, which had declared simply that the infant died within a year of coming to the parish and that the bearing-sheet was his best piece of clothing and so due as a mortuary. The issue, presumably on the property in the sheet, was found against Hunne on the evidence of witnesses, and Tunstall pronounced in favour of Dryffeld.

Dryffeld was principal defendant to the *praemunire*, but joined with him as *abbettatores excitatores procuratores fautores & consilarii*

---

[1] *E.H.R.*, xxx, 477.

[2] Public Record Office KB 27/1006 m. 37.

[3] *Supplicacion of Soules*, in *Works*, 1557, p. 297.

[4] J. Gairdner, *The English Church in the Sixteenth Century*, p. 36 ; A. Ogle, *The Tragedy of the Lollard's Tower*, p. 52. Mr. Ogle also thought that the *praemunire* was intended to throttle not the heresy proceedings but the suit for the mortuary (*ibid.* pp. 51, 54, 55, 60) ; and Gairdner may have thought the same (*op. cit.* p. 25 ; but *cf.* p. 36). A. F. Pollard rightly took it that the mortuary suit was over before the *praemunire* started: *Wolsey*, p. 32.

were his proctor,[1] his doctor advocate,[2] the witnesses,[3] Marshall, and Charles Joseph the summoner, later to be suspected of Hunne's murder. They pleaded in justification, telling the story with the part played by each, and asserting that the whole process was lawful. To this Hunne demurred : *minus sufficiens est in lege*.

According to the roll the question of law so raised was never decided. The case was repeatedly adjourned *quia curia domini Regis hic . . . nondum advisatur*, the last such adjournment being from Michaelmas 1514 to Hilary ; but by then Hunne was dead, and nothing more was entered. That nothing had happened, however, seems unlikely : More[4] tells us that the heresy charge was held up ' till it appered clerely to the temporall judges and all that were anye thinge learned in the temporall lawe, that hys suite of ye premunire was nothing worth in ye kinges law.' And his theory about Hunne's death depends upon the outcome being clear :[5] Hunne was

> a man highe mynded, & sette on the glorie of a victorye, whiche he hoped to have in ye premunyre, wherof he muche boasted as they sayd, among his familiar frendes, that he trusted to bee spoken of long after hys dayes, and have his mater in the yeres and termes called Hunne's case. Which when he perceived would goe agaynst his purpose, and that in the temporal lawe he should not winne his spurres, and over that in the spiritual lawe perceived so much of his secrete sores unwrapped and dyscovered, that he beganne to fal in feare of worldly shame. It is to me much more likelye, that for werinesse of hys lyfe, he ridde hymselfe out therof . . .

More's words, read in the light of the record, suggest that the demurrer had been argued in the Michaelmas term and effectively decided against Hunne, and that the formal judgment would have been entered in Hilary ; but this is a guess which may be plausible only because we know so little of the relationship in this period between what went down on the plea roll and what happened in court.

The *praemunire* was not Hunne's only attempt to win his spurs in the temporal law ; it is preceded in the roll by an action against the same Henry Marshall for slander.[6] In a bill[7] sued out on 25 January a.r. 4 (1513) Hunne complains that on the preceding 27 December, being in the peace of God and of the king, he went to the church at Whitechapel to hear vespers ; and Marshall, ready in his surplice to say them,

---

[1] Thomas Gotson.
[2] Walter Stone.
[3] Thomas Lambe, Thomas Esgore, Robert Kylton, and William Awdley.
[4] *Supplicacion of Soules*, pp. 297–8.
[5] *Dialogue concernynge heresyes* . . . , bk. iii, cap. 15, in *Works*, 1557, p. 239.
[6] KB 27/1006 m. 36.
[7] There is no mention of privilege or of *custodia marescalli*.

ex sua malicia precogitata . . . *excelsa voce dixit ista obprobriosa & minatoria verba ad procuracionem litis et ad dampnum tam corporis quam bone fame ipsius Ricardi Hunne*. . . . Hunne thowe arte accursed and thowe stondist acursed and therfore go thowe oute of the churche for as long as thowe arte in this churche I wyll sey no evynsong nor servyce *ubi in facto predictus Ricardus Hunne non est nec adtunc fuit excommunicatus* . . . ;

whereupon Hunne *ad evitandum magis malum & ob metum lesionis corporis sui* left the church *et vesperas ejusdem diei & festi* . . . *totaliter amisit*; and his good name and credit were so damaged that the merchants with whom he ordinarily dealt dared not and would not trade with him. To this bill the defendant demurred ; and again the record ends with a series of adjournments, the last being to the term after Hunne's death.

The writer should explain in conclusion that his own interests are in the law ; these entries were found by chance, and the questions they may suggest have not been pursued. Whatever their importance as pieces of the Hunne puzzle, it is the slander action which legal historians will wish had gone into the ' yeres and termes ' ; a report of argument on a demurrer in so early a case [1] would be very instructive.

---

[1] There are earlier examples of slander in the rolls, but I have not seen one trenching so obviously as this on the ecclesiastical jurisdiction.

REASON IN THE DEVELOPMENT OF THE COMMON LAW

PLUCKNETT's death has made this a sad occasion. I shall not now venture upon a formal tribute: his books are there, and the volumes of the Selden Society for which he did so much. But perhaps I may record my own belief that for him the voices in the year books were real, and that it was not only the lawyers he heard but also their lay clients. His contribution was to bring legal history back to the task so clearly seen by Maitland of placing the law in its social and intellectual setting. The intellectual influences at work in the earliest days of the common law, and the isolation into which so early and so wilfully it plunged itself, were a theme of Plucknett's two latest books, the lectures in Cambridge on legal literature and in Belfast on the criminal law; and the interest was foreshadowed in his inaugural lecture here. But my own favourite is the volume of Oxford lectures on the statutes of Edward I, in which those laborious technicalities become the answers to real problems in a real society.[1]

What Plucknett was after in that book, as his preface explains, was to show how legal history could help general history. And for one chiefly interested in the Middle Ages, this is the aspect of the subject which comes to seem most important. If I may intrude a rueful note of autobiography, one can spend much time on the technicalities of a law-suit before tumbling to it that what one does not understand are the underlying facts, and even more time gingerly talking with social and economic historians only to find that they do not understand them either, and that your law-suit offers the best hope of finding out. And so a technical inquiry into, say, the workings of an action about rights of common turns itself into an effort to imagine a routine of life.

But though this is the aspect of legal history which has come to give me most pleasure, and which, largely because of Plucknett's work, is today most valued, it is only one aspect of the subject; and it is one which a student of the eighteenth century will find less insistent than a student of the thirteenth. Partly, of course, this

---

* An inaugural lecture given at the London School of Economics on May 20, 1965.

[1] Plucknett: *Early English Legal Literature* (C.U.P., 1958); *Edward I and Criminal Law* (C.U.P., 1960); " The Place of the Legal Profession in the History of English Law " (1932) 48 L.Q.R. 328; *Legislation of Edward I* (O.U.P., 1949).

is because the strictly legal sources form a diminishing proportion of the evidence available to the social and economic historian. But it is also because, as the law moves further from its customary beginnings and becomes a wholly professional business, the legal sources become a less sensitive record of everyday circumstances. Indeed, the growth of common forms of pleading, the associated development of fictions, and the use of the jury to give a general verdict for one side or the other without ever saying what happened —all these things rebuff the inquirer who chiefly wants from his report or his plea roll just a simple slice of life.

Nor is this just a matter of the state of the evidence. The legal sources reflect the conditions of life less well because the law itself responds to those conditions less directly. The professional handling which singled out English customs for transmutation into a major system of law necessitated an increasingly artificial relationship between law and society; and the legal historian must become more and more of a lawyer. His attention shifts from relatively static social facts to problems of change. A change made by legislative act will be straightforward for him; there is a direct and visible relationship between social ill and legal remedy. But from the end of the thirteenth century to the beginning of the nineteenth, legislation played a tiny part in the development of private law. Nearly all of it was done in the courts; and judges do not, as does Parliament, make avowed changes in the law in response to argument about social needs. They do not make avowed changes at all; and that is the point.

Legal change under these conditions has the appearance of a conjuring trick: out of the old hat there comes a new rabbit. It is one of the mechanisms of this that I wish to talk about today; and I have chosen it because it illustrates an old-fashioned aspect of legal history which seems to me to need re-emphasis at the present time. The subject is more than a branch of social history. It is also a legal study which has a relevance for lawyers beyond the claims of piety and curiosity. The legal historian has not finished his job when he has identified the pressures which compelled a change; it is obviously not enough to say, for example, that a law of consensual contract came into being because a mercantile community needed it. He must get inside the court-room and hear how the lawyers did it. It was not a vegetable response but required argument, and not social argument but legal argument, legal analysis. And this is what I mean by the title of my lecture. There has been no plan in the development of the common law, even less, as I shall hope to illustrate, than legal historians have some-

(497)

times thought. On the contrary, the absence of plan has been a condition of progress. But each step has involved an intellectual problem to be solved by the application of elementary legal ideas. However much it looks like mumbo-jumbo, we have generally not understood a change until we have heard an argument which would have been at least intelligible, perhaps with a little preparation before and a little grumbling after, to Ulpian or Holmes.

That this argument is likely to have important effects, in the real world as well as in legal theory, may seem self-evident; but it has been variously denied. Holmes is here a relevant name. " The life of the law has not been logic: it has been experience." [2] Whole philosophies were built upon his good sense, and what they came to in their most extreme form was that the logic merely clothes the result and is entirely without consequence. Even this was perhaps only to make uncomfortably explicit some comfortable assumptions behind our talk of an inductive empirical system, and our picture of continuous and painless adjustment to social change. Logic is not so obliging. However small a part it plays in deciding the single case—and that is a controversy I would not dare to enter—it plays a large part in legal development. The reasoning adopted yesterday may not have caused yesterday's result; but it governs the terms in which today's dispute is put to a court, or is not put because the lawyers cannot now make a case of it. The " necessities of the time " make demands which cannot always be met; and when they are met, the effectiveness of the response depends upon the logic of the time.

When the demand is, to speak loosely, for regulation in some new area, it can often be reached easily enough from neighbouring premises; though I shall suggest later that the most accessible premises are not always the most appropriate. But the reversal of principles which have been positively established is quite another thing. Logic is directly matched against experience, and shows its strength most obviously in the rarity of such reversals and the difficulty with which they have been brought about. In the nature of the case, there must be resort to fresh premises. The old principles and reasoning are not controverted but abandoned, and the question is approached with a different set of legal ideas. To anticipate my example, the rules of contract yield a result which is no longer acceptable, so ideas from tort are used instead. But though logic is defeated with its own weapon, its strength is shown again in the consequences. What was unacceptable about the old principle was the result; but the approach probably represented the natural

[2] *The Common Law*, p. 1.

analysis of the problem. Using ideas from tort to reconstruct the law of contract is likely to cause both oddities in contract and deficiencies in tort. Fictions and the like are only a symptom of the deep conceptual artificiality into which logic has forced the common law. And this in turn, or so I shall suggest, has affected and may still affect its capacity for natural response even to new demands.

Such change then is indeed more like a trick than the direct magic which the legislator commands: the rabbit is really taken from a different hat. But in one respect the analogy is seriously misleading: the stage cannot have been prepared. Change becomes possible when two lines of reasoning which have developed, as it were, in different compartments, happen to have come sufficiently close for a situation which has traditionally fallen under the one to be represented as within the other. When they reach into the new compartment the lawyers may be acting deliberately and even disingenuously; something like a legislative intention can be imputed to them. But earlier developments in that compartment cannot have been directed. There have been few strategists on the Bench, and none at the Bar: one seeks an argument to win his case, not to pave the way for a change which is probably beyond imagination. Looking back on it, however, the legal historian will see an unbroken line of development; and he can more easily than any other sort of historian be beguiled into supposing that the end was aimed at when early steps were taken. Obvious though the trap is, it is one into which I, at any rate, repeatedly fall; and I shall later try to show it up in connection with the early steps of the process by which our law of contract was won from the ideas of tort.

But first I must justify the proposition that the compartments involved in this method of change have always been conceptual, that events in say the fifteenth century were not different in nature from modern developments by which the law of contract, supposedly about promises, has been altered by resort to the law about statements. The point has been obscured, and a good deal of seeming mumbo-jumbo introduced into legal history, by excessive deference to the formal aspect of the forms of action. Of course, the existence of boundaries between actions made a difference to the problem of change, which presented itself as a matter of rival forms. But it did not necessarily make change more difficult, because the old rule could be left untouched, harmlessly in force. In the action of debt, for example, the debtor by simple contract could make a general denial of indebtedness, and wage his law on it, until 1833. But from the early seventeenth century this was of no consequence in real life, because he would always be sued in a form of action which required jury trial. Again it followed from the availability of wager that his personal representatives could not be sued at all; and again the practical result was reversed, although the old rule was left standing in the disused enclosure formed by the action of debt. The abolition of the forms of action may well have made major change more difficult for the courts, by making it harder to reverse the result without openly reversing the rule. The continued existence of a partially formal barrier between law and equity may be a condition of the continued potency of equity as a means of law reform; its *in personam* operation has always been the most artless means of making a change without actually saying so. But within the common law itself, the abolition of the forms has left us with purely conceptual compartments, and especially with such textbook headings as tort, or the individual torts, and contract. And in this respect, our position is not very different from that in the early days of the common law. No writ, no remedy; no remedy, no right; slogans such as these have made the forms of action appear as though they were primary entities in the law, with the writs playing the part of a law-giver's code. But the writs were attached by red tape to actions which were mostly there first; and the actions themselves, as their names show, mostly represented elementary legal ideas. It is the names, of course, that have caused the trouble. Trespass and covenant became just the names of actions, or at most of very narrow concepts; and so it became possible to read the report of a discussion five hundred years old as being just about the propriety of an action, when it was really about the analysis of the facts. The nearest modern equivalents would be tort and contract; but these would not be exact, and something must be said of the history of the names as such.

" Covenant " presents the fewer problems. Let us start in the middle. From the early fourteenth century, the king's courts applied an invariable rule to actions of covenant brought before them: the plaintiff had to produce a deed sealed by the defendant witnessing the promise. This rule was the outstanding feature of covenant as an action; and it is easy to assume that if the action embodied any concept it was that of a formal contract under seal. But the rule was an adoption and not aboriginal even in the king's courts; and it was not followed in all local courts, for example in London or in Bristol. There is therefore no reason to withhold from the word its dictionary meaning, *conventio*: it is about the enforcement of agreements or promises. A lawyer today might say of a gratuitous oral promise that a claim would sound in contract, even though he added that by the rules of our law of contract it would fail—and that perhaps the matter might be formulated in deceit or estoppel. What the rules of covenant were in local courts, or indeed in the king's courts before a seal came to be necessary and sufficient, we do not yet know. No doubt they varied from place to place, though one would suppose at least that a plaintiff who had performed his side of a bilateral arrangement would be in a strong position.

This introduces one particular in which not merely the rules but the concept of covenant was narrower than our contract. We regard as contractual most claims arising out of most kinds of transaction; covenant was confined to the purer notion of enforcing agreements or promises. The chief difference comes with the kind of obligation which Roman lawyers would describe as contracted *re*. The medieval lender of money for example did not think of himself as relying upon a promise for its return; and this kind of obligation seems to be the original sphere of the word " contract." The complementary nature of the two categories is illustrated in many claims of jurisdiction by franchise-holders, which mention both covenants and contracts. Both are embraced by our modern contract, because in the revolution of the sixteenth and seventeenth centuries both covenant and debt were replaced by *assumpsit*; and it is an odd twist that while we commonly rationalise even the lender's claim in terms of agreement, the informing notion of covenant, it is " contract " that became the generic name. This must be because " covenant " was disabled by its attachment to a form of action, and because in the course of time it acquired the connotations of that attachment, the promise under seal. Consider for example an early eighteenth-century textbook statement: " A Covenant properly is a Specialty, but by Custom *Conventio ore tenus facta* is binding in *Bristol*." [3] It makes sense only in terms of the action; and the writer would no doubt have been incredulous if told that the special custom of Bristol was a survival from the old general law of what we would call contract.[4]

Even more devious is the history of the word " trespass "; and though I have bored legal historians with it before,[5] this gives me a chance to state the results in less indigestible form and, in some particulars, more correctly. At first trespass meant just wrong, *transgressio*, its dictionary sense. It was more vague than covenant,

---

[3] *The Law of Covenants* (1711), p. 2.
[4] Our usage would probably not have been accepted by the writer: *cf.* p. 15 where, however, he is quoting a case of 1590; 1 Leon. 208. Blackstone uses " contract " as a generic term including covenants under seal; *Commentaries* (5th ed., 1773), Bk. 3, pp. 153, 155; *cf.* Bk. 2, p. 465.
[5] (1958) 74 L.Q.R. at pp. 195, 407, 561 , here pp. 1-90.

as tort is more vague than contract; and like tort it could probably have been defined only in terms of what it was not—not contract and so on. Even that negative approach would leave much of what we can separate off as crime, though the public authority inherent in the notion of crime would not always be the king: in a manor court it might be the lord for a breach of agricultural routine, and in London it might be the city for a marketing offence. The procedural separation of crime is a process which I can lament, but cannot trace—at any rate today. But it starts from the same point as our present story: a legal wrong can be seen as offending not merely any individual who may be harmed but also the authority whose law has been broken. In thirteenth-century England there were many such authorities; and the rule was that trespasses, wrongs, whether prosecuted by public authority or the injured party, were matters for the king's court only when the king was, as it were, the appropriate authority. This appropriateness may be all that was at first meant by the phrase " the king's peace " as opposed, for example, to the " sheriff's peace " of the shire court. But the king's peace was most readily broken by a breach of the peace in the modern sense, so that nearly all trespasses coming before the king's courts were wrongs in which force and arms were alleged. One truly complaining of forcible wrong could seemingly choose whether to make these allegations and bring his case before a royal court, or omit them and sue in his shire court. But the victim of a wrong involving no force had ordinarily no choice: he had to sue in his shire court.

In the fourteenth century the position became artificial. On the one hand, even when force was alleged, the king's interest in the breach of his peace became nominal. A fine was still taken from a convicted defendant, and continued to be taken for centuries. But the stringent process by *capias*, originally given to secure this redress for the king, was now treated as being for the plaintiff's benefit and to secure his damages. And on the other hand, some wrongs involving no possible force could be brought within the jurisdiction by careful wording. My favourite case concerns the buyer of a cask of wine, who left it for later collection, and complained that in the meantime his seller, against the king's peace and with force and arms, to wit with swords and bows and arrows, drew off some of the wine and substituted water.[6] I like to picture the honest cask resisting so stoutly. But artificiality might not have provoked a change had it been for the courts to make it. Presumably, however, the decision lay with the Chancery; and in the third

[6] Y.B. 10 Ed. II, Seld.Soc., Vol. 54, p. 140.

quarter of the fourteenth century they began to seal writs returnable in royal courts for the redress of wrongs in which a breach of the king's peace was not even alleged. Perhaps some lost warrant permitted this; an analogous change concerning nuisances was made by statute in 1382.[7] But so far as our evidence goes it just happened.

Trespass could now come before royal courts with no pretence of royal interest. And because there were no standard forms and a special writ had at first to be composed for each case, the writs, and later the actions and even the wrongs, were distinguished by the name of trespass on the case. But trespass on the case was not at first a legal entity any more than trespass *vi et armis* was. They were all just wrongs, and the jurisdictional accident which had divided them might have been without consequence but for a further accident. It has already been mentioned that in trespass *vi et armis*, originally because of the king's interest, process could be by *capias*. But so convenient did this prove that it was extended to purely private law-suits, first to account, and then by a statute of 1352 to most other important personal actions, which were enumerated.[8] But trespass was not mentioned because in 1352 only trespasses *vi et armis*, which had always had such process, could come into the king's courts at all. A generation later, when other trespasses began to come in, there was therefore no warrant for process by *capias*; and the gap was not formally repaired until 1504.[9] By that time the damage had been done. For more than a century it had continued to matter whether or not a trespass writ was formulated with *vi et armis* and *contra pacem*; and since these phrases had become artificial even when jurisdiction hinged on their use, a criterion for their propriety was hard to find.

The search for a common factual feature of trespasses *vi et armis*, by a process which did not end until the eighteenth century, generated a new legal concept, the oddest artefact of the common law: direct forcible injury. And since the search had been for a distinction between trespass *vi et armis* and trespass on the case, commonly shortened to trespass and case, this concept was attributed to the word " trespass." Large consequences followed both

---

[7] Stat. 6 Ric. II, st. 1, c. 3, made the old viscontiel writs of nuisance returnable in royal courts at the plaintiff's option. In the case of trespass there was a period of confusion when *contra pacem* was capriciously alleged; above, pp. 30, 57-60, 63; and below, p. 161, n. 24.

[8] Account: Stat. Marlborough (1267), c. 23; Stat.Westm. II (1285), c. 11. Debt, detinue and replevin (but not covenant, see n. 26, below): Stat. 25 Ed. III, st. 5, c. 17.

[9] Stat. 19 Hy. VII, c. 9. Process in actions on the case was to be as in debt and trespass. The wording shows that case is regarded as an entity distinct from trespass. It is at about this time that *transgressio super casum* begins to appear as a term of art in the plea rolls.

in law and in legal history. In law trespass became a unitary wrong, to be committed with anything from a deliberate punch to a straying cow; and what reason made out of a pair of chronological accidents may have caused widespread injustice. And though in cases of straying shots and straying motor-cars the courts have lately walked through this ghost—eighteenth-century Gothic, perhaps, rather than medieval—it will probably be some time before the clanking of its chains dies away altogether.[10] In legal history, the assumption that " trespass " had always had its modern meaning elicited from the year books a detailed, coherent and anachronistic account: the law could at first comprehend only the simplest physical injuries, and case was a series of developments by analogy, perhaps with statutory aid, to reach more sophisticated wrongs. It is a plausible sequence, but in the dark age of a legal system and not in fourteenth-century England.

In much the same way as " covenant," then, the word " trespass " became disabled from doing its original work; and " tort " was recruited in its place. The noun and its adverb, *atort*, in Latin *injuria* and *injuste*, appear in the claims and defences of every kind of action from the time of our oldest formularies, and were so used as long as these formal phrases were spoken. In the same wide sense the noun turns up in the year books and early reports, and that is the sense it had for Coke.[11] As late as 1677 a treatise alphabetically arranged, the *Doctrina Placitandi*, uses " Tort " for one of its headings; but what is there discussed is the replication *de injuria, de son tort demesne*, the common answer to a plea in justification.[12] This heading has disappeared from a publication of 1771 passed off as including a translation of the *Doctrina Placitandi*, the author of which used the word rather as we would; one of his paragraphs begins: " There is a great difference between torts and contracts." [13] It was precisely in pointing this difference that the modern usage was first foreshadowed. The *Regula Placitandi* of 1691 says that a plea of Not Guilty is not necessarily fatal in *assumpsit*, " and the reason is because *Tort and Deceit* is alledged "; and it also reports an argument in which counsel says: " Here is

[10] *Fowler* v. *Lanning* [1959] 1 Q.B. 426; *Letang* v. *Cooper* [1964] 2 Q.B. 53; [1964] 3 W.L.R. 573. Cattle-trespass is an illuminating oddity. In the Middle Ages it might be deliberate, part of a dispute over rights of common; but the same writ was used to bring accidental escapes before a royal court when *contra pacem* had still to be alleged. This being established, a straightforward writ on the case was never invented; and a proposal in 1953 to make the equivalent change, basing liability on negligence, was rejected when it turned out that the strict liability was more convenient for farmers than delving into questions of fault; Cmd. 8746.
[11] Co.Litt., f. 158b.
[12] *Doctrina Placitandi*, p. 343.
[13] *A System of Pleading*, p. 444.

neither Contract nor Privity betwixt the Parties but *Tort* and Wrong." [14] The writer of 1720 who called his book *The Law of Actions on the Case for Torts and Wrongs* must have been using the word in much our sense; but he still felt it necessary to add the " and wrongs " in explanation.[15] Blackstone speaks of " *torts* or wrongs "—italicizing the " torts " in my edition [16]; and according to Winfield the earliest American textbook on the subject, published as late as 1859, was likewise called *Law of Torts or Private Wrongs*.[17] As our term of art, then, the word is late, later than the contraction in the sense of " trespass," itself an indistinct process. Coke says " trespasser " where we should say " tortfeasor," [18] but he expressly equates trespass *simpliciter* with trespass *vi et armis*.[19] There seems to have been a verbal interregnum in the seventeenth century; and if it follows that lawyers were not using the concept itself, the conclusion is not unacceptable or even surprising. Though useful, tort is not an indispensable idea as is contract. It is not one of the elementary particles of the law, but a class, and a residuary class at that. The practical lawyer deals with individual wrongs, and uses the class only when distinguishing other kinds of legal claim. In the seventeenth century most other kinds of legal claim had lately been taken over by the forms of action in what had been called trespass and would later be called tort, and for the time being such distinctions could hardly be drawn. They were the frontiers over which the conceptual war had been fought and lost.

But in the fourteenth and fifteenth centuries such distinctions were being drawn; and what to hindsight look like the earliest battles in that war were probably no more than arguments about the proper analysis of situations which had never before needed to be analysed. Take first the case of the promise ill performed, for example the doctor who undertakes a treatment and does it so badly that his patient is made worse. Today, at least if he is a private doctor, the patient may sue either in tort or in contract; and

---

[14] *Regula Placitandi*, pp. 191, 201. Italics as printed.
[15] The book is by no means the same as *The Law of Actions* (1710), as stated in Winfield, *The Province of the Law of Tort*, p. 8, n. 1 (a misreading of *Bibliotheca Legum*).
[16] Blackstone, *Commentaries* (5th ed., 1773), Bk. 3, p. 117.
[17] Winfield, *The Province of the Law of Tort*, p. 8.
[18] *Isaack v. Clark* (1614) 2 Bulstrode 306 at p. 313: " . . . it should be a hard case, to make him by this to be a Trespasser, and subject unto an Action upon the Case for a Trover and Conversion, onely by his Denyer to deliver them, being demanded, but there ought to be some other act done by him, to make him thereby to be such a Trespasser. . . ." But earlier in this judgment Coke does use the phrase " Trespassor upon the case."
[19] *The Case of the Marshalsea*, 10 Co.Rep. f. 68b at 76a. *Cf.* 2 *Inst.* p. 170, commenting on Stat.Westm. I, c. 6 (amercement " *solonque le quantity del trespasse* ") where he expressly notes the old wide usage. The statute of 1504 extending *capias* to actions on the case uses trespass in the narrow sense; n. 9 above.

normally it does not matter, so we do not worry about the analysis. Nor did it matter in the local courts which at first necessarily heard such cases. There was no seal to ground an action in covenant before the king's courts, and no royal interest to admit it as a trespass. But neither mattered in local courts; and though in London, for example, there seems to have been a remedy at least since the early fourteenth century, nothing would turn on its classification as trespass or covenant.[20] In the king's courts, that was to be crucial. As a trespass it could come in, and did, as soon as the requirement of a royal interest was dropped; but the requirement of a seal in covenant never was dropped. So it is no wonder that the surgeon, the horse-doctor, the ferryman who overloaded his boat and lost its cargo, figure in the earliest trespass actions heard in royal courts with no royal interest, and no wonder that they all argued for the matter being analysed as covenant. Some local courts might have thought them right, though the question would perhaps occur only to the enrolling clerk who had to give the action a name. In 1325, for example, in Littleport, when the owner of grain sued a maltster for malting it badly, the bishop of Ely's clerk called it covenant.[21] And although the king's judges consistently held that such claims were well laid in trespass, there is no reason to suppose either that they were affirming the obvious or that they were conniving in an obvious cheat, still less that they saw themselves as making a first move towards the replacement of one form of action by another. Certainly they saw both the force of the defendant's argument, and the practical inconvenience of accepting it: " . . . this action of covenant is necessarily maintainable without specialty, because for such little things one cannot always have a clerk to make a specialty." [22] But the discussions are of a genuine problem, of the same nature as those provoked in more recent times by, for example, a statute governing a successful plaintiff's right to costs by reference to the principal sum he recovers, and then

---

[20] An entry of 1300 looks as though an action in covenant had been bought off; *Cal. of Early Mayor's Court Rolls of the City of London, 1298–1307*, p. 81. But an action of 1320 entered on the City's unprinted Sheriff's Court roll must be in trespass: the defendant *usurpando sibi officium surgici* undertook to cure the plaintiff's feet and applied *diversa medicamenta sua . . . contraria* so that she could not walk; and then, perhaps after a refusal to pay, he *vi et armis* entered her house and made off with her goods. For discussions of the early development of this sort of liability, see Kiralfy, *The Action on the Case*, pp. 138–139; and (1958) 74 L.Q.R. at pp. 571–572., here pp. 71–72.

[21] *The Court Baron*, Seld.Soc., Vol. 4, p. 140. *Cf. Sel.Cas. Concerning the Law Merchant*, Vol. i, Seld.Soc., Vol. 23, pp. 103–104, a St. Ives action in 1317 for building with inferior materials; but substituting inferior materials for those supplied by the plaintiff was called trespass in London in 1300; *Cal. of Early Mayor's Court Rolls of the City of London, 1298–1307*, p. 82.

[22] Y.B. Hil. 48 Ed. III, pl. 11, f. 6 at f. 6d, *per* Cavendish.

fixing different sums for contract and for tort. A class-room question suddenly becomes of practical importance.

I wish I thought I understood so clearly what was going on in the cases in which the defendant did not act upon his promise at all. We can hardly be concerned with a frontier incident here. This is the capital city of covenant; and in the end it fell, and trespass actions became generally available. My campaigning metaphor reflects the pervasive assumption that what happened was somehow intended, that there was throughout an aim to circumvent the requirement of a seal. But this is unconsciously to assume a legislator. The minds we want to get inside are the minds of the lawyers who advised plaintiffs to bring trespass actions. They were not out to reform the law, and they are unlikely often to have proffered the desperate chance that a fundamental rule would be reversed for the benefit of one who had foolishly neglected to comply with it. Even if the occasional obstinate client insisted on fighting a hopeless case, his lawyer had to make an argument. Two kinds of argument have been detected in the year books. In three cases between 1400 and 1425 the plaintiff seems to rely on a simple analogy with the cases of ill performance.[23] And, though it comes astonishingly close to success, this evidently fails on the obvious ground that mere failure to perform a promise cannot be anything but a matter of covenant. Success begins to come with a more sophisticated argument that the defendant has deceived the plaintiff. But for a long time this only works when the defendant has actively done something which disables him from performing his undertaking, for example by conveying to a third party land promised to the plaintiff; and this is generally regarded as a handle by which the matter could be dragged into the ambit of ill performance.

Even though they did not in fact succeed, the earlier cases, before there was talk of deceit, provide the greater puzzle. To sue in trespass for the failure to carry out a promise seems just impudent; and if there was no more to it than a smart lawyer trying on an analogy with ill performance, one would expect it to be treated with contempt. But it was not treated with contempt, and chronology suggests that it was not an attempt to push onwards from ill performance seen as an established base. Although the earliest such action reported by the year books was in 1400, it appears from the plea rolls that they were begun a generation earlier, while the base was being established. In Michaelmas term 1370, for example, writs against bad smiths, bad shepherds and a bad tiler are matched by others complaining of a failure to carry

[23] Y.BB. Mich. 2 Hy. IV, pl. 9, f. 3d; Mich. 11 Hy. IV, pl. 60, f. 33; Hil. 3 Hy. VI, pl. 33, f. 36d.

grain and a failure to sow land; and in Easter term 1391 there are six writs for failure to build or repair buildings and one for failure to mow.[24] The rolls of the Common Pleas for these two terms alone occupy the skins of more than a thousand sheep, so that the numbers of such actions are relatively tiny; and it may mean little that I have not found one actually carried to a hearing earlier than the earliest year book example. Even if there were none, it still looks as though there must have been something more in the background than a false analogy to make trespass actions for breach of covenant seem plausible. Something must have obscured the boundary between trespass and covenant, either generally or in a particular class of case.

That it was something in the class of case is possible. All the early plea roll examples mentioned are of the same nature as the earliest year book cases, failure to build or to repair buildings, to carry, or to perform some agricultural operation. Promises for services may have been peculiar in several ways. For one thing, they must have been the chief casualties of the common law requirement of a seal: promises to pay money and to deliver goods would, in suitable circumstances of mutuality, be enforceable without contractual formality in debt and detinue; but an oral promise to serve would not be actionable in covenant in a royal court even though the promisor had been paid. This would at least be a motive for exploiting any confusion caused by opening the jurisdictional barrier. Then again the labour legislation may have introduced confusion of a different kind by treating refusals to serve and departures from service as wrongs. Indeed, the year books themselves suggest that the early cases may possibly be explicable as actions intended to be based on the Statutes of Labourers, but defective for not expressly saying so; if so, it all began with incompetence in plaintiffs' lawyers rather than their effrontery.[25] Or again we may be up against a more deep-seated source of confusion, something to do with status and contract. Outside the common law failures to carry out agricultural operations, at any

[24] CP 40/440, mm. 70 (smith); 260 (marshal); 204d (bailee of sheep; *contra pacem* incongruously alleged, as to which see n. 7 above); 309 (shepherd); 520 (tiler, *contra pacem*); 630d (failure to carry by water); 407d (failure to cultivate and sow). CP 40/521 has many misfeasance actions, including several for bad building. Failures to build are: mm. 96d, 201d, 481 (houses); 340 (mill). Failures to repair: mm. 291d, 387d (both mills). Failure to mow: m. 276.

[25] Confusion could arise over the need to recite the statute when counting in an action based on it; Y.B. Hil. 5 Hy. V, pl. 26, f. 11. The close relationship between covenant and the statutory action against the departing servant is often made clear: *e.g.*, Y.BB. Mich. 41 Ed. III, pl. 1, f. 17; Mich. 41 Ed. III, pl. 4, f. 20; Mich. 45 Ed. III, pl. 15, f. 15; Hil. 46 Ed. III, pl. 10, f. 4d; Mich. 47 Ed. III, pl. 23, f. 16.

rate, must have been treated as manorial offences far more often than as breaches of covenant; and apart from tenure, the relationship of employer and employee may not always have seemed legally any more than socially the matter of agreement between persons in some sense equal that an apprenticeship was.

A quite different kind of explanation, not restricted to service agreements, would look particularly to the common law. Since trespass was, as tort is, essentially a residuary category, an uncertainty over its boundary with covenant must have its source in covenant. The outstanding fact about covenant in royal courts, indicated by the year books and driven home by the plea rolls, is that after about the first half of the fourteenth century hardly anybody ever used the action except for the purpose of levying a fine. Agreements in general were given force by conditional bonds, in which the performance desired was not itself promised, but made the condition of avoiding a promise to pay money; and litigation was in debt and not covenant. Promises as such, other than promises to pay money, were not being enforced in the king's courts; so that although the name and the action of covenant embodied one of the most basic legal concepts, that concept was not in fact being put through the refinery of professionally conducted litigation. This whole area of the law was lying waste.

This disuse is itself a likely cause of uncertainty about the scope of covenant; but it may be the product of another. Why was the conditional bond universally used instead of the direct deed of promise? If you had to have a deed anyway, one by which your carpenter promised you a large round sum if he had not built the house by Christmas was no doubt more effective (until equity began to disallow penalties) than one by which he simply promised to build it by Christmas. But it takes two to make a contract, and why should the carpenter always agree? It is possible that this mode of contracting, which contemplated redress for failure to perform, was adopted precisely to avoid the writ of covenant which contemplated no such thing. The writ took shape at a time when almost the only kind of agreement important enough for anybody to want to bring to the king's court was an agreement concerning land, and it embodies the most literal notion of enforcing promises: *praecipe quod teneat conventionem*. The words are appropriate for compelling a performance which is still possible, and inappropriate not only for recouping a loss caused by ill performance but also for recouping a loss irremediably caused by failure to perform, for example failure to plough in time for sowing. Whether or not this inappropriateness was a cause of the rise of the conditional bond

(509)

and the decline of covenant,[26] it may well have combined with it to produce uncertainty about the proper remedy for an irremediable breach, and to make colourable the use of trespass actions. Surely it was in the minds of those, arguing in 1425 for the propriety of a trespass action for failure to build a mill, who put the extreme case of physical damage flowing from a breach of promise, rain spoiling furniture because of a failure to roof, or floods destroying crops because of a failure to ditch.[27] Surely too it played its part in the disablement cases. As early as 1284 the draftsman of the statute of Wales thought it right to deal expressly with the case of one who promises to convey land to the plaintiff and then conveys it to another; the plaintiff cannot have other redress in his writ of covenant, the statute says, than damages.[28] But in 1442 it seemed a reason for allowing a tortious remedy on those facts: to what end, asked a judge, would the plaintiff have a writ of covenant, even if he had a deed, when the defendant cannot keep his covenant? [29]

For these early cases, I have proposed too many answers, probably all wrong. But the question must be right: the plaintiffs' lawyers did not mean to make history, so what were they up to? It is much easier to see what was in their minds when they started talking of deceit in the disablement cases. At first sight this too looks like a dodge, a second and more sophisticated attempt to pass off as a trespass what was really a breach of covenant. But that is to credit the lawyers with too much vision. Deceit in this context was not snatched from the air, or dragged across from fields as remote as the abuse of legal process or even the giving of false warranties on sale. Such illusions are due to the same accident as befell trespass. That you can wrong a man by tricking him into doing something disadvantageous, was as obvious as it is to us; and in local courts proceedings for this kind of trespass were familiar, sometimes at the instance of public authority, as with a seller dubbing his basket of wares, sometimes at the instance of the party aggrieved. But there was no royal interest in such matters, and so deceit did not generally appear in royal courts. The point

---

[26] After this lecture was given, Mr. C. A. F. Meekings kindly suggested to me a quite different kind of explanation for the disuse of covenant, namely that its popularity as the basis of fines had appropriated it to the conveyancer. Once suggested, a connection seems compelling, and it may perhaps have been through the ubiquitous process. That debt did and covenant did not have *capias* would be a motive for using the conditional bond; and the omission of covenant from the statute extending *capias* in 1352 (n. 8 above) may well have been in the interest of the conveyancer.

[27] Y.B. Hil. 3 Hy. VI, pl. 33, f. 36d, *per* Babington and Cokayne.

[28] Stat. Wales, c. 10.

[29] Y.B.Trin. 20 Hy. VI, pl. 4, f. 34 at f. 34d, *per* Newton. The " even if " translates *mesque*; it has sometimes been rendered as " unless " which destroys the force of the passage.

appears clearly from an entry of 1280: a woman had been tricked out of her land by a promise of marriage, and justices were ordered to hear her complaint, whether it was to be classified as a plea of land or trespass or deceit.[30] One particular kind of case regularly came in, however, namely where the court itself was deceived; and so the appearance of deceit in purely private affairs after the requirement of a royal interest was dropped, such as the action on a warranty, has been regarded as a development from the process for deceit of the court like the development of case from the mythical trespass.

The result, as with case, has been to represent as legal inventions or the stretching of analogies what were just early appearances in royal courts of claims familiar elsewhere; and the disablement cases turn out to be another example of this. They are generally taken to begin in 1433, when the defendant was a lawyer retained by the plaintiff to arrange a conveyance of certain land to him; and instead he disclosed the plaintiff's plans and arranged a conveyance to a third party.[31] The accident that he was a lawyer has facilitated a derivation from the old process for deceit of a court. In 1442 the defendant was just a landowner who agreed to convey to the plaintiff, and instead she conveyed to another. When sued in deceit, she staked her case on the proposition that the action should be in covenant; and this was argued out in the Exchequer Chamber.[32] To hindsight the plaintiff's action looks like a clever step on the path to a tortious remedy for non-performance of a promise; but the cleverness may just as well have been in the defendant's objection. The claim was not new even in royal courts. As early as 1401 a manorial steward agreed to arrange a customary tenancy for the plaintiff, and then caused the lord to convey the land to a third party; he is sued in deceit, and in the reported argument it is not even suggested that covenant would be appropriate.[33] Nor is there any hint that this was an innovation; nor was it. In 1382 the would-be founder of a lunatic asylum agreed to buy a suitable property and paid for it; and then the vendor sold it to another.[34] The facts

---

[30] *Sel.Cas. in King's Bench*, Vol. i, Seld.Soc., Vol. 55, p. 65. " *Dominus rex iniunxit Radulpho de Hengham et Waltero de Wymburn' viua voce quod audirent et terminarent querelam Agnetis de Sperkeford versus Willelmum de Pateny, siue esset de placito terre siue transgressionis seu alicuius collusionis vel decepcionis Agnetis de Sperkeford. . . .*" The proper remedy on such facts was evidently a puzzle; *Brevia Placitata*, Seld.Soc., Vol. 66, p. 122; *Casus Placitorum*, Seld.Soc., Vol. 69, p. 30/3. It seems to have become settled as the writ of entry *causa matrimonii praelocuti; cf. Novae Narrationes*, Seld.Soc., Vol. 80, p. cxxxii, n. 4.
[31] Y.BB. Hil. 11 Hy. VI, pl. 10, f. 18; Pasch. 11 Hy. VI, pl. 1, f. 24; Trin. 11 Hy. VI, pl. 26, f. 55d.
[32] Y.B. Trin. 20 Hy. VI, pl. 4, f. 34; Kiralfy, *The Action on the Case*, p. 227.
[33] Y.B. Mich. 3 Hy. IV, pl. 12, f. 3.
[34] *Cal. of Select Pleas and Memoranda of the City of London, 1381–1412*, p. 23.

are indistinguishable from those which sixty years later went to the Exchequer Chamber; but they happened in the city of London, whose courts had no requirement of a seal in covenant. Calling the action deceit rather than covenant was therefore not a dodge but the natural analysis. And as with the simple cases of ill performance, though not so promptly, a genuine difficulty arose when actions came into a jurisdiction where the analysis mattered, where covenant was restricted by a formality.

I cannot today go either forwards or backwards from this point. By going backwards, I mean exploring the boundary between covenant and deceit in local jurisdictions. Perhaps there was none, in that a complaint could be double; even if there was, it is unlikely that the promisor's state of mind was decisive, or indeed that there was any single test. In London it looks as though one would not call it deceit unless at least two conditions were satisfied: that the promisee had paid for the promise, and that the promisor had disabled himself from keeping it, as by conveying land to another. If the promise could still be kept, the action would probably be called covenant and judgment would be for specific performance, which remained, where practicable, a normal remedy in the City. Any idea lingering in the common law that the essence of covenant lay in compelling actual performance may therefore have had a more fundamental origin than the mere words of the writ. On the other hand disablement probably did not amount to deceit in London if the promisor had not been paid. In 1366 a plaintiff had agreed to buy land, giving God's pennies but not paying the price, and had bought timber and made arrangements with a carpenter to build; and his action against the defendant, who had sold to another, was apparently in covenant.[35] Obviously the essence of deceit was being tricked out of something. And it may be—to cast a glance forward in the common law—that the general trespassory remedy for failure to keep a promise, at first apparently available only when the promisee had paid or done his part, was just the simple application of this idea suggested by Ames; and hence the doctrine of consideration. Even if so we still need to find out at what point, if ever, it became a mere matter of chicanery. The development of *indebitatus assumpsit*, for example, whereby a trespassory action could be used to recover debts, looks from its beginning like a brazen manoeuvre to avoid using the action of debt with its wager of law. But it may not be coincidence that centuries earlier we find talk of deceit in London actions against

---

[35] *Cal. of Plea and Memoranda Rolls of the City of London, 1364–1381*, p. 56.

buyers who have induced their sellers to rely on special arrangements for payment.[36]

I have spent time on these early questions because they interest me most, and because like many inaugurals this is really a sermon; and to the extent that it is directed to legal historians its message, right or wrong, is now obvious—so obvious that I would not presume to state it if it did not constitute a confession of past and probably future guilt. Only at the most minute level of detail can our question "How did it happen?" correspond to a contemporary "How can it be brought about?" It is difficult even to see from a distance what to the lawyer of the time was a life-sized problem; and if we are to see it through his eyes, we have to furnish his mind. Our knowledge of later happenings, the false background of one looking backwards, must be taken out; and the implications of this are as hard to reckon with as those of most truisms. Instead there must be put in a background which includes a framework of elementary legal ideas accommodating the practice of local courts as well as the forms of action available in the king's courts. The making of the common law has too often been imagined as consisting of two distinct phases: first it earned its name by absorbing local custom; and then, having collected all the materials it was ever to have and arranged them into the pattern of the forms of action, it sealed itself off, and developed by rearranging the pattern. Lawyers are credited with more than human cunning, and less than ordinary sense.

But the morals which my lecture is chiefly meant to point are for those who practise and those who teach a system of law which has been capable of exploits, however small the stages by which they were brought about, like the reconstruction of contract out of materials taken from tort. It is a method of development which produces great logical strength in detail and great overall disorder; and in particular, barriers which seem fundamental in other systems are insubstantial in ours. A topical example is our propensity to convert an obligation about an object, such as a matrimonial home, into a proprietary right over it.[37] Lack of symmetry in itself is not

---

[36] *Cal. of Early Mayor's Court Rolls of the City of London, 1298–1307*, pp. 170–171. *Cf.* the fragment of a thriller at p. 247.

[37] *National Provincial Bank* v. *Hastings Car Mart* [1965] 3 W.L.R. 1. The recent history of licences in general is a good example of development by reaching into a seemingly inappropriate compartment of ideas. For some reason such as the Rent Restriction Acts, the appropriate rules, those concerning leases, yield an undesirable answer; so a new starting point is sought in contract. The special dexterity of equity in making rights *in rem* out of rights *in personam*, that is to say in reaching third parties, depends upon its nominal basis: conscience is a matter of undifferentiated wrong, and the cage of privity is replaced by the illusory tether of notice. But if a property right is created, considerations of true wrong are expelled; consider *L.C.C.* v. *Allen*

of course a defect requiring action; but nor is it a virtue, a sign of good sense to be modest about. It is a fact to be reckoned with, and an important one. Abandoning the natural approach to a problem for transient reasons has compelled a capricious use of legal resources, and elementary ideas have been exploited because they were accessible rather than because they were apt. Over the centuries the landscape has been ruthlessly transformed: whole conceptual areas have been laid waste, and others have been made to support activity beyond what they will naturally bear.

This may be illustrated by a more cavalier raid into history, to collect some remoter consequences of the development of which we have examined the earliest stages in such detail. In contract itself there is the odd career of consideration. At any rate so far as the common law is concerned, it began in *assumpsit*; and it may have been, as Ames thought, the promisee's damage when he expresses the matter as a deceit. But it came to seem so much the essence of contract, that some jurisdictions abolished what they took to be the intrusive binding property of the promise under seal. On the face of it they were extirpating the last trace of our original law of contract; and they incidentally set themselves in its most acute form the general problem of the gratuitous promise for which ideas of justice or policy demand enforcement. Now it is the new rules of contract that have to be evaded; and resort is made more or less whole-heartedly to estoppel, an idea again springing from statement rather than promise. And there is another sense in which none of this may be as novel as it looks. We know little enough about the process by which a seal became necessary, and almost nothing about its becoming sufficient. But it did not begin as a contractual formality; and the magic was surely first seen as precluding discussion rather than as directly giving force to a promise.

Less familiar, but not less striking, are some of the consequences in other parts of the law. *Assumpsit* and the action for breach of warranty absorbed the concept of deceit, and carried it off into contract; and the obvious gap left in the law of wrongs was repaired as late as the eighteenth century by what was regarded as the invention of a new tort of deceit. But more fundamental damage had been done. When deceit was diverted into contract, it was

[1914] 3 K.B. 642. In the common law, the strict liability in conversion is similarly the result of expelling fault from a personal remedy to make it serve a proprietary purpose. It should be added that the common law, although not as productive as equity, has manufactured property rights: the passing of property on a sale of goods came about in a mysterious way; but the lease was a simple matter of adding to a contractual right tort remedies against third parties.

also sterilised: if the actions were to enforce promises, their allegations of deceit had to be emptied of meaning. Deceitful conduct as such was left without specific effect in the common law; and the elaboration of fraud as one of the great categories of equitable jurisdiction reflects this. But it is important not to misread the story. That fraud fell to Chancery and Star Chamber can be taken, especially in association with the old misunderstanding about trespass and case, as showing a primitive poverty of ideas in the early common law, which could comprehend a taking or a blow or duress but nothing so subtle as cheating. This is deeply anachronistic. Deceit miscarried in the king's courts because the lawyers were too clever rather than too stupid, and it had flourished in the local jurisdictions from which the common law was drawn. We cannot be sure whether in those jurisdictions it was seen as a distinct entity which could exist outside a contractual context, but the question would not often arise; that is why the common law was able to manage so long without the tort. Deceitful statements, whether about the quality of goods or otherwise, are generally made to induce a contract; and in London, at any rate, it seems that a natural remedy was to undo the transaction.[38] In this matter the Chancellor was no innovator in substance or in treatment.

So far-reaching have been the consequences of this particular development that it may be instructive to cast up a balance sheet. In place of a single idea we have at least three: warranty denatured by absorption into the contract, representation operating outside it, and the resurrected tort. And there are secondary complications about honest misstatement, which may be disposing us to leave deceit once again without specific effect in civil actions. The tendency to use and then supersede the idea like this deserves thought. It is of course convenient to fix liability on a cheat without having to call him so. But the pressure seems never to have been directed to this end, but to generalising the liability; and it is an accidental result that the cheat comes to mingle unmarked among others caught by the general rule. In the end the elementary concept, a moral as well as a legal one, is used as a foundation which disappears under the rules built on it. And it may be that the idea of negligence is playing a similar part in the law today.

As with deceit, though not so profoundly, the history of negligence has been affected by the interaction between contract and tort; though in this case the story begins with ill performance. This was remedied, as we have seen, by actions which the king's

[38] *Cal. of Plea and Memoranda Rolls of the City of London, 1364–1381*, p. 126 (sale of entailed property as fee simple; the defendant was also imprisoned).

courts categorised as trespass. But the writs generally used the magnetic word *assumpsit*, and the idea of negligence was thereby attracted—not to speak too definitely—into the contractual sphere of influence. In this century there was still some ghost of privity to be laid in fixing a manufacturer with liability to the ultimate consumer of his product; and the story is not over yet. So great is the difficulty of proving negligence in such cases that in some jurisdictions attempts are being made to resort to the idea of warranty. The frontiers are to be crossed again. Either privity must be eluded, and the matter smuggled back into contract, or warranty itself must be returned to its first home in tort.[39] Such an attempt to reverse history has of course a more substantial motive than the difficulty of proof. The situation is one in which the language and concepts of specific individual fault may come to seem inappropriate for governing the incidence of loss. It is at first sight curious that the common law, which makes so little use of deceit, should do so much with negligence as a basis of liability; and the historian, at least, is tempted to wonder how far this owes more to its accessibility than to its fitness for all the purposes which we make it serve. To hold that there is a duty of care in a new kind of situation is the modern equivalent of sanctioning a new writ. But since negligence became a tort, instead of the convenient title for a miscellany, it has been possible for us to go on believing in the difficulty of creating new torts without seeing an incongruity in the growth of negligence; and it has been easiest for us to establish new liabilities, new duties, in terms of duties of care. The tort of negligence is the residuary legatee of the action on the case, itself the residue of the residuary category of tort; and we may, like the clerk who files all accessions under Miscellaneous, be overloading the idea.

And this leads me to my conclusion. Questions like the desirability of reaching the manufacturer by means of negligence are asked more easily in the United States, because the conceptual frontiers are less closely guarded. Multiple jurisdictions and discordant precedents keep authority in its place; and on this side of the Atlantic it may be that we must increasingly rely on legislation for major change. Since I have been at pains to show some of the unreasonable things that reason has made case law do, perhaps I should welcome this prospect; but in some areas, at least, I believe that we should be the losers. The common law has traced odd patterns by following its nose; but this is because it has by and large turned, however clumsily, to tasks needing to be done. There

---

[39] See generally, *Prosser on Torts*, 1955 ed., p. 506. I am indebted to Professor Samuel Donnelly of Syracuse Law School, N.Y., for pointing out to me the relevance of these warranty questions during a session last summer at N.Y.U.

will always be enough such tasks for us to want all means of doing them; and I personally would like to see the welcome proposals for improving our legislative machine supplemented by a relaxation in our rules of precedent. But the growing stiffness of the common law in England may not derive so much from authority as from the submissive attitude authority produces. The chief benefit of more obvious choice is to compel more elementary thought, both about results and about reasoning. The lesson has been tardily learnt, and in this School we are particularly trying to apply it, that the lawyer must attend to the results in real life of his reasoning; but the reasoning remains his special business. It is not enough to turn out a student who merely knows the rule, and not much better if he is merely discontented with it. Whatever is to be the balance between legislation and precedent, the vitality of the law depends upon the enterprise of lawyers in exploiting their elementary materials. And if they have never thought about any law but English law, or any period but the present, they may neither guess the range and qualities of those materials, nor even understand that their business is not to find answers but to make them.

7

LAW AND FACT IN LEGAL DEVELOPMENT

I

LAWYERS inquire into the history of their rules and institutions to find out how things came to be as they are, and they generally assume that the facts behind each development are in themselves well known to historians. Historians search the legal sources for some trace of those same elusive facts, and their assumption is that the relevant law is well known to lawyers—or at any rate to legal historians, who are thus condemned to unanswerable questions from both sides. The mutual misunderstanding is like that which, in England at any rate, exists between academic lawyers and practitioners. Academic lawyers are supposed to think of purely legal problems arising out of clear facts, practitioners of clear law as the background to disputes about what happened. But neither in the single case nor in the mass and over the centuries are the law and the facts so separate that either can be seen as the fixed background to an examination of the other.

This essay is about the beginnings of the common law as an intellectual system, and its premiss is that legal development consists in the increasingly detailed consideration of facts. If so, the limit at any time is the extent to which the legal process presents the facts for legal handling. Academic or juristic speculation may go beyond the problems of daily life, but it cannot imagine the unimaginable or excogitate questions of a different order from those which actually arise. Legal development in Rome arose from the jurists on the one hand and the praetor's control of the formulary system on the other. But this combination of systematic thought and actual authority perhaps depended upon the nature of the formula itself. A dispute remitted to the deciding body with instructions in some such form as: "If you find this, then, unless you find that, condemn the defendant to pay so much," has been reduced to the same terms as those used by the speculative lawyer; and they are almost the terms of substantive statement. The form of litigation at common law has never attained such clarity, and approached it only sporadically and late.

A previous stage was represented in Roman law by formulae appropriate to the more ancient type of claim in which the main assertion, instead of being essentially one of fact, such as that the plaintiff had sold the defendant a slave, was one with a very high legal content: "If you find A to be owner *ex jure Quiritium*" or "If you find B *dare oportere*." This question was sent undigested to the *judex*, and answered by a bare decision for the one party or the other. For our present purpose, this pattern of litigation seems to be at the same level of development as litigation under the historical *legis actiones*; and we shall see that something like it was long predominant at common law. Apart from the bare classification of the claim, any legal analysis there may be of the facts is not formally brought out, but goes on in the mind of the *judex* or other deciding body, or is at best made explicit in the form of advice to the *judex* from a jurist or directions to the jury from a judge.

But at least the decision was taken by a rational being who could seek the facts and be guided or, as we shall see, misled by them. There is no direct evidence of a yet earlier stage in Roman law. But in *legis actio per sacramentum*, which Gaius describes as having been the general form of action, the rational *judex* looks as though he might be a modern substitute for something archaic. The parties made formal assertion and formal counter-assertion, not of course about simple facts but about ownership *ex jure Quiritium* or *dare oportere*; and the function of the *judex* was to settle a bet on which was right. If the assertions had been oaths, and if the decision between them had been made not by a human *judex* but by some test understood to convey the judgment of the gods, the pattern would be that prevailing in England when law first emerges into the light of connected evidence—a thousand years and more after the time of Gaius, to whom such a stage, if it had ever existed in Rome, was not even a memory.

This was the logic of the ordeal, which disappeared in England in consequence of a decision taken by the church some twenty years after the earliest of our series of surviving plea rolls.[1] It was also the logic of trial by battle the first inroad on which, the Grand Assize, was still in its infancy when that roll was written. And up to a point it was the logic of compurgation, a reality through the Middle Ages, which could be regarded rationally, but which had much the same effect on legal thinking as ordeal and battle. It is solely with the development of legal thinking that this article is concerned: not with the working of these ancient modes of trial, nor the details of their replacement, but just with the fact that our evidence allows us to watch the intellectual development of a system of law from so early a stage of litigation. How much law can there be when a law-suit is settled by testing a comprehensive oath affirming the justice of the one cause or the other, however rational or irrational the test? How much more law will come into being when the same comprehensive question of right between the parties is put to a jury? How did the common law courts get facts before them to think about? Such questions are easier to ask than to answer, and the danger of anachronistic thinking is enhanced by a disparity between the state of legal process in the early part of the story and the sophistication of the men

---

[1] The fourth Lateran Council in 1215 forbade clergy from taking part in the necessary ceremonies for ordeals. Apart from the oaths involved, the ceremonial of battle was not ecclesiastical in character.

who worked it. *Brevia Placitata*,[2] a manual giving the bare forms of litigation, is perhaps a year or two later than Bracton's book; and it is half a civilization earlier.

II

In one respect the English law-suit seems always to have brought out more facts than did the earlier Roman pattern. So far as we know the plaintiff never said just "I claim to be owner of this thing" or "I claim that the defendant owes me so much." His writ might be no more informative than that (though some, such as the writs of entry and writs on the case, were very informative); but the writ was just administrative drill referring the plaintiff's claim to the appropriate tribunal. There he was required to begin, as apparently he had before writs existed, with a formal statement of his case; and this set out a lot of facts. In the writ of right, for example, the demandant's count would run, in effect, "I claim this land to be mine, because such a one, my ancestor, was seised of it in the reign of such a king, and from him the right descended to such another, and from that other to me"; and in a writ of debt, "I claim that the defendant owes me so much, because on such a day I sold him a horse for that amount and he has not paid it."

These facts were not set out by way of argument or evidence to persuade, because there was no one to be persuaded. They were an integral part of the law-suit; and the oath which would be taken by or on behalf of one of the parties, and which, by being put to a divine test, would decide the action, was explicitly in affirmation or denial of the whole of the count. It follows that, while some facts were always asserted in the count, no others could emerge so long as litigation was strictly in this mould. The social historian interested just in the facts will ask in vain how, in a writ of right, the land had got into the wrong hands, or whether, in a writ of debt, there had ever been a sale, or whether it was of a cow rather than a horse, or of a horse that immediately died, or whether the defendant had paid, or what had happened. And conversely the legal historian interested just in the law will ask in vain whether the heir of one who had been tricked into granting his land away could ever get it back again, whether the buyer of a moribund horse was obliged to pay for it, and so on. And this is not because of the nature of legal records but because of the nature of law-suits. The court that heard the case knew no more of the facts. Could it know more of the law?

The kind of law which such a framework can support may be described, in childish terms, as being about claims and not about defences. The circumstances in which a man is to be put to answer can be elaborated and classified. But the answer will be an impenetrable denial, its possible basis locked up in the judgment of God. Consider, for example, an old argument

[2]Edited as Volume 66 of the Selden Society series.

among legal historians: did medieval man act at his peril, or could he plead accident and the like? Straws have been taken to point the one way or the other, but perhaps the only real evidence is that there are just straws. Until surprisingly late, the legal sources are virtually silent.[3] They could not be otherwise so long as law-suits were on the ancient pattern. The defendant swears he is not guilty, and his oath is tested and found true: who is to ask whether he did not do the deed, or did it but did not mean to? The question does not arise.

The field of contract affords no such single clear-cut example. But the persistence of wager in the action of debt was not just a symptom of social backwardness: it seems also to have been a cause of the retarded intellectual growth of that branch of the law. The legal historian trying to reconstruct substantive law finds many elementary questions that he cannot answer, and the reason turns out to be because the facts raising them would not be specially pleaded but subsumed under *Nil debet*. If the defendant waged his law, it was in his conscience that the rule sought actually operated. And when the historian has realized this he ought to ask—and one at least must confess that he has not always done so—how far a rule on the matter could have had definite existence. It might, of course, have come up in some other way: but within this framework, the matter would emerge into the light of legal discussion only if an opinion were sought on the propriety in conscience of wager.[4]

A simple example of an undiscoverable rule is that in *Pinnel's Case*.[5] Was a debt discharged by acceptance of a lesser sum in full satisfaction? The earliest discussions are late and hesitant,[6] apparently because the question would not squarely arise. If the defendant had executed a deed, and on his side had a deed acknowledging receipt of a lesser sum but releasing the whole debt, the release would be effective anyway. If there was no deed on either side, the defendant would probably wage his law. The question was perhaps only brought out by cases like *Pinnel* itself, in which the payment of a sum was the condition of avoiding a penal bond, and the question was whether the condition was satisfied by the acceptance of less than the sum it named.

Similar doubts may arise over the creation of debts. It is generally agreed, for example, that the sale of goods became a "consensual" contract long before assumpsit had done its work, in the sense that debt and detinue

---

[3] Short discussions which refer to the principal literature are: Plucknett, *Concise History of the Common Law* (5th ed.), 465 *et seq.*; Fifoot, *History and Sources of the Common Law*, 187 *et seq.*

[4] See e.g. YB. P., 21 Hy VI, pl. 2, f. 35, at f. 35d, where a suggested wager is said to be *malveis & perilous en conscience*; Brooke, *Abridgment*, *Ley Gager* 93. It would be nice to know more of the "good admonition and due examination of the party" said in Coke's report of *Slade's* case to be preliminary to the waging or making of law; 4 Co. Rep. 92b at 95a. Probably it was a standard formality.

[5] 5 Co.Rep. 117a. Cf. Simpson, "The Penal Bond" (1966), 82 *L.Q.R.*, 392 at 405.

[6] YBB. M., 33 Hy VI, pl. 32, f. 47, at f. 48; M., 10 Hy VII, pl. 4, f. 4; Dalison, 5 Eliz., pl. 13, p. 49.

became respectively available to the seller who had not delivered and to the buyer who had not paid, provided in each case that the plaintiff was willing to deliver or pay. But it seems impossible to find out when this happened. Year Book discussions are again late and hesitant, and include, for instance, a dispute about the sale of land which has a distinctly academic ring.[7] And the plea rolls tell us nothing, unless it is that there was nothing to tell. Suppose such an action by a seller for his money: almost certainly it would be enrolled among all the others in which a count that the defendant *emisset* something for the sum demanded is met by a blank *Nil debet*. But if that was the way in which the matter would be pleaded, it would come up for legal consideration indirectly and slowly; and the curious obliquity of Year Book discussions on this and other points is fully explained. Indeed it is possible that differing local customs were given indirect force, and that on identical facts one defendant might conscientiously wage his law when another, his conscience informed by different rules, would regard himself as liable. In the nature of the thing we shall not find direct evidence of this. But it would help to explain certain apparently incongruous claims found on the plea rolls, and it would reduce the anomalies we are otherwise compelled to imagine as resulting from the 40-shilling barrier between royal and lesser jurisdictions.

Local customs about contract serve to introduce a different aspect of the kind of law generated by the ancient pattern of law-suit. If the answer must be a blank denial, legal refinement and indeed common sense can only go to work on the claim; and the law will be largely about the obstacles which have to be surmounted by a plaintiff before he can put the defendant to make the answer. This is particularly clear of contract in local jurisdictions, where many kinds of rule went to the preliminary proofs or guarantees of good faith with which a plaintiff had to be armed.[8] The contractual effect of the deed under seal began in rules of this nature. And in all actions at common law the *secta* tendered at the end of the count was in principle a verification of the assertions contained therein. To begin with it seems that the defendant could stake his case upon some examination of the *secta*.[9] But in most kinds of action in royal courts the institution was already vestigial when the Year Books began; a fact we should remember when we are tempted to think wager of law merely absurd.

At this first stage, then, the law will consist in kinds of claim, modes of proof appropriate to each, and conditions to be satisfied before the claim can be put to the proof. And although the second and third of these, at any

---

[7]For the references see Ames, *Lectures on Legal History*, 140, n.3; and for a bewildered account of the matter see Milsom, "Sale of Goods in the Fifteenth Century" (1961), 77 *L.Q.R.*, 257, esp. at pp. 271 , here 119 *et seq.*

[8]See e.g. *Borough Customs*, Vol. 1, Selden Society Volume 18, 167 *et seq.*, 202 *et seq.*; Henry, *Contracts in the Local Courts of Medieval England*, *passim*.

[9]YBB., 2 & 3 Ed II, Selden Society Volume 19, 195; 17 & 18 Ed III, Rolls Series, 73. In actions *De nativo habendo* the suit, which consisted of relatives of the alleged villein, continued to play a real part; *Novae Narrationes*, Selden Society Volume 80, cxlvi.

rate, have a procedural look, they presuppose an essentially substantive classification. Consider the matter through the eyes of the two earliest groups who can in some sense be called professional lawyers. The *narratores* or counters were concerned with the making of claims, and their special skill was in fitting the facts alleged by their clients into the appropriate mould and, no doubt, advising about such things as *secta* and proof. All this involves abstraction and classification. Then there are the administrator-judges, viewing the same proceedings from above, concerned largely with the system for dealing with claims, with jurisdiction. They were to contribute some Roman ideas and Roman language, to our confusion and perhaps to their own; but the first practical result of their approach was the generalization of the writ system, the need to begin many kinds of law-suit by getting, as it were, a chit from head office referring the dispute to the appropriate tribunal. Since the writ had to indicate the nature of the dispute, this necessitated a further degree of abstraction, the production of master-moulds. Some of these bore names representing elementary ideas, though their tortuous later history made it seem unthinkable that covenant once meant just agreement and trespass just wrong, and so lent colour to a purely formalistic view of the early common law.[10] Even the earliest procedural framework of which we have any knowledge seems to have supported an elementary jurisprudence.

III

But of course it was not our jurisprudence, and our present concern is with its limitations. Consider what was evidently a fundamental concept, the right. If a claim sounded in the right, certain consequences followed: from the administrator's viewpoint the feudal rules of jurisdiction came into play, and so important would be the outcome of the action that the formidable delays of the essoin *de malo lecti* must be accepted; from the counter's viewpoint, he must tender on his client's behalf not only *secta* but also *dereyne bone*, and he must have a champion available. But just what was involved in the right and just how it passed from one person to another were questions there was no occasion to ask: they were lost in the battle.

Or take what seems to us an elementary failure, the blurring of property and obligation implied by the late separation of debt and detinue. So far as the formalities of litigation went, this separation may never have been completed. A writ of debt normally alleged that the defendant *debet et detinet*: of detinue just that he *detinet*. But if the claim was for chattels, even for fungible chattels like so many measures of unascertained barley (or even for money when the action was against, for example, an executor), *debet* was omitted. Since the pleadings followed the writ, "debt in the *detinet*" is formally indistinguishable from detinue. In an action for corn

---

[10] For a brief survey of the history of the words, see Milsom, "Reason in the Development of the Common Law" (1965), 81 *L.Q.R.*, 496, at 500 , here 153 *et seq.*

lent, the historian may guess that the loan was probably for consumption rather than for use, and may deduce that the action is debt rather than detinue. In an action for corn bought, or cows bought, he can make no guess; and his only hope seems to be to work from the other end and find what the action was called. The plea rolls do give the names of actions, not, unhappily, when the pleadings are enrolled, but at certain subsidiary and often remote stages, for example when a party makes an attorney or has himself essoined. But it turns out that even hunting for these will not help here: Year Book statements of 1343 and of 1413 disclose that such entries describe detinue as *de placito debiti*.[11] Perhaps then there is still only one action? But no: the 1343 report tells us these entries are only form, and "les accions sount diverses." The bewildered historian then turns to his prime catalogue, the printed *Register of Writs*: and detinue vanishes once more. All writs claiming chattels are intermingled with those claiming money, and placed under the rubric *De debito*: only what we call detinue of charters is segregated as *De cartis reddendis*.[12] But in the two great commentaries, the old and Fitzherbert's new *Natura Brevium*, detinue is there again, a heading separate from debt and comprising claims for chattels as well as charters.[13]

Legal thinking has clearly outstripped legal forms. The lawyers have arrived at a distinction which is not fully reflected in the work of the clerks, whether those who issue writs in Chancery or those who enrol pleas in court. What matters to us is not that this did happen—there is nothing remarkable about officialdom overtaken by events—but that it could happen. The clerks' law represents the procedural framework, the formal steps in a lawsuit, what could actually be done. But unless we are to suspect the lawyers of wanton jurisprudence, there must have been some room in which their extra, unofficial law could operate. Perhaps, once more, the problems first arose and were first dealt with behind the capacious screen of that blank denial.

To begin from the purely factual point, it seems likely that the specific or unascertained quality of goods would just not matter so long as the denial remained truly blank. What can make it matter is a possible defence, that the goods were specific and that they have perished in circumstances which should absolve the defendant. Bracton in a significantly Roman passage states this clearly as the *magna differentia* between a loan for consumption and a loan for use. And, though Fleta successfully follows him here, Britton, perhaps equally significantly, botches it: he seems to think that the debtor who is robbed may in suitable circumstances be excused.[14] Britton has

[11]YBB., 17 Ed III, Rolls Series, 141; H., 14 Hy IV, pl. 37, f. 27d, at f. 28d.
[12]*Registrum Omnium Brevium* (ed. 1634), f. 139 (*De debito*), f. 159d (*De cartis reddendis*).
[13]*La Vieux Natura Brevium* (ed. 1584), f. 60d (*Dette*), f. 63 (*Detinue*); *Le Novel Natura Brevium* (ed. 1588), f. 119 (*Dette*), f. 138 (*Detinue*).
[14]Bracton f. 99; Fleta, II, c. 56 (ed. 1685, 120; Selden Society Volume 72, 186); Britton, I, c. 29, 3 (ed. Nichols, Vol. I, 157).

gathered that there may be a question about liability, but not that it depends upon the factual difference. In one way, his treatment is like that of Glanvill, who also states the difference and does not draw any conclusion from it.[15] But Glanvill states the opposite rule, imposing a strict liability upon the borrower for use; and he seems entirely clear-headed about it. For him, writing in a language in which the two transactions have different names,[16] the factual difference cannot be ignored, although in the law about which he is writing he thinks nothing turns upon it. It is not our present concern to speculate about which of these, if any of them, most nearly represented English law, or to give them marks for their understanding of Roman law, or to ask whether their Roman learning brought fault into the liability of English bailees, but simply to take them all into court with us and watch for a case. It may happen under our eyes and we shall not see it, nor will there be anything in the clerk's record to identify it. The question discussed by our authors will probably have been raised and decided, if at all, in the mind of a defendant who pleaded *Non detinet*.

But though rules which so operate will be tentative, hard for us to discover, and easy for unconscientious litigants to evade, still they are real. And slowly they will come into the open: perhaps juries on a plea of *Non detinet* will ask for directions; perhaps special pleas will put the facts formally before the court for discussion; and eventually visible clerks' law will grow up, but still on a foundation invisible because within the blank denial. The further history of the bailee's liability and the development of trover appear to be examples of this, though in the nature of things part of the story is hidden. The paucity of Year Book evidence on bailees' liability suggests that the usual way out was to plead *Non detinet*.[17] But it seems that this became improper, and wager on it effective perjury. Instead the bailee should make a special plea; and this necessity represents the difference between detinue *sur bailment* with its element of obligation, and the purely proprietary detinue *sur trover*. The bailee could not in honesty be allowed a *Non detinet* which meant just "I have not got it," and hence the growth of special pleas about loss without fault for those compelled in conscience to confess a bailment but believing that further facts avoided their liability. But for the mere neutral possessor of another's goods, who had entered into no transaction and against whom a purely proprietary claim is being made, *Non detinet* can indeed be allowed its literal sense. For him, typified in pleadings as the finder, we do not find in detinue special pleas of loss without fault. Instead

---

[15]Glanvill, X, 12–13 (ed. G. D. G. Hall), 128.

[16]See the important observations of Mr Hall in his edition of Glanvill, xxxvii.

[17]For general discussions and references to the medieval authorities see Fifoot, *History and Sources of the Common Law*, 158 *et seq.*; Holdsworth, *History of English Law*, Vol. III, 336 *et seq.*; Fletcher, *The Carrier's Liability*. Observations in the Year Books are jejune, the point being generally raised indirectly. It is interesting, for example, that so much weight should be put on the *Marshalsea Case*, YB. H, 33 Hy VI, pl.3, f. 1. The jailer's liability in debt for an escape may well have been thought to be governed by the same substantive rules as the ordinary liability of the bailee: but there was a large difference in practice, namely that the general issue was never open to the jailer.

we find tort actions against him in situations in which he has lost possession wrongfully, for example sold the goods and converted the proceeds to his own use.[18] But for our present purpose the interesting point is that the considerable body of substantive law represented by this correlation, if indeed it is right, all depends upon the differing content of the same blank denial, *Non detinet*. Only an extraordinary chance would let us see through this in record or report, or indeed, if we could be there, at the hearing itself; and in this case our only direct indication is a stray Year Book note.[19]

What it comes to is that lawyers, thinking as it were off the record, or rather about facts which on the record were at first encapsulated within the denial, have divided detinue from debt, and then subdivided it so as to enforce two quite different kinds of liability. And, looking at the process as a whole, one cannot help feeling that they might have done a better job if the procedural framework had brought the facts less indirectly to their attention. The forms represent, and that not quite consistently, the crudest factual distinction between money, which can be owed, and goods, specific or other, which can only be detained. The perishability of specific but not of generic goods then caused a division between actions which does not coincide with the forms: generic goods can be owed for the purpose of calling the action debt, but the writ still cannot say *debet*; hence "debt in the *detinet*" for fungibles such as corn.[20] And finally, on the detinue side, it turns out that the point about perishability does not permit all claims even for specific goods to be treated alike: although the word *debet* cannot be used, there is an element of obligation in the bailee's position which must be catered for. The lawyers have evolved a distinction between actions which does not coincide with the clerks' forms, and then evolved concepts which do not coincide with either. At every point there is sound legal logic; but a great over-all disorder seems to be the result of the piecemeal way in which the facts leaked out from *Non detinet*, so that the logic could set around one before the next emerged for consideration.

---

[18]This view of the beginnings of trover was first stated in Ames, *Lectures in Legal History*, 80 *et seq*., esp. at 84. For what was meant to be a clearer statement, with some amplification, see Milsom "Not Doing is no Trespass," [1954] *Cambridge L.J.*, 105 at 113, here 99-102. The element of obligation in detinue *sur bailment* was of course what largely anchored detinue to debt; see e.g. YB., 20 & 21 Ed I, Rolls Series, 189, at 191.
[19]YB. P., 27 Hy VIII, pl. 35, f. 13. The note is cast in terms of substantive law rather than of pleading, but it is difficult to see how any other sense can be given to it. The discussion goes on with a pure pleading query: can one charged as bailee plead specially that he was finder and had parted with the goods before action brought? One speaker says not, because that is tantamount to the general issue. The other says yes, *per laweroust*, (doubt) *des laies gentz*. For another view of the whole matter, see Simpson, "The Introduction of the Action on the Case for Conversion" (1959), 75 *L. Q. R.*, 364 *et seq*., esp. at 371-2. And for the meaning of the word conversion see Milsom, 77 *L. Q. R.*, 278, here 126, n. 42; Bracton's *Note Book*, pl. 687; Bracton f. 91d.
[20]The other kind of "debt in the *detinet*," typified by the action against a specialty debtor's executor, is in part an outlier of detinue: the executor's liability depends upon the continued existence of a specific fund, the debtor's property; and significantly the executor can only be sued in his personal capacity if he has "converted" that property to his own use, and the writ will then be in the *debet*; see 77 *L. Q. R.*, 278, here 126, n. 42.

IV

We have, of course, gone far beyond the time at which the ancient modes of trial were exclusive, and in debt and detinue it may be that even this degree of progress is partly due to the defendant's option of a jury. But the effect of the jury on legal development in general was curiously indirect. One who turns from the plea rolls of the fourteenth century to those of the thirteenth may feel that in between a chance was missed, that in the later years of Henry III and the earlier of Edward I there was what might have been the dawn of a golden day. Then the fog came down again. The passing gleam lies in the amount of facts which find their way into the plea rolls. The historian of today can quite often tell in detail what had happened in a case; and the lawyer of the time could therefore have thought about it in the same detail. Consider an example in print, and one relevant to what we said earlier about liability for accident. In 1290 two defendants are sued for burning the plaintiff's house down.[21] The writ makes it sound like arson, but the count says they were guests and caused the damage by foolishness with an unwatched candle. The defendants expressly plead accident, and a jury explains that when the second of the two went to bed that night a third guest would not let him blow the candle out, and later himself left the room: the candle fell over, and the house was destroyed with everything in it. From a marginal note we gather that the jury was then asked to assess the damages in case the defendants were held liable, and fixed them at £100, half the amount claimed but still a fortune. And there the enrolment ends.

We know now, and the court knew then, the whole story of this calamity in Devon on the night of August 20, 1288. One party or the other must have been ruined, and which it was to be is a good legal question. But we do not know the answer, and perhaps the court never gave it. Perhaps, indeed, they did not like being confronted with what might have been a problem in a law school examination six hundred years later and more. Not until modern times would common law judges again be presented with facts in this comprehensive and relatively informal way. In between they had been protected from such embarrassment by what our books unanimously call the perfection of the rules of pleading; and the main rule was that, so far as possible, the defendant and the jury must be prevented from divulging facts to the court.

The sequence of events can be considered in terms of this same case. A century earlier few if any such actions had reached royal courts, and the plaintiff would probably have sued in the county court of Devon. It is not inconceivable that his count would have resembled that in 1290 in expressly alleging carelessness; but the defendants' answer could only have been a blank denial, tested by compurgation or the like. That is to say that county

[21] *Select Cases in the Court of King's Bench*, vol. I, Selden Society Volume 55, 181.

customs may have recognized what we should call a tort of negligence with fire; but there could be no more definition than the formula of the claim. Or that formula may have been just "he burned my house down," its blankness relieved only by pejorative but imprecise adverbs. In either case the actual question whether this defendant was liable would not have been for the men of Devon to decide: the refinements of law as well as the questions of fact were lost within the judgment of God.

To explain what is, for our present purpose, an irrelevant source of confusion, we must now revert briefly to the case itself. There is an incongruity between the count, alleging carelessness, and the writ, which alleges breach of the king's peace. This is a jurisdictional point.[22] Until the "origin of the action on the case," which was no more than the Chancery beginning to issue writs returnable in royal courts for purely private wrongs, those courts were supposed to hear only wrongs affecting the king's interests; hence the allegations of breach of the king's peace in writs commencing trespass actions in royal courts. The writ in 1290 is therefore one symptom of the tangle of red tape which later enmeshed the common law in the mysteries of "trespass" and "case." But our present concern with the entry is the huge step forward it shows in legal thought, or rather in opportunity for legal thought. Not God inscrutably, but the court of King's Bench in words, with all the facts before it, was to settle a problem of pure substantive law.

A century later the law has stepped back again. The proper way of dealing with the matter, and teachers in 1290 were probably already saying this,[23] was for the defendant to make his ancient answer, "Not guilty" and for the jury to pronounce him "Guilty" or "Not guilty." Indeed, from the historian's point of view, the law has in this kind of case taken two steps back. Defendants' lawyers, taking any point that offers, have made capital of the irrelevant incongruity between a writ alleging breach of the king's peace and a count alleging carelessness like this; and the count will now match the writ in suppressing the carelessness, so that the affair looks like a charge of deliberate arson and a simple denial of the fact. From the fourteenth-century plea rolls, one could therefore deduce that fire-raising was a common English pastime, as, apparently, was putting cats among pigeons;[24] and only some leakage will show that we are concerned with humdrum accidents. In 1368 and 1374 actions for burning the plaintiff's house down with force and arms and against the king's peace were both answered by the standard "Not guilty," and we know what happened only because the juries told their stories instead of giving the usual general verdict.[25] In the later action, indeed, they were questioned in order to bring up

[22]Milsom, "Trespass from Henry III to Edward III" (1958), 74 *L. Q. R.*, 195, 407, 561. See also 81 *L. Q. R.*, at 501 *et seq.* Respectively 1-90 and 154-57 above.
[23]*Brevia Placitata*, Selden Society Volume 66, 207 (*Cas marvellous sur vee de naam*); YB., 21 & 22 Ed I, Rolls Series, 29 (*De Vasto*; it looks like a teacher's problem).
[24]There are two writs for this wrong in *Registrum Omnium Brevium* (ed. 1634), at f. 106. The plaintiff's neighbours or tenants were probably seeking to protect their crops.
[25]YBB., 42 Lib. Ass. pl. 9, f. 259d; M., 48 Ed III, pl. 8, f. 25.

a quite different point of law: the defendant was again a lawful occupant of the house who had been careless, and the question was whether she was tenant at will, in which case this action was proper, or tenant for years, in which case she should be sued in waste. In the earlier the defendant was a neighbour and the fire had spread from his own house; and in this kind of case the formal artificiality appears to have become intolerable, and to have provoked the acceptance of an action on the case in which the true nature of the charge was set out in the writ and count.[26]

Our present concern, however, is not with the artificiality gratuitously added in what we should call tort by jurisdictional considerations, but with a more fundamental failure: the lawyers have retreated from the facts by going back to the ancient pattern of law-suit. The question of law, which in 1290 was freely brought out by allowing the full story to come formally onto the record, has so far as possible been locked up again with the facts themselves, not indeed in the judgment of God but in the jury room. The historian can hardly ever tell what happened: his plea rolls tell him the verdict was "Guilty" or "Not guilty," but not how it was reached; and even if that process was regarded as legally interesting, the *Nisi Prius* system usually kept Year Book reporters away from it. But the historian of today is not alone in the dark. He has cheerful company in the lawyer of the time. The matter is once more outside the process of pleading, and therefore outside his formal learning. At best it is unofficial law, scarcely more articulate, until the formal direction of juries was regular and recognised as legally important, than considerations about the circumstances in which wager might imperil a defendant's salvation.

Whether a genuine chance had been missed is unanswerable. The kind of maturity which, to hindsight, seems to have been within reach in the thirteenth century was not to be attained until the nineteenth, and perhaps it was necessary that an elaborate and constricting procedural framework should be painfully built, painfully altered, and painfully discarded. Perhaps if the jury had been fully exploited early on, as looked possible, the rudimentary conceptual framework would have collapsed under the welter of facts, and perhaps Roman ideas would have gained a real ascendancy in our law. This is to carry speculation beyond the meaningful; but it suggests questions which are real, though they cannot be answered. Did the retreat reflect the passing of the clerical tradition of Bracton and his kind, whose Roman learning, good or bad, was on this view important not for its own sake but because, being enured to legal analysis, they were able to face facts? Was it a conscious victory for such as the compiler of *Brevia Placitata*, or just that their promotion dragged the king's courts down to the immemorial level of most local jurisdictions? Or was it that the king's judges

---

[26] For the early history of these actions concerning fire, see above 19-21 and 82-3; for the emergence of this and some other kinds of action on the case from under the artificial cover of *vi et armis* writs, see above 85-7.

found their lists silting up with cases adjourned for thought, or that they did not like thinking?

The entry of 1290 is, of course, a particularly striking example. The rolls of the time are not full of cases which might well have happened in 1890. But they do reflect a certain modernity in the mechanics of litigation. The first response to the innovation of the jury was the natural one: the facts which parties thought told in their favour were often directly put forward in pleadings. Had this procedure continued, the law would have developed directly, and Year Book discussions about the admissibility of pleas would have been immediately recognizable to us as concerned with substantive law. But actual development was dominated by the rule that the general issue must be taken whenever possible. We have already seen that progress, at first informal and tentative in nature, had largely to be made within the general issue itself, through the direction of juries, argument about the propriety of wager and the like. And we shall finish by indicating, in the barest outline, how it might be made by prizing the general issue open and taking out for formal discussion a single point previously contained within it.

V

Broadly speaking this might happen in two ways: the defendant might exceptionally be allowed a special plea; or, which is less obvious and much less common, the plaintiff might be allowed a special action. Both may be illustrated by a series of pictures of a claim for freehold land. In our earliest picture D, the demandant, claims the land as his right, of which A, his great-grandfather, was seised in the reign of such a king, and of which the right descended from A to B, from B to C, and from C to this D. The tenant, T, makes his blank denial, and the action will be settled by a battle which formally tests the truth of an oath by D's champion (whose own ancestor is supposed to have witnessed the seisin of A). What had actually happened, how T came to be there at all, we do not know: no more did the court. Now for our second picture let us make T choose the Grand Assize. The knights will no doubt discover these things; and Glanvill suggests that they might if they wished tell the facts to the court, and leave the court to decide the case.[27] But certainly the normal practice came to be a general verdict in favour of the one party or the other. Usually, therefore, we shall know no more of the facts than when there was a battle, though the court may have. For our third picture let us postulate a fact, namely that T is there because the land was granted to his ancestor by B. T is now in the difficulty that the assertions in D's count, namely the seisin of A and the subsequent pedigree, are all true. He would probably like to make a special plea, and get a verdict solely on the grant by B, but this is not allowed. He must plead

[27]Glanvill, II, 18 (ed. Hall, 35).

the general issue on the right at large, and the only concession to his predicament is that he may have a mise, a formal joinder of issue, which points out that he claims the right by virtue of B's grant.[28] To pleas like this we shall come back. Then for our last picture let us postulate a further fact in the same story, namely that B was mad when he made the grant under which T claims. Now it is D who is in a difficulty. If T goes to the Grand Assize, D will succeed provided he can tell them of B's madness—and provided the court tells them that madness invalidates a grant. But T may in this case choose not the Grand Assize but battle. To enable D to avoid this possibility a new remedy is evolved for him, the writ of entry *dum non fuit compos mentis*, in which he will start not from A's seisin but from B's defective grant.

This last picture illustrates a splitting of the general issue in the interest of the demandant or plaintiff by extracting one of the questions formerly latent within it and providing a distinct action. But the point of law must have first emerged from under the blank denial; and in this case it seems likely that grants made by incapable persons could only have come up for regular discussion in court after the introduction of the Grand Assize.[29] The writs of entry provide the clearest example of law becoming explicit in this kind of way, if only because the formal common law, the clerks' law, was still malleable. But we have already suggested that the division of detinue from debt, and the sub-division of detinue, were not dissimilar processes, although the clerks' forms could not then adapt themselves to the lawyers' distinctions. Similar in another way are those actions on the case which gave expression to liabilities earlier apparently enforced in royal courts under the guise of *vi et armis* writs.[30] One of these we have mentioned, the action against a neighbour for negligently keeping his fire so that the plaintiff's house was burnt down. So far as the king's courts are concerned, the facts, seem first to emerge for judicial consideration because a jury may ask questions about the general issue in a general action; then later, as with the writs of entry, a narrower and more explicit claim is fashioned. But here it seems that the relevant law was not in the ordinary sense being made by the king's judges because the liabilities were generally recognized in local

[28]*Novae Narrationes*, Selden Society Volume 80, xxxvi. Perhaps significantly, no such special mise has been found admitting the fact of A's seisin but denying its rightfulness; and reflection on the mysteries of any form of "ownership" suggests the wisdom of preserving an ultimate inscrutability here.

[29]See e.g. *Curia Regis Rolls*, vol. VII, 296. At least one of the common law writs of entry gave a remedy where a writ of right may have given none, namely *causa matrimonii praelocuti*. The immediate ancestor seems to have been proceedings in deceit; *Select Cases in the Court of King's Bench*, vol. I, Selden Society Volume 55, 65; vol. II, Selden Society Volume 57, 20; vol. III, Selden Society Volume 58, xcix; vol. IV, Selden Society Volume 74, lxx; *Select Cases of Procedure without Writ*, Selden Society Volume 60, xlvii, n.2. But since land was in issue, a writ was necessary, and the writ of entry was probably composed in consequence. For a very early case of a woman complaining that she was wrongly induced to make a grant, by a man who *tam per minas quam per estucciam* (guile) *et per pulcrum loqui tantum fecit quod ipsa eum amavit et ipse illam*, see *Curia Regis Rolls*, Volume I, 388–9.

[30]The examples detected are listed in 74 *L. Q. R.*, at 585–7, here 85-7.

custom. If so, the acceptance of explicit actions, though in one sense it made parts of the common law, was primarily the removal of a jurisdictional artificiality. In a wider sense though, all actions on the case, and not just those which first came into the king's courts in disguise, illustrate the point which this essay seeks to make. We are often told that the great advantage of case was that it carried jury trial; and to a plaintiff in a situation which might come within one of the older actions like debt, this made it more likely that the facts would be considered. But on a larger view it is surely no accident that so much of the modern common law should have been built up within a framework which expressed the claim, not in terms of ancient mysteries like the right or even like *debet*, but just in terms of what had happened. The facts are formally on the record, and they have to be dealt with.

VI

A much more complicated process, and one about which little modern work has been done although it is largely what the Year Books are about, was the splitting of the general issue in existing actions by letting defendants make special pleas. We have already suggested that the difference between the plea rolls of the later thirteenth century and those of the fourteenth may be the measure of a lost chance: the law might have been developed directly by exploiting jury trial to the full and allowing parties to put formally before the court whatever facts seemed to them relevant. Another measure lies in the difference between all but the earliest Year Books and their corresponding plea rolls. When a fact is discussed in the Year Books, the argument is not about its substantive effect in law but about how it is to be pleaded, and, in particular, whether it should not be contained within the general issue. Usually it should: and in the plea rolls, at any rate after about the middle of the fourteenth century, we find that in all kinds of action there is a small number of standard pleas, and that in most kinds of action the general issue is by far the most common. What we see in the Year Books, and so in the learning of the time, is therefore a kind of looking-glass world in which the legal relevance of facts is uncertainly reflected in discussion about whether they can formally be disclosed.

So far as there was a single guiding principle, it was that facts should be specially pleaded only in circumstances in which the general issue opened some clear possibility of injustice, because a jury was particularly likely to go wrong in fact or law. Our series of pictures about an action for freehold land has already provided an example of facts which might mislead: a writ of right in which everything in the demandant's count about the seisin of his ancestor and about the pedigree was true, but in which the tenant was allowed to draw special attention to an additional fact, namely that somebody in that pedigree had granted the land to one of his own ancestors. But even this was not a true special plea: the right as a whole had to be put in issue, with the special matter mentioned as a concession to the fallibility of the Assize. This kind of compromise became common. We have already seen that in debt there was normally no special plea of payment: it was contained within *Nil debet*. But there were refinements.[31] If the debt was contracted in Kent and paid in Surrey, the defendant was permitted to mention the payment, but still had to "conclude to the *debet*." His plea would be "paid in Surrey, and therefore *nil debet*." This was a variant of the general issue, and would go to a Kentish jury; but he was at least allowed to tell them of what could not be within their own knowledge. But if the debt was alleged to have arisen in one of the exceptional ways which excluded wager of law, for example if it was for the rent due on a lease or for the arrears found due by auditors on an account, the defendant could make a true special plea, "paid in Surrey," without concluding to the *debet*. This admitted the creation of the debt, and anything else that he might have put to a Kentish jury on the general issue; and he staked his whole case on the payment, which was referred to a jury within whose knowledge it lay, namely one from Surrey.

Two distinct points are illustrated by these convolutions over pleading payment. One is that the mere availability of wager had a muffling effect, even when it was not actually used. The truly special plea of payment in Surrey was allowed in the last case because wager was not available, and was not allowed on an ordinary simple contract debt because it was. The defendant who was obliged to conclude to the *debet*, and so to have a Kentish jury, was at no hardship because he need not have had a jury at all. His own knowledge was not confined by the county boundary, and he could have waged his law on a plain *Nil debet*. The second point illustrated is the extreme logical compulsion needed before a defendant was allowed to unpack the general issue and take out a single fact for truly separate handling.

Reflection suggests that the possibility of extracting a question of law must similarly have been raised by the substitution of a fallible jury for the ancient modes of trial. And if weight can be given to a silence by the author of Glanvill, the rules of inheritance form a striking example. In describing the Grand Assize, probably no more than a decade old when he wrote, he explains that when the tenant has chosen the assize, the demandant may object on the ground that the parties are of the same stock of descent; if this is admitted, there will be no assize and the case will be determined by the court itself.[32] But in his account of what happens when the tenant chooses the more ancient battle, no such possibility is mentioned.[33] Once

---

[31]Good cases on what follows are: YBB. H., 11 Hy IV, pl. 27, f. 50; H., 22 Hy VI, pl. 1, f. 36; M., 10 Hy VII, pl. 4, f. 4; M., 11 Hy VII, pl. 16, f. 4d.

[32]Glanvill II, 6 (ed. Hall, 26–28). For examples see *Curia Regis Rolls*, vol. IV, 256–7; vol. V, 75.

[33]Glanvill II, 3 (ed. Hall, 22–26). At II, 19 (ed. Hall, 36) it is said that there can be no battle where there cannot be an assize *nec e conuerso*. The statement is out of

the point had been brought out, of course, it would soon be seen as equally applicable to battle: and in the thirteenth century we can watch an elementary distinction between fact and law being grasped and refined, so that even brothers may get to the battle if one of them claims by purchase.[34] Perhaps a corollary of this process, perhaps even a part of the dawn which in that century seemed possible, was the notorious tender of the demi-mark, by which a tenant could stake his case on the factual detail at the very base of the demandant's claim, namely the seisin of the ancestor in the reign alleged. But the distinction, obvious as it must seem in the case of such legal law as the canons of descent, was perhaps only brought up by the introduction of the assize. When there was only the battle, we must not assume that anybody consciously saw it as deciding a question of fact about the ancestor's seisin and a separate question of law about the rules of inheritance. It decided who swore truly about the packaged right. Even centuries later, when we see in the Year Books the final perversities of colour,[35] the acceptance of disingenuous factual pleadings in order to prevent the jury from getting a patently deceptive point of law wrapped up in the general issue, though we can be sure that lawyers now think there is a clear distinction between law and fact, still we must not assume that the particular point raised by each case had long been known and labelled. The general issue was as prolific of new legal questions as are human quarrels.

VII

And this takes us back to our starting-point. The only reality before the court was the dispute, and the only need was to settle it. The law which emerged was only a construction made from the facts, and the facts which emerged were only the hypothesis from which the law was made, a selection and arrangement of suppositions. A court in the Year Book period, let alone at any earlier time, knew even less than today what had really happened; and in one respect the procedural framework was less deceptive. Judges could not in general state what look like given facts and then seem, as a separate process, to draw from them legal conclusions; they could at best pronounce upon single hypotheses: if this, then that. But the clarity which the rules of pleading would have produced, both for lawyers at the time and for historians today, was blurred by the primacy of the general issue. This represents a survival of, partly a reversion to, the most ancient

---

context, and may relate to II, 13, which sets out the kinds of claim (land, services, advowson, etc.) for which the assize was available. It is anyway striking that an account of battle, placed first, should be completed without mentioning the exception. The canons of descent were perhaps mainly formed not in litigation *ex post facto* but by lords (including the king) deciding whose homage to take.

[34]*Brevia Placitata*, Selden Society Volume 66, 3, 43–44, 155; *Casus Placitorum*, Selden Society Volume 69, lxxxii/64, 2/11.

[35]See Thayer, *Preliminary Treatise on Evidence*, 232. This fundamental book contains much material about the background to the questions here discussed.

pattern of law-suit: the claim, the blank denial, the test of rightness. Latent in this rightness were questions which became separated: truth in fact, and justice in law. This separation, and the true beginnings of the law as an intellectual system, could only be brought about by the possibility of more detailed assertions than the blank denial.

The door was opened by the introduction of the jury, and not quite closed again by insistence on the general issue. Apart from the sanctioning of new kinds of claim, law could then develop in two ways. First it could develop in what would have been the natural way, by the sanctioning of special pleas. But discussion of these was not directly about their substantive validity, but about whether the matters raised must not be left wrapped up in the general issue; and the usual question was whether the unopened parcel was so deceptive that a jury might be misled. Even when it was so deceptive, there was long thought to be no injustice if wager of law was available to the defendant; and this was one reason for the relatively slow growth of the law of contract and personal property within the actions of debt and detinue, whose very separation was itself retarded. But wager of law also impeded legal development by the other route, namely discussion within the general issue itself. In the nature of things a defendant was less likely than a jury to ask for directions; and he could not insist on returning a special verdict. And it was in these ways, all except the rare special verdict off the record, that law had to be made within the framework of the general issue.

But of course these two methods of development were not truly distinct. The problem associated with *Pinnel*'s case, for example, could have been brought up by a scrupulous and pedantic defendant wanting to know whether wager was safe in conscience, or by a jury asking for directions on the general issue; or it could have been brought up on a special plea in the very special circumstances of a particular kind of transaction in one county followed by an alleged discharge in another. But also, and this is why the later Year Books tell us so much more than their corresponding plea rolls, it could have been brought up on discussion of a special plea which was proposed but finally thought inadmissible. If this was so held on demurrer, of course, a bit of official law had been declared. If not, if the proposed plea was just withdrawn, as it usually was, then the law made was again off the record and in a sense unofficial. The mere possibility of special pleas therefore generated much more law than those which were actually made and enrolled. And the relative creativity of this process, compared with discussion on the general issue itself, may be one of the things reflected in the poverty of the criminal law, in which the supremacy of the ancient denial was never challenged.

The unofficial nature of much of the law produced by these mechanisms explains many things. Most obviously it explains the failure of the writ of error as an appellate process: law which exists off the record cannot be corrected on it. Then it explains the difficulty in getting answers from the Year Books, and the extraordinarily hesitant and oblique way in which fundamental questions are treated in them. It also explains the adoption of written pleadings and the decline and ending of the Year Books themselves: the process of litigation and therefore the learning of lawyers were adjusting themselves to the form in which the law now existed. The common law had been pushed into greatness because its practitioners could not quite stop each other talking about what had actually happened.

8

AN OLD PLAY IN MODERN DRESS

A Review of Grant Gilmore, *The Death of Contract*

The reviewer determined to complain about something had better pick on the title. The death in question, like Mark Twain's, may turn out to have been exaggerated. Mr. Gilmore's book is as much about the birth of contract as its death. And in a deeper sense it is not about the death of anything, but about the way in which the common law lives, perhaps the way in which any system of law lives.

To this improbable reviewer, a legal historian practicing mostly in the Middle Ages, it has given that rare and unnerving pleasure experienced by lecturers who suddenly, in full cry, understand what they are saying. From time to time, pretending that he belongs in a law school, the medievalist puts on a course with some such title as "mechanics of legal development." Part of it goes like this. The law is a reiterated failure to classify life. There have always been categories like tort and contract (the medieval words were trespass and covenant); each cycle begins with fact situations being pinned up under the one or the other without much need for thought. Under each heading, the preoccupations of the formative period dictate more or less clear rules; and the system as a whole acquires mathematical force. But as soon as the force is compelling, the system is out of date. Both the classification itself and the rules within each category formed around yesterday's situations; when today's are pinned up on the same principles, they are subjected to rules and yield results no longer appropriate. The individual lawyer cannot hope to get the rules changed for his client, but he can often try to have his case reclassified. No doubt a promise is a promise: but it may also be or imply a statement, and if the rules of contract do not effectively enforce the promise, the statement may still trigger essentially tortious rules about reliance. This is how *as-*

sumpsit began, not, of course, as the conscious device of a profession suddenly aware that its rules of contract were out of date, but as a back door to justice in a few hard cases. For the front door, the law of contract governing at the time, you needed a document under seal; this once sensible requirement of proof for large transactions was being forced upon small ones by economic and jurisdictional changes, hitting first and worst those who themselves acted on their agreements but had no document with which to attack the other side. It was for such victims that lawyers first sought out a backdoor "tort theory." But the inappropriateness of sealing wax for daily business turned it into the main entrance: most agreements were made on the footing that any litigation would be in *assumpsit,* and the document under seal came to be used only for special transactions. And so our first law of contract died its death, and there was conceived that which was to flourish in the late 19th and early 20th centuries and to die so opportunely under the eyes of Mr. Gilmore.

The medievalist's offering is of course a little fraudulent: already uncomfortable as the 17th century looms up, he never reaches the 19th, let alone today; names like 'promissory estoppel,' and 'products liability' have hitherto been dropped to suggest that it all belongs together and that the past can illuminate the present.[1] Now it turns out that it all does indeed belong together, and that the present can also illuminate the past. One might say that Mr. Gilmore has almost produced this play again in modern dress, but with the richness of ascertainable detail, the immediacy of Corbin's recollections, and the solidity of Mr. Fuller's reliance cases[2] instead of those shadowy early *assumpsits.* But one difference deserves discussion. The mechanism depends upon there being clearly separate categories within which rules are insulated, and the early *assumpsit* cases seem to have been truly seen or at least truly presented as trespass rather than covenant, in our language tort rather than contract. It was this that warded off the requirement of a seal, and development would have been crippled by a suggestion which left some traces in the year books: that even in the tort action a plaintiff relying upon the contract as a factual ingredient, must prove it appropriately.[3] The modern analogue, presumably, would be a holding that reliance entitled you to reliance damages, but did not absolve you from the need to prove consideration.

1. On all the foregoing, see the present reviewer's HISTORICAL FOUNDATIONS OF THE COMMON LAW (1969) and *Reason in the Development of the Common Law,* 81 LAW Q. REV. 496 (1965), above p. 149.
2. Fuller & Perdue, *The Reliance Interest in Contract Damages,* 46 YALE L.J. 52, 373 (1936).
3. Y.B. Mich. 2 Hen. 4, f. 3d, pl. 9; Y.B. Mich. 11 Hen. 4, f. 33, pl. 60.

But the development described by Mr. Gilmore began entirely in contract, the separate categories being epitomized by two sections of the first *Restatement of Contracts,* § 75 (consideration) and § 90 (reliance). His account of their genesis is perhaps the most absorbing passage in this absorbing book. He also gives as good an explanation as we can hope for of the paradoxical fact of the two sections in the same document: the text and illustrations of § 90 suggest "that no one had any idea what the damn thing meant";[4] it was compelled by a line of cases won by plaintiffs who could plainly show no consideration within the meaning of § 75, in many of which the courts had resorted to talk of estoppel, "which is simply a way of saying that, for reasons which the court does not care to discuss, there must be judgment for plaintiff."[5] Section 90, in short, represents a sensible, practical view taken in hard cases. "A sensible, practical view it may be," wrote the greatest of legal historians about a very different development, "but legal principle avenges itself."[6] Mr. Gilmore mentions recent suggestions that a recovery based on the principle behind § 90 is not a contract recovery at all.[7] As a practical matter, of course, such recovery accommodates plaintiffs who lack some component in the contract package other than consideration; it would also lead to greater flexibility over damages (a need, incidentally, which seems to have helped the beginning of *assumpsit*). But the compulsion to intellectualize is surely playing its part. Of §§ 75 and 90 Mr. Gilmore says that "these two contradictory propositions cannot live comfortably together: in the end one must swallow the other up."[8] Or push it out into a different compartment of the law? The animals can live at the same time provided they are in separate cages.

And it remains astonishing that they have for quite a long period lived together as incompatible principles in the same compartment; and here a geographical rather than a historical comparison may be helpful. This vigorous coexistence has not happened in England, and could not have happened. The English promissory estoppel is an anemic creature able only to release obligations; it cannot replace consideration in creating liability. Mr. Gilmore charitably attributes this difference to a more relaxed English view of consideration,[9] but the

---

4. G. GILMORE, THE DEATH OF CONTRACT 65 (1974) [hereinafter cited to page number only].
5. P. 64.
6. F.W. MAITLAND, THE COLLECTED PAPERS OF FREDERIC WILLIAM MAITLAND I, 447.
7. Pp. 66, 72.
8. P. 61.
9. P. 100; *see also* p. 129 n.145.

offended reaction when the pale English estoppel was introduced, less than 30 years ago,[10] suggests that here he is overgenerous. The likely explanation, and one which gives the story a new juridical twist, is that the English have been hidebound enough never to do anything about sealing wax. It remained possible to embody an agreement in a document under seal, and so long as the forms of action mattered the chief result was that litigation would be in one of the old actions rather than in *assumpsit*. The chief result today is that one can make a promise binding without any consideration. The kind of case in which American courts first resorted to promissory estoppel, for example, the promised benefaction, would therefore look less hard in England: the benefactor could have made a binding promise under seal, and the beneficiary relied on anything less at his own risk.

But what actually happened or not is less important than what could have happened, and however pressing the need, things could not have happened in England quite as they did in the United States. There could not have been a *Restatement* enunciating contradictory principles because there could not have been a *Restatement* at all. It is a larger proposition than it sounds. There is no room for a *Restatement* in a single jurisdiction with a clear hierarchy of courts and the rigid adherence to a monolithic precedent that is its product. There is no room either for that vitalizing competition between ideas and approaches so strikingly exemplified by the American story. Multiplicity of jurisdictions does not alter the basic mechanism of change, but it enables it to respond much faster.

The English experience may be relevant to another aspect of Mr. Gilmore's story, namely the 19th-century appearance of contract as a system, a subject in itself. He attributes to Langdell's casebook, first published in 1871, and in particular to a summary appended to the second edition in 1880, "the idea that there was—or should be—such a thing as a general theory of contract,"[11] and to Holmes and then Williston the enunciation and elaboration of that theory; Holmes's formulation in particular is beautifully expounded. But these system-builders may have found more spadework done than is here suggested, and more by way of foundations already laid. Mr. Gilmore[12] remarks that many of Langdell's cases were English, and that the jurisdictional unity in England makes for doctrinal coherence. "English case law is manage-

---

10. Central London Property Trust Ltd. v. High Trees House Ltd. [1947] K.B. 130.
11. Pp. 13-14.
12. P. 13.

able in a way that American case law has never been."[13] Another adjective would be "stifling." But it is certainly manageable for the writers of textbooks, and a cursory glance suggests that they may by the date of Langdell's book and summary have come closer than their American counterparts to formulating a theory of contract, or at any rate to assuming that there was such a thing. Where did the idea come from? It may not be irrelevant that among the earliest treatises on contract to be published in English were translations of Pothier.[14] But we would be as wrong to think of a civilian idea being casually taken up, as Mr. Gilmore may be wrong in seeing a like idea as coming out of the blue to Langdell. History had left a vacuum to be filled and lawyers' thinking necessarily requires the kind of classification with which this review began.

The Middle Ages had a concept like our contract, or rather had two concepts. Their "covenant" was about the enforcement of agreements as such. And their "contract," confusingly different from ours, was something like the Roman contract *re:* it was about the duties arising when certain transactions were executed on one side, most obviously loans. But these concepts were submerged by *assumpsit,* which expressed the matter in tort: even in the early 19th century, for example, the contractual defendant would be charged with deceit, though so formally that he did not even take offense. This made the old concepts unusable. Trespass and covenant became the names of actions and for a century or so legal thought proceeded in terms not of separate abstract categories but of separate "forms of action." The assumption that such thought is as old as the common law writs has done much to make our legal history seem unsatisfying; indeed the thought itself must have been unsatisfying too. The rise of our own ideas can be traced in the titles of books. 'Tort' was a newcomer in such a role and at first needed a subtitle explaining torts as wrongs.[15] But 'contract' had only to be expanded from its old sense. Powell in 1790 on the *Law of Contracts and Agreements* was followed in 1807 by Comyn

---

13. P. 55.
14. The earliest translation of R.J. Pothier's *Treatise on Obligations* was American but was presumably done not just to satisfy juridical curiosity: It was published in 180 by F.X. Martin, who also wrote on the laws of North Carolina and of Louisiana. Another translation was published in London in 1806 by W.D. Evans, who admired the cosmopolitan learning of Lord Mansfield and saw the value of comparative study; this edition was reproduced 20 years later in Philadelphia.
15. The lateness of books on torts is interesting. The earliest was American. F HILLIARD, LAW OF TORTS OR PRIVATE WRONGS (1859). In England, instructive titles are C.G ADDISON, WRONGS AND THEIR REMEDIES, BEING THE LAW OF TORTS (1860) (15 years after hi contract book); A. UNDERHILL, LAW OF TORTS, OR WRONGS INDEPENDENT OF CONTRACT (1873) Even F. POLLOCK, LAW OF TORTS (1887) has a subtitle referring to 'Civil Wrongs.'

on *Law of Contracts and Agreements not under Seal,* and the additions were evidently needed to bring in the original idea of 'covenant.' But for Chitty in 1826, Addison in 1845, Smith in 1847 and Leake in 1867, *Law of Contracts* by itself was enough to mark out the field. Pollock in 1876 and Anson in 1879 both expressly endowed it with "principles." Pollock, in fact, took a further step relevant to Mr. Gilmore's theme: he went into the singular with *Principles of Contract*.[16]

Pollock must bring us back to his great friend Holmes, and to another dimension of a book which could take on a team of reviewers and entice each into a different sort of irrelevance. This notice has sought to place Mr. Gilmore's insights about contract in the context of centuries. To others, the main interest will not be in contract at all, but in his picture of the American legal scene in the last hundred years. It comes almost in throwaway sketches: Williston and Corbin; the making of the *Restatements;* Holmes's dramatic lectures on the common law. A line here and a line there, and that is what people were like and how things happened. The life of the law may be all sorts of solemn things, but in court and classroom it can also be seen as something which hardly ever comes through in print: sheer pleasure in predicaments and solutions, in the economy of ideas. It is this which makes Mr. Gilmore's so perceptive as well as so enjoyable a book.

16. A subtitle notes that references are made to American law, as well as to Roman and European law and to the Indian Contract Act of 1872.

9

THE NATURE OF BLACKSTONE'S ACHIEVEMENT

That Pembroke College should devote its annual Blackstone Lecture to Blackstone himself in the bicentenary year of his death is entirely proper. On reflection, I am not sure that the Selden Society will further its objects by going in much for the commemoration of individual lawyers.[1] It may encourage legal historians in their chronic error: we attribute too much to particular causes and expect too much, as it were, of particular people. Because we know that law is the product of people thinking about problems, it is curiously hard to avoid imagining its history as a kind of Pilgrim's Progress, with a single professional mind addressing the problems raised by a changing world. The mistake is one of scale. The changes the historian can see were too large to be seen by the lawyers he is thinking about; and the problems the lawyers were thinking about were too small for the historian to see. The mechanism of common law response has been indirect, involving a kind of market in ideas. What the large change does is to concentrate demand, raising small daily problems in a particular area; and small and marginal solutions accumulate into central changes. There are no great ideas, and in that sense no great lawyers. An anonymous profession serves its day, or not.

Legal writers, of course, do not. They serve the servants; and their business is to arrange yesterday's results in whatever way will be most convenient for those working on today's problems. But you can order the past about more confidently than the present; and the writer's arrangement of yesterday's results may reach further into the future than the results themselves. We have lately, I think, attributed too little to Blackstone. He first gave his lectures in 1753. The syllabus was published in 1756,[2] and the *Commentaries* themselves between 1765 and 1769. Excluding, of course, reprints of that first edition produced for the antiquarian and scholarly markets in recent years, working editions appeared in England until about about the time of the Judicature Acts, in the United States until about the turn of the century. And of Stephen's version, first produced between 1841 and 1845 as a more up-to-date survey especially for students, an edition was actually produced after the second world war.

---

1 Pembroke College sponsors an annual Blackstone Lecture in Oxford. The Selden Society sponsors occasional lectures which are normally given in Lincoln's Inn. This lecture, in commemoration of Blackstone's bicentenary, was jointly sponsored by the two bodies, and was given in Oxford on 31 May 1980.
2 *An Analysis of the Laws of England* by William Blackstone, Esq.

For something of the order of a century the book played a central part. Then for a similar period it was a classic venerated by professional tradition, little discussed except to echo or to doubt the views of Bentham. And lately, partly in the wake of renewed interest in Bentham and partly because the time always comes for having a go at a classic, legal historians have begun to read the *Commentaries* in the way of business.³ They do not actually say they are disappointed, but they seem puzzled, particularly about the arrangement. Perhaps it was just defective;⁴ or perhaps some deeper end was being served.⁵ There is no denying the success of the book; and so far there has been little question about its influence, especially in the United States. But what was great about this urbane account of the common law system?

Our chronic mistake of scale has a corollary which is equally hard to avoid: we patronize lawyers of the past for failing to deal well with what we see as their problems. Blackstone's book looks so easy. Just think how easy it would be today to write its equivalent or to give the equivalent of his lectures. All you would have to do would be to string together epitomes of all the existing legal materials. Or would it? Who would find such a work useful? It might be useful to the practitioner needing to get his bearings quickly in some unfamiliar area of the law, provided he could quickly find his way about the book. The alphabet comes to mind, and another encyclopaedia would be in the long tradition of the *Abridgment* which enabled Viner to found Blackstone's chair. But who would be served by a compilation which strung together in however rational an order condensations of the existing law books? It would be no use to lawyers, and make no sense to laymen; and it would not be an enterprise of a nature even comparable with Blackstone's *Commentaries*.

Blackstone was addressing laymen, trying to make sense of the formal structure and rules of society for those who would play laymen's parts, and also for those who might decide to become lawyers. Would that be an easy thing today? We certainly do not do it. Even for law students, their university course is just the beginning of their professional training. From the beginning we lock them up inside the legal system, teaching them to think like lawyers about selected areas of technical doctrine, largely those which had become well established by the second half of the nineteenth century. The twentieth century and other aspects of reality, like how law-suits work, will dawn upon them later. They will know more and more law as lawyers know it; and they will learn to criticize it as lawyers criticize it, in terms of the existing framework and the existing assumptions. They will never have that overall view from the outside that Blackstone tried to give, and

---

3 There had of course been some earlier studies seeking to 'place' Blackstone; see e.g. D. J. Boorstin, *The Mysterious Science of the Law* (1941).
4 See e.g. the strictures of the scholars introducing books of the *Commentaries* in the facsimile edition issued by the Chicago University Press in 1979: A. W. B. Simpson in vol. II viii, xiii, xiv; J. H. Langbein in vol. III iii.
5 D. Kennedy, 'The Structure of Blackstone's Commentaries', 28 *Buffalo Law Rev.* (1979) 209.

never have the basis for the kind of radical reconsideration which followed Blackstone's work.

What the view from the outside requires is that the expositor should consciously reject the arrangement which generations of patchwork treatment have imposed upon the law, and somehow organize his materials around the relationships of life. Today the most intractable difficulty would be that a mixed economy has generated two intersecting systems. There are the horizontal relationships between citizens, in which private rights are conceived of as having some absolute existence. And there is the vertical system of social regulation and dependent benefits, in which the citizen can have only claims or expectations as against authority rather than abstract rights. If, as seems likely, the vertical system is superseding the horizontal, perhaps a new *Commentaries* is indeed impossible until the process is complete. Or perhaps the very attempt would hasten its completion. Imagine the reaction of a new Bentham if a new Blackstone were successfully to integrate the traditional learning about land law with planning, rent control and the like, or indeed the traditional learning about property in general with taxation and national insurance. Might he not pillory the traditional learning as circuitous fiction, and demand that the law should more directly represent the realities? But perhaps we are not quite there yet; and perhaps a good conservative had better stop trying to indicate a measure for Blackstone in terms of the present, and hurry back into the past.

* * *

Blackstone's difficulty was certainly not an overlapping between the horizontal system of abstract rights between citizens and any vertical system of benefits truly dependent upon a superior, whether feudal lord or welfare state. For five centuries and more the relationship between lord and tenant had been one of abstract rights fixed by the king's courts. The tenant's rights had been independent of any discretion in the lord; and even those fixed rights of the lord which had real value had been abolished more than a century before the *Commentaries* were published. It is of some interest that Blackstone could still write of the Act for the abolition of military tenures as 'a greater acquisition to the civil property of this kingdom than even *magna carta* itself'.[6] But for him tenures were relics, to be discussed as to our shame we still have to discuss them today, together with estates. He did not find it necessary to follow Hale, from whom the arrangement of the *Commentaries* was largely borrowed, in allocating a separate section to the relationship between lord and tenant, and another to that between lord and villein.[7]

Still less, of course, did Blackstone have to question, as we do, the absolute and abstract character of the private rights that he discussed as being somehow dependent upon the state. They were not less rights because they might be invaded by the Crown, or because the victim's remedy against the Crown would then be at best by petition. Nor were the laws less laws because they could not

6 *Commentaries* II 77.
7 *An Analysis of the Civil Part of the Law*, Sections XIX, XXI.

contemplate a wrong done by the king himself. He could not 'misuse his power, without the advice of evil counsellors, and the assistance of wicked ministers,' who were themselves answerable for what was done.[8] And although Blackstone mentions only indictment and impeachment, the year in which his first volume first appeared was also the year in which *Entick* v *Carrington* was decided.[9] The individual minister or agent had no special defence to a civil action brought by the victim of governmental abuse. This was a horizontal system of private law in its purest form.

It is with Blackstone's articulation of that system that this lecture is concerned, and not with the constitutional load that it was to carry. I believe that what he did was immensely difficult, that it was a turning-point in the development of Anglo-American law, and that it has its place in a longer and wider history. Large propositions do not become unimportant because they become stale. The western world has produced only two original systems of law. Perhaps there was some quirk in the Roman and the English character, or perhaps the necessary coincidences of circumstance are just rare. But what I am afraid may be rare is the condition of security and relative prosperity necessary for a society to develop law as we understand it. Private law supposes an economy based upon the exercise of private rights, as opposed to the management of resources understood to be ultimately at the disposal of authority. Between the development of the Roman law and that of the common law there lay the desperate times that forced societies into feudal structures, as we in turn are being forced into new forms of dependence. Against authority perhaps legal protection can in the end be only procedural: the feudal judgment of peers, our own rules of natural justice, wider ideas of due process. We shall, I am afraid, see.

What the Roman law and the common law both did was to progress beyond procedure, beyond rules about how law-suits should be conducted, and to develop substantive rules purporting to regulate in some detail how people should behave, to analyse the relationships of life into a comprehensible system of rights and duties. So far as we can see (which is further with the English materials, although much more scholarly effort has been devoted to the Roman) the two systems passed through similar stages of development. In the case of the common law (and here I do not say English law, because I think the United States were at that point a little ahead of us) the culmination came in the nineteenth century, with the appearance of text-books systematically presenting the substantive rules of contract and the like with as little reference as possible to the procedures by which they were enforced. So compelling was the result that we cannot imagine how things were ever otherwise. We think as though such books had always somehow existed: it is just that they were not written. And we judge Blackstone, who in a sense made them possible, as having made a rather pedestrian job of summarising them.

* * *

8 *Commentaries* I 237.
9 *Entick* v *Carrington* (1765) 19 St Tr 1030; 2 Wils KB 274.

In one area, of course, my chronology is wrong. Ever since Littleton there had been what can properly be called a text-book of land law; and by the eighteenth century there was a great body of intricate substantive rules for which Blackstone's task was indeed to summarize and simplify. This is not the occasion to discuss the distinct mechanism by which those rules had first came into being. It was a by-product of the process which had, as I believe, made the beginning of the common law possible, the process by which the relationship between lord and tenant was subjected to the superior jurisdiction of royal courts and so became one of reciprocal private rights rather than of dependent allocation. Consider inheritance. By using visual aids, Blackstone managed to compress into a single chapter the mass of detailed rules which would in every possible case identify who a man's heir was. For him these were the central rules about title to land. When a land-owner died, his heir so designated was automatically entitled; so that (until 1897) no process of vesting by human hand was needed.[10] And if the wrong person had got in on the death of a land-owner long ago, then his and all derivative rights must yield when the proper rule is now belatedly applied. But abstract title devolving according to fixed rules of law had been an unconscious creation of royal courts. It was what they had made of feudal customs by which, on the death of each tenant, lords' courts had taken a once-for-all decision about whom the lord should admit in his place: the allocation of that tenement was thus decided, and conclusively decided, just for another lifetime, at the end of which the lord would similarly allocate the tenement to yet another tenant. The transfer of jurisdiction made abstract rights out of claims to be allotted what was at the management's disposal, and turned what were by nature customs of good management into instant law.[11]

That is why something like a text-book, almost certainly intended even then as an introduction for students, could be written as early as the fifteenth century. But complications multiplied, Littleton was buried beneath Coke's disorderly gloss, Coke in turn was lost under sedimentary annotation, and no other general book was written about the land law as a whole until after Blackstone's death. Learning of theological elaboration was to be gathered mainly from the cases and from the considerable literature produced for conveyancers; and his simple account is an extraordinary expository feat. But essentially it summarizes established learning. People may have thought more clearly about the land law because of his work, perhaps more critically: but they did not think about it in a different way.

If property law emerges from customs about the allocation of resources, most other law emerges, by slower mechanisms with which I have bored audiences before, from procedures for settling disputes.[12] This lecture will suggest that important consequences for the law followed because Blackstone was addressing laymen and not lawyers. Those consequences oddly mirror much earlier

10 Land Transfer Act 1897 s. 1.
11 S. F. C. Milsom, *The Legal Framework of English Feudalism*. The matter will be (I hope) more simply explained in the forthcoming new edition of *Historical Foundations of the Common Law*.
12 S. F. C. Milsom, 'Law and Fact in Legal Development', 17 *U. of Toronto L J* (1967) 1, here 171.

consequences that had followed from the use of laymen in judicial proceedings. In the evolution of Roman law, the productive process was the remission of a dispute by the magistrate to a lay judge, with a formula of instruction: if you find that this happened then, unless you also find that something else is the case, order the defendant to pay so much. The sentence is almost ready to be written into a textbook or a code; and substantive rules were directly stated with clarity and economy. The English jury was handled less tidily. Questions particularly likely to confuse them might be isolated in special pleas: 'it is true that I pulled his house down, but only to stop the spread of a city fire'. Single substantive rules were thereby made explicit, but only sporadically because for various reasons special pleas were rare. More akin to the Roman formula was the judge's direction to the jury. But this was an informal *ad hoc* affair, not even recorded; and it was not at all regularly reflected in reports until a way of questioning its propriety developed in the seventeenth and eighteenth centuries.

It was through these two mechanisms and their procedural variants that, outside the area of land law, the common law grew from what was in effect a list of causes of action into a modern system. But they did not generate a system. They generated what we can see as single rules, materials which would one day be assembled into text-books of contract, tort and the like. But no lawyer wrote the books, or even thought much in those terms about the law. Why should he? He wanted the practical information in the form in which it appeared: 'yes, that is a good plea' or 'on these facts a jury should not hold you liable'. It was deposited chronologically in reports, and marshalled alphabetically in abridgments; and the only systematic arrangement of any use would be in procedural terms, in annotated formularies, pleading books and the like. I once bought a little book which has for title on its spine 'Torts and Wrongs', and the date 1720. But the title-page soon dashed my hopes: 'The Law of Actions on the Case for Torts and Wrongs, being a methodical collection of all the cases concerning such actions, viz'. (and it lists trover and certain other actions), 'to which is added Select Precedents of Declarations and Pleas'—and even the adjective 'methodical' seems to mean little more than that the cases are indeed distributed under the various actions. It is a detached bit of abridgment. But, outside the land law, it was as close to being a text-book as anything available to Blackstone.

But we are still not at the bottom of his difficulty. If he wanted to explain the law to laymen, to give as it were a consumers' view of the law, then of course as far as possible he must expound the substantive rules without reference to the procedural framework in which they existed for lawyers. But if the various kinds of action reflected the kinds of way in which one person could do wrong to another, then the procedural framework would itself provide a basis for exposition. If you had one kind of action against a defendant who knocked you down, another against a defendant who took your property, and a third against a defendant who failed to do what he had promised, it would surely be enough to state the rules which had emerged in each action without explaining the procedural setting. You would end up, as we did end up in the nineteenth century, with a classification of the law in terms of elementary legal ideas like contract and tort. But they are elementary precisely because, in a sense, they classify life. In the eighteenth century, however, the kinds of action did not directly reflect elementary relationships or the kinds of way in which one person could do wrong to another. The medieval actions had more or less done so; but, for reasons of procedure and proof, those which protected contractual and proprietary interests had been largely replaced by other actions which sounded formally in tort. For most situations there were at least two actions available: a natural one which was intelligible but did not work, and an artificial and unintelligible one which did.

Even if Blackstone had been able to overcome that difficulty, as those who stood on his shoulders later did, I am not sure that he would have thought the solution a good one. Consider his treatment of contract, which has particularly vexed some modern commentators because it is thin and distributed between three separate places.[13] Book III, 'Private Wrongs' is not about torts but essentially about the remedies by which private rights are protected; and it naturally includes a short account of the contractual actions.[14] Book II, 'Rights of Things' is essentially about property; and the major treatment of contract is as a means of acquiring personal property.[15] But, as Professor Kahn-Freund pointed out in his Blackstone lecture for 1977, there is almost nothing about contracts of employment here, because the employment relationship is dealt with in Book I, 'Rights of Persons'.[16] Having dealt with the '*public* relations of magistrates and people', Book I turns to '*private* economical relationships', the household relationships of master and servant, husband and wife, parent and child, and guardian and ward. To us it seems perverse so to divide a 'natural' category of the law. But a legal historian of the future, looking back and seeing how many rights and duties of the parties today do not flow from the contract of employment, how far we have moved back from contract towards status, may think it is our judgment that is perverse. Certainly to the young gentlemen in Blackstone's audience, taking on a coachman was very different from bespeaking a coach or buying a horse. And from Blackstone's point of view, to divide an abstract category of the law (if, indeed, he would have thought of contract in that way) may have seemed less damaging than to divide the various aspects of a daily relationship, putting the justice's powers of labour regulation in one place, actions *per quod servitium amisit* in another, implied terms about duration in a third and so on. He was, after all, not the only elementary expositor of a legal system to find a section on Persons useful.

Nor was Blackstone the first writer since the Middle Ages to address himself to a general account of English law. Finch in the early seventeenth century and Wood in the early eighteenth had written such books, and Hale in the late

---

13 See e.g. A. W. B. Simpson in his Introduction to vol. II of the Chicago facsimile edition of the *Commentaries*, xiii, xiv.
14 *Commentaries* III 153–66.
15 *Commentaries* II 442–70.
16 *Commentaries* I 410–20; O. Kahn-Freund, 'Blackstone's Neglected Child: The Contract of Employment' 93 *LQ Rev* (1977) 508.

seventeenth century had planned one; and all three had struggled with the arrangement.[17] Finch had proceeded upon a definite philosophical basis of division and subdivision of the kind which can be represented in the tabular form beloved by Hale and which actually lies behind Blackstone's *Commentaries*;[18] but Blackstone wisely kept the tables out of the book, and they are given only in the *Analysis* which was first published as a syllabus for his lectures.[19] While acknowledging all three predecessors,[20] he actually based himself upon Hale's *Analysis*; and to the extent that Hale and Wood looked to an exemplar other than Finch, it was to the Roman institutional arrangement. Both confess to the sense of despair with which they addressed their task of ordering the law. '[The] particulars thereof are so many, and the connexions of things so various therein'—and who but Hale could even have expressed the difficulty in so few words—'that as I shall beforehand confess that I cannot reduce it to an exact logical method, so I must declare that I do despair at the first, yea, the second or third essay . . .'. His hope was that his attempt would at least show the task to be possible.[21] 'It has been thought Impracticable to Bring the Laws of England into a Method' writes Wood, 'and therefore a Prejudice has been taken up Against the Study of Our Laws, even by Men of Parts and Learning, as if there was no Way to attain to the Knowledge of them, but by a Tedious Wandring about, or with the Greatest Application and Long Attendance on the Highest Courts of Justice . . .'; and at first he was 'utterly Discouraged from the Attempt'.[22] Finch's was a work of great originality, but neither he nor Wood quite got the upper hand of the technicalities in detail; and both books read a little like abridgments rebelling against the alphabet. Hale made his plan, but he did not write the book; and we may wonder whether he too would not have become entangled, particularly in the antiquarian detail. Blackstone did it. He was thirty years old when he first gave his lectures, and only a young man could have had the strength to reduce to an order what Wood, with the clarity of despair, had described as 'this Heap of Good Learning'.[23]

* * *

Just as hindsight has obscured the achievement, so do I think that it may have obscured the consequences. I shall not speak about the movements for reform or about Blackstone's complacency or otherwise. Simple exposition necessarily attracted attention to the fiction and artificiality which devious development had left behind; and reaction was inevitable. But I believe that other things that

17 H. Finch, *Law, or a Discourse thereof* (1613); for his various works and the relationship between them, see the article cited in the following note. T. Wood, *An Institute of the Laws of England* (1720). M. Hale, *An Analysis of the Civil Part of the Law* (1713).
18 W. Prest, 'The Dialectical Origins of Finch's *Law*' [1977] *Cambridge L J*, 326.
19 W. Blackstone, *An Analysis of the Laws of England* (1756). The tables are made to serve as a table of contents to the *Analysis* and, from the 6th edition (1771), to the *Commentaries* themselves.
20 See the Preface to his *Analysis*, vi-viii.
21 M. Hale, *An Analysis of the Civil Part of the Law* (4th ed 1779) Preface (unpaginated).
22 T. Wood, *An Institute of the Laws of England* (2nd ed 1721) Preface i.
23 Ibid.

happened may have happened in consequence. Giving the Blackstone Lecture for 1976 Sir Rupert Cross said that Blackstone was not, as Bentham was, one of those who changed the way in which people think.[24] But—if lawyers count as people—I am not so sure. His work was certainly followed by a new kind of legal literature. It happened even in the highly developed area of the land law. Conveyancers began to write not primarily for the practical purposes of their business, but in scholarly and almost speculative vein. Phrases like 'fee simple' had been used by lawyers for centuries to serve particular purposes, commonly to distinguish other arrangements like 'fee tail'. But to the conveyancer those were not terms of art to be used in documents: rather were they symbols making compendious reference to the possible results of their handiwork. And before Blackstone tried to explain them to laymen, with incomparably more success than such predecessors as Wood, it had not occurred to anybody that they were worthy of scientific discussion as things in themselves. Fearne's *Essay on the Learning of Contingent Remainders* first appeared in 1772, Cruise's *Essay on Fines* in 1783, and Preston's *Elementary Treatise by way of essay on the quality of Estates* and Sanders's *Essay on the Nature of Uses and Trusts* both in 1791. Finally, in 1804, there came Cruise's *Digest of the Laws of England respecting Real Property*. 'It is but of late years', he says in his Preface, 'that this mode of treating legal subjects has been adopted. Our abridgments and treatises on particular titles of the law formerly contained little more than a collection of the adjudged cases, that had been determined on each Title; disposed without much method, and without establishing or deducing any general principles'. He then refers to Fearne, to his own essay on fines, and to his growing conviction 'that the true mode of treating legal subjects, as well as other branches of science, is by a systematic distribution of abstract principles, illustrated and supported by adjudged cases'. Then he quotes Sir William Jones: 'If law be a science ... it must be founded on principle. ... But if it be merely an unconnected series of decrees and ordinances, its use may remain, though its dignity be lessened; and he will become the greatest lawyer who has the strongest habitual or artificial memory'.[25] Roman lawyers will wince, but what Fearne and Cruise had been caught by was the juristic impulse.

Sir William Jones takes us outside the land law, and is even more revealing. His *Essay on the Law of Bailments*, published in 1781, is self-consciously juristic in spirit; and one feature is the considerable element of comparison with other systems which became so common in the best English legal writing of the nineteenth century. Today, of course, we regard comparative law as a subject in its own right to be consigned to specialists, and we have grown out of the notion that English lawyers might regularly learn from other systems. But the present interest of Jones's book is his own account of its genesis. The law was uncertain, with many apparently discordant judgments: and he thought that study of these

---

24 R. Cross, 'Blackstone v. Bentham', 92 *LQ Rev* (1976) 516.
25 W. Cruise, *Digest*. The quotations are from the preface to the 1st edition as reprinted in the 3rd edition, v-vii. Cruise's quotation of Jones is from the *Essay on the Law of Bailments* (1781) 123-4.

and comparison with other systems would bring to light 'their true spirit and reason'. And this would be especially useful because 'our excellent Blackstone, who of all men was best able to throw the clearest light on this, as on every other, subject, has comprised the whole doctrine in three paragraphs, which, without affecting the merit of his incomparable work, we may safely pronounce the least satisfactory part of it . . .'.[26] I wonder, in passing, whether it could have occurred to any earlier writer to use the phrase 'the doctrine of bailments'.[27] But I interrupted just as Jones was coming to a more general statement about Blackstone. 'His commentaries', he says, cribbing from Coke upon Littleton, 'are the most correct and beautiful outline, that ever was exhibited of any human science; but they alone will no more form a lawyer, than a general map of the world, how accurately and elegantly soever it may be delineated, will make a geographer'.[28]

The geographical image is Blackstone's own, taken from his inaugural lecture 'On the Study of the Law' which became the first section of his Introduction to the *Commentaries*. The 'academical expounder of the laws', aiming to make intelligible to laymen and beginners, 'should consider his course as a general map of the law, marking out the shape of the country, its connexions and boundaries, its greater divisions and principal cities: it is not his business to describe minutely the subordinate limits, or to fix the longitude and latitude of every inconsiderable hamlet'.[29] What Blackstone contemplated was an outline map of the law seen as territory already known and mapped in detail in reports, abridgments, and practice books of various kinds; and it was from those, and not from books like his, that he thought you could 'form a lawyer'. What Jones contemplated was something quite different. Those detailed maps existed in the sky; and the law could be stated in the same kind of terms as in Blackstone's summary, only in more detail. That is what the nineteenth-century text-books sought to do. They had not existed for Blackstone to summarize. They are expansions from his reduction and simplification of the mechanical learning of practitioners. In trying to give laymen a view from above the procedural technicalities, he had given lawyers a new vision of the law.

It was not really a new vision of course. I keep interrupting when Jones is telling us something. Having said that you could not make a lawyer from Blackstone's *Commentaries* any more than you could make a geographer from an outline map of the world, he goes on like this '[If], indeed, all the titles which he professed only to sketch in elementary discourses, were filled up with exactness and perspicuity, *Englishmen* might hope at length to possess a digest of their laws . . .'.[30] The only italic type or capital initial is for '*Englishmen*'; but he is of course thinking of the *Commentaries* as an English equivalent of the *Institutes*, and

26 W. Jones, *Essay on the Law of Bailments* (1781) 3.
27 Ibid., 2.
28 Ibid., 3–4.
29 *Commentaries* I, 35.
30 *Bailments*, 4.

envisaging the production of titles in a digest like that of Justinian; though each title would apparently consist of works such as his own essay on what he calls the 'title' of bailments.[31] Justinian's were of course the *Institutes* that he would have read: his essay was published thirty-five years before the discovery at Verona. But there is an unconscious echo in his possessive reference to 'our excellent Blackstone': Justinian's men spoke of *Gaius noster*.[32]

The comparison between Blackstone and Gaius has often been made: generations of lawyers were introduced to the law by their writings. But one who is no Roman lawyer may wonder whether there is not more to it than that. Both produced their works at the end of a period of legal creation lasting some centuries, and at the beginning of a period of literary creation in which the legal results were reduced to coherent substantive systems. Perhaps the Roman law in the second century and the common law in the eighteenth were at about the same stage of development. Perhaps in both it was a stage at which a teacher of no great importance in the world, trying only to make sense of it for beginners and laymen, could make this new sense of it for lawyers too. But even at the time and even to the writers themselves the innovation would not be visible. The statement in substantive instead of in procedural terms would command the assent of instant recognition: 'of course; and he has explained it wonderfully well—except that this bit does not seem quite right'. That is Jones's reaction (and by an odd coincidence a Roman Jones could have made a similar complaint about Gaius's treatment of what my Roman law teacher would not let me call Roman bailments). Perhaps both writers were affectionately 'ours' not just as the authors of elementary books which all lawyers read, 'the old friend of our student days',[33] but, as it were, as spokesmen. The 'incomparable work' of 'our excellent Blackstone' had articulated what in the process became familiar, obvious.

Once again—and this must be the last time—I did not let Jones finish his sentence. The English digest to which he looked forward 'would leave but little room for controversy, except in cases depending on their particular circumstances; a work, which every lover of humanity and peace must anxiously wish to see accomplished'.[34] His vision is of a system of principles in the sky having its 'true spirit and reason', a vision of right answers which could be worked out and would, as it were, be final. Jones was more inclined than his successors to wear his heart upon his sleeve; but I doubt whether we can understand the legal history of the nineteenth century unless we reckon with such a vision. We have felt entitled to patronize those judges who used to say that they were not making law, only finding it: silly chaps. And conversely, we have not given much credit to the writers of nineteenth century text-books: dull chaps, they were just writing out some body of known doctrine. Of course both were making it up; but there was a sense of discovery, of intellectual compulsion. The writers saw themselves as

---

31 Ibid., 3, 4.
32 e.g. *Inst.* 4, 18, 5.
33 F. de Zulueta, *The Institutes of Gaius* Part II, 3.
34 *Bailments*, 4.

finding the pattern which fitted the rules, the judges as finding rules which fitted the pattern. Something absolute was emerging.

Of course never articulated, the vision was for a time seen from both sides of the Atlantic. But something must give way: either life or the text-books. In the United States, the text-books were put in their place. In England, Blackstone's successors as writer have joined with his successors as judge; and not just rules but even classifications, approaches to problems, have been subjected to the deadly touch of authority. But once more the historian had better hurry back into the past. No doubt the common law would have had its classical period any way. But just as procedural reform was provoked, so do I believe that the transformation of the law into a substantive system was precipitated by Blackstone's effort to make sense of the law for laymen. Nothing that he could have had occasion to say to lawyers would have changed the way in which lawyers talked to each other. And if he could not see how much more of a 'science' the law would become than he had intended, we cannot see the magnitude of what he did intend. Having interrupted Sir William Jones so often I must ask him to finish my lecture for me and pay tribute to 'our excellent Blackstone'.

10

THE PAST AND THE FUTURE OF JUDGE-MADE LAW

Many years ago an English student law society was addressed by a much-respected judge on the merits of judge-made law; and at the end questions were invited. There followed one of those silences in which the students are gripped by shyness and the senior members rack empty brains. This time it was broken by a student: did the speaker not agree, he asked, that for judges to make law was very undemocratic. It is the faces that I chiefly remember; the embarrassment of most of the company; the unthinking confidence of the questioner; the hunted look of the speaker as he wondered how to explain, without unkindness, that democracy had nothing to do with the matter. Perhaps the scene really lodged in the mind of a legal historian as a kind of *tableau* of changing assumptions. Almost the first thing an English law student is taught is that the law springs from two comparable sources, that judges make it in somehow the same sense, though not at all the same way, as Parliament. What he is not told is how recent that understanding of things is.

The largest legal changes are precisely in the understanding of things, in the assumptions upon which the system rests. And since it is the point of assumptions that one does not think about them, it follows that the largest changes are never visible until they are all over. The legal historian is generally tolerated by lawyers on a false basis: he is thought somehow to testify that all the wisdom of the ages is behind the present arrangements. But in fact the only distinctive service he can do for his own day is to raise doubts. And my aim in this lecture is to say something of the different mechanisms by which, as a matter of history, law has been in some sense "made" in legal proceedings, and then to wonder whether some ancient and beneficent process is indeed continuing.

The starting-point is a distinction which has been resisting formulation in speculative literature for centuries, and which today is lost for practical men behind jurisprudential dispute about the basis of any law. But in the framework within which the common law first grew, it was practical enough. There were two kinds of legal question: questions about the arrangements

---

* Wilfred Fullagar Memorial Lecture delivered 5 August 1981 at Monash University.

of life, which might require human adjustment, and questions about right and wrong which were beyond human reach.[1]

Let us begin with the arrangements of life. Battles must be won and food harvested; and if fighting men and ploughmen held land of their lords in return for their service, then questions presented themselves to lords' courts not in the terms of ownership of property but in those of management; and the customs of such a court were more like good managerial practices than rules of law. They were of course understood to have some more authoritative basis; and at least at the higher levels of society, the customs were largely seen as general and as resting upon the obligations of good faith imported by the almost sacramental act of homage. You could, for example, get rid of the tenant who failed in his obligation of loyal service, and take back the land which you had allocated to him by way of pay. But by custom he had tenure in the modern sense, so that you could do this only by due process, by the judgment of your court which consisted of all his peers, his equals as tenant. Again the custom was that when your tenant died you gave the place—land and job—to his eldest son. But suppose the eldest son was incapable; perhaps your court decided to pass him over as though he did not exist, and give the place to his younger brother; or perhaps it agreed to give it to the younger brother immediately, but upon the terms that when he came to die it would go to the issue (if any) of the incapable elder brother. In all this the court was in ultimate control, dealing as best it could with the situations that life threw up. The customs might give rise to confident expectations: but there were no rights and no law beyond what the court actually decided. Jurists of the realist school would have felt at home; and so perhaps, since these were decisions of all those affected, would the student of my recollection who worried about democracy.

But all this was transmuted into something very different by economic and jurisdictional changes. Instead of buying men with land, you bought land with money. To the tenant, his holding ceased to appear as an income conditional upon his performing a real service, and became instead a capital which was unconditionally his; and managerial discretions in the lord fell away—or in some cases were pushed. The power to get rid of a tenant, for example, finally disappeared because the King's courts would interfere at his instance to enforce upon lords' courts their own ancient customs of due process; and the enforcement was so rigorous that lords contented themselves with lesser means of securing what were now just fixed economic rights in the nature of servitudes. Nor was such control the end of the jurisdictional change: from holding lords' courts to their own customs, the King's courts took to deciding all disputes themselves. And the customs,

---

[1] For the historical matter which follows see S. F. C. Milsom, *Historical Foundations of the Common Law* (2nd ed., London, Butterworths, 1981).

which had been criteria for decisions of a managerial nature, had then to work in a world in which there was no management. They worked very differently. What had been a custom whereby on the death of a tenant the lord would ordinarily give the place to his eldest son now became an inflexible rule conferring a direct legal right. Not only must the eldest son always inherit, capable or not: it became an automatic event transacting itself in some juristic sky, and the lord had not even a formal part to play.

The change cuts deeper yet. Managerial questions are about what to do now, but law is not confined to the present tense. That automatic event must have happened in the sky to give something to the eldest son a century ago, although some mishap on the ground had given the land itself to his younger brother. Lawyers were driven to think of some sort of ownership and of its devolution; and such concepts can raise new puzzles affecting the future as well as the past. Consider the kind of arrangement mentioned in connection with the incapable elder son, which had become common in many situations: land was to go to A for life and then (say) to the heir of B. It had been in the nature of an agreement, something that the management now agreed that it would implement in the future. There is nothing arcane about that; and it raised no intellectual problems. But in its new habitat there was no management: if the arrangement was to survive, as unfortunately it did, it could only be as a present grant reaching into the future. That was magic enough, but even magic can make difficulties: if the grant was to A for life and then to the heir of B, where was that ownership now, if B was still alive and his heir unknown? Was it still lurking in the grantor, or could it subsist in the clouds?

Of course I have chosen a particularly absurd question to make my point. But I did not invent it. The King's judges really worried about it, and others like it: and it is largely to worrying of that nature that we owe our earliest considerable body of "judge-made law". What had happened—although of course nobody at the time could see it in the way I am describing it—was that the judges found themselves in charge of a great many rules which were not of their own making; and the only terms on which they could treat them were those of intellectual coherence. They were making sense, not of people's lives, but of rules and concepts. And so the practical arrangements of a feudal society were embalmed in logic, having only the kind of flexibility that tax planners exemplify today: the law could be manipulated, but it could not directly respond to changing needs. Landowners were indeed forced to provide for many of their needs by withdrawing land from these rules altogether, and to reintroduce a managerial capability for themselves by handing it over to friends whom they could trust to carry out their instructions. Much of the future lay there—and a weird future some of it was. But that underlying logical structure was to last until now. I like to think that a splendid denunciation by the greatest of legal historians had something to do with the final abolition of the heir-at-law.[2] But that was done as recently as 1925; and far too much of the ancient apparatus survives in many common law jurisdictions today. I have an uncomfortable theory that once any body of law can be written out in a text-book, it is incapable of true response; and there was what can be regarded as a text-book of the land law as early as the fifteenth century.[3]

For text-books of contract, tort and crime, however, you have to wait until the nineteenth century; and we now turn back to that other kind of legal question, questions about right and wrong. Such law-suits also moved, more gradually, from communal to royal courts; but, though some damaging oddities resulted from the move, there was no transformation such as that from feudal custom to instant law. There were indeed no substantive customs to transform, only customs about proof. Law-suits worked at first in the King's courts as they had been working for centuries in community meetings. The plaintiff made his claim in set terms, the defendant denied it at large, and this general issue was put to proof—not evidence to convince somebody, but an oath on the one side or the other to be submitted to supernatural test. If he had killed by accident, perhaps the ordeal would declare him Not Guilty: but accident was not a question for the court. There were no degrees of homicide or laws about *mens rea*. There was just a claim for unlawful killing, perhaps understood to rest upon some clause in a code like "Thou shalt not kill"; and lawyers had nothing to do with that.

The critical happening here was independent of jurisdiction, and may have happened at other times to trigger development in other systems of law. The supernatural tests were replaced by human deciding mechanisms, in England by juries; and jurors can be puzzled or misled. Should they say "Guilty" or "Not Guilty" if their man had killed by accident? The single rules that would in the nineteenth century be assembled into text-books mostly came into being slowly and piecemeal in consequence of that second Fall of Man. Questions about right and wrong were asked, and somebody had to answer them. But who, and how? Was this law really made by judges, and if so where did they get it from?

A realistic answer would require separate examination of each of the procedural contexts in which questions could arise; and it is important to remember that even in those in which the historian can see the judges as most clearly "making law", the judges themselves were thinking in procedural rather than in substantive terms. Here it will be possible only to mention the most important. In principle it would be for the judges alone to decide any questions arising on the pleadings, that is to say about the

---

[2] F. W. Maitland, "The Law of Real Property" (1879) *Westminster Review*, reprinted *Collected Papers*, Vol. I, p. 162.
[3] Littleton's *Tenures*.

formal propriety of the plaintiff's claim or the defendant's defence. In the Middle Ages it was rare for any but the established claims to be made. The first questions, those reflected in the earliest law reports known as the year books, were about novel kinds of defence; and they were being put up precisely because jurors could be misled. The defendant sued for battery by the trespasser he had ejected would be in obvious danger if he pleaded that previously invariable Not Guilty; and he sought to confess the battery and avoid liability by express reliance upon his justification. It was the chance that jurors would say Guilty just because he had done the deed that induced judges to allow such departures from the old general denial, and it was that rather than "the law" that they were worrying about. But still in sanctioning such pleas they were writing little sentences—few and easy ones—that would centuries later find their place in a text-book of torts; and their answers seem essentially to have been those of common sense.

The converse process, the appearance in substantial numbers of novel claims, was brought about in the sixteenth century by changes having in themselves little to do with jury trial. On the one hand the allocation of work as between the King's central courts and local jurisdictions now depended largely upon a fixed monetary limit; and the falling value of money brought in a flood of small claims, some of which were put in ways new at least to the King's courts. And on the other hand, to an extent that is only now becoming apparent, the events surrounding the Reformation brought in claims of a nature previously at home in the church courts. But there was no preliminary filter: personal actions could by this time generally be commenced without a writ; and anyway the Chancery would now seal almost any writ presented to it, leaving the defendant to contest its validity in court if he chose. In the common sequence of events, a defendant would first plead the general issue and try his luck with a jury; and the jury, as we shall see, might exercise hidden influence on these new claims. But the defendant who lost with the jury could still take advantage of a procedural relaxation which was then relatively new. He could by "motion in arrest of judgment" make what was in effect an *ex post facto* objection to the intrinsic validity of the claim. To that question, the verdict actually obtained was irrelevant: it was for the judges alone to decide whether the plaintiff had a good cause of action on the facts as he had formally stated them in the document initiating his case. They were not concerned with truth or—and the importance of this will appear in a moment—with untruth. Nor of course were they often deciding upon right and wrong in the abstract. Most of the wrongs alleged were in principle familiar in other jurisdictions; and the question was often not whether this was a wrong, but whether it was a wrong the King's court should remedy in this way. But substantial bodies of the common law were indeed "made" by this mechanism, most obviously the tort of defamation and the doctrine of consideration in contract; and though both were later forced into more or less systematic frameworks, both exhibit some of the catalogue-like quality which, as this lecture will later suggest, may be associated with judges making law directly out of raw facts.

Consideration in contract, however, introduces another and more startling aspect of this flood of novel claims, and another dimension to "judge-made law". These new claims did more than establish themselves in areas with which the common law had not previously dealt: they came to supplant the old remedies of the common law itself, and the process appears to involve the most extraordinary formal dishonesty. One example must serve for all. In the old action which a creditor would bring against his debtor, one of the ancient tests still survived: the debtor could in effect swear himself out of liability; and the end of the story is that that action was replaced by another which had to go to jury trial. But that end was not imagined, let alone intended, when the new action was first used. One version can best be seen in the context of the new actions for defamation, among which injury to mercantile credit played a part. Suppose a debtor to be in default; and when his creditor threatens to sue he makes the kind of specific promise for payment on a future date that hard-pressed debtors often do make. And now suppose that the creditor, relying on that promise, contracts to purchase other goods from a third party, which he intends to pay for with the money he will have from his debtor. The debtor lets the creditor down; the creditor has to let the third party down; the third party goes about telling others not to trust the creditor; and the creditor sues the debtor for that injury to his mercantile standing. It is a genuine cause of action in something like the modern tort of deceit; and it has nothing to do with the action to recover the original debt itself. But by the end of the century it (with many variants) is being used for just that purpose, and the promise to pay and the third party have receded into fiction. It was a development bitterly opposed by the conservatives—who are always the good lawyers. But they were defeated, as I believe, in this and in all the parallel developments, by jurors out to do justice. Until the eighteenth century—for the most part, indeed, until the nineteenth—damages were entirely for the jury's decision. Not only were there no rules about measure: there was no way of discovering how a jury had made their measurement. But the juridical difference between my two claims can only manifest itself in figures: so much is the amount of the debt, and so much for the injury to the plaintiff's credit. In a claim for the second, the plaintiff should not recover the first. But juries gave it to him, and everybody knew it. And so "the plaintiff in this action on the case . . . should not recover only damages for the special loss (if any be) which he had, but also for the whole debt". Those are the words in which Coke recorded the victory of the newer action; and they enabled the judges to remove what had become the obvious anomaly by ruling that the one action would bar the other.[4] But who had brought about the change? Clever lawyers? Not really. Once it became clear that juries were reckoning the debt in their award of damages, lawyers were almost under a duty to their clients to put the claim in this way. The judges were concerned only with the propriety of the claim on the facts as stated, not with the truth of those statements. If they were not true, all the defendant could do was to deny liability, and throw the matter to the jury. And the jurors probably had no idea that they were spoiling the symmetry of the law by finding as they did; but they knew very well that they were doing justice between the parties.

And that brings me to the last and most fruitful of the mechanisms by which law became explicit, namely the direction to the jury. Our very language betrays our own assumption about the relationship. The judge "directs" or "instructs" the jury; and sometimes we speak of jury "nullification", by which we generally mean the acquittal of a man who did the act charged because the jury, however carefully "directed" on the law, do not think it is fair. Our vision assumes, as it were, a text-book on the judge's desk. But that book was the end product of this process; and that cannot have been the relationship before there was any book.

Of even the elementary historical facts we know too little. For administrative reasons, the trial of an issue of fact by a jury did not take place before the full court which had presided over the pleadings and which would, when the verdict was reported to it, give judgment. The trial was delegated to a single judge and separated in time and place; and it was of no interest to reporters. It is the point that whatever happened at that stage was not "law". For centuries all that we have is the clerk's enrolment of the bare verdict. Nor did the full court itself have anything more: there was reported to it just the answer "Guilty, to the plaintiff's damage of so much" or "Not Guilty"; and that was all it needed to give judgment.

Common sense suggests that the trial judge must sometimes have been asked for guidance if, for example, the defendant had done the deed while drunk. But the most such dialogues can have done was to contribute to professional tradition among lawyers. They could not create law until they could formally be made the basis of a judgment by the full court; and it was not until the seventeenth century that it became regularly possible, at the stage at which the verdict was reported to the full court, to raise any questions about the basis upon which it had been reached. Various mechanisms then came into being, of which the simplest was the "motion for a new trial" on the ground that the judge had misdirected the jury: the defendant, for example, had produced evidence that the harm was accidental and the judge had told the jury that that was legally irrelevant.

---

[4] *Slade's* case (1602) 4 Co. Rep. 92b, 94b; 76 E.R. 1074, 1077.

Nor is the previous blankness of the verdict just a small fact about the history of the common law. There could be no law about all those questions which had been left to the jury within the general issue. The opportunities for departing from it, for making a special plea, had been remarkably limited; and the guiding principle had been the risk of confusing jurors, and not what modern lawyers would regard as the intrinsic importance of the question. Why is it, for example, that questions of fault in the law of torts are not discussed in law reports until the seventeenth century—and mostly much later? Is it really that civilisation was only then dawning, dispelling some primitive darkness of "absolute liability"? Of course not. The questions had always been there, among all the other questions left to juries in the general issue. But it was only now that they were becoming questions of law.

This basic fact about the late emergence of so large a proportion of the possible legal questions is, I hope, by now familiar to legal historians. I have been boring them about it for some time.[5] But consider its implications for our assumption that the answers to all those questions became "judge-made law". It is true that the full courts made them into law when they articulated the answers in judgments concerning, for example, the propriety of the single judge's direction. But where did they get the answers from? Were they, and was the single judge, evolving them by some process of introspection? Had they suddenly annexed right and wrong to themselves? Surely not. The answers were not first given by judges at all. So long as the questions were understood to be for the jury, he was not telling them: he was helping them to focus their own ideas of right and wrong. There are still traces in the law today. The reasonable man, for example, first lived in directions to juries, where he was indeed an aid to focussing their minds. Nor did he begin as a sort of Mr Average: in legal English the word "reason" was slow to lose its French connotations, and the reasonable man began as the rightful man. What lawyers first articulated, and then appropriated, had begun as something more than the decent instincts of society: it had been the same right and wrong that had once been brought to bear within ordeals, then found by jurors searching their conscience.

The appropriation of right and wrong by lawyers led into another process. As enough individual propositions of law became, as it were, explicit, there was the intellectual impulse to fit them together into a system; and as with the land law four centuries earlier, the end of that was the exposition of substantive rules of law as an object of study for their own sake in text-books. The whole of the law was becoming seen as a discipline akin to mathematics, in which answers could often be worked out; and for better or worse intellectual coherence was now a criterion in its own right. There

---

[5] See also S. F. C. Milsom, "Law and Fact in Legal Development" (1967) 17 *Uni. Toronto L.J.* 1, here 171.

followed, culminating in the late nineteenth century, a kind of golden age. Propositions were being made explicit and fitted into a framework; and there must have been that wonderful sense of finding right answers that comes to those who do crossword puzzles, and sometimes even to scholars. In today's climate, perhaps it is only an insistently literal mind like mine that can believe in the sincerity of all those judges who used to say they were not making law, only finding it. But I believe in it, and believe also that our modern view of judge-made law is possible only in a society which understands itself to have grown out of ideas like right and wrong. But I anticipate.

That golden age can itself be seen as the end of a cycle of legal development. Right and wrong had been captured and written down in books. The logical thing to do then, as some lawyers at the time thought, was to write them down in a code, so that ordinary people could see and understand at least the basic principles of the law. But most lawyers supposed that development would go on; and for them there was a different logical thing to do, as some thought in England and many more in the United States. Text-books could hardly be banned, but they could be treated as without authority, no more than slightly disreputable cramming aids for students facing examinations.[6] English judges for a time clung to the whimsical barrier that living authors could not be cited to them; but in England, and I think in the whole common law world, though least of all in the United States, text-books have been allowed to get the upper hand. And in England, at any rate, we have the worst of both worlds. The textbooks do nothing to make the law accessible to ordinary people; but the systems they perpetuate are as constricting as any code.

I shall leave my golden age with one last observation. It is about the texture of the law, the strength and simplicity of its judgments. Consider *Rylands* v. *Fletcher* just over a century ago. A new problem had arisen about fault in the law of torts; and of course I have chosen it as one aspect of a wider problem to which this lecture will return. If a large-scale operation is carried on with all due care, but is such that accident may bring large-scale disaster to outsiders, who should bear the loss if such accident befalls? For the particular kind of situation before them, the Court of Exchequer Chamber gave a clear answer in a judgment occupying ten printed pages, and the House of Lords affirmed it in six, citing three cases.[7]

Comparisons are odious, and I hope I shall not be understood just as saying that there were giants in those days. But compare reports since, say, the Second World War. Decisions of that order of magnitude are not found. Longer judgments cite more cases to settle smaller questions less clearly. Sometimes indeed the reader (or at least one reader) finishes without

[6] See for example Sir Frederick Pollock, *A First Book of Jurisprudence for Students of the Common Law* (2nd ed., London, Macmillan 1904) p. 312 fn. 1.
[7] (1866) L.R. 1 Exch. 265; (1868) L.R. 3 H.L. 330.

knowing quite what has been settled, sure only that the intention was not to be "wrong" in the sense of being inconsistent with the numerous authorities discussed. It is an intellectual process, and a very expensive one. And just as the growing mass of authority adds to the running expense of the process, so does the expense add a moralistic force to authority: since litigation is ruinous, it is argued, the worst thing a judge can do is to introduce any uncertainty about what is already settled. The abdication of responsibility for adjustment to change would perhaps be a price worth paying if one could be sure of what seems to be the underlying hypothesis, namely that each point decided reduces the number of possible legal disputes. But if, as I fear, the process is essentially one of descent into lower levels of detail, then each detail settled will allow yet smaller details to come into question, and the benefit is largely illusory.

But the historian should stick to his past; and my aim is to enquire whether this change in the texture of judge-made law can be related to other changes. Firstly there is a series of mechanical changes all intended only to make the system cheaper and more efficient. One of them is too obvious to need much discussion. Reorganization of our courts in the later nineteenth century produced for the first time a single hierarchy; and authority has not since been kept in check as in most other great common law countries by a multiplicity of jurisdictions. The same reorganization made a change which is less obviously relevant. The old full courts were abolished, their effective place being taken by the Court of Appeal; and the single judge, who previously had just presided over the jury trial, became in his sole person a sitting of the court. Before this change a few reporters had begun to interest themselves in his doings; but such reports were understood to be of little authority. It is otherwise now: judge-made law is the product of many individuals working separately, and not just of more or less stable groups; and the number of reportable decisions is of course greatly increased.

Nor is it just that the single judge decides without colleagues on the bench. He now also decides civil cases without a jury; and I believe this to be a far more important change. Of course nobody had anything in mind except to make law-suits cheaper. After all, the law was now written out in books, and it seemed wasteful to make the judge explain it to the jury so that they could apply it to the facts that they would find, when judges could find the facts just as well for themselves. But the consequence, I believe, was that the common law broke, without noticing, through a natural boundary between law and fact, and began that descent into ever lower levels of detail. The boundary had been the need to explain to laymen all the law possibly involved in a dispute within a reasonable compass, and on the basis that it was then for the laymen to decide what the facts actually were and to apply to them the law so explained. Roman lawyers will see an analogy with the formulary system. It was the need to comprehend all the factual possibilities within a direction which the laymen could understand and remember that kept the law at a certain level of abstraction, and made for simplicity and strength. But today's judge finds his own facts and finds them first; and then he can pick upon any detail and make it legally relevant to his decision.

In one sense of course, it makes no difference to the realities of deciding the individual dispute. Somebody must apply his mind to the details. But under the old system the law itself was stated in terms which left the details to the discretion of the jury; for them, the question might be whether the defendant had behaved as a reasonable man. The weight given to the details was confined to the jury room, and not stated in the verdict or fed back into the system to make new law. Today's judge, however, has a book which lists all the things that his predecessors have decided the reasonable man does or does not do, and the details upon which he now picks will add to the list, add another little rule to the law. The question is whether society or justice is served by this particularisation.

One mechanism of adjustment to the times must surely be lost. Rules stated in terms which left details to discretion were, so to speak, "index-linked". The jury's reasonable man, for example, was a standard which changed automatically with the times. But if you write down all the things he should and should not do, you have rules that can be changed only by legislation. Detailed statement makes for rigidity. But there is a more important aspect of this, one which introduces another change in the texture of judge-made law; and this change has nothing to do with procedure. The law that had to be reducible to directions to laymen had to be law which they could understand and respect, which laymen could feel under some moral duty to obey. But can we really think today that ordinary people go about trying to obey the law of torts? On the contrary, if there is an accident followed by a law-suit, the loser commonly regards the law-suit as a blow of fate as capricious as the accident itself. The judge, talking only to other lawyers, does not have to and does not state the law in terms acceptable to laymen. Nor is this just a matter of inadvertence, a lapse from simple statement because it was the discipline of formulating directions that kept statements simple. There is an independent change in quality. To an increasing extent the law is indeed no longer about how people should behave, but about whose insurance company should pay.

I am not quite changing the subject in turning to another possible loss suffered by the law with the disappearance of jury trial. It carried an inherent ability to adjust only so far as the law was stated in terms which, like the "reasonable man", left juries to apply their own standards. But it was also a means by which ordinary people could at least signal to lawyers their sense that adjustment was needed. In the last days of civil juries in

England, judges and other lawyers kept grumbling that tort actions were going wrong: there was no evidence of such fault in the defendants as would make them liable according to the law in the books, but the verdict had gone against them apparently because they were a rich corporation or because the jury had somehow learnt that they were insured. It was a form of "nullification". But instead of grumbling, perhaps those lawyers should have wondered about the law in the books. Perhaps the message of those juries was essentially the same as one that in England we are now picking up at second-hand from across the oceans, and considering whether to embody in legislation. Modern technology has made fault hard to locate, and capable of causing damage out of all proportion to the fault itself; and the law of torts everywhere is moving away from fault and towards utilitarian considerations like who can be expected to insure. The particular changes which have followed in other common law jurisdictions, and which may follow in England, would hardly be possible without legislation. Even vision and strength like that behind *Rylands* v. *Fletcher*[8] could hardly have overcome *Donoghue* v. *Stevenson*[9] to reach to "product liability" and other recent manifestations of the "no-fault" idea. But still those juries might have made us think.

My present concern, however, is not so much with legal adjustment as with the change in the nature of the law shown by these developments. Even in those areas of the law which were "judge-made" in the usually accepted sense, we seem indeed to have grown out of right and wrong. Instead of justice between man and man in the single case, we think in utilitarian terms or those of social good. But it has been a thesis of this lecture that nobody saw judges as making right and wrong: they were articulating, or in their own language "finding", something absolute. And to that kind of "judge-made law", the worry of my student questioner about democracy was irrelevant indeed. But utilitarian considerations and those of social good belong to that other kind of legal question from which this lecture started, and to which the whole body of the law is now returning: questions are about the arrangements of life, and they require a response which is partly managerial. What is the place of judge-made law with such questions? One possible answer is for judges to accept the responsibility in full: to treat authority as no more than an argument, and openly to take account of other arguments based upon policy considerations. We know it can be done, but perhaps only on the basis of a constitution which is understood to commit a new absolute right and wrong to the care of the judiciary. The logical alternative is to accept the student's dogma in full, and to see judges as applying but not making law. The practical consequence would be a measure of codification, followed no doubt by the growth of a

---

[8] Ibid.
[9] [1932] A.C. 562.

new but less cumbersome case law about the interpretation of the code. But again we seem in England to have the worst of both worlds by carrying on upon the old assumptions. It is understood that judges do make law; but they almost always bow to that student of mine and say that its adjustment is not their business. Legislative resources, in time and otherwise, are insufficient. And the great apparatus of case law remains in being although it can do little more than refine authority into yet further detail.

But the serious harm is not just in ineffective adjustment to change. It is in the loss of moral authority suggested by the student's question, a loss which I have mostly discussed in terms of the disappearance of the civil jury, although of course the shift from a moral basis for the law itself had its own separate causes. English judges are now confronted by a task incomparably more important than any further development of their traditional areas, precisely because of the changed basis and texture of the law. Most legislation today does not adjust the law in the traditional sense. It withdraws matters from it, and hands them over to managerial bodies. The logical end of the "no-fault" movement in torts has already been demonstrated: you can simply abolish much of your law of torts, and have the job done by a system of national insurance. Or consider what is happening in England to that law of real property which crystallised out so early. Nobody now really thinks of bringing it up to date: but it is beginning to slip into irrelevance. The real economic interests in a piece of land depend increasingly not upon the formal legal rights, but upon the decisions of the planning committee, the rent control officer, and similar authorities. And that itself is only a part of the process by which the traditional forms of property are losing importance to the institutions by which people really live, the national health service, social insurance benefits and the like. At different speeds, much of the Western world is moving back to dependent structures of which the feudal unit was a simple model. In such a structure the obligations of society are not between man and equal man: they are, as it were, in the vertical dimension, between manager and managed, between those with the power to allocate and those with some entitlement to allocation. So long as the legislature casts those entitlements in terms of definite rules and rights, of course, there is no problem about judicial control. But one of the pressures behind the whole shift is that which has pushed the law itself off principles and into details. Complexity defies specification. There are too many details, too many possible factors; and in the end you have to leave it to somebody's discretion. In this respect, too, the fevered imagination of the historian can see history running backwards: but now the discretion is that of administrators, not juries. But juries were generally thought to do justice in a way which may be beyond the most detailed rule of law. Let me make my point in terms of a dreadful heresy. The more you refine your law of taxation to stop avoidance, the more you catch situations which might more justly have been left alone, and the more economic distortion you produce as people arrange their affairs with an eye to the revenue rather than the natural market. But you do not stop avoidance, or produce among people at large the belief that justice is being done. Society pays a great price for its rule of law in this area, not least in disrespect for the law itself. Perhaps even in so central a citadel it would be wiser and more just to accept guidelines for a discretion rather than a capricious multitude of rules, and to concentrate the law upon ensuring that the discretion is properly exercised.

It is in such control that the important future lies for judge-made law. A historian who has in his time tried to teach more law than he ever knew, remembers wondering what it was about administrative law that made it more absorbing than any of the traditional subjects. It is today's legal history. Such control can of course only be procedural, exactly the kind of due process by which, as I believe, the King's courts first imposed control upon feudal courts more than eight centuries ago. But history was on their side then. And the due process which they used as their instrument, the judgment of peers, was not their creation: it was universally accepted in feudal custom. Our judges, beginning from slender materials and to that extent unconstrained by authority, have already worked elementary ideas of fairness up into an impressive body of law. The question is whether, in a secular world and without the external authority of a fundamental document, they will be understood as articulating a new right and wrong for the new relationships of society.

FORMEDON BEFORE *DE DONIS*

THE classical entail was protected by three writs of formedon. If the issue in tail came to an end and no remainder had been limited, the grantor or his heir recovered by formedon in the reverter; formedon in the remainder secured the analogous position of one to whom a remainder had been limited after the entail; and the issue in tail enforced their rights by formedon in the descender. The state of the common law before the statute *De Donis Conditionalibus* of 1285 [1] has in certain particulars been doubtful, and the questions mainly canvassed have been about the existence of these writs before that date. When the existence of any writ is established, it becomes equally important to ascertain the uses to which it was put.

There has never been much doubt that formedon in the reverter existed before *De Donis*,[2] and its evolution can now be traced. It began, at least as early as 1219, as a writ of entry explaining fully why the land *debet reverti*.[3] About the middle of the century it adopted the language of escheat [4] and, like the writ of escheat itself,[5] lost the form of a writ of entry [6]; so closely did it then resemble its twin that it was even known as a writ of escheat.[7] Maitland found that it still occurred in this form late in Henry III's reign, but was rare; and that it had parted from escheat and taken its final form, and also become quite common, immediately before the statute.[8] No example is in print, and this opportunity is taken to publish one, with the writ in its final form, pleaded in 1275. The first of the two cases below is transcribed from the roll of the Common Pleas for Hilary term, 3 Edw. 1.[9]

Whether formedon in the remainder existed at common law was the subject of a famous dispute. Challis [10] said it did not, arguing that there could be no remainder after a conditional fee:

---

[1] Stat. 13 Edw. 1, c. 1.
[2] The statute itself says "Breve per quod donator habet recuperare suum, deficiente exitu, satis est in usu in cancellaria." See the references in Holdsworth, H.E.L., Vol. III, 5th ed., p. 18, note 1.
[3] Bracton's *Note Book*, pl. 61.
[4] See the writs appended by "the annotator" to Bracton's *Note Book*, pl. 487; and *Casus Placitorum*, S.S. Vol. 69, p. 30, writ. 1.
[5] For examples of escheat in the form of a writ of entry see Bracton's *Note Book*, pll. 402, 462, 597.
[6] Maitland, Coll.Papers, Vol. II, p. 143; *Brevia Placitata*, S.S. Vol. 66, pp. cxiv, 203.
[7] Maitland, Coll.Papers, Vol. II, p. 143.
[8] P. & M., Vol. II, p. 28; see also p. 23, note 2.
[9] C.P. 40/8, m. 4
[10] *Real Property*, 3rd ed., pp. 428 *et seq.*

Maitland [11] pointed to the mass of grants which purported to create such remainders, and urged that their authors "knew their own business, and were not devising futilities." The issue seemed to be settled when Mr. Humphreys [12] printed in the *Cambridge Law Journal* what looked like a formedon in the remainder from a register earlier than the statute; but Professor Bailey [13] questioned his interpretation of the evidence, and it cannot be taken as proving the point.[14] There are, however, other grounds for the same conclusion. A form of the writ occurs, next to an early version of formedon in the reverter, in a manuscript of *Casus Placitorum* [15] which contains no formedon in the descender. Again, Britton [16] and Fleta [17] both say that if the grantee in tail dies seised, the heir in tail may recover by mort d'ancestor; but if there is no heir in tail, the remainderman must use a formedon. Both were writing a few years after the statute; but there is some reason to think that in these passages they did not take it into account.[18] What they say about the availability of mort d'ancestor was true before the statute, and was later said to have become untrue because of it; the heir had been given formedon in the descender and could no longer use the assize.[19] Britton and Fleta, moreover, are only repeating a passage in Bracton,[20] the sole difference being that they refer to formedon by name while he speaks of *aliud breve*. It may therefore be that formedon in the remainder, or something like it, is as old as Bracton. The writer has seen no example in the plea rolls, but he has not been seeking formedons and found those printed below only by accident.

[11] Coll.Papers, Vol. II, pp. 174 *et seq.*
[12] *Cambridge Law Journal*, Vol. VII, pp. 238 *et seq.*
[13] *Cambridge Law Journal*, Vol. VIII, p. 275, note 9. Professor Bailey suggests that the writ may have been for the survivor of two joint tenants in tail; this seems more likely than Mr. Humphreys' interpretation.
[14] Professor Plucknett has told me, with particular reference to this writ, that manuscript registers often make mistakes in using initials for the parties.
[15] S.S. Vol. 69, p. 30, writ 2. This manuscript was transcribed early in the fourteenth century (p. xiii); but if the writ had been interpolated then, one would suppose that it would have been in its final form, and also that a formedon in the descender would likewise have been interpolated. Writ 1 is a formedon in the reverter, speaking in terms of escheat, and still in the form of a writ of entry; and is very like a specimen given by the compiler of Bracton's *Note Book* (see note 4 above). If they are indeed contemporary, writ 2 may be approximately the one which Bracton promised to give but did not (see note 20 below).
[16] Ed. Nichols, Vol. II, p. 120.
[17] Ed. 1685, p. 288.
[18] *Cf.* Nichols, in his edition of Britton, Vol. I, p. 236, note 1.
[19] Y.BB. 3 & 4 Edw. 2, S.S. Vol. 22, pp. 112–115; 6 Edw. 2, S.S. Vol. 34, pp. 43–44; 10 Edw. 2, S.S. Vol. 52, pp. 132–138, all *per* Bereford. But see Plucknett, *Statutes and their Interpretation in the Fourteenth Century*, p. 130; and *The Medieval Bailiff*, p. 20, note 1.
[20] ff. 262b, 263. At f. 69 he says he will give the writ, but does not; see Bracton and Azo, S.S. Vol. 8, p. 243. The writ in *Casus Placitorum* may be of about this date; see note 15 above.

The existence of formedon in the descender at common law became a matter of doubt soon after the statute and has continued so until the present day. Opinions expressed in the Year Books [1] are as definite as they are contradictory. Coke affirmed it in one place,[2] denied it in another,[3] and in a third [4] took refuge in the sentence " some have holden that there was a Formedon in the Discender at the Common Law." Reeves [5] thought that it did not exist, Maitland [6] that it did, Holdsworth [7] that it did not. In fact it did. The second of the two cases below is a formedon in the descender pleaded in the same term as the formedon in the reverter; it is likewise transcribed from the roll of the Common Pleas for Hilary term, 3 Edw. 1.[8]

It is important that this evidence should not be misunderstood. The statute was not declaratory. Nobody had any remedy before 1285 if the tenant in tail had issue and, being under no incapacity, conveyed the land away. The formedon in the reverter printed below was brought by the heir of the grantor upon the death of the grantee *sine herede de corpore suo legitime procreato*. The tenant's vouchee pleaded that the grant had been in fee simple, and a jury found that it had. There is no way of telling how the vouchee had come to the land. It seems likely that both formedon in the reverter and formedon in the remainder were available against the grantee's alienee if no issue had been born, against his heir general if he had died seised leaving no issue, and against a disseisor or intruder. That is to say, they probably provided what protection there was before the statute. Formedon in the reverter doubtless evolved, together with the writ of escheat, from special writs of entry [9]; and Bracton's *aliud breve* may have been some earlier variant of formedon in the remainder [10]: but there is no reason to think that situations covered after the statute by these writs were previously covered by other general writs.[11]

---

[1] Y.BB. 21 & 22 Edw. 1, R.S., pp. 321–325; 3 & 4 Edw. 2, S.S. Vol. 22, pp. 40–45; *ibid.*, pp. 112–115; 6 Edw. 2, S.S. Vol. 34, pp. 43–44; 9 Edw. 2, S.S. Vol. 45, pp. 10–12 (for further proceedings in this case see K.B. 27/236, m. 103); 10 Edw. 2, S.S. Vol. 52, pp. 132–138, and Holdsworth's comment at p. xiii; 3 Edw. 3, Mich., pl. 2; 5 Edw. 3, Mich., pl. 7. See also the Y.B. references in note 15 below.
[2] Co.Litt., 19a.
[3] 2 Inst., 336.
[4] Co.Litt., 60b.
[5] 3rd ed., Vol. II, p. 321.
[6] Coll.Papers, Vol. II, p. 160, n. 2.
[7] H.E.L., Vol. III, 5th ed., p. 18.
[8] C.P. 40/8, m. 53. The case had started earlier; C.P. 40/5, m. 36d.
[9] See above, and the references in notes 3 to 8, p. 223.
[10] See above, and notes 15 to 20 above.
[11] The remainderman's rights must have depended wholly upon his formedon. For the reversioner, a writ of right or a writ of entry would *a priori* seem possible: but if the writer is correct in thinking that formedon in the reverter

The contrary is true of formedon in the descender, which seems to have been put to a very limited use at common law. No writ was available if the grantee had alienated; protection in that case was the innovation of the statute. There is no direct evidence about the remedy of the issue if the grantee had been disseised [12] or had alienated while lacking capacity [13]; but a writ of entry would seem appropriate,[14] except perhaps if the issue was not heir general. Finally, if the grantee had died seised, the issue normally had mort d'ancestor.[15] In this case, however, if the issue was not heir general, as where the grant was to the grantee and the issue of his second marriage and there was a son by his first marriage, mort d'ancestor would not on principle suffice.[16] Whether it was brought against the heir general himself or one claiming through him, or against a stranger, the issue entitled by the *forma doni* would lose on the points of the assize; he was not *propinquior heres*. In 1561 Serjeant Bendlowes [17] suggested that formedon in the descender existed before the statute to meet just this case, which must have been rare, of the issue not being heir general. After the confusion in the Year Books [18] there can hardly have been a reliable tradition, and we can only speculate whether he had looked at old plea rolls or was making a brilliant

---

itself evolved from a writ of entry, both possibilities are accounted for; one would not resort to a writ of right when he could have the lower remedy.

[12] Holdsworth, H.E.L. Vol. III, 5th ed., p. 18, suggested that mort d'ancestor was available here; but this suggestion must have been made *per incuriam*.

[13] When Coke, Co.Litt., 19a, said that formedon in the descender did exist at common law, this was the use which he attributed to it.

[14] This suggestion is an inference from the availability of mort d'ancestor if the grantee died seised. It is to some extent borne out by a passage in Constable's Reading on the statute in 1489; *Readings and Moots at the Inns of Court*, Vol. 1, S.S. Vol. 71, at pp. 199 *et seq*.

[15] Bracton, ff. 262b, 263; Britton, ed. Nichols, Vol. II, p. 120; Fleta, ed. 1685, p. 288; Y.BB. 30 & 31 Edw. 1, R.S., p. 14; 1 & 2 Edw. 2, S.S. Vol. 17, pp. 79–80; *ibid*., p. 170; 3 Edw. 2, S.S. Vol. 20, pp. 133–134; 3 & 4 Edw. 2, S.S. Vol. 22, p. 10; *ibid*., pp. 27–28; *ibid*., pp. 112–115; 5 Edw. 2, S.S. Vol. 63, pp. 76–94; 11 Edw. 2, S.S. Vol. 61, pp. 34–41; 12 Ric. 2, A.F., at pp. 48–49; Reeves, 3rd ed., Vol. II, p. 321. *Contra*, Y.BB. 5 Edw. 2, S.S. Vol. 31, pp. 120–122; 6 Edw. 2, S.S. Vol. 34, pp. 43–44; 10 Edw. 2, S.S. Vol. 52, pp. 132–138, *per*, respectively, Bingham, Inge, and Ingham (in each case his seems a minority view). Record evidence is unlikely to be found because the record of an assize would not normally disclose the form of the grant. In 1231 the issue entitled under a *maritagium* brought a writ of entry; Bracton's *Note Book*, pl. 487. In the light of what follows, it is perhaps interesting that the tenant in this action was the mother's second husband, who was claiming curtesy; an assize might have led to difficulty.

[16] Maitland found a case of 7 Edw. 1 in which the issue in tail actually recovered in mort d'ancestor against the heir general, but questioned whether he could have done so if the latter had "wisely abstained from special pleading"; P. & M., Vol. II, pp. 28–29.

[17] In *Willion* v. *Berkley*, Plowden, pp. 223 *et seq*., at p. 239. The suggestion was noted by Booth, *Real Actions*, at pp. 139–141, and by Hargrave in his Note 5 to Co.Litt., 19a. Challis, *Real Property*, 3rd ed., at p. 84 n., referring to Hargrave, thought the suggestion " plausible."

[18] See the references in note 1, p. 225, and note 15, above.

conjecture.[19] Whichever it was, he was right. At any rate this was a situation in which the writ was used; others may emerge. The second case printed below is a formedon in the descender brought by the heirs *per formam doni* against the heir general, who asserts that the original grantor had the land only in right of his wife, that after his death the latter recovered it from the grantee in tail, and that she then made a new grant to the same grantee but in fee simple. This is denied, and issue is taken on the facts.

Buk' *A formedon in the reverter, 1275* [20]

Bartholomeus de Sulley petit versus Johannem filium Reginaldi de Grey manerium de Swynestone cum pertinenciis, exceptis quinque virgatis terre in eodem manerio, quod Ocuel de Sully, consanguineus predicti Bartholomei cujus heres ipse est, dimisit Galfrido de Chauz et heredibus suis de corpore suo legitime procreandis, et quod post mortem predicti Galfridi ad predictum Bartholomeum reverti debet per formam donacionis predicte, eo quod predictus Galfridus obiit sine herede de corpore suo legitime procreato etc.

Et Johannes venit. Et alias vocavit inde ad warantum Reginaldum de Grey, qui modo venit per summonicionem et ei warantizat. Et defendit jus suum quando etc. Et dicit quod predictus Johannes tenet sexdecim solidos et decem denarios redditus cum pertinenciis in predicto manerio per manus quorundam liberorum tenencium in eodem manerio scilicet [the names of the tenants follow], de quo redditu predictus Ocuel nunquam fuit in seisina ita quod illum dimittere potuit predicto Galfrido, et hoc offert verificare sicut curia consideraverit.

Et predictus Bartholomeus dicit quod predictus Ocuel fuit in seisina de predicto redditu tempore quo dimisit predicto Galfrido predictum manerium, et de hoc ponit se super patriam. Et Reginaldus similiter. Ideo preceptum est vicecomiti quod venire faciat hic a die Pasche in xv dies xii etc. per quos etc. et qui nec etc. ad recognoscendum in forma predicta quia tam etc. [A gap is left for the *postea*; but the verdict on this point is enrolled below with that on the other issue.]

Et de residuo predictus Reginaldus petit quod sibi ostendi quid habet de forma predicte donacionis. Et predictus Bartholomeus dicit quod carta de predicta donacione tradita

---

[19] The report gives a reference which the writer has not traced.
[20] C.P. 40/8, m. 4.

fuit predicto Galfrido quando positus fuit in seisina de predicto manerio et penes ipsum remansit sicut debuit; set quod predictus Ocuel dimisit predicto Galfrido predictum manerium in forma predicta offert verificare per patriam.

Et predictus Reginaldus dicit quod predictus Bartholomeus proponit predictam formam donacionis in brevi suo tanquam jus et racionem sue petitionis, unde, desicut nichil profert de predicta forma donacionis nisi simplex dictum suum, petit judicium si aliqua verificacio debeat inde fieri per patriam.

Postea a die sancti Johannis Baptiste in xv dies venit predictus Reginaldus et dicit quod predictus Ocuel dedit predictum manerium predicto Galfrido et heredibus suis simpliciter et non in forma predicta. Et de hoc ponit se super patriam. Et Bartholomeus similiter. Ideo preceptum est vicecomiti quod venire faciat hic a die sancti Michaelis in unum mensem xii etc. per quos etc. et qui nec etc. ad recognoscendum in forma predicta quia tam etc.

Postea a die Pasche in xv dies anno regni regis nunc quarto coram Rogero de Seytone apud Dunstapelle veniunt juratores de consensu parcium electi, qui dicunt super sacramentum suum quod predictus Ocuel, de cujus seisina predictus Bartholomeus petit, fuit in seisina de predicto redditu sexdecim solidorum et decem denariorum redditus die quo fecit predictam dimissionem. Set revera dicunt quod predictus Ocuel, consanguineus predicti Bartholomei, nunquam dimisit predictum manerium predicto Galfrido de Cauz et heredibus suis de corpore suo procreandis, immo illud dimisit ipso Galfrido et heredibus suis quibuscumque absolute et sine alicujus condicionis adjectione. Ideo consideratum est quod predictus Reginaldus inde sine die. Et predictus Bartholomeus nichil capiat per breve suum, set sit in misericordia pro falso clamore etc.

A formedon in the descender, 1275 [1]

Linc'

Adam le Keu et Amabilia uxor ejus, Henricus filius Julie de Scrobby, Phillippus filius Roberti et Milisentia uxor ejus petunt versus Rogerum de Scrobby unum mesuagium et unam bovatam terre, exceptis quinque acris terre et quinque acris prati, in Scrobby; et versus Galfridum Rape unam acram terre cum pertinenciis in eadem villa; et versus Willelmum filium Roberti de Maubertorpe tres acras terre cum pertinenciis in eadem villa; et versus Hugonem de Rollesby duas acras

---

[1] C.P. 40/8, m. 53.

prati cum pertinenciis in eadem villa; et versus Willelmum de Rollesby unam acram terre cum pertinenciis in eadem villa; et versus Priorem de Markeby unam acram terre cum pertinenciis in eadem villa; et versus Gwydonem de Wodethorpe duas acras terre cum pertinenciis in eadem villa, que Robertus de Chaucumbe dedit Phillippo Wyloke et Avicie uxori ejus, et que post mortem eorundem Phillippi et Avicie ad prefatos Amabiliam, Henricum et Milisentiam descendere debent per formam donacionis etc.

Et Rogerus et alii per attornatos suos veniunt. Et predictus Rogerus de tenemento versus eum petito petit inde visum, et habeat. Dies datus est eis a die sancti Trinitatis in xv dies. Et interim etc.

Et Galfridus et omnes alii de tenementis versus eos petitis vocant ad warantum predictum Rogerum, qui presens est et eis warantizat. Et defendit jus suum quando etc. Et dicit quod predicta tenementa fuerunt jus et hereditas predicte Avicie matris sue, post cujus mortem ipse successit ei in eisdem ut filius ejus et heres. Et dicit quod nichil eis descendere potest per formam donacionis etc.

Et Adam et alii dicunt quod predictus Robertus de Chaucumbe dedit predicta tenementa predictis Phillippo et Avicie et heredibus ex corporibus procreandis, et quod eedem Amabilia, Milisentia et Henricus sunt heredes ipsorum Phillippi et Avicie; unde dicunt quod predicta tenementa eis descendere debent per formam donacionis predicte.

Et Rogerus dicit quod predicta tenementa fuerunt jus cujusdam Julie, quondam uxoris predicti Roberti de Chaucumbe, que post ejus mortem recuperavit eadem tenementa versus predictam Aviciam; et inde fuit in bona seysina; et postea inde feoffavit predictam Aviciam tenendam sibi et heredibus suis. Et de hoc ponit se super patriam etc.

Et Adam et alii dicunt quod predicta Julia nunquam rehabuit seysinam suam de predictis tenementis postquam predictus Robertus de Chaukumbe predicta tenementa dedit predictis Phillippo et Avicie ita quod ipsam Aviciam inde feoffare posset, immo eadem Avicia semper statum suum continuavit, absque hoc quod predicta Julia aliquam seysinam inde haberet. Et de hoc ponunt se super patriam. Et Rogerus similiter. Ideo preceptum est vicecomiti quod venire faciat hic ad prefatum terminum xii etc. per quos etc. et qui nec etc. ad recognoscendum in forma predicta quia tam etc.

12

INHERITANCE BY WOMEN IN THE TWELFTH AND EARLY THIRTEENTH CENTURIES

Inheritance and Family Provision: The Background

Inheritance and family provision in the twelfth and early thirteenth centuries were affected by two kinds of interest. The family interest had no doubt produced many differing customs, and at a humble level some survived to appear in the manor court rolls of the late thirteenth century.[1] At higher levels and in the king's court more pressure was exerted by what may be called the feudal interest; and questions were asked and answered in feudal terms. The feudal dimension has been explored elsewhere.[2] Its essence is that land was not owned, but allocated by lord to tenant in return for service. The customs were not about abstract rights, metaphysical name tags stuck into the earth. They were about powers and obligations, about what individual people could and should do.

Who should do what when a tenant dies? At least formally the lord could take the land into his own hand. But if the tenant had done homage and left an heir, the lord could not keep it for himself. That he must make a new arrangement with whomever his court decided to be the heir was a settled consequence of homage before rules were settled determining in every case who the heir was. Suppose the simplest case. The tenant had been married once, had two sons and one daughter, and is survived by all three children and by his wife. However clear it is that the elder son gets the land, he gets it not by operation of law but because the lord gives it to him.

But it does not follow that the elder son is entitled to enjoy for himself the whole of what the lord has now given to him. He may be under a similar obligation to honor allocations made from it by his father. When the father married, he would have made an allocation to his wife by way of dower. That was an internal arrangement, no concern of the lord's: and now that the father is dead, the obligation to honor it falls not upon the lord but upon the heir. Similarly, the father may have made an allocation to his daughter. Normally he does this when she marries, and the land is said to be given "with" the daughter to her husband. We shall return to the language, but may mention here the difficulties that arise when a father tries to provide for his daughter before her marriage. There is nobody to whom the land can physically be given, so he keeps it for her

---

1. George Caspar Homans, *English Villagers of the Thirteenth Century* (1941; reprint ed., New York, 1960), chaps. 8–14.
2. S. F. C. Milsom, *The Legal Framework of English Feudalism* (Cambridge, 1976).

as *custos*; and then it can be argued that the allocation was never made.³ If the father's allocations were properly made, the son must warrant both the daughter's *maritagium* and the widow's dower; and it is in his court, not the lord's, that both must make their claims.

The claims of widow and daughter against the heir are of the same nature as the heir's own claim to be given his inheritance by the lord. But there is a difference in intensity. For the heir's claim to his inheritance, there is a kind of external sanction flowing from his father's homage. When we read that homage is not done for dower or *maritagium*, we are not being told just that homage does not feature in the list of incidents associated with two "estates" whose properties are independently fixed. Homage is a prime force, and its presence or absence determines many features of the relationship. In the case of *maritagium*, what we read is that the arrangement somehow changed its nature when the third heir from the original donee entered, and also that he was the first to do homage to the donor or his heir. But in reality homage could be taken at any time: the only magic about the third heir was that by custom he could require it to be taken.⁴ Whenever it was taken, two consequences followed. The less important was that the land must now bear its share of the service due to the lord from the inheritance as a whole: if the *maritagium* had been *liberum*, there would have been no such obligation before. The more important consequence was that homage transformed a provisional family arrangement into a tenure as durable as that by which the heir himself held the inheritance of the lord.

Suppose that after the father's death the daughter and her husband die leaving an only son, who does homage to his elder uncle, the present tenant of the inheritance. If now the daughter's son himself dies childless, his land must go to his heir; and if we think in terms of abstract rules of inheritance, that would be the same elder uncle. But those are the wrong terms. The uncle is lord, debarred from having the land by the homage he has taken, obliged to give it to whoever is heir on that basis: and in our case it will be his own younger brother.⁵ The land originally given to the daughter cannot reunite with the inheritance itself. It was precisely to avoid that result that homage was normally not taken so early. Provision for the daughter was at the expense of the heir, a subtraction from the resources available to sustain the services due to the lord. But until homage was done, it was not a permanent subtraction: if the daughter herself died childless, or if her issue failed before homage was done, the land simply came back to the heir of the donor. As the daughter's issue lengthened out, it was increasingly unlikely that it would fail, that this land would any way revert to the parent inheritance; and so there was no harm in stabilizing the situation by homage. It is now a purely feudal and not a family arrangement.

The special feature of the daughter's *maritagium* was therefore the

3. Ibid., pp. 145–46.
4. Ibid., p. 143.
5. Ibid., pp. 139–43.

obligation on her father's heir to maintain it, even beyond her own lifetime, although her husband had not done homage. This obligation existed in the heir's own court; but it had also an independent sanction. As against the father and his heirs, the daughter could claim in the church courts on the basis of a breach of faith.[6] But the feudal interest did not permit any such provision for the younger son. The father could make him an allocation, and the elder son could choose to maintain it. But there was no custom like that of dower or *maritagium* whereby the father could oblige the elder son to maintain his allocation, even for the life of the younger son. The only way in which the father could guarantee the younger son's enjoyment was to take his homage; and this he often did.[7] But the effect lasted beyond the life of the younger son and beyond the continuance of heirs issuing from him. So long as there was any other heir, the land could never come back to the parent inheritance. It was to avoid that result that grants came to be made to a man and the heirs of his body: the fee tail could mitigate the family hardship of primogeniture without permanently detaching land from the inheritance. But this paper looks backwards rather than forwards. The integrity of the inheritance was important because of the nature of the central transaction. When he first made his grant, the lord was not just allocating resources within his control. As the word and the act of homage remind us, he was securing for himself a man.

Women Inheriting

A lord would never have made his initial arrangement with a woman. Is he obliged to renew it with a woman? So long as the question was asked in those terms, and not in terms of the devolution of property, uniform answers would be slow to develop. But it is not only that uniform customs of inheritance seem to be later for females than for males. They are different in nature.

Let us begin with some familiar learning of the thirteenth century. If a military tenant left an infant male heir, the lord should at once take the infant's homage and so acknowledge his own absolute obligation to deliver the land to this heir.[8] But he did not make livery, and before 1176 did not necessarily take homage, until the heir came of age; and meanwhile he held both land and heir in *custodia*. At any rate at first, that *custodia* was not some special entity peculiar to this situation: we have seen that the father allocating land to his daughter before her marriage

---

6. *Tractatus de legibus et consuetudinibus regni Anglie qui Glanvilla vocatur*, ed. and trans. G. D. G. Hall (London, 1965) (hereafter cited as *Glanvill*), VII, 18 (p. 93).

7. *Glanvill*, VII, 1 (pp. 72–73); Milsom, *Legal Framework*, pp. 137–42.

8. *Glanvill*, IX, 1 (p. 103); Assize of Northampton, c. 4. For the latter text see William Stubbs, ed., *Select Charters and Other Illustrations of English Constitutional History . . .*, 9th ed., rev. by H. W. C. Davis (1913; reprint ed., Oxford, 1946), pp. 179–81.

would hold the land himself as *custos*.⁹ Now suppose that the military tenant died leaving only an infant daughter. The lord cannot take homage, and so commit himself directly to her. His obligation is still that flowing from the homage he took from her father: he must not keep the land for himself and must hand it over to the father's heir, but he has not foreclosed discussion of who that is. Again, he holds land and daughter in *custodia*; but this *custodia* is not going to end when she attains some age, and he is never going to make livery to her. What he should do when she comes of age is to arrange a marriage for her; and then he will deliver land with daughter to the husband, and take the husband's homage for her inheritance. Whose now is the land? It is an anachronistic question to which this essay seeks terms appropriate to the time. Parts of the answer are that the husband has become the lord's man, and that his holding of his wife's land can be described, like the lord's own before the marriage, as in *custodia*.

Now let us turn to some familiar documents. The interior changes by which tenure ceased to be something like a contract of service and became something like an ownership of land left few visible traces in the way of demands for conscious adjustment. The most obvious are about the regularization of inheritance and its corollaries. Not counting initial assurances to the church, this is the concern of the first three clauses (in the conventional numbering) of the Coronation Charter of Henry I,¹⁰ and of the first seven clauses of the Great Charter of John.¹¹ Both charters address themselves to the most fundamental point of all, the fixing of reliefs.¹² The earlier has to express the matter in elementary terms: the heir must not be made to buy back his land. Both address themselves also to what looks like a detail: widows should not be compelled to remarry. King John contemplates that the widow may have *hereditas* as well as dower and *maritagium*;¹³ and though he was probably denying himself only an income from sales, it is worth recalling that even in the thirteenth century the husband's death left a widow in control of her inheritance for the first time. From her father it had passed directly into the *custodia* of the lord or his nominee, and thence into the *custodia* of the husband. Henry's undertaking extends in terms only to dower and *maritagium*.¹⁴ He does not mention the widow with *hereditas*. Perhaps she was omitted by mistake, and he reckoned that she could make provision for the services due from her inheritance. That she could make such provision for the services due from her husband's inheritance is the assumption behind Henry's seeming liberality in conceding *custodia* to her or some

---

9. See above, pp. 231-32.
10. Cc. 2–4. For this text, see Stubbs, *Select Charters*, pp. 117–19.
11. (1215) cc. 2–8; (1225) cc. 2–7. For these two texts, see J. C. Holt, *Magna Carta* (Cambridge, 1965), pp. 316–37, 350–58.
12. Coronation Charter, c. 2; Magna Carta (both versions), c. 2.
13. (1215) cc. 7, 8; (1225) c. 7.
14. Coronation Charter, cc. 3, 4.

other relative.[15] This remained the logic of socage wardships. It was only when the value of military service visibly lost all relation to the actual revenues of the land that a lord would invite bids for a *custodia* or keep the revenues for himself; and that left consequential problems of waste for John's charter to deal with.[16]

But other explanations are possible for the silence of Henry's charter about the widow with *hereditas*. The simplest is that Henry would indeed compel her to remarry, in the sense of depriving her of the inheritance if she refused. The most fundamental is that he did not contemplate that she would hold the inheritance anyway. Dower was meant to be the widow's provision for life. So, as a minimum even if there were no children, was *maritagium*. Perhaps *hereditas* was hers to transmit rather than to enjoy for herself. In their dealings with baronies, it was an attitude still sometimes taken by Henry's grandson and great-grandson. Redbourne was the inheritance of Maud, granddaughter of the Domesday tenant. Maud was married to Reginald de Crevequer, who died between 1165 and 1172, and was herself still living in 1185. But her inheritance passed on Reginald's death to one of their sons; and before Maud died it had passed again to the issue of another.[17] Later, as we shall see, these events were to be rationalized in other terms.[18] But they happened. Again, when William de Mandeville died in 1189, the "heir" to his great barony of Pleshy was his aunt Beatrice de Say, who still had some eight years to live. But Richard I at once gave the inheritance to one of her two sons, then took it back and gave it to the issue of the other.[19] In each case the disposition actually made will be of interest in other contexts. But the disposition that was not made may be even more significant. The king's dealings with his tenants-in-chief seem to have been exceptional only in continuing what had been the understood powers of lords in general; and in passing over the widows, Henry II and Richard may have done what Henry I assumed that any lord would do. His charter is silent because the question has not arisen.

On the question of women inheriting in the first place, John's charter is silent for the converse reason: so far as concerned the dealings of lords with their tenants, the question seemed to be settled. But Henry's Coronation Charter has to deal with it; and it is worth reminding ourselves of the nature of such a document. The king is neither legislating nor

15. Coronation Charter, c. 4.
16. Magna Carta (both versions), cc. 4, 5.
17. *Curia Regis Rolls* (London, 1922–) (hereafter cited as *CRR*), 2:218, 223–24; *CRR*, 3:317; *The Earliest Lincolnshire Assize Rolls, A.D. 1202–09*, ed. Doris M. Stenton, Lincoln Record Society, vol. 22 (1926), pp. lxxx–lxxxii; I. J. Sanders, *English Baronies: A Study of their Origin and Descent, 1086–1327* (Oxford, 1960), p. 74.
18. See below, p. **239**.
19. *Ancient Charters Royal and Private, prior to 1200*, ed. J. H. Round, Pipe Roll Society, vol. 10 (London, 1888), pp. 97–99 (no. 59); Sanders, *English Baronies*, p. 71. Cf. Sidney Painter, *The Reign of King John* (1949; reprint ed., Baltimore, 1964), p. 263: "But no king was likely to take seriously the claims of an elderly widow to the great Mandeville barony."

codifying. He is giving undertakings about his own use of his powers as lord of his own men, and commanding them to treat theirs in the same way. But until that command is regularly enforced, there is no law in these matters except what he and other lords actually do. He may be setting up as the model what he thinks the best of current practice. But he makes law only to the extent that his model is followed in current practice. For the parties to any individual dispute, it is not even current practice that matters: it is what the court dealing with that dispute actually decides.

The Coronation Charter first deals with the living tenant arranging a marriage for his daughter or other female relative. He should speak with the king or other lord, who, however, is not to demand payment, and not to refuse consent unless the proposed husband is an enemy.[20] Some ninety years later, Glanvill makes a more stringent statement. He confines it to the tenant having only a daughter or daughters, and says that he may be disinherited for arranging the unlicensed marriage.[21] For Glanvill, there is a rule by which the daughter automatically inherits her father's land; and only by disinheriting the father can the lord be saved from having to accept the homage of one who may be an enemy. For Henry I, his more relaxed provision suggests that there was some choice about a woman inheriting. One with an unacceptable husband could simply be passed over. But customs were becoming established, and it was better that the difficulty should not arise.

Henry's charter states one custom that he proposed to follow: "si mortuo barone vel alio homine meo filia haeres remanserit, illam dabo consilio baronum meorum cum terra sua."[22] This contemplates that a daughter can in some circumstances be *haeres*: but it does not show an automatic inheritance according to fixed rules, let alone the particular rules that came later to be fixed. In terms it is a promise about the marriage of a lone unmarried daughter; and she will be *haeres* in the sense that the land will be given with her to the man chosen as her husband. Nothing indicates that several unmarried daughters would all be *haeredes*. And it is possible that *filia haeres remanserit* confines the inheritance to the unmarried daughter who had remained with her father, to the exclusion of those already married. Suppose the father had three daughters, and had married off two in his lifetime. Those two would each have received *maritagium*; and even from the family point of view, it would make sense to leave the married daughters with what they had, and allow the remaining one to inherit what was left. This is an aspect of the matter to which we shall return in the last section of this paper.[23] Our present concern is with the lord's own interest; and though he might have consented to the earlier marriages, this solution would give him the homage of the man whom he himself had chosen. Nor is this pure

20. C. 3.
21. *Glanvill*, VII, 12 (p. 85).
22. Coronation Charter, c. 3.
23. See below, p. 252.

speculation. King John had so granted the whole inheritance of William de Buckland with the youngest of his three daughters; and when the two elder and their husbands sued in 1218 for their shares, the youngest and her husband sought to have the question postponed until Henry III was of age. It was, they said, a right that all his predecessors had enjoyed in such circumstances to give *postnatam filiam que remaneret in hereditate patris sui* to one of his knights with the whole inheritance.[24]

The contention was limited to the king and apparently to the lifetime of the favored daughter; and anyway it was unsuccessful. But that was in 1218 when regularization was far advanced and all daughters understood to be entitled to their shares; and there is no reason to think it was without basis in the earlier practice at least of kings. Henry's charter contemplates a single daughter, and we shall return to the question of sharing. But even when sharing was clearly established, we sometimes find that a claim is by an elder sister or her issue against a younger.[25] Generally, of course, we do not know what had happened when the ancestor died, how the younger came to get the whole. But we do know in a case of 1201–3 concerning a royal serjeanty, a tenure in which the actual service has continued to matter. A tenant dying under Henry II had left two sisters, and the issue of the elder are suing the son of the younger. He relies simply upon Henry's charter granting the whole to his father as husband of the younger sister.[26]

We do not know whether Henry II had arranged the marriage in that case or had chosen between already married husbands. Only if the youngest daughter was the only one unmarried would she be in a specially favorable position. The general principle, if anybody thought in those terms, was perhaps that the father's homage constrained the lord to choose one of the daughters; but which he chose would depend upon her husband, as much as her seniority. In one sense, as we shall see, he chose a single daughter until well into the thirteenth century; but regularization prescribed that he should choose the eldest. With holdings of mesne lords, we only once find it argued that the lord's disposition is in itself conclusive.[27] But for baronies the king clearly chose a single sister, and supposed that his choice was final. We have already mentioned the case of the great Mandeville barony of Pleshy, when Richard I passed over the widowed Beatrice de Say, made and revoked a grant to her younger son, and gave it to the issue of her dead elder son. That son had left two daughters, Beatrice II, who was married to Geoffrey fitz Peter, and

---

24. *Bracton's Note Book*, ed. Frederic W. Maitland, 3 vols. (London, 1887) (hereafter cited as *BNB*), no. 12.

25. (a) *Three Rolls of the King's Court in the Reign of King Richard the First, 1194–1195*, ed. Frederic W. Maitland, Pipe Roll Society, vol. 14 (London, 1891), pp. 6, 30–31, 49, 54; *Rotuli Curiae Regis*, ed. Francis Palgrave, 2 vols. (London, 1835) (hereafter cited as *RCR*), 1:13; (b) *CRR*, 5:46–47, 149; (c) *CRR*, 9:14, 284–85; *CRR*, 10:19, 20, 54, 177; *BNB*, no. 302; (d) *BNB*, no. 12.

26. *CRR*, 2:25, 68, 232; *CRR*, 3:40.

27. *CRR*, 6:119, 133, 190, 199–200, 295 (inheritance partitioned earlier, dispute over land formerly held by widow in dower).

Maud, who was married to William de Buckland (whose own inheritance, as we have seen, King John was to grant to the youngest of his daughters, to the exclusion of the two elder). King Richard gave the barony to Beatrice II, or rather to Geoffrey fitz Peter; and Maud got nothing. That was in 1191. It was not until 1218 that Maud felt able to claim her share, and even then the case disappears with an adjournment "eo quod consilium domini regis non audet facere judicium super cartas domini regis."[28] In the Mandeville case the sister preferred was in fact the elder. But consider what was done and what was said in the case of Aldington. William fitz Helte had died in 1180 leaving three sisters. In 1206–8 we find the son of the middle sister suing a third-party contender, who argues that he need not answer unless the heirs of the other two are joined. To this the demandant has his answer: "dominus rex reddidit ei jus quod fuit Willelmi Helte sicut recto heredi pro ccc. marcis argenti."[29]

The Mandeville case, and that of Redbourne, also already mentioned for the immediate grant of a widowed heiress's own inheritance to her issue, both exemplify another choice that a lord might have between possible heirs. In each the sisters concerned were daughters of a dead elder son, and there was a living younger son. An important study of the *casus regis* is expected soon; and little can be said with confidence until it comes. But the question probably seemed different when one of the possible heirs was a woman. Consider King John's own case. When Richard I died there was another claimant to the English crown: Arthur of Brittany was the twelve-year-old son of John's dead elder brother Geoffrey. A few years later Arthur died, and John is generally believed to have seen to that.[30] But for Arthur's sister Eleanor, John and his son after him judged it sufficient to keep her an honored and unmarried prisoner.[31]

28. For the original disposition see references in n. 19. For the 1218 case see *BNB*, no. 8; *CRR*, 8:117, 236; *CRR*, 9:247. Maud's claim is based on the seisin of her and Beatrice II's father, who had however died long before the Mandeville inheritance fell vacant. There is no mention of the agreement dividing the father's inheritance, apparently made in 1185 after the sisters were married (cf. *Rotuli de Dominabus* [1185], ed. J. H. Round, Pipe Roll Society, vol. 35 [London, 1913], pp. 49–50), confirmed in 1198 (*Ancient Charters*, pp. 108–10 [no. 66]), and entered on the pipe roll at Geoffrey fitz Peter's instance a few months later (*Pipe Roll, 10 Richard I*, ed. Doris M. Stenton, Pipe Roll Society, n.s., vol. 9 [London, 1932], p. 139). The confirmation is less emphatic than the enrollment about releasing Maud's rights, but it saves to Beatrice her *antenatio*. From the pedigree in *The Earliest Lincolnshire Assize Rolls*, pp. lxxx–lxxxii, Redbourne would appear similarly to have been granted to one of two sisters; but compare *Testa de Nevill*, Record Commission (London, 1807), p. 344, with *Book of Fees* (London, 1920–31), 1:189. Another barony giving rise to relevant disputes was Barnstaple. See *RCR*, 1:45; *RCR*, 2:179–80; *Pleas before the King or His Justices, 1198–1212*, 4 vols., ed. Doris M. Stenton, Selden Society, vols. 67 (London, 1948), 68 (1949), 83 (1966), 84 (1967) (hereafter cited as *PKJ*), 1, nos. 2093, 2473, 3198; Sanders, *English Baronies*, p. 104.

29. *CRR*, 4:140, 161; *CRR*, 5:19, 282; *PKJ*, 3 and 4, nos. 1746, 1785, 2120, 2374, 3159; Sanders, *English Baronies*, p. 1.

30. Painter, *King John*, p. 85: "John himself saw to Arthur."

31. Her English lands were held in *custodia*; cf. (a) *CRR*, 9:13, 237–38, 328; *CRR*, 10:215; (b) *CRR*, 9:142–43.

King John's future predicament cannot have been envisaged by Henry II in his dealings with Redbourne: they were all over before Geoffrey of Brittany was dead or Arthur born. And it is very unlikely to have been in Richard's mind when he disposed of the Mandeville barony in 1189 and 1191. Both kings first chose the living younger son in preference to a daughter of the dead elder son; and both changed their minds. In the Mandeville case, Richard's first choice of Geoffrey de Say may have owed a little to the wishes of the widowed Beatrice: but the inheritance was granted to him in return for a proffer and transferred to his niece for default of payment. When Geoffrey and his son revived his claim in 1212–14, they relied upon an alleged seisin of Beatrice and upon the short seisin of Geoffrey himself; but the claim fails on an irrelevant ground and the *casus regis* question is not mentioned.[32] It could not be directly relevant to the lawsuit that was brought about Redbourne; but a view is implicit in an argument that deserves notice for another reason. Henry II's dealings had been even more high-handed. The inheritance was Maud's; and it is relevant that she outlived not only her elder son and her husband, who died in that order, but also her younger son. This was Simon de Crevequer, to whom the inheritance was granted on the death of his father, Maud's husband. Simon enjoyed it all his life; and only when he died leaving an infant son was it transferred to his niece Cecily and her husband. In 1203, Simon's son seeks to recover it in mort d'ancestor, on the basis that Simon had died seised; and so he had. But Cecily claims that his enjoyment had been only in right of Maud, who had really been seised of her inheritance throughout.[33] By 1203 inheritance was seen as a matter of rules, and rules that were supposed always to have existed; and a widowed heiress was left in possession subject only to a possible condition of having to remarry at the lord's will. Cecily had herself been a widow for some five years, and seems to have controlled the barony until her death. Looking back on what happened from that framework, her interpretation was a natural one. But it would have surprised Henry II, who was dealing in facts rather than abstractions.

Except for the fact that she had got in, the niece in each of these cases was in the situation of Eleanor of Brittany; and King John's court could hardly have allowed the abstractions to be declared in her favor. Nor should we be misled by our own label of "representation" into assuming that from the beginning the niece's claim was indistinguishable from the nephew's. The lord's need of a man merged into a general preference for the male line. A less exalted case of 1220 shows that the younger son had again got in; and his niece, perhaps for the political reason, bases her claim on special facts. On the occasion of the elder son's marriage, she says, the father of the two sons resigned (*se demisit*) the inheritance in his favor; and the father held thereafter only by grace of the elder son. On

---

32. For other aspects of the matter see references in nn. 19 and 28. For the 1212–14 case see *CRR*, 6:270; *CRR*, 7:57, 110–11.

33. See above, n. 17.

that basis the elder son died seised, although in his father's lifetime, and his daughter makes her claim in an assize of mort d'ancestor. The assize finds that the elder son did not die seised; and the younger son is left in possession with no direct discussion of the point of principle.[34] But in the same year, in a case brought on the king's own behalf as guardian, the king's court has no hesitation in affirming that the son of a dead son is to be preferred to living and married daughters: "quia . . . ipse est de masculo, consideratum est quod . . . majus jus habeat in terra illa."[35]

Sharing the Inheritance

The early understanding seems to have been that a lord would grant the whole inheritance to the husband of one daughter, but might have some discretion in choosing which. This section will consider how these two propositions changed. The next will try to make out the properties of the husband's holding.

First, the lord's discretion became restricted to his control over the marriage of any daughter. He still had a voice in choosing husbands, but lost any power to choose between them. The eldest daughter and her husband acquired a right. This change could not be complete until the king's court would regularly override whatever other disposition the lord and his court had in fact made; and it is one aspect of the invisible change that came over all inheritance. If a past choice can be overridden, you cease to think in terms of choice or even of controlling choice: you think in terms of an abstract right, passing independently of what people have actually done. There is a formula in which pedigree and chronology are the only variables. By 1200 it is assumed that the eldest is automatically entitled.[36] But we have already mentioned cases about that time in which it is an elder sister who is having to sue a younger;[37] and the uniform assumption may not be very old. How did it grow? In lords' courts the natural preference would be not for the first-born but for the eldest who was unmarried when the father died, the first whose husband would be a man of the lord's own choosing. But there is enough talk of *esnecia* (which comes in many spellings) to suggest that the first-born was thought to have some inherent claim; and she was the obvious choice for a single formula. In early usage *esnecia* sometimes denotes the right of an elder son as against a younger,[38] and Glanvill's only use of the word also refers to males. He says that an inheritance partible between males will

---

34. *CRR*, 9:178–79, 322; *CRR*, 10:136–37, 267(?); *CRR*, 11, no. 658(?); *BNB*, no. 1462.
35. *CRR*, 9:268–69; *CRR*, 10:61.
36. *CRR*, 1:250–51. Cf. the obscure *CRR*, 12, no. 1839.
37. See above, nn. 25, 26.
38. (a) *CRR*, 7:338; *RCR*, 2:88–89; *CRR*, 1:179, 180, 226; *PKJ*, 1, no. 2973; (b) *RCR*, 1:363.

Inheritance by Women

be divided "saluo tamen capitali mesagio filio primogenito pro dignitate ainsnecie sue."[39]

The word is most commonly used in connection with a changed reality in female inheritance. The lord loses any choice, but his choice ceases to be important. The invariable right of the eldest daughter is subject to a kind of trust in favor of the others. *Esnecia* is used to denote whatever features of that arrangement are under discussion in the case.[40] Glanvill's reference to an inheritance partible between males makes a good starting point. With military tenures the capital messuage was never just a matter of *dignitas*. It was the headquarters of a fee.[41] Here the lord paramount would distrain the lord of the fee; and here the lord of the fee would hold court for his own tenants. It was the heart of the inheritance, not to be allocated in dower (the usual context of its mention in lawsuits) or in *maritagium*. And when the inheritance came to be partitioned between sisters, this was something that the eldest must keep for herself, although reckoning its value as part of her share.

The essence of the parage arrangement is well known.[42] The lord still had a single tenant. The whole inheritance was held of him by the eldest sister and her husband; and it was the eldest sister's husband who did homage and who was responsible for the whole service. So far as the lord was concerned, that was that. Provision for the younger sisters was an internal arrangement within the inheritance like dower and *maritagium*. The younger sisters held of the eldest, and they and their husbands reimbursed the eldest and her husband for their share of the services. But the husband of a younger sister did not do homage to the husband of the eldest.[43] As in *maritagium*, homage would not be done for a younger sister's share until her third heir entered; and this must have been for the same reason as in *maritagium*. Suppose there were three sisters, and the husbands of the two younger did homage to the husband of the eldest: if the second sister died without issue, her third share could only pass intact

---

39. Glanvill, VII, 3 (p. 75).

40. (a) *Three Rolls of the King's Court*, pp. 6, 30–31, 49, 54; *RCR*, 1:13; (b) *Memoranda Roll, 10 John*, ed. R. Allen Brown, Pipe Roll Society, n.s., vol. 31 (London, 1955), p. 109; *RCR*, 1:147; *CRR*, 1:50, 80; *CRR*, 2:92; (c) *CRR*, 1:350; (d) *CRR*, 1:225, 447–48, 453; (e) *CRR*, 4:162; (f) *CRR*, 5:46–47, 149; (g) *Rolls of the Justices in Eyre for Yorkshire, 1218–19*, ed. Doris M. Stenton, Selden Society, vol. 56 (London, 1937), no. 304; (h) *CRR*, 8:145, 185, 213–15; *BNB*, no. 86; (i) *CRR*, 8:387; *CRR*, 9:214, 294; *CRR*, 10:17, 196; *CRR*, 11, no. 394; cf. *CRR*, 8:24–25; (j) *CRR* 10:17–18, 106; (k) *CRR*, 10:166–67, 196; (l) *CRR*, 11, no. 1223; *CRR*, 12, nos. 360, 866, 914, 1576, 2045; (m) *CRR*, 12, nos. 249, 1771; (n) *CRR*, 11, nos. 2019, 2682; *CRR*, 12, no. 256; *BNB*, nos. 924, 1053. For *antenatio*, see *Ancient Charters*, pp. 108–10 (no. 66); for the context of this document see above, n. 28.

41. (a) *CRR*, 7:25, 41, 48; (b) *BNB*, no. 1207.

42. Glanvill, VII, 3 (p. 76); Sir Frederick Pollock and Frederic W. Maitland, *The History of English Law before the Time of Edward I*, 2d ed., reissued with a new introduction and select bibliography by S. F. C. Milsom, 2 vols. (Cambridge, 1968) (hereafter cited as *P&M*), 2:274–78.

43. Glanvill, VII, 3 (p. 76); IX, 2 (p. 106).

to the youngest; and if issue of the youngest then failed, her two-thirds would have to go to a younger son of the eldest line. The homage would prevent the eldest sister and her heirs from increasing their original third share until there were no other heirs of the younger sisters. After three generations it was unlikely that the inheritance would reunite anyway, and so the dependent tenures might as well be stabilized by homage.

Except that shares are equal, the relationship between the eldest sister and her husband and the younger sisters is exactly that between a male heir and his sisters having *maritagium*; and both arrangements are a compromise between family provision and the lord's interest in the integrity of the inheritance. That interest depended upon his vision of a tenure as a source of service, the same vision that allowed Henry I to concede *custodia* to an infant heir's mother or other relative on the understanding that she would arrange for the service to be done.[44] It was the increasingly obvious unreality of military service compared with the actual revenues of the land that gave independent value to what became thought of as the separate "incidents of tenure." In the language of investment, *custodia* and escheat were the lord's residuary interest in the equity of the land. When they were what mattered, and when the integrity of the inheritance did not matter, the parage arrangement worked against a lord's interest. An infancy in a younger sister's holding properly brought no wardship either to the eldest sister or to the lord: the eldest just continued to take contribution to the service. An infancy in the eldest sister's holding could therefore bring little more than her share to the lord. Rather belatedly, parage vanished and the lord came to take homage in respect of all the sisters' holdings. But that is not our present concern.

There are many reflections of the living reality in the early records. The commonest is an express reservation of *esnecia* in claims or arrangements for partition,[45] or a reservation of the capital messuage,[46] or some reference to tenure between sisters.[47] But litigation might turn on the tenurial details of the arrangement. The question may be between the lord and the representative of the eldest line. In 1223 it concerns the power to sanction a marriage in the younger line.[48] In 1220 the lord has been distraining on the younger line, and the eldest sues to stop it; and a fine dating from Henry II is recited, which sets out the parage in detail.[49] Or

---

44. See above, n. 15.

45. (a) *Rolls of the Justices in Eyre for Yorkshire*, no. 304; (b) *CRR*, 10:166–67, 196; (c) *CRR*, 11, no. 1223; *CRR*, 12, nos. 360, 866, 914, 1576, 2045.

46. *BNB*, no. 137. Cf. (a) *CRR*, 4:162; (b) *CRR*, 10:17–18, 106.

47. (a) *RCR*, 1:147; *Memoranda Roll, 10 John*, p. 110; (b) *PKJ*, 1, nos. 2085, 2475, 3488; *CRR*, 1:157; (c) *CRR*, 10:97–99, 187, 281–82; *CRR*, 12, nos. 507, 1751; (d) *CRR*, 11, nos. 523, 1065, 2029; cf. *CRR*, 6:161, 200–201, 254, 282–83; *CRR*, 7:47, 194–95, 235, 298; (e) *CRR*, 11, no. 2090.

48. *CRR*, 11, nos. 132, 420, 742, 1331; *BNB*, no. 1596. Maitland thought the marriage concerned was that of the son of a younger sister (*P&M*, 2:277). Some mistake may have been made by the plea roll clerk; but the nature of the dispute is clear enough.

49. *CRR*, 8:387; *CRR*, 9:214, 294; *CRR*, 10:17, 196; *CRR*, 11, no. 394. Cf. *CRR*, 11, no. 869; *BNB*, no. 1639.

the question may be between the two lines. In 1225 the representative of the elder has to sue the younger for contribution to the relief he has paid to the lord for the inheritance.[50] In 1221 yet another tenurial level comes into it: the question is whether a tenant of the inheritance still holds of the eldest or has been attorned to a younger.[51] Another case in the same year shows that in this context, as in that of *maritagium*, it is not only historians who have found the three degrees confusing.[52] A quarrel about the share of a dead sister brings into question also the original sharing; and the representatives of the younger sisters offer homage to the lord, which the grandson of the eldest resists, saying, "ipse exiuit de primogenita sorore et fuit ad tercium genu et ideo debuit ipse facere homagium."[53] Degrees made a difference in the younger line, not the elder; and the difference they made was in the matter of homage to the eldest, not to the lord. But the case is interesting as well as odd, and serves to introduce a serious question. It was to the lord that all parties turned, proffering large sums for his protection. And it was the lord who in the end arranged an equitable partition, putting out the eldest whom he had himself put in. The action in the king's court is an assize of novel disseisin brought in consequence by the eldest against the lord. The assize returns a special verdict setting out the facts, and justices itinerant are sufficiently uncertain to adjourn the case to Westminster. Judgment is eventually given for the defendant lord, but it is more or less expressly based on the merits rather than on the law.

How and when did the younger sisters come to acquire their right to a share, and how was it protected and in what court? We will begin with the last of these questions. The lord's action in the case just considered, proper or not, was extrajudicial. Could the representatives of the younger sisters have brought a writ of right patent to his court? If the tenure was not military, so that each parcener would hold directly of the lord, that was clearly proper; and this seems to be the situation envisaged by most early precedents of the writ of right *de rationabili parte*.[54] But a younger sister claiming in parage could not bring her writ patent to the lord. Such a writ "must be directed to him of whom the demandant claims to hold, not to anyone else, not even to the chief lord."[55] On Glanvill's principle, the writ should go to the eldest sister. In the case of dower, also a dependent tenure within the inheritance, we know that the widow's writ of right

50. *CRR*, 11, nos. 2019, 2682; *CRR*, 12, no. 256; *BNB*, nos. 924, 1053.
51. *CRR*, 10:106–8; cf. *CRR*, 9:5; *CRR*, 10:99.
52. Cf. *CRR*, 4:2, 76, 118, 187, 219–20; *CRR*, 5:3.
53. *Rolls of the Justices in Eyre for Gloucestershire, Warwickshire, and Staffordshire, 1221–22*, ed. Doris M. Stenton, Selden Society, vol. 59 (London, 1940), nos. 1036, 1115, 1133.
54. *Early Registers of Writs*, ed. Elsa de Haas and G. D. G. Hall, Selden Society, vol. 87 (London, 1970), CA.2, CC.2–3, R.19–21. The writ in *Glanvill*, XII, 5 (p. 138), is untypical: a rent-paying messuage is held of the king, and the addressee may be a royal bailiff. Even the operative command is *facias habere*, not the usual *plenum rectum teneas*.
55. *Glanvill*, XII, 8 (p. 140).

must be directed to the heir.⁵⁶ We are not expressly told this in the case of the daughter's *maritagium*. But in an early claim by a daughter against her brother and a third party, the clerk by mistake enrolled the writ: it is directed to the brother himself.⁵⁷ Such accidents are rare, and only one early action between sisters has been found in which the legal records themselves tell us what the writ was: the actual document, dating from 1199, is one of the few early writs to survive.⁵⁸ It is not a writ patent at all, but a *precipe* bringing the dispute directly into the king's court. A parage arrangement seems to be involved, but because the land is held of the honor of Boulogne and had been the subject of an earlier fine in the king's court, no general conclusion can be drawn from that.

We have, however, information of another kind. When Miss Hurnard set out to discover how far the *precipe* was being used improperly before Magna Carta, she correlated entries in the pipe rolls of payments due for *precipe* writs with entries in the plea rolls of lawsuits between the same parties. She did not count claims for dower in which, though the plea roll often does not say so, the *precipe* of the pipe roll was probably a writ of dower *unde nichil habet* and therefore proper to the king's court.⁵⁹ But of the kinds of claim that she did count, that between sisters turned out to be the most frequent. The absolute number is not large, seven.⁶⁰ But because the pipe roll does not note all *precipe* writs, at most only those issued on credit,⁶¹ and because actions between sisters are relatively uncommon on the plea rolls, even this small number is significant. It does not in itself tell us anything about parage, because once in the king's court the parage would not be relevant to the claim for a share, and we should not and do not see it. But it does tell us that before the Charter, claims between sisters were being started by *precipe* when strict propriety would require a writ patent to the eldest in parage and to the lord in other cases.

Magna Carta placed a general restriction on the *precipe* that restored the elementary principle in its full rigor.⁶² One claiming right in land must always begin with a writ directed to the lord of whom he claimed to hold it, no matter how clear it was that the lord's court could or would do nothing, so that the claim would reach the king's court only after the

---

56. *Glanvill*, VI, 4 and 5 (pp. 60–1); *Early Registers of Writs*, CC.6 and note preceding it, R.16 and *Regula* preceding it.

57. *Memoranda Roll, 10 John*, pp. 105 (writ), 100–101; *CRR*, 1:41; *CRR*, 7:346. *Glanvill*, VII, 18 (p. 94), makes a procedural comparison in general terms with dower.

58. *PKJ*, 1, no. 3488 (writ; fine and confirmation also printed by the editor), 2085, 2475; *CRR*, 1:157.

59. N. D. Hurnard, "Magna Carta, Clause 34," in *Studies in Medieval History presented to Frederick Maurice Powicke*, ed. R. W. Hunt, W. A. Pantin, and R. W. Southern (Oxford, 1948), pp. 157–79, at p. 164.

60. Ibid., p. 166. Miss Hurnard suggested a different kind of explanation; but see Milsom, *Legal Framework*, pp. 69–70.

61. Ibid., p. 165.

62. Magna Carta (1215), c. 34; (1225), c. 24.

Inheritance by Women 245

roundabout tolt and *pone*. The old undifferentiated *precipe* disappeared, and came to be replaced by special forms with clauses explaining why the particular *precipe* did not deprive a lord of jurisdiction.[63] The *precipe in capite* and *quia dominus remisit curiam* explain themselves to us as well as to contemporaries. The entry clause in a writ of entry showed that the dispute was between the demandant and one claiming to be in as the demandant's tenant, and therefore that the demandant's lord would not be concerned.[64] No such explanatory clause could have made a *precipe* obviously proper for the claim between sisters, which must be a claim to hold either of the eldest or of the lord; and one might expect that the claim would be driven back into the ambit of writs patent. But no: a new writ was developed, one not formulated with a *precipe*.

The action known as *nuper obiit* is first found in the earliest records to survive after the Charter.[65] Before the Charter a sister might possibly resort to mort d'ancestor.[66] For all the sisters against lord or stranger this was appropriate; but between sisters it was not appropriate, as a case soon after the Charter pointed out: *perquirat se alio modo si voluerit*.[67] It looks as though a new need prompted the hasty provision of a new writ, which does not, as does mort d'ancestor itself, define its own scope. It says only that the ancestor "died lately." There was doubt about the permissible remoteness of the relationship between ancestor and parties;[68] and a remarkable range of limitation periods was proposed.[69] Other restrictions came to be adopted for which there is no warrant in the words of the writ. One is taken from mort d'ancestor: the ancestor must have died seised. Another has the appearance of being taken from dower *unde nichil habet*: the demandant must have no part of the inheritance.[70]

If we think in our own terms of abstract rights and possessory remedies, it is possible to explain *nuper obiit* as extending to the parcener the rapid protection that the heir had in mort d'ancestor and the widow in

---

63. M. T. Clanchy, "Magna Carta, Clause Thirty-Four," *English Historical Review* 79 (1964): 542–48.

64. Milsom, *Legal Framework*, pp. 88–102.

65. *BNB*, no. 12. Bracton refers to a case now lost *in rotulo de primis placitis post guerram* (*Bracton De Legibus et Consuetudinibus Angliae*, ed. George E. Woodbine, trans. with revisions and notes by Samuel E. Thorne, 4 vols. [Cambridge, Mass., 1968–77] [hereafter cited as *Bracton De Legibus*], fol. 77 [2:224]). A possible forerunner is *CRR*, 4:290; *PKJ*, 3, no. 2219. And the phrase is used in an action started by different means in *CRR*, 10:166–67, 196.

66. (a) *PKJ*, 3, no. 860; (b) *CRR*, 4:79, 157–58 (against lord having other sister in *custodia* and alleging bastardy of demandant).

67. *Rolls of the Justices in Eyre for Yorkshire*, no. 322 (actually son of one sister against other sister). Cf. *Glanvill*, XIII, 11 (p. 155).

68. *Britton*, ed. Francis Morgan Nichols, 2 vols. (Oxford, 1865), III, ix, 3 (2:83).

69. *Novae Narrationes*, ed. Elsie Shanks, completed with a legal introduction by S. F. C. Milsom, Selden Society, vol. 80 (London, 1963), p. cxi. To the references there given, add *Early Registers of Writs*, note following CC. 186b.

70. *Novae Narrationes*, pp. cxii–cxiii.

unde nichil. But the promptness is hard to square with a hesitation about *aiel* and *cosinage* some twenty years later, to which we shall return.[71] And even Bracton, who saw remedies in terms of possessory protection, did not see *unde nichil* itself in that light. He has a different explanation which, as has been remarked elsewhere,[72] can be extended to cover *nuper obiit*. If dower is being refused because the marriage is denied, the issue must go to the church courts; and perhaps it was only the king's court that could demand an answer.[73] The same difficulty would arise if one claiming as parcener was being refused any share on the supposition that she was a bastard. But in neither case is there factual support for the explanation. In the earliest records, which do not reach back to the creation of *unde nichil*, dower actions are very common and denials of the marriage rare.[74] The records do reach back some twenty years before the appearance of *nuper obiit*; and though actions between parceners are not frequent, we can be sure that bastardy allegations were not a pressing problem.[75] The similarity between the two actions seems even odder now that *nuper obiit* turns out to be a substantially later creation.[76] Perhaps with *unde nichil* itself Bracton was only rationalizing the result of some different and forgotten logic.

The immediate occasion for *nuper obiit* was the restriction placed on *precipe* writs by Magna Carta. The logic of that was the logic of tenure itself. A claim to land is a claim to be the lord's tenant and must be addressed to the lord: hence the writ of right patent. But before the Charter, immediate action in the king's court was accepted as proper when there seemed no room for dispute, when the lord himself was keeping out one with a direct right against him in defiance of his obligations. We know from the legislation creating it that this was the original role of mort d'ancestor.[77] It was conceived for use against the lord himself; and legislation about damages nearly a century later still treats that as the principal case.[78] And when some twenty years after Magna Carta (and also after the creation of *nuper obiit*), the principle of mort

---

71. See below at n. 79.
72. *Novae Narrationes*, pp. cxii–cxiii.
73. *Bracton De Legibus*, fols. 296–96b (3:357).
74. Examples noted in the plea rolls before Magna Carta are: (a) *RCR*, 2:56; (b) *CRR*, 1:233, 322; (c) *CRR*, 2:41; (d) *CRR*, 2:63; (e) *CRR*, 2:79; (f) *CRR*, 3:150; (g) *CRR*, 4:2–3, 38–39; (h) *CRR*, 6:153; (i) *CRR*, 7:99, 275; (j) *CRR*, 7:101. Cf. (a) *CRR*, 1:309; (b) *CRR*, 6:301, 391–92. Even if many have been missed, the proportion is minute in relation to the number of dower actions.
75. (a) *CRR*, 4:79, 157–58 (mort d'ancestor against lord having other sister in *custodia* and alleging bastardy of demandant; writ to bishop); (b) *CRR*, 12, no. 1537 (*nuper obiit*; issue to jury).
76. G. J. Turner, in *Brevia Placitata*, ed. G. J. Turner, completed by T. F. T. Plucknett, Selden Society, vol. 66 (London, 1947), pp. xciv–xcv, thought the two writs might be the creation of the same chancellor.
77. Assize of Northampton, c. 4 (Stubbs, *Select Charters*, pp. 179–80); *P&M*, 1:148 and 2:57, n. 1.
78. Stat. Marlborough (1267), c. 16, reaffirming Provisions of Westminster (1259), c. 9.

Inheritance by Women

d'ancestor was extended to cases omitted because the dead ancestor was too remote, a wider "abstract" remedy was expressly resisted by the magnates. They were prepared to sanction the new *precipe* writs of aiel and cosinage only as against the lord himself or one who could vouch him.[79] The direct remedy is given, in the latter case by *precipe*, precisely because the lord himself is defaulting on his obligations.[80]

When dower is seen as a dependent tenure within the inheritance, the writ *unde nichil* falls into similar place. The widow claims not an abstract property right, but the benefit of an obligation falling upon the heir. If she has nothing, it is not just that he has not fulfilled his obligation: he must be repudiating or defying it. Instead of setting up a separate procedure like mort d'ancestor, the king exercises the discretion attributed to him by Glanvill and issues a *precipe* writ.[81] Like mort d'ancestor, the writ named the tenant of the land but did not identify his tenurial position; and this obscured the logic. Both came to be used against other tenants, no doubt for the same reason: if another tenant was in, that itself was the responsibility of the lord in mort d'ancestor, of the heir in dower *unde nichil*. The husband's grantee holds of the heir, is warranted by him, just as the widow claims to be. In both cases the extension had happened before the time of Glanvill, but in the case of dower the logic is expressly recollected. Whoever is named as tenant, the book warns immediately after giving the writ *unde nichil*, the heir himself must be present *qui mulieri petenti de dote sua respondeat*.[82] And though the logic was not known to Bracton, it was probably still remembered at the time of the Charter: the *precipe* writ with its explanatory clause seems not to have been questioned.

What about the other dependent holdings within the inheritance? There is little evidence linking the *precipe* with *maritagium*:[83] but normally there is no need for action when the father dies, because the daughter and her husband already have the land. But in parage it is the eldest sister who gets the land; and the claim she faces from a younger sister is exactly akin both to the mort d'ancestor claim of heir against lord and to the *unde nichil* claim of widow against heir. These are the two remedies from which *nuper obiit* takes its properties. And this is a situation in which the use of the *precipe* before the Charter would have had the same

---

79. *BNB*, no. 1215 (1236–37), with amended reading suggested in Milsom, *Legal Framework*, p. 84, n. 6. Notice the linking of aiel with mort d'ancestor, *nuper obiit*, and writs of entry in the objection of the tenants in *Select Cases in the Court of King's Bench under Edward I*, vol. 2, ed. G. O. Sayles, Selden Society, vol. 57 (London, 1938), pp. clvi–clvii (1239).
80. Cf. Milsom, *Legal Framework*, pp. 85–86.
81. *Glanvill*, I, 5 (p. 5); notice also the availability for claiming free tenement as well as fee.
82. *Glanvill*, VI, 15 and 16 (p. 66).
83. See Hurnard, "Magna Carta, Clause 34," at p. 166. Miss Hurnard explained these cases differently; they do not seem to be claims against the heirs; and anyway the number is hardly significant considering the frequency of actions involving *maritagium*.

justification as the *precipe* writ *unde nichil*: the eldest sister must be repudiating or defying any obligation to the younger.

But *nuper obiit* was not, and the earlier use of *precipe* writs may not have been, confined to this claim of a younger sister against the eldest; and the logic of parage may have had powerful reinforcement in a practical difficulty resulting from its mere existence. It is not just that subinfeudations reaching down to a humble level might leave parties uncertain whether or not there should be parage, and so whether or not there should be a writ patent to the lord. Suppose there should clearly be parage, but it is the youngest of three sisters who has the whole: what writ patent should the middle sister get, and what the eldest? Make the problem harder, and suppose that the inheritance is held of the king: should the eldest get a *precipe*, and should it claim just her beneficial third or the whole? Perhaps somebody actually tried to draft those writs, and decided that the niceties must be cut through. We have met the case before. It is that of the daughters of William de Buckland in 1218; and it seems to be the earliest surviving example of *nuper obiit*.[84]

These procedural questions about the established parage all reflect an earlier and substantial question: how did it become established in the first place? Let us assume a lord to have given the whole inheritance to the eldest sister and her husband: to whom did the younger sisters first turn? It cannot have been the lord, not just because they did not claim to hold of him, but because he needed a single tenant and an undivided tenement. In his court, the right thing had been done and there was an end of it. And in an important sense, there indeed was an end of it. The eldest was not disturbed in what the lord had given to her, and the rights of the younger sisters were strictly dependent. It is equally self-evident that those rights could become regular only when the king's court would regularly intervene. But should we think in terms of a customary right having, like the *maritagium*, some earlier existence in the court which the eldest sister would hold as lord of the inheritance? Or should we think of an almost legislative creation, with the king's court intervening from the beginning with some mechanism like the *precipe*?

In either case the motive force no doubt came from family arrangements customary before there were lords to upset them. And the willingness of the church courts to treat as breach of faith a failure by the heir to honor a gift in *maritagium* suggests that they saw an underlying moral duty to make such provision. But *maritagium* became a customary institution in lay courts because it was customarily given. The younger sisters may have had a moral claim well established in family custom, may sometimes even have been in the inheritance. But the only gift actually made was the lord's gift of the whole to the eldest; and hers was the only "legal" right.

That there was at some time something in the nature of a legislative act or declaration of right by some authority is a fact that we learn by

---

84. *BNB*, no. 12; above, p. 237. Cf. above, n. 65.

accident. A charter attributed to about 1145 refers, in passing and with tantalizing obscurity, to a *statutum decretum* by which if there is no son, daughters are to share "by spindles"; "nec potest maior natu iuniori medietatem hereditatis nisi vi et iniuria auferre."[85] Whether or not the words by which this ruling is described, *statutum decretum*, suggest some church participation, the words in which it is expounded do not suggest a legislative act providing in modern terms for the legal division of property rights. It must have declared that the elder sister would do wrong in depriving the younger of her share. The language is that of obligation; and two echoes in detail, though much later, are insistent. The formula *defendit vim et iniuriam* is common form in the plea rolls, but not in "proprietary" actions: it is the standard denial in all personal actions. Another echo is in the writ *nuper obiit* itself: it is not a *precipe*, and the operative words are *ostensurus quare deforciat*. The *ostensurus quare* formula is most at home in actions for wrongs. What the lost ruling seems to contemplate is the wrongful exercise of an undoubted power. The land is the eldest sister's, but she is under an obligation to allow the younger her share. Parage is the expression in tenurial terms of something like a modern trust.

The significance of this casual recital is further sharpened when it is placed in its context. The charter is one by which a considerable lord confirms a gift that his tenant has made to a religious house; and it recites that the tenant's daughter joined with her father in placing the land upon the altar by means of a symbolic knife, which daughter was heir of the tenant for that land "iuxta statutum decretum quod ubi filius non habetur terram patris filie per colos parciuntur nec potest maior natu. . . . " The father is still alive; and if he has a younger daughter, it must be the point of the recital that she will have no "legal" right, that the consent of the elder to this grant will be binding on the inheritance. But nothing suggests that there was in fact a younger daughter, and probably the recital of the part of the enactment relating to younger daughters was only for the sake of completeness. As a matter of syntax, the entire recital is to explain why the lord who is issuing the charter feels himself entitled to treat the daughter as heir at all: "que scilicet Agnes heres erat Walteri . . . iuxta statutum decretum quod ubi filius non habetur. . . . " Whatever the ruling was, it probably did more than state a duty to share. It took some step beyond Henry I's Coronation Charter in establishing female inheritance itself, perhaps in recognizing that an unmarried daughter herself had a right, and not just an expectation that the lord would give the land with her to whomever he chose as her husband.

---

85. F. M. Stenton, *The First Century of English Feudalism*, 2d ed. (Oxford, 1961), pp. 38–41, 260–61 (app., no. 5). Cf. *Regesta Regum Anglo-Normannorum*, vol. 3, 1135–54, ed. H. A. Cronne and R. H. C. Davis (Oxford, 1968), p. 39 (no. 106).

The Husband's Interest

The important change was in the sense in which women inherited. The husband contemplated by Henry I in his "*illam dabo . . . cum terra sua*" is himself a grantee. When the land is the woman's by operation of law, the husband's right is derivative, flowing from the marriage. But the woman's automatic right was also, if she had sisters, a shared right; and the sharing itself had practical consequences which may have affected the way in which the husband's right was seen. We shall therefore start with those.

The most obtrusive consequence of sharing, from the husband's point of view, is that the acquisition of an inheritance by marriage becomes less simple. He, or his father, had better buy the marriages of all the daughters. When Richard de Lucy of Egremont died in 1213 he left a widow and two daughters. The widow married Thomas de Multon; and Thomas acquired from the king the *custodia* of both daughters and married them to his own two sons. Egremont was, in fact, granted whole to the elder couple; but Multon won something else for the younger. Richard de Lucy had inherited Egremont from his mother, the middle of three sisters who had each inherited a barony from their parents. When the youngest died childless in 1215, the whole of her barony of Papcastle was taken by the representative of the eldest line. Multon, acting in the king's name, recovered half (and arranged a partition in which *esnecia* was reserved to the eldest line); and it was this half that went with the younger Lucy, daughter to his own younger son.[86] Just a hundred years later their grandson was granted the other half of Papcastle, which had escheated to the crown, a delayed bonus over and above what Multon had striven for.[87]

Such calculations did not always work out. A tenant of the earl of Winchester died leaving two daughters and, though the facts were disputed, *custodia* of the inheritance and of both daughters seems similarly to have been acquired by the father of two sons. The elder son married the elder daughter all right; but a church on the inheritance fell vacant, "*et placuit . . . postnato filio melius promoveri in ecclesiam illam quam uxorem ducere.*" Something had to be done, and the elder son did it: he placed the younger daughter in a nunnery. But it was not a very secure one; and she contrived to send for a man friend and, on their own account, he married her then and there in the nunnery. When some news reached the elder son, he arranged for her to be removed to a more secure house; and on the way the party passed her new husband. The husband's account is no doubt colored—or deliberately colorless—because he is facing an action in the earl's name for forcible abduction. He says she called to him for help, "*et ipse vidit multitudinem gentium et respondit ei*

---

86. *CRR*, 11, no. 1223; *CRR*, 12, nos. 360, 866, 914, 1576, 2045; Sanders, *English Baronies*, pp. 115 (Egremont), 134 (Papcastle), 142 (Skipton).
87. Sanders, *English Baronies*, p. 135.

quod noluit pro ea pugnare," whereupon she threw herself from her horse and went off with him on her own initiative, "et tali modo recuperavit ipse uxorem suam." The melodrama fades away, and later we find the two couples getting down to litigation over the division of the inheritance.[88]

But it is not just a stirring story. The sequence of events may not have been uncommon; though there were not necessarily two sons, and it might from the beginning be intended to dispose of the sister by making her a nun. Of one such case we have only fleeting glimpses; and it is by accident that we learn that in the end the plan failed and the lady was married without question.[89] Another such case gave rise to bitter litigation, ecclesiastical and lay, lasting some twenty-five years. The younger sister says that the elder and her husband placed her in the nunnery when she was five years old, and that she properly returned to the world when she reached the age of discretion. Properly or not, she was excommunicated; and the earliest proceedings were in church courts. The father had apparently died under Henry II. Her claim for her share of the inheritance is first seen in the king's court in 1201, and it is eventually compromised in 1220.[90] She might have had a better life without it.

Another aspect of sharing brings us back to the relationship between inheritance and *maritagium*. At all levels of society some provision was made for a daughter on her marriage, whether in land or in goods and money. If somebody else inherited, most obviously her brother, then no question arose on the father's death. But a question did arise if the daughters themselves inherited; and family equity allows two kinds of answer. Either the benefit received must exclude the beneficiary from sharing in the inheritance, or the inheritance must be shared on the footing that the benefit falls into hotchpot.[91] The question always arises with partible inheritance, and many variations of detail are possible. With impartible inheritance, the underlying question arises in another form: what lifetime gifts are permissible within the family? That is a major question for Glanvill; and his discussion, particularly of the gift to a younger son, shows family sense at odds with the feudal burden borne by the inheritance.[92] Unfortunately he discusses *maritagium* only in the same context of a male heir, and not in the context of daughters sharing the inheritance; and here it is possible that the feudal and the family forces had for a time pulled in the same direction.

---

88. *CRR*, 9:65–67; *CRR*, 10:92 (both concerning the abduction); *CRR*, 9:91; *CRR*, 11, nos. 190, 293(?), 306, 344, 346, 686 (all concerning the inheritance).

89. References in Milsom, *Legal Framework*, p. 156, n. 4.

90. *CRR*, 2:81; *CRR*, 3:41, 178, 334–35; *CRR*, 4:80, 155, 252, 318; *CRR*, 5:79, 79–80, 123, 171, 183–86; *CRR*, 7:108–9, 180, 246; *CRR*, 8:173, 184; *CRR*, 9:222, 241, 381–82, 385; *PKJ*, 3 and 4, nos. 171, 1654, 1724, 2117, 2695, 2783.

91. For a survey see Jack Goody, "Inheritance and Property and Women," in *Family and Inheritance: Rural Society in Western Europe, 1200–1800*, ed. Jack Goody, Joan Thirsk, and E. P. Thompson (Cambridge, 1976), pp. 10–36.

92. *Glanvill*, VII, 1 (pp. 69–71); Milsom, *Legal Framework*, pp. 121–22.

At humble levels it is clear that some customs excluded daughters with marriage portions from inheriting.[93] If the tenement barely supports a family, portions are likely to be given from family savings in goods and money; and this must be the first home of the "hearth-child" who will inherit the tenement itself. But even at higher levels, where marriage portions are generally in land, this is an approach acceptable to family feeling. By confining inheritance to unmarried daughters, it is also an approach that leaves the lord to choose the husband who will be his tenant. This is something we have already noticed as possibly relevant to the *filia haeres remanserit* of Henry I's Coronation Charter, and to the disposition that King John made of William de Buckland's inheritance: he acted on an alleged prerogative to give *postnatam filiam que remaneret in hereditate* with the inheritance to a man of his choosing.[94] Even the words in which the lost enactment about sharing is described would be consonant with an exclusion of elder daughters having *maritagium* and a division of the residue of the inheritance. It is not *primogenita* but *maior natu* who is to share *per colos* with her junior.[95] Suppose a tenant to die leaving three daughters, of whom only the eldest was married. The *maritagium* of the eldest would be balanced by the tenurially similar parage of the youngest; and apart from a possible inequality of share,[96] the only thing "wrong" with the result would be that it is the middle sister who has become the lord's tenant, not the eldest. Cases in the king's court in which it is an elder who is having to sue a younger for her share, in some of which there is also an express claim for *esnecia*,[97] do not necessarily reflect lords who simply ignored the family situation.

Even when all questions come to the king's court, we should not think too simply in terms of "the law." If the eldest, or her husband, is always to be the lord's tenant, then that in itself implies a different approach to *maritagium*. If *maritagium* does not exclude from the inheritance, the question must arise of its falling into hotchpot, and that is the result toward which the king's court works. But problems arise piecemeal. When was a grant by the father sufficiently independent of the marriage to be exempt?[98] Was a grant even on the marriage exempt if the land had

---

93. (a) *CRR*, 11, nos. 298, 1273, 1460, 2386, 2878; *BNB*, nos. 951, 988; (b) *CRR*, 11, nos. 1743, 2407, 2905; *BNB*, no. 1018. See also *Borough Customs*, vol. 2, ed. Mary Bateson, Selden Society, vol. 21 (London, 1906), p. 133; Homans, *English Villagers*, p. 141. Cf. the concord made in a seignorial court in the time of Henry II, *CRR*, 2:112–13.

94. See above, n. 24 and accompanying text.

95. See above, n. 85 and accompanying text.

96. *Glanvill*, VII, 1 (p. 69), says that one can give "quandam partem terre sue cum filia sua uel cum alia qualibet muliere in maritagium siue habeat heredem siue non." Both this, and the feudal burden on the inheritance, suggest that the permissible size of the gift would be the same whether there was a son or not. So long as a *maritagium* remained *liberum*, there would be compensation for any shortfall in the actual share.

97. (a) *Three Rolls of the King's Court*, pp. 6, 30–31, 49, 54; *RCR*, 1:13; (b) *CRR*, 1:225, 447–48, 453; (c) *CRR*, 5:46–47, 149. Cf. Bracton *De Legibus*, fol. 75 (2:218).

98. (a) *Rolls of the Justices in Eyre for Lincolnshire, 1218–19, and Worcestershire,*

Inheritance by Women

been the father's own purchase rather than his inheritance?[99] Nor could rules be stated in the abstract: it depended upon who was suing whom. Unless both parties agreed to exclude their lifetime benefits,[100] a demandant clearly had to bring her *maritagium* in.[101] But the sister enjoying handsome *maritagium* will not be demandant: she will feature as tenant being sued.[102] Can she be made to give up any excess beyond her mathematical share?[103] And if what she has is the whole, can she hark back to the other approach to the problem and argue that there is no inheritance to divide?[104] In the early rolls, and indeed in Bracton, it looks as though the questions are somehow new.

Just as sharing affected the calculations of a husband seeking to acquire an inheritance which will descend to his issue, so does its relationship with *maritagium* affect our understanding of his own personal tenure of the land. His right to enjoy the land for his whole life, if issue had been born of the marriage, comes to be known as curtesy. Glanvill describes it, though not under that name or indeed any name; but his description comes in his account of *maritagium*, and nothing is said about the wife's inheritance.[105] Most scholars, though not all, have followed Maitland in supposing that at that time it did apply to inheritance,[106] as it does for Bracton.[107] Maitland indeed thought that inheritance was the prime case, that Glanvill can be understood as saying that the right applied "even" to *maritagium*.[108] To that proposition we shall return. But the ramifications of sharing suggest that the question itself may be oversimplified. On an obvious factual level, if there was ever a decision to be made about *maritagium* falling into hotchpot, whether in general or in a particular case, a possible change in the husband's entitlement would be at least

---

1221, ed. Doris M. Stenton, Selden Society, vol. 53 (London, 1934), no. 1040; (b) CRR, 11, nos. 2201, 2793; BNB, no. 934. Cf. Bracton De Legibus, fol. 77 (2:224–25); Britton, III, viii, 8 (2:79).

99. *Memoranda Roll, 10 John*, p. 109; RCR, 1:147; CRR, 1:50, 80; CRR, 2:92. Cf. Glanvill, VII, 1 (pp. 70–71). According to Bracton De Legibus, fol. 77 (2:224), it makes no difference.

100. CRR, 12, nos. 249, 1771.

101. CRR, 11, nos. 2201, 2793; BNB, no. 934. Cf. Bracton De Legibus, fols. 77 (2:223–24), 428b (4:331).

102. (a) CRR, 6:161, 200–201, 254, 282–83; CRR, 7:47, 194–95, 235, 298; CRR, 11, nos. 523, 1065, 2029; (b) *Rolls of the Justices in Eyre for Lincolnshire*, no. 1040; (c) CRR, 10:166–67, 196; CRR, 11, nos. 219, 1374. Cf. Bracton De Legibus, fol. 77 (2:223–24).

103. Bracton De Legibus, fols. 76b–77 (2:223–24); Britton, III, viii, 8 (2:78–79).

104. Bracton De Legibus, fols. 76b–77 (2:223); Britton, III, viii, 8 (2:78–79).

105. Glanvill, VII, 18 (pp. 92–93). But the discussion of homage and its consequences at least contemplates that a husband may continue to hold his wife's inheritance after her death: "nec primus maritus premortua uxore, terram illam iterum releuabit" (IX, 4 [p. 108]).

106. P&M, 2:420, n. 1. Followed by G. D. G. Hall, in Glanvill, p. 93, n. 1, and apparently by T. F. T. Plucknett, *A Concise History of the Common Law*, 5th ed. (Boston, 1956), pp. 548, 568. Doubted by G. L. Haskins, "Curtesy at Common Law," *Boston University Law Review* 29 (1949): 228, n. 5.

107. Bracton De Legibus, fols. 216 (3:151), 437b–38 (4:360).

108. P&M, 2:420, n. 1.

relevant. But there is a deeper complication. Any difference between inheritance and *maritagium* might be expected to flow from the husband's homage. But if there were two or more sisters, only one husband would do homage. The tenure of the younger sister in parage is like *maritagium*. Indeed, if, as seems possible, sharing was first confined to younger and unmarried daughters, leaving the elder undisturbed with their *maritagium*, the parage of the youngest may have been consciously modeled upon the *maritagium* of the eldest. If there ever was a difference between *maritagium* and inheritance over curtesy, it is unlikely to have survived a general principle of sharing the inheritance.

Curtesy was the right of the surviving husband to hold the land so long as he lived, provided only that a child capable of inheriting it had been born of the marriage. It did not matter that the wife had left sons by an earlier marriage so that the heir being kept out was not the husband's own child.[109] Nor did it matter that the heir, even by an earlier marriage, was an infant so that the wife's lord was losing a wardship; nor, indeed, that any child had already died, so that the person being kept out was either a collateral heir of the wife's or the lord awaiting his escheat.[110] When inheritance is automatic and when women are understood to inherit in the same sense as men, the right looks generous to the husband and hard on the wife's heirs. We inevitably think about it in the same terms as dower.

That it was not like dower is most obviously shown by the comparative frequency with which the two things figure in early litigation. The widow had in a ceremonial sense been given dower on her marriage, but, even if the land had then been specified, it remained within her husband's control. Her action to recover dower after the husband's death from his heir or grantee is one of the most frequent of all actions on the early plea rolls.[111] There was no action by which the husband could claim curtesy, and he never had to sue for it. He had had the land ever since the marriage. If he granted it away, after the wife's death or before,[112] or if after his own death it was taken as his own inheritance,[113] then of course there might be litigation between the persons claiming under the wife and

---

109. *P&M*, 2:416–17, and references there given. *Glanvill*, VII, 18 (p. 93), expressly places the second husband on the same footing as the first; *Bracton De Legibus*, fol. 438 (4:360), reports a contrary view, which is followed in *Britton*, II, xii, 3 (1:289), and in *Fleta*, ed. and trans. H. G. Richardson and G. O. Sayles, Selden Society, vols. 72 (London, 1953) and 89 (London, 1972), IV, 3 (3:54). There may of course be what will later be called "special tail" (*CRR*, 14, nos. 395, 1067; *BNB*, no. 487; *Bracton De Legibus*, fol. 168 [3:34]).

110. Maitland thought the remarkable fact about curtesy was its priority over the lord's wardship and escheat (*P&M*, 2:417). That depends upon a thirteenth-century view of the "incidents" as of prime importance to a lord, as opposed to the services. See below, p. 258.

111. Cf. the review by G. D. G. Hall of *CRR*, 12, in *English Historical Review* 74 (1959): 107–10, at 108.

112. *Glanvill*, VII, 3 (p. 76). Examples: (a) *RCR*, 2:202–3; *CRR*, 1:330–31, 466; *CRR*, 2:30–31; (b) *CRR*, 7:31, 109, 158, 290; (c) *Rolls of the Justices in Eyre for Yorkshire*, nos. 167, 1132; (d) ibid., no. 292 (customary power of husband to sell).

113. (a) *CRR*, 7:177, 180; (b) *CRR*, 8:335.

those claiming under himself. But curtesy was never as such the object of litigation. When the wife died, her heir might claim the land in mort d'ancestor; and because the points of the assize would presumably be answered in favor of the heir, one would expect that the case would always be recognizable from an exception made by the husband. But such assizes are not common.[114] What we find a little more often is an assize of novel disseisin brought by the husband against one who has simply taken the land on the wife's death.[115] This may be the wife's heir; and in the case of *maritagium*, which can be inherited only by issue, he is necessarily the issue of an earlier marriage.[116] Other possible defendants are the donor of *maritagium*,[117] the donor's heir,[118] or, if the land was the wife's inheritance, the lord of whom it was held.[119] In the examples found of the latter situation, in which the defendant is the woman's father or brother taking the reversion after *maritagium*, or is her lord taking his escheat, the facts again appear from an exception that he expressly pleads. But it is possible that this was unnecessary, and that other such cases are hidden behind general verdicts for the one party or the other. When the defendant is the woman's heir, we generally learn the facts only because the clerk has enrolled an explanation given by the recognitors for a general verdict. Any question about the husband's entitlement, for example, whether or not children had been born alive, goes to his having or not having free tenement,[120] and is therefore within the points of the assize. He was or was not disseised of his free tenement, and the explanation upon which the historian depends was for those concerned at the time gratuitous.

Taking all these kinds of action together, in the first thirty years after the earliest surviving plea roll the total number of cases visibly involving curtesy is of the order of one or two a year. Unless we can make that mere fact tell us something, it follows that the rolls themselves will not tell us much about curtesy. They are not even as clear as might be hoped about

---

114. (a) *RCR*, 1:432 (see below, n. 141, for another stage of this dispute); (b) *RCR*, 2:202–3; *CRR*, 1:330–31, 466; *CRR*, 2:30–31; (c) "Roll of the Justices in Eyre at Bedford, 1202," ed. G. Herbert Fowler, in *Bedfordshire Historical Record Society*, vol. 1 (Apsley Guise, 1913), pp. 144–247, at no. 65 (pp. 160–61); (d) *Rolls of the Justices in Eyre for Gloucestershire*, no. 1090. For mort d'ancestor in this situation see *Bracton De Legibus*, fols. 271 (3:293), 278 (3:311). For a special action see ibid., fol. 438b (4:362–63). Cf. (a) *CRR*, 1:182, 249–50, 294, 452, 476; (b) *CRR*, 6:11–12.

115. *Bracton De Legibus*, fols. 168 (3:34), 169b–170 (3:38), 206 (3:124–25), 216–16b (3:151–52); cf. fol. 404b (4:259).

116. (a) *CRR*, 6:333–34; (b) *Rolls of the Justices in Eyre for Yorkshire*, no. 309; (c) *Rolls of the Justices in Eyre for Gloucestershire*, no. 534. Cf. *CRR*, 7:7, in which it is not clear who the defendants are.

117. *Rolls of the Justices in Eyre for Yorkshire*, no. 22.

118. *CRR*, 3:66. Cf. *CRR*, 10:73–74.

119. (a) "Roll of the Justices in Eyre at Bedford, 1202," no. 63 (pp. 158–61); (b) *Rolls of the Justices in Eyre for Lincolnshire*, no. 357.

120. (a) *Rolls of the Justices in Eyre for Yorkshire*, no. 309; (b) *Rolls of the Justices in Eyre for Gloucestershire*, no. 534.

the application to inheritance as well as *maritagium*. Most cases in which the wife's interest is stated do involve *maritagium*, but at the higher levels many more women would have *maritagium* than would inherit. At the humblest level, where marriage portions would be in goods, woman heirs would be relatively more common; and many of the early cases, including some of those in which we can see that the land was indeed inheritance and not *maritagium*, are from humble levels.[121] The earliest clear allegation of curtesy from a military inheritance relates to some period before 1200; but the allegation itself is made as late as 1219, and then in litigation in which the curtesy is barely in issue.[122] Only one case has been found in which it may possibly have been argued that something turned on the distinction. It is an assize of mort d'ancestor in 1200. Walter and his wife Richolda had a son William and a daughter Maud. After Richolda's death, Walter gave some of her land in *maritagium* with Maud, and William, as Richolda's heir, is now claiming it from Maud's husband; but Maud's husband is warranted by Walter, so that the real dispute is between William and Walter. According to one enrollment, "Willelmus dicit quod non licuit patri suo dare hereditatem matris sue cum filia sua: e contra Walterus pater ejus dicit quod ipse duxit ... Richoldam uxorem suam cum maritagio suo. ..." But probably nothing turns on William's use of *hereditas* to describe Richolda's land as against Walter's use of *maritagium*, because Walter goes on to conclude that "ex consuetudine Anglie debet tenere hereditatem ejus et warantizare tota vita sua." Another enrollment shows William denying that he had consented to the gift by Walter, and his real concern clearly goes beyond Walter's lifetime.[123]

Walter's phrase *ex consuetudine Anglie* is as near as the early rolls come to a formula specifically denoting curtesy. In the previous year we find *secundum consuetudinem regni*;[124] and some twenty years later, that and *per legem terre* come into more general use.[125] "Curtesy" itself is much later. Nor is it just that there is no special name for this right of the husband. It has to share a name with other things. Among its other uses,

---

121. (a) *RCR*, 1:359, 427–28; *RCR*, 2:65, 196; *CRR*, 1:136 (lord recovering land of dead wife *salvo jure heredum illius terre*); (b) *Rolls of the Justices in Eyre for Lincolnshire*, no. 357.

122. *CRR*, 8:152, 333; *CRR*, 9:20, 57, 87, 370–71, 379; *CRR*, 10:253. Cf. *CRR*, 8:213–15; and Sanders, *English Baronies*, p. 22 (Bulwick). Robert de Courtenay was married to his second wife, Alice of Papcastle, by 1200 (*CRR*, 1:265). The suggestion that the heir was sufficiently seised to endow his wife during his father's lifetime may be an infection from dower (Milsom, *Legal Framework*, p. 145).

123. *RCR*, 2:202–3; *CRR*, 1:330–31, 466; *CRR*, 2:30–31. A similar confusion of language may be seen by comparing *RCR*, 1:432, with *RCR*, 2:124–25 (see below, n. 141, for this dispute). In one sense *maritagium* became *hereditas* when issue was born.

124. *RCR*, 1:359, 427–28; *RCR*, 2:65, 196; *CRR*, 1:136.

125. (a) *Rolls of the Justices in Eyre for Yorkshire*, nos. 167, 1132; (b) *CRR*, 13, no. 311; *BNB*, no. 266; (c) *CRR*, 8:152, 333; *CRR*, 9:20, 57, 87, 370–71, 379; *CRR*, 10:253; (d) *Rolls of the Justices in Eyre for Gloucestershire*, no. 534.

custodia is used of the husband in relation to his wife's land, whether she is alive[126] or dead.[127] When she is dead the *custodia* is sometimes specified as *cum pueris*,[128] when alive as *cum uxore*[129] or *per uxorem*.[130] But it might be neither: in one early case the issue was whether the husband had held after the death of both wife and child *ut de feodo an ut de warda*.[131] We shall ask later for whom in such a case he might be holding in *custodia*. Our immediate concern is with the lack of a specific name.

It is a fact to be placed beside the scarcity of litigation. A state of things which does not give much practical trouble and has not earned for itself a name cannot need much discussion. Glanvill devotes a book to dower, and five sentences to curtesy.[132] They come in his chapter on *maritagium*, at the end of his book on inheritance and alienation. That book is a remarkable achievement of substantive analysis;[133] and it is possible that this passage has misled us into overlooking the absence of a name and antedating curtesy as a legal entity of the same nature as dower. Even Bracton, who uses *per legem Angliae* as a name, makes only scattered procedural statements.[134] He considers problems, mainly of proof, that may arise if the husband brings novel disseisin or faces mort d'ancestor or an action in the right; and even in these short references space is devoted to monsters heard to roar as opposed to children heard to cry.[135]

We cannot solve the various problems of curtesy, but we may reduce them by starting from this point. There is no name and no need for substantive discussion precisely because the husband needs no action, does not have to formulate a count. He is in, protected so far as the king's court is concerned only by novel disseisin; and he is within the protection of the assize because he has free tenement. How was he protected before novel disseisin was introduced? It has been argued elsewhere that the assize was originally intended to protect tenants against action by their lords in breach of the customs governing the tenurial arrangement.[136] To

126. (a) *RCR*, 1:253, 393; (b) *PKJ*, 2, no. 455; (c) *The Earliest Northamptonshire Assize Rolls, A.D. 1202 and 1203*, ed. Doris M. Stenton, Northamptonshire Record Society, vol. 5 (1930), no. 450.

127. (a) *CRR*, 7:31, 109, 158, 290; (b) *CRR*, 8:152 (full references above, n. 125). It is not always clear whether the wife was at the relevant time alive or dead: (a) *CRR*, 2:37, 221; (b) *CRR*, 8:335.

128. (a) *CRR*, 1:182, 249–50, 294, 452, 476; (b) "Roll of the Justices in Eyre at Bedford, 1202," no. 65 (pp. 160–61).

129. *PKJ*, 2, no. 455.

130. *RCR*, 1:253, 393. Cf. *The Earliest Northamptonshire Assize Rolls*, no. 450.

131. *RCR*, 1:359, 427–28; *RCR*, 2:65, 196; *CRR*, 1:136. Cf. *CRR*, 7:31, 109, 158, 290.

132. *Glanvill*, VI, (pp. 58–69) (dower); VII, 18 (pp. 92–94) (*maritagium* including curtesy).

133. G. D. G. Hall, *Glanvill*, p. xxiv.

134. *Bracton De Legibus* (on novel disseisin) fols. 168 (3:34), 169b–170 (3:38), 206 (3:124–25), 216–16b (3:151–52), 404b (4:259); (on mort d'ancestor) fols. 271 (3:293), 278 (3:311); (on action in the right) fols. 437b–39 (4:360–63).

135. *Bracton De Legibus*, fols. 438–38b (4:361–62). Cf. fols. 216 (3:151), 271 (3:293).

136. Milsom, *Legal Framework*, pp. 8–25.

have free tenement was to be such a tenant, to be protected by these customs in the lord's court. The husband is simply the lord's tenant, and entitled to the same protection as any other tenant.

The conclusion is obvious enough: but obvious propositions are sometimes worth emphasizing. Dower and *maritagium* were special entities partly because they were "tenures" as much as "estates." Curtesy was not a tenure. Consider the wife's inheritance and assume for simplicity that she is an only daughter. The husband becomes the lord's man in the same way as a son would have: the lord makes livery to him and takes his homage. The tenure is that by which the wife's father had held. The lord is securing a man and his service. For Maitland it was a great puzzle that the husband's curtesy should keep out the lord's wardship if the wife died leaving an infant heir.[137] But that is a thirteenth-century puzzle. When it was his services that a lord desired, he would naturally continue to look to the husband. We have seen that Henry I was prepared to look to the widow or other relative of a dead male tenant:[138] like socage *custodes*, they could have *custodia* of the land provided they arranged for the service to be done.

All this applies equally to the second husband. Unless Magna Carta was making an otiose promise,[139] there had been a time when the widowed heiress might be compelled to take a new husband so that the lord might have a new man. If she herself wished to remarry, the lord must be asked to consent:[140] but the absence of consent could not affect the fact of a marriage, and the sanction must have been that the husband would not become the lord's man and would not get the land. But here novel disseisin probably wrought a real change: the lord had to put up with him. A case of 1199 shows one who was actually the donor of *maritagium* proceeding in the king's court against a second husband to whom he had not consented, but the terms of his challenge are those of a lord: *in feodum suum intraverat sine ejus assensu*.[141]

Questions about the second husband suggest a yet earlier stage. We have seen that the Coronation Charter of Henry I makes no promise about the marriage of a widow with *hereditas*.[142] Perhaps he might compel it. But dealings with baronies suggest that if, when the husband died, there was a male heir of full age, the inheritance might be given directly to him even though the woman was still alive.[143] Perhaps to begin with the husband was indeed seen as tenant of the wife's inheritance like any other tenant. The most that any tenant could have was the lord's war-

---

137. *P&M*, 2:417.
138. Coronation Charter, c. 4; see above, pp. 234-35.
139. Magna Carta (1215), cc. 7, 8; (1225), c. 7.
140. *Glanvill*, VII, 12 (p. 86).
141. *RCR*, 2:124-25. This case is discussed, and full references given, in Milsom, *Legal Framework*, p. 51. See also above, n. 114, for an earlier stage of the dispute. Cf. the action brought by the dead woman's lord in *RCR*, 1:359, 427-28; *RCR*, 2:65, 196; *CRR*, 1:136.
142. Coronation Charter, cc. 3, 4; see above, p. 234.
143. See above, p. 235.

ranty and protection for life, together with the obligation imposed on the lord by homage that when the tenant died the land would be given to an heir. If homage was taken in the wife's name, this last obligation would be toward her heirs. But if the husband was indeed the lord's tenant like any other tenant, it was his life that mattered, not hers; and the real puzzle is not why the husband could keep the land if issue had been born but why he lost it if not.

It is not impossible that this rule grew up as one of the customary properties of the *maritagium*, and was generalized in the uniformity of the king's court. At the higher levels of tenure, the *maritagium* was certainly of more frequent occurrence than the inheritance coming to a woman; and on the view taken in this essay, it is likely also to have been the earlier. And because it was a product of the family interest undistorted by feudal logic, and in particular did not attract the preordained consequences of homage, the customs may just reflect the implied terms of an arrangement that was desired. Although with *maritagium*, as with inheritance, the land is said to be given "with" the woman to the husband, the donor was providing for the woman: we have seen that he might try to make his gift before any marriage was in prospect, himself holding it as *custos*.[144] To him it was always the woman's life that mattered, not her husband's; and an understanding that he would no longer warrant the husband if there was no child at the woman's death would be entirely intelligible. But then suppose that a child survived its mother but quickly died? The practical desire for certainty could have produced the all-or-nothing conclusion that the mere birth was decisive. But it is hard not to suppose some deeper connection with the later idea of a "conditional fee."

Let us return to the case of inheritance and consider the husband's position in terms of an arrangement with the lord, rather than of the properties of some "estate" as a known entity. Even in 1219 it could be an arrangement on special terms. Because the wife had died childless a lord retook the land; but at the time of the marriage the lord's predecessor had conceded that the husband should hold for life *siue haberet heredem de ea siue non*, and so the husband recovered in novel disseisin.[145] We can be sure that in that case the lord was taking his own escheat: his predecessor could not have made such a concession at the expense of collateral heirs of the wife.[146]

A century and more earlier, what were the likely terms of the arrangement contemplated in "illam dabo . . . cum terra sua"?[147] The lord is under an obligation imposed by homage toward the dead tenant's heirs. Instead of giving the land to, say, the dead man's brother, he is making the daughter's husband his man. What has induced him to do so? Suppose the dead tenant had left a brother and a grandson by a dead daugh-

---

144. See above, pp. 231-32.
145. *Rolls of the Justices in Eyre for Lincolnshire*, no. 357.
146. For an arrangement with the heir see CRR, 6:11-12.
147. Coronation Charter, c. 3; see above, p. 236.

ter:[148] surely the lord would have felt obliged to the grandson; and if the grandson was an infant, would he not accept the dead daughter's husband as holding in *custodia*? So should not the living daughter have her chance to transmit the inheritance? But she cannot be heir in the same sense as a man; and the lord cannot take her homage and regard the matter as closed until her own death, when he will ascertain who is her heir. Her capacity is just to transmit the inheritance; and all the time there is another heir in the dead tenant's brother. If these were indeed the terms of the lord's problem, they necessarily become the terms of the arrangement he makes. It is a conditional arrangement. The homage he takes from the daughter's husband is itself conditional, obliging him to the heirs of the marriage if there are heirs. Until there are, perhaps the daughter has nothing and the husband only a *custodia* for whomever the heir will turn out to be. If children have not been born when the wife dies, nothing can keep out the alternative heir of her dead father. If a child is born, the husband's homage takes its full effect: he becomes the lord's man indeed, but still in *custodia* for the heirs of the inheritance and not his own heirs.

Direct evidence for any such proposition is so unlikely that one must be suspicious when it seems to turn up. In a case of 1199–1200, the suspicion is that lost facts would disclose some quite different explanation, such as a fine. But we have more facts than usual, because the central figure wrote a letter to the justiciar, who quoted it in a letter to the justices that has survived. She was a widowed heiress who had granted an advowson in frankalmoign to a religious house, and this grant is being contested by her son-in-law. What the letter says is that the grant was made from what had descended to her from her father, and was made before her daughter's marriage. But later she contradicts herself on the second point, and admits that the grant was made after her daughter had married and had children. As against the religious house, the son-in-law had argued that the lady could not warrant the grant, and this appears to be vindicated by her admission.[149] It is hard to imagine any basis other than a lingering idea that an heiress primarily transmits the inheritance.

---

148. *Glanvill*, VII, 3 (p. 77).
149. *PKJ*, 1, nos. 3063, 3104, 3475 (the letter); *RCR*, 1:239, 313, 397; *RCR*, 2:53–54, 226; *CRR*, 1:44, 65, 142, 143, 201 (the letter contradicted), 301.

F.W. MAITLAND

IN my college library the *Proceedings of the Academy* are so shelved that a search through the volumes is least inconveniently conducted on the top of a ladder, and the results may be precarious too. Of those admitted to the pantheon formed by the Master-Mind Lectures, Maitland lived more recently than any except Bertrand Russell, and he is the only one who in his lifetime was an Ordinary Fellow of the Academy. If one does not count the philosophers, indeed, there are few scholars in the humanities. Of historians there are only three: Carlyle, Gibbon, and Bede. And although there are several persons who had to do with the law— Cicero, Bacon, Bentham, even Bagehot—only Grotius is there as a lawyer. All this is partly explained by the terms of the endowment. The benefactress referred to such as philosophers and poets: it did not occur to her, and rightly not, that law or scholarship as such could yield a master mind. So I climbed down from my high place to set Maitland in more accessible company, among his peers as the first Fellows named in the Academy's charter of incorporation in 1902. Of which of the historians would today's average history graduate probably have heard? Of Lecky, I suppose, and perhaps of John Morley and Cunningham; but only just. The lawyers might fare better, with Anson, Pollock, and Dicey. But that would be partly because of the practice by which law books are kept alive artificially. Anson on Contract, for example, is hale and hearty and 101. In a world in which nothing much must be seen to change, the old name is a comfort; and it sells the book. It is an odd twist that Pollock's name is most widely known in 1980 because it is on the title-page of 'Pollock and Maitland', and that a reason for keeping it there in 1895 was to help sales in the United States. But though he contributed little to the *History of English Law*, Pollock was, and perhaps is, a larger figure in his own field than most of those first Fellows. A historian and a lawyer among them

* British Academy Lecture on a Master-Mind delivered 5 November 1980.

exemplify the usual ends of innovative scholars: Cunningham, Maitland's student friend and rival, was a pioneer of economic as Maitland was of legal history; and his work is all but forgotten, honourably buried under the work of those who followed. Dicey's work is not forgotten; but it is remembered not for the questions he asked but for the reputations which were so long to be made by picking holes in his answers. For a longer after-life you have to climb back up the ladder: Gibbon's work lives, but not as scholarship.

Names have been dropped around that ladder because the oddity of a familiar fact is a hard thing to communicate; and Maitland's standing today must be among the odder facts in the history of history. His work has not been buried or picked to pieces, and does not survive just as literature. Indeed, apart from lectures which he would not himself have published, it has never been much read except by other historians. But by them it has been regarded, and still is, almost as revelation; and Maitland himself has been, and still is, not just revered but loved. He died in 1906, his consequence measured for the world at large by a meagre and inaccurate obituary in *The Times*, for the academic world by the address of condolence which Oxford University sent to Cambridge University. Such addresses were regularly sent to sovereign or family when a royal personage or the University's Chancellor died: but for this, the immediate precedent was an address to Berlin University on the death of Mommsen. In the aftermath of Maitland's death there were published two books about him, one almost incoherent in its admiration, and a three-volume collection of his papers; and these things were not at that time out of the way. But personal reminiscences were sought as long as they were available. Fifteen years after Maitland's death W. W. Buckland wrote of him in terms astonishing to one who remembers the rather mathematical pleasure of Buckland's teaching. Thirty years later, marking the centenary of Maitland's birth, came a more formal tribute from H. A. Hollond, who also secured the publication of a private memoir written long before by Maitland's sister. And in 1957 there appeared the enchanting recollections of Maitland's daughter Ermengard. But Maitland's death, on Miss Ermengard's nineteenth birthday, was then fifty years in the past. Personal affection could surely play no further part. Yet, in that same year, a new collection of his papers was published by Helen Cam, who had been an undergraduate at Royal Holloway College when Maitland died and never knew him: but there is something like devotion in what she wrote. Since then books have been dedicated to him; his letters have been published; there have been a book about his work (by one who confessed to having fallen under a personal spell), a full-length life (something of which the thought, suggested by accident, seemed grotesque to Maitland himself), and lesser hagiographical writing—and all this for a scholars' scholar dead almost three-quarters of a century. And today, however ill the task is done, the Academy acknowledges that he was more than that, and places him on its own list of immortals.

What was it about Maitland that has made time stand still? He is not even a dead immortal, one whose contribution, however great, is measurable and past. Some of the peripheral writing in that extraordinary range has of course been overtaken, like all other historical work done so long ago. But his work on the history of English law is largely untouched, untouchable. 'Maitland's analysis . . . remains dominant, and it is hardly conceivable that the primacy of his work will ever be displaced': the magisterial tone is that of *The Times Literary Supplement* a year or two ago. 'That's not what Maitland said, is it?' The question was put to Professor Thorne on a recent visit from his Cambridge to ours. 'No', said Thorne. 'Well I don't believe it then', said his questioner. Both remarks were occasioned by the appearance of a book which proposed an altogether different interpretation of matters central to Maitland's subject; and by an irony it is the author of that and other heterodox work who had been set to fathom his unfathomable quality. Your lecturer is the lonely figure in some Bateman drawing, the man who thinks that Maitland was wrong. People have been kind about it, as about any other eccentricity. But that is how Maitland stands.

His life was in the ordinary sense uneventful. The surprising thing in retrospect is that the period of achievement was short and began late and almost casually. It began at about the same time as what seems to have been an unusually happy marriage, and as the recognition of an illness which could only bring the life slowly to its end. Personally reticent, I think he would have resented a stranger poking about, even if only by way of explaining his own admiration for the man as well as his mind; and I shall mention only such details as seem relevant. The family was well-to-do. Maitland's grandfather's grandfather and father had made money in the city of London; and by marriage the latter had acquired land in Gloucestershire. A sufficiency of both was to descend through the next three generations, and to allow their lives to shape themselves as they did. Maitland's grandfather was first called to the Bar: then he was ordained and took a cure of souls. But that did not last long either; and although he was for a time Librarian of Lambeth, his life was essentially that of an independent scholar, an ecclesiastical historian of some distinction. Maitland's father did well enough at Cambridge to become a Fellow of Trinity College; and he too was called to the Bar. But though his life was long centred on Lincoln's Inn, it was one of leisure and cultivated interests until, only a few years before his early death, he became Secretary to the Civil Service Commissioners.

This was the tradition that Maitland followed. The need was not for a career so much as for an activity in which the talents could be used; and often, of course, as with his undoubtedly talented father, they were not used to great advantage. It is an aspect of Maitland which was naturally apparent to his family: his sister wrote her memoir 'to show how he gradually settled down to work and gradually discovered the work that it was best for him to do'. For me it is symbolized—as is much about the law itself—by a book on my shelves, Maitland's copy of Littleton's *Tenures*. For the subject which he created, this fifteenth-century account of the land law is an important source: but Maitland did not acquire it as a legal historian. The name on the flyleaf is that of his father; and when Miss Ermengard gave it to me, she pointed out that it might well have been first acquired by his grandfather. It was natural for a gentleman to be called to the Bar, and therefore to have a copy of Littleton—and not just out of antiquarian interest.

Other family circumstances made for independence of mind. Maitland was born in 1850. His mother died soon after, and he and his two sisters were devotedly brought up by a sister of hers. Shortly before his thirteenth birthday his father also died; and it was his mother's brother who a few months later took him to Eton. Half-way through his time there his paternal grandfather died, the ecclesiastical historian; and the family property came to Maitland when he was sixteen.

He spent six years at Eton, gaining no identifiable acquirements except a love of testing exercise, especially rowing and running, and a distaste for the Greek language. In 1869 he went up to Trinity College, Cambridge, as a commoner; and such efforts as he made in his first year must have gone to the rowing and the running. They cannot have gone to mathematics, which he was reading, because he did badly in an examination at the end of the year. Why mathematics? He probably never thought of contenting himself with an ordinary degree, as many commoners did then and much later. And if he was to seek honours, only the classical and mathematical triposes carried prestige or any chance of a fellowship: his father's had been the reward for doing well in both. But Eton had put paid to the classics; so he made the only conventionally respectable choice.

What else was there? Not history. The History Tripos was created the year after Maitland went down, the subject having been ejected first from the Moral Science and then from the Law Tripos. Plucknett in a printed lecture on 'Maitland's view of law and history' was dismayed—even affronted—that Maitland's inaugural lecture should have looked to the Bar to advance legal history. But for once Plucknett's own historical sense had deserted him, and he was placing Maitland in his own world. But Maitland did not read law either. It is ironical that Cambridge had a Law and History Tripos exactly for the time that he was up. Another Maitland of Trinity took it; and the *University Calendar* and *The Times* obituary both confused the two. Our Maitland turned from mathematics to what he must have seen as an almost defiantly unconventional choice, one which he could afford. The Moral Science Tripos carried no prestige, and no college would contemplate electing a Fellow on the basis of success in that alone. 'The standard of a first class is low because the most able and industrious men do not devote themselves to the study; they do not devote themselves to the study because it is not rewarded, and it is not rewarded because the standard of a first class is low.' That was how Henry Sidgwick saw the tripos in 1870, the year that Maitland turned to it. Perhaps his regard for Maitland was partly for the first of a succession of remarkable men who turned to it for something other than the conventional reward, and so gave it standing.

What first attracted them may have been admiration for the stance which Sidgwick had taken in the preceding year, by resigning his Fellowship because he no longer believed the declaration required by the religious tests. Maitland recalled going to listen on 'the idle whim of an idle undergraduate'; but the lectures were one of the important experiences of his life, and near its end he remembered Sidgwick as 'one to whom I owe whatever there is of good in me'. Sidgwick had paid for the readership which brought him back to Cambridge, a debt acknowledged in the dedication of *Bracton's Note Book*, and had given him frequent encouragement, but Maitland's language goes beyond such things: this was his only master. If the influence was ever specified, it may have had to do with the quality that so impressed him about Sidgwick's lectures, a transitive truthfulness, a determination to communicate his understanding of things. It was not just a habit of scrupulous statement, though in Maitland himself that became automatic. You could almost devise a linguistic metal-detector which, passed over his pages, would tell you where to dig in legal history: a change into the more accommodating passive mood, for example, may be the echo of a doubt. The special thing for Sidgwick was the communication: in our horrid but helpful jargon, he had always to 'get it across'. And Maitland's own most obvious power is the directness with which he speaks to you through the printed page. My language is mixed, but for once not by accident. We know that his lectures were always written and always read; and we have Miss Ermengard's near certainty that he spoke his words as he wrote them 'or at any rate heard them very clearly . . . he never merely wrote or read—he taught by word of mouth'. He lectured with an intense nervousness of delivery and gesture which dissolved for hearers into their own preoccupation with his subject-matter. But the force that drew them in was not generated by the performance. It had already been caught on the page, and you can hear him still.

Success came and went for Maitland with Sidgwick's subject. He became president of the Union and an Apostle. And in 1872 he shared with Cunningham the first place in the first class of the Moral Science Tripos. But he knew that that could not qualify him to follow his father in a fellowship, and was tantalized by another chance. In 1875 Trinity offered a fellowship in philosophy to be awarded by dissertation. Of the four candidates Maitland, Cunningham, and James Ward were all to be among the first Fellows of this Academy; and it was James Ward who won the Trinity fellowship. Maitland had his dissertation printed as for publication, but was later careful to insist that he had not in fact published it; and it shows none of his strength. One could wonder why Sidgwick thought so highly of him if Sidgwick had not explained his own reason for doubt: it was because Maitland understood Sidgwick's mind so well. It is not just that he dealt better with the concrete than with the abstract, would have made more of Wilkes than of liberty. It is that you cannot sympathize with abstractions; and the visions he communicates with such power are of people whose situation he sees so clearly that he feels their feelings.

Perhaps he was seeing them with the eyes that so struck contemporaries. Buckland mentions them in connection with Maitland speaking in the Senate House, and particularly his speech in 1897 in favour of women's degrees. Maitland was on the losing side, but at least he put paid to a scheme for fobbing the women off with a university of their own. The place for that, he suggested, would be the waiting-room at Bletchley Junction. But 'you could not oblige the women to take the Bletchley degree. You would be waiting, waiting, waiting in the waiting room, and they would be waiting, waiting, waiting outside... You wait there; but you do not wait there always. You change for Oxford and Cambridge.' Perhaps just wit. But those two waiting groups are dramatizing a conflict in the same way as three individuals—to take one of dozens of examples from 'Pollock and Maitland'—in a passage discussing how the representation of litigants in court first became permissible. 'John may fairly object that he has been summoned to answer not the circumspect Roger but the blundering Ralph.' An explanation is then offered: 'The captiousness of the old procedure is defeating its own end, and so a man is allowed to put forward some one else to speak for him, not in order that he may be bound by that other person's words, but in order that he may have a chance of correcting formal blunders . . .'. This is congruous with the only relevant fact, which is that early pleaders might be disavowed by their clients. But there is no other evidence, and Maitland scrupulously put a 'perhaps' before his summarizing sentence: 'Perhaps the main object of having a pleader is that one may have two chances of pleading correctly'. But I am sure that he was convinced as, for what it is worth, am I—convinced by John and Roger and Ralph.

It is not for a lawyer to discuss the place of imagination in historical studies at large. But the legal historian must reckon that his law had no abstract existence, that his subject-matter makes sense only in terms of people involved in some real or imaginary conflict, and that the conflicts that matter to him are the ones that were somehow difficult. 'Persons who can never be in the wrong are useless in a Court of Law', wrote Maitland; and so are persons who are obviously in the wrong. The legal historian has not only to visualize the dispute, but to feel some sympathy for both sides. There is another metal-detector to pass over his pages: if he condescends to the people he is writing about, he has misunderstood the matter. You rarely get a signal from Maitland's work on that machine. Whenever a question is reduced to the scale of a visualized dispute, the litigants and their lawyers take credible attitudes. But you cannot do it always: and it is when questions are not reduced to that scale that even a Maitland can go wrong.

But you have to ask more of your imagination than to serve as a check on your understanding of the evidence. The evidence tells you what disputes were about in the superficial sense; but it does not tell you in detail what had happened, let alone how each side saw his grievance. And that is the essence of the subject. Legal development comes down to articulations of the nursery cry: 'Not fair'. The immediacy and realism of Maitland's work stem, I think, from the sympathy which induced him to visualize so much in those terms. The quality can only be a gift of fortune. But if the habit owed anything to any other person, a nursery may have had to do with it. All the compelling work was done after his marriage; and his wife peopled their daughters' world with all kinds of creature, animal and human, real and imaginary, all with distinct characters and all articulate. Her Mrs Gravelrat and Maitland's Mrs Josiah Smith (the Ermengard of his fancy was to be the reliable wife of a reliable clergyman) and the waiting groups at Bletchley and Roger and Ralph all lived in the same mind.

We left him after a failure. Another was to come. He had joined Lincoln's Inn as a student in 1872, perhaps meaning to go to the Bar only in the way his father had. The years after he left Cambridge were leisurely. He lived in the house in Kensington to which his sisters and aunt had moved some years before. He travelled, especially for musical occasions in Germany. It could so easily have been an honourable and unfruitful life like his father's. But he went into chambers on his call in 1876 and until 1884 sought practice as a conveyancer. In 1884 he was elected to the Cambridge readership which had been established by Sidgwick's generosity; and since his first book on legal history was published and his second projected all about the same time, it is agreeable to think that he left the Bar because he saw his future as a legal historian. But he had applied for a readership at Oxford in the preceding year, before his first visit to the Public Record Office and before there was any thought of editing the Gloucester plea roll, let alone *Bracton's Note Book*; and although he had published three papers about the early history of the criminal law, they do not show the sense of mission which was to possess him. There may have been negative reasons for the change. The Kensington household broke up with the death of his aunt and the marriage of his elder sister. The agricultural depression left the Gloucestershire lands little more than self-supporting. There was other money of course: he was able to pay for the publication of both the *Gloucestershire Pleas of the Crown* and *Bracton's Note Book*—and it is to his having to do so that his beloved Selden Society probably owes its existence. But he was never again to feel quite so secure as he

(272)

had; and unease would be intensified if he already had any suspicion about his health. 'Slowly it is doing for me; but quite slowly. . . .' In 1899 he said that a doctor had diagnosed the condition so described more than ten years earlier. And in 1889 he wrote 'Many things are telling me that I have not got unlimited time at my command' . . . and wondered whether he had even another year to live. The earliest recorded physical break-down was in 1887; but the Bar has always demanded great stamina, and the 'many things' may have begun to raise doubts about that.

The change was more than a change of career: it was almost a change of character. Except for the running and the rowing and the work inspired by Sidgwick, it had so far been an easy-going life. And now at the age of thirty-four he began to work with an intensity that only illness would interrupt and only death would end. Whatever the excitement of those materials that Englishmen had so neglected, he must have made an unrelenting effort of will; and the sense of mortality surely played its part. But there was something else. 'I should never have succeeded if I had not failed once.' He often said that; and his sister took it to refer to his first mathematical failure at Cambridge. But she tells also of his growing disappointment with the Bar, and links it with a passage in his inaugural lecture: 'The day may come when in the bitterness of his soul he will confess that he is not going to succeed, when he is weary of waiting for that solicitor who never comes . . .'. The lecture then makes the suggestion that so offended Plucknett, that perhaps it was failed barristers who would write the history of English law. It is how Maitland saw himself.

What was he like as a barrister? After his death, the master with whom he had read in chambers recorded the opinion that he would never have succeeded because he would not have pushed enough. But of Maitland as a lawyer he wrote in terms which must be quoted:

he had not been with me a week before I found that I had in my chambers such a lawyer as I had never met before. I have forgotten . . . where and how he acquired his mastery of law; . . . certainly . . . not in my chambers: he was a consummate lawyer when he entered them. Every opinion that he gave was a complete legal essay, starting from first principles . . . and . . . coming to a conclusion with the clearest grasp of legal points and the utmost lucidity of expression . . . [His] opinions, had he suddenly been made a judge, would have been an honour to the Bench.

This has been discounted as undiscriminating eulogy. But to those who have ever had to do with a particular kind of lawyer, it reads like a simple description. I have had the humbling fortune to encounter two such more than casually, both now dead: one was briefly and in some formal sense my student; the other was my master when I read in chambers—by coincidence the editor of the last version of Maitland's *Equity*. From elementary propositions and in few and simple words a pattern was built up which disposed of the question. Reference to authority seemed superfluous: you could only say 'of course', and wonder how it had seemed difficult, and reflect that this man should go straight to the bench. But rare and impressive as it is, the talent by itself makes little difference in ordinary practice. It is not even particularly satisfying to its possessor: the law is too easy a material for that kind of power, and life keeps spoiling the patterns. The phenomenon must have to do with the mathematical affinities of the law. The pattern that seems to come from the sky is conjured up by the problem; and its conclusive effect is partly that of internal coherence and partly because it fits the fixed points. No doubt the computer had been offering other patterns to the fixed points; and had one of those fitted, an equally definitive opinion would have been based upon different elementary propositions—different in the sense not of contradicting those actually chosen, but of being about something else. That is how the law works, and largely how it changes. The change is in the premises from which a matter is approached.

Would the possibility that Maitland was that kind of lawyer throw light on the historian? It would explain the speed at which his work was done. But in attributing even speed to the pattern-finding ability of this particular kind of lawyer, I am venturing on to contentious ground; and from this point on you must reckon that your lecturer can no longer quite separate his attempt to explain Maitland's talent from his own beliefs about what will always be regarded as Maitland's subject. For me the question is how historical reconstruction can be so convincing, even so beautiful, and yet, as I have no doubt that it is, fundamentally wrong. The conviction is of two kinds. At the level of detail there is that human conviction: abstract propositions are reduced to disputes between people whose attitudes seem entirely natural. Then there is the intellectual conviction of the patterns into which the detail is arranged: they are always coherent and satisfying and they fit the fixed points.

I think back to my master in chambers, and hear echoes. You could only say 'of course'. It was hardly conceivable that the opinion could be wrong. And indeed things that are obvious cannot be slightly wrong: like the movement of the sun, they can only be fundamentally wrong. In the law the coherence of the pattern itself is hardly ever in question. The question is which of two patterns fits more closely: you look at the facts this way instead of that way, and an equally compelling answer flows from different premises. But what have the shifty workings of the law to do with honest history? The legal historian also is finding patterns which fit the fixed points of his evidence. He has a mass of original documents produced for business purposes; but they do not explain the ideas and assumptions underlying the business. Unless you have some general account, such as an elementary book for students, you have to reconstruct those for yourself, to find a pattern which fits the detail.

But the shiftiness of the law goes deeper than that. It is not just that more than one pattern may fit. It is that wrong patterns are actively pressed upon the historian. Until modern times the law rarely responded to change with overt changes of its own. Change was absorbed so that those affected never quite saw what was happening, and historians cannot easily see it either. To take the simplest example of often complex mechanisms, a word changes its meaning; and there is nothing obvious to warn you against reading back the later sense and seeing the later pattern of elementary ideas. All historians are subject to that kind of anachronism; but I think it is only legal historians who are systematically deceived by the nature of their evidence.

'We must not be wise above what is written or more precise than the lawyers of the age.' Of course Maitland saw the danger. But consider a passage, for once incautious, that he wrote to explain why 'Pollock and Maitland' stopped with the accession of Edward I.

> So continuous has been our English legal life during the last six centuries, that the law of the later middle ages has never been forgotten among us. . . . Therefore a tradition, which is in the main a sound and truthful tradition, has been maintained about so much of English legal history as lies on this side of the reign of Edward I . . . We are beginning to discover that it is not all true . . . Its besetting sin is that of antedating the emergence of modern ideas . . . But in the main it is truthful.

No historian would dare to write that today: yet all the standard works until recently have been based upon that assumption. You look back on centuries of material generated on the premise that nothing much must be seen to have changed, and write a book saying that nothing much changed. What you project back are features of a later world, not just its law but the assumptions of its society.

Accident made mischief. Except for his Rede Lecture on *English Law and the Renaissance*, which has long been questioned and lately stood on its head, Maitland published little about the law of any period later than the early fourteenth century; and his view of tradition should not have mattered. But he acted upon it in writing a series of seven elementary lectures on the development of the common law remedies. And like his lectures on constitutional history, which we know he would not himself have published, these were published after his death under the title *The Forms of Action at Common Law*. A very short text seems to encapsulate everything important about the subject. It has been by far the most widely read of Maitland's books on legal history; and it provided the framework upon which scholarly work was based for half a century after his death.

Even in such lectures I do not think Maitland would have formulated the view they convey but for another accident, this time one of chronology. The last vestiges of the forms of action themselves were not abolished until the judicial system which had grown since the Middle Ages was at last replaced by a single and almost rational structure. The Judicature Acts took effect in 1875, and even then many years were to pass before they worked their way down into professional assumptions. Maitland joined his Inn in 1872, and was called in 1876. The law that he learnt, and to a large extent the law that he practised, were seen within a framework which had had a truly continuous existence from something close to a beginning. He was still within the tradition upon which he relied, and we are not.

The misunderstanding was serious. Legal development was seen in almost ecological terms. Writs and actions were the original entities of the common law, multiplying by a kind of parthenogenesis and competing for survival. In retrospect, one can attribute its long acceptance only to the authority of Maitland's name, but of course it had some of his strength. Coherent patterns were discerned by reading much earlier materials with the nineteenth-century sense of such words as 'trespass' in mind. They made grammatical sense, but it would have been hard to make human sense if Roger and Ralph had been enlisted and set to argue out disputes, and harder still not to feel that tell-tale condescension towards their lawyers. Instead of new formulations of 'Not fair', you hear less reasoned nursery cries of the order of 'Shall' and 'Shan't'. But Maitland, hurrying through seven centuries in as many hours, had no time for Roger and Ralph.

The damage done to his subject by that act of piety after his death was mainly to what may be called the intellectual history of the law, especially the post-medieval law. You cannot make much of people shouting 'Shall' and 'Shan't' at each other: few scholars took up legal history; and other historians decided, by and large, that the subject was not worth attention. But a historian working in the Middle Ages cannot put the law aside so easily. It is more obviously central to the rest of life, and much of the medieval evidence in England is legal evidence. But here Maitland had not been hurrying, or at least not hurrying in the same way—there was just the bizarre need to finish 'Pollock and Maitland' before Pollock could write any more of it. But disputes are visualized so that detail carries human conviction; and the patterns into which the detail is arranged are, as always with Maitland, compelling in their coherence. You can only say 'of course'.

But the patterns now seem wrong, and for the same kind of reason. The idea of the forms of action was itself carried back, so that the logic underlying medieval lawsuits was not so much missed as seen back-to-front. Modes of proof, the true focus of attention, were associated with kinds of action rather than with kinds of assertion; and some contemporary reasoning was hidden behind an assumed formalism. The distortion is not altogether confined to our picture of legal thinking: the early history of the criminal law, for example, has been bedevilled by our mistaking a legislative change in modes of proof for a much grander invention to secure public order. But for the period upon which Maitland truly worked, as well as for the long sweep of those short lectures, these misunderstandings went more to the intellectual history of the law than to our picture of society.

That is not true of another set of patterns, about which I must say something even on Guy Fawkes night when there will be bonfires handy for a heretic. The formal continuity of legal materials proved deceptive in another way. Let us start from Maitland's copy of Littleton. For his father, and perhaps for his grandfather, it was probably one of the books read to learn the land law. By the time Maitland himself went to the Bar, there was a modern textbook. But he had a bad time with it; and when about 1890 he advised Cambridge students on preliminary reading for the subject, Littleton was among the books he mentioned. But his principal recommendation was that they should read the second volume of Blackstone. Many rules had since been altered, he warned them, and some of the history was untrue. But they were not to worry about either the history or the later changes: 'I recommend it to you as the easiest and pleasantest way of making yourselves familiar with the technical terms and the elementary ideas of our property law'. There was no antiquarian bias in the law teacher's advice. Ten years earlier, while still at the Bar, he had published anonymously a breath-taking attack on the law of real property; and though anger was muted in this talk to students, you can still hear his distress at the continued domination of a system of ideas as unsuited to the time as 'tenure'. But dominant they still were, and students must learn to work with them.

Perhaps it was their unfitness for his own time that suggested to the historian immutability in the ideas themselves. 'Tenure' is the crux. Copyhold tenure in the nineteenth century was visibly the vestige of an order in which the holding of the tenant was truly dependent upon his lord. The eighteenth century had envisaged a similar starting-point for freehold, and this Maitland utterly dismissed. For him there had of course been erosion of the rights and powers of lords: but at their earliest and most ample they were limited, in the nature of servitudes over what was always the property of the tenant. It is now clear, at least to a heretic, that at their beginning they added up indeed to the proposition that as between the two the land was the property of lord rather than tenant, or rather to the more fundamental proposition that this was an arrangement between them to which the language and ideas of property are inappropriate. For our understanding of the society the difference is large, and hence the heretic's unease about bonfires. But so far as the legal evidence goes, and most of the evidence is legal, it comes down to the familiar difficulty of telling cause from effect. A series of remedies was provided by the king's courts. The heresy sees these as, in origin, external controls working upon the jurisdiction of lords, and generating abstract rights of property in the same kind of way as today the external control of the European Court is beginning to produce abstract 'human rights'. When a governmental unit ceases to be sovereign, whether feudal lordship or modern state, its practices cease to be conclusive. But for Maitland the tenant had always had an abstract ownership; and these new royal remedies represent only competition with feudal jurisdiction, not control. Jurisdiction was all the king wanted, and better mechanical protection was all the tenant got.

Maitland was again, of course, writing within the tradition. Tenants were owners, and even the limited economic rights of thirteenth-century lords had finally disappeared with the

(278)

abolition of military tenures. There was nothing to suggest a yet earlier time when those rights were not in themselves desired, when, for example, the succession of an infant tenant was not a benefit bringing wardship of the land but an interruption leaving the lord without a man, when a tenure was indeed an arrangement over which the lord exercised a true control. Such control is paradoxically easier for us to envisage as 1984 approaches than it was for Maitland in 1895. We can see the language and ideas of our own property law being rendered inappropriate by governmental powers of the same juristic nature as those once exercised by lords. You are less of an owner when you cannot effectively realize your property without planning permission, for example, in the same way as you had not quite become owner so long as you needed your lord's licence to alienate.

But these changes of our own day teach another relevant lesson. They have been separate responses to separate problems; and there was no moment at which the over-all social change could be resisted for what it was. So it was with the transformation of feudal society. The over-all change was absorbed by the law, concealed again in such simple ways as the changing meaning of a word. For Maitland 'seisin' was a mystery because it had for centuries been an abstract idea of the same nature as our 'possession'. If you think in those terms, 'to be seised' must denote a relationship, however mysterious, between a person and a piece of land; and 'to be disseised' probably denotes an act of disorder. It does not occur to you that the mystery, the disorder, and the uneven syntax may all disappear if you introduce another person, the lord who had first to put the tenant in seisin and who might later put him out. He disappeared from the language as he lost real control. But his going is not signalled in the evidence. It makes grammatical sense when you read back the later meaning, and the only warning you have is a matter of human sense: since disseisins were very common you seem to be shown a remarkable degree of disorder.

This is the routine deception of legal records, of law itself. It was abetted by another and larger accident, of the nature of an archaeological find recorded as having turned up too deep. The kind of development which English law was beginning in the twelfth century had been completed by Roman law something like a millennium earlier; and there was in England book learning and even, in the church courts, practical experience of a sophisticated system. That infection from another world is the salient fact about the thirteenth-century treatise on English law known by the name of Bracton. It is not the actual Roman learning that matters, right or wrong. It is the familiarity with substantive rules and abstract concepts proper to a fully developed system. English legal historians have this treatise, written indeed in the thirteenth century but informed by a sophistication of ideas that English law itself would not attain until the eighteenth. Maitland, writing within a still-living tradition, seemed to have warrant for the continuity of that blend of abstract ideas and formalism. Nor is it just that the treatise was available together with all the other sources. For him another accident had given it pre-eminence. 'Pollock and Maitland' was conceived in 1889. In 1887 Maitland had completed his first big task in legal history, his edition of the collection of transcripts from plea rolls known as *Bracton's Note Book*; and for that purpose he had immersed himself in the treatise. Its assumptions had become his own.

Another of his early works might have raised questions, as indeed it raised a passing doubt about the view of contractual development which was to be propagated in *The Forms of Action*. This was a formulary of claims and defences which Maitland edited for his Selden Society in 1890, and it shows clearly the primitive pattern of litigation; but he may have discounted it as coming from the humble level of manor courts. The pattern was of a claim made and denied in almost sacramental phrases; and the one or the other would be sworn to, and the oath tested by compurgation or battle or—until the church interfered—by ordeal. In the king's courts departures from that pattern were compelled as the supernatural testing of oaths made by or on behalf of the parties was replaced by a more rational mechanism. Disputes came to be settled by submitting them to the oath, the sworn verdict, of a jury. But on some constellations of fact, there was obvious danger that a jury would go wrong if the dispute was put to them at large on the old unanalysed general denial of liability. In some circumstances a special plea had to be allowed; and the discussions in court generated by this new possibility became exciting enough to be reported in what have come down to us as the Year Books. Only near the end of his life did Maitland turn to editing those, and only then did he pay them the kind of attention that the editorial task compels. 'A stage in the history of jurisprudence is here pictured for us, photographed for us, in minute detail. The parallel stage in the history of Roman law is represented, and can only be represented, by ingenious guess-work: acute and cautious it may be, but it is guess-work still.' The words come from his first Year Book introduction, and sometimes

I encourage myself with the fancy that they show a sudden doubt: perhaps the world on which he had worked was younger than *Bracton* had led him to believe. But it was too late.

And now the dwarf must stop grumbling about his vantage-point on the giant's shoulder and climb back up his library ladder. Maitland had nothing to stand on. There was no legal history worth the name. There were only the documents for the details, and a mendacious professional tradition and an even more mendacious *Bracton* for the patterns. In some branches of history you can study details in isolation and add the results together. In legal history that does not work. The detail makes little sense in isolation: you have to proceed upon some hypothesis about the patterns, about the framework of ideas and the relationships of society. Maitland's framework enabled him to conjure up a richly detailed world. If the framework is indeed wrong, the detail is not; and progress in his subject is likely to be by successive rearrangements. But nobody will need the qualities that were needed to make a start.

A start towards what? Of course not just the history of doctrine and technicalities, or even of society if that means just a structure. In his introduction to *Bracton's Note Book*, Maitland quoted lines from *The Ring and the Book*:

> Justinian's Pandects only make precise
> What simply sparkled in men's eyes before,
> Twitched in their brow or quivered on their lip,
> Waited the speech they called but would not come.

That Bractonian twist in time seems to infect even the verse: long centuries of making things precise lay behind Justinian. But Maitland was writing about people indeed near a beginning, near that second fall of man by which right and wrong, no longer manifested in divine judgements, had to be articulated into a workaday system. He knew what he was after, and looked forward to a time when 'the thoughts of our forefathers, their common thoughts about common things, will have become thinkable once more'. But all the resources of scholarship will not achieve it without some touch of his sense for common feelings as well. It is this Shakespearian quality that exacts devotion even from the unbeliever: 'Others abide our question'.

T.F.T. PLUCKNETT

T. F. T. PLUCKNETT—his formal signature was as characteristic as his formal dress, and to no more than two or three friends did he become Theo—was born on 2 January 1897 in Bristol. The name is an old one in Somerset; and perhaps he was descended from those early Plucknetts he was to meet in the Year Books, and from whose lawsuits and others like them he was to learn so much. But in his home the distinguished historian of the future would have seemed only a little less remote than the great family of the past. Intellectual inquiry was not absent, however. His father was Frank Plucknett, a master of shoe manufacturing processes and of the theory behind them, who taught in a series of technical colleges and is remembered as a pioneer in this branch of technical education. Frank Plucknett wrote two books on his subject, and there is about these a strength and directness, and a concern to make sense of detail from first principles, which it may not be fanciful to identify as sources of his son's quality. In more concrete terms, it seems certain that Plucknett, who was the only son, had the support and encouragement of his father in his ambitions; and there is some reason to think that when he was accepted as a full-time student at University College, London, his father sought employment in London to make the venture financially possible.

The household had then moved several times since Plucknett's birth, and nothing is known of his earliest education. Between the ages of 11 and 16 he was at Alderman Newton's School in Leicester, and for the two years after that at the Bacup and Rawtenstall School at Newchurch in Lancashire. Even as a schoolboy, however, he went about things in his own way. Whatever the weather or season, as a lady still living in Newchurch remembers, he was never without a rolled umbrella. And whatever occupation his contemporaries found for their free time, Plucknett was qualifying himself for an external degree. He matriculated at London University in 1913; and in 1915, when he was 18 years old, he graduated with second-class honours in history. When in the following year and within a week or two of his nineteenth birthday he became a full-time internal student at University College, it was not therefore as an undergraduate but as a candidate for the M.A.; and this degree he had obtained before he was 21.

The striking thing, however, is not so much the rapidity of his start as its independence. Although, after getting his first degree by private study, he spent seven years as a graduate student in London and the two Cambridges, those years were devoted to research. He seems to have undergone no formal courses of instruction, and to have had little guidance beyond whatever was involved in the supervision of his theses. The only known exception is that while in London he had some instruction from Hubert Hall in editorial techniques, and in his last years he remembered this with pleasure. Otherwise he can have had little time for anything but the work out of which came his M.A. thesis, supervised by Pollard and Miss Jeffries Davis, and the Alexander Prize Essay for 1917. In 1918 he went to Cambridge with a research exhibition in history at Emmanuel College. And though this led in 1920 to the LL.B. degree, it was awarded for research under regulations superseded when Cambridge adopted the Ph.D. His thesis on the early statutes was supervised by Hazeltine and published as the second volume in Hazeltine's series of Cambridge Studies in Legal History. After a further year at Emmanuel working on medieval canon law, Plucknett was nominated by Cambridge to the Choate Memorial Fellowship at Harvard. There he went to the Law School, which kept him for a second year as a student and then took him on to the staff. But as a student he again spent his time in historical research; and though no doubt he had some guidance from Pound, he attended no courses of any kind.

That the professor of legal history seems to have had no formal university instruction in either law or history is a pleasing fact; but it may also be relevant. The legal historian is fortunate in having an abundance of truly original materials which, though often complex and intractable, can be relied upon to give consistent answers when asked the right questions; and a major difficulty is to avoid anachronism in framing the questions. The formal continuity of our law and its language and institutions distorts the vision of an inquirer who brings the simplest assumption to his material. Plucknett allowed himself few assumptions, and the extent to which he had from the beginning found things out for himself must have had to do with this. For him, as he says in discussing Maitland's work, history was an adventure; and, though he does not use the adjective, the adventure was a solitary one. He went out among his sources and listened until they made their own sense to him; and his reports were in the definite terms of one who had been there. This sense of immediacy, which impressed his pupils from his earliest lecturing days, distinguishes his writing from much other work on legal history in two special respects. He did not go in for theories, propounded with particular pieces of evidence neatly deployed, though he sometimes attacked them in that way to clear the ground: either he knew, because his answer fitted a great mass of evidence, or he kept silent. And he did not go in for abstract connexions between the technicalities of one generation and those of another: what he listened for was the complaint of the lawyer's client, the mischief faced by the legislator or administrator.

The germination of these qualities, and of Plucknett's interests, can be seen in the work of his graduate student days. His M.A. thesis exists only in typescript; but there is a natural overlapping with his Alexander Prize Essay, 'The Place of the Council in the Fifteenth Century', which is printed in the *Transactions of the Royal Historical Society* for 1918. Although the prize was awarded to Plucknett when he was 20, there is no sign of youthfulness unless it is joy in the investigation and in the use of words to state the results. The work of other scholars has been digested, but it is not discussed. The political ideas of the time are allowed their place, but as the 'vague, hazy notions of the clerk in the office and the baron at court' rather than as large theories. What mattered were administrative routines, and the points in them at which power could in fact be brought to bear. And the directness of the approach is matched by the dexterity with which these things are reconstructed from the scattered remains. Such results as the discovery of the struggle for control of the royal seals are exciting in themselves; but they are by way of bonus to what would anyway have been an exciting inquiry. The same cannot be said of *Statutes and their Interpretation*. This is a dull book, and the dullness is that of the Ph.D. thesis: the author is not in full control of his materials. If Plucknett was ever intellectually a young man, it was when he did this, his second piece of work, at Emmanuel.

But the cause was in the subject rather than in the writer, and the book is important. For one thing it made a legal historian of Plucknett. How far this was intended, and by whom, can no longer be established. Hazeltine had not yet left Emmanuel for the Downing Chair when Plucknett went there; and whether or not Plucknett entered for his studentship at Emmanuel in order to work under him, he must have influenced the choice of subject. Rarely can an unhappy choice have had such happy results. At the outset Plucknett probably saw his question as a constitutional one; and both he and Hazeltine may have supposed that it could be answered by seeking statements in the Year Books. But for one of Plucknett's cast of mind it is impossible to be content with statements whose contexts are not understood. And so he found himself confronted with a multitude of individual problems which, for all the connexion they had with each other, might as well have been picked at random from the whole field of private law. Treated in this way the task was gigantic, something that a legal historian might attempt towards the end of his life, something indeed that Plucknett was to do again, and triumphantly, in his Ford Lectures. The triumph of the beginner was in getting the upper hand of his materials enough to make a book of them at all. But what matters in retrospect is the beginning.

Plucknett had now qualified himself in two areas. He had chosen to make a particular reconnaissance in constitutional history, and had done it with distinction and grace. In the history of private law, whether he had chosen to enter it, or had been directed there, or misdirected, he had in some sense found himself lost; and though he had made his own way through, and written an account of considerable value, the struggle had evidently been a weary one. That he went back there, and spent much of his life proving the wealth of this difficult country, is his chief contribution. But his constitutional interests never left him, and they account for many of his publications. Apart from the general survey which he undertook in editing *Taswell-Langmead*, when his usual materials became inaccessible during the second war, these mainly fall into three related groups. There are the institutional studies; the Alexander Prize Essay; 'The Lancastrian Constitution' contributed in 1924 to the celebratory volume for Pollard; and the study of parliament in the first volume of *The English Government at Work, 1327-1336*, published in 1940. He also became a member of the Editorial Board of the History of Parliament, when that project finally took shape. Then secondly there is a series of articles, ranging from 1937 to 1953, about the judicial aspect of government: impeachment and attainder, and state trials generally. And thirdly, and showing even more clearly than these how much of a piece Plucknett's interests really were, there are the studies in which he followed up, one by one, ideas that had come to him when he was writing *Statutes and their Interpretation*. The constitutional question from which that work seems to have started, seen as central in the United States and quietly smothered in England, is about the relationship between legislature and courts and the idea of fundamental law. To this Plucknett came back in an article in the *Harvard Law Review* on *Bonham's Case*, published in 1926 but the result of long cogitation, and remembered after his death by Mrs. Plucknett as a kind of Moby Dick. The legalistic shadow of this question, a matter which English lawyers can allow to be discussed so long as no conclusion is reached, is statutory interpretation itself. Plucknett returned to this in a public lecture of 1933 which was not itself printed but which formed the basis of his contribution to the studies in honour of Edouard Lambert in 1938; and here is a survey of one of the woods lost in the trees of his first book. And then there is the exploitation of the trees for their own sake, the use of legislative history to display the underlying social facts. From this came an article in 1936 about measures suggested before the enactment of the Statute of Uses, the Ford Lectures in 1947, and, in a sense, all Plucknett's work on the history of private law.

But in 1920, notwithstanding the book destined for the Cambridge legal history series and the rather misleading LL.B. which it had won, it is not clear that Plucknett saw himself as a legal historian in this sense. His third year at Emmanuel was spent on a point which had caught his attention when working on the statutes. But, although it again set him digging into the details of private lawsuits, he may first have seen it as a rather similar institutional problem. This was the treatment of canon law in the English royal courts; and the fruits of his inquiry were an immediate article in the *Cambridge Law Journal*, the acceptance of a dimension to be reckoned with in all his later work, and an interest in canon law as such which was to grow toward the end of his life. Even his earliest publications from the other Cambridge carried him no further into the sphere of private law. But if any external event finally drew him in, it was the award of the Choate Fellowship and his attachment to the Harvard Law School. Plucknett was, and he always firmly remained, an historian and not a lawyer; but the American and particularly the Harvard approach to the law would probably have been more congenial to him at that time than the English. The historian concerned to detect the mischiefs at which rules were originally aimed will at least understand the language of lawyers determined to approach rules from mischiefs; and they will understand his. More specifically, there was the influence of Pound. More specifically still, in the rather surprised words of Plucknett's own recollection, there was the fact 'that in September 1923 Roscoe Pound stood me for the first time before a university class, with a general direction to teach legal history'. And so began his career of just forty years as a professional legal historian, for most of that time, as he used to lament, the only one in the common-law world.

Harvard was good to Plucknett. His Choate Fellowship lasted only one year, but the Law School provided for another with one of their own scholarships. And it was no doubt his appointment in April 1923 as Instructor from September that enabled him in that year to marry. His wife was Marie, the daughter of Ferdinand Guibert of Clermont-Ferrand, and they met while she was teaching French in the Massachusetts Cambridge. They were married at her home in France, which became a second home for Plucknett, to be visited every year except when war or illness intervened; and there he is buried. His marriage was presumably also responsible for his taking ancillary employment in Cambridge, as Instructor in History at Radcliffe College; but this lasted only twelve months, and he seems never again to have allowed himself to be distracted by undertaking paid jobs outside his principal field of interest. From 1926 until his resignation and return to England in 1931 he was Assistant Professor of Legal History in the Law School. When he left, the Faculty gave a luncheon for him, and presented him with a set of the Year Books. It was a remarkable gesture to make to a junior colleague of eight years standing, now aged 34 and leaving to go to a new post in his own country.

But the Harvard Faculty had done more than give him a good send-off. His reputation at the time rested not only on his publications but also on the news they spread about him and about the course he gave. This was a general course for graduate students, uncompromisingly entitled 'History of English Law' and uncompromisingly requiring the use of original materials, Latin, black-letter, and all. Its impact may be recorded in words written after Plucknett's death by Dean Griswold, who in 1928–9 attended not as an enrolled member of the class but for interest's sake. It was 'one of the great experiences in my legal education'; and 'he made everything alive and interesting'. Whatever the feelings of piety, curiosity, or resignation with which members joined what must have looked like an arduous excursion into the unreal, some evidently came back believing that they had seen things both real and relevant. The everyday problems of another society had been conjured up around, and largely elicited from, its legal technicalities; and this was the kind of sense they wanted their twentieth-century law to make. It was this approach to his subject, little proclaimed and springing from a powerful sense of reality rather than from any *a priori* doctrine, that made his work exciting; and it was probably this that came in particular to the ears of Harold Laski, who played some part in bringing Plucknett to the London School of Economics. And so it came about that his quality as an historian made Plucknett one of only four full-time professors in the law faculty of London University. His was the first university post in England devoted to legal history, and there is still no other; and in 1931 London had no full-time professor in either Roman law or jurisprudence. It was an imaginative appointment; and there is irony in the reflection that towards the end of his life concern with the social context of the law, which had seemed a self-evident need to the medievalist, should have arrived after a slower crossing of the Atlantic to be a reforming cry in English legal education.

At Harvard Plucknett had written two books and had been partly responsible for a third. This, the earliest, was a new edition of the *Readings on the History and System of the Common Law* originally compiled by Pound, and it is one of two visible memorials of the association between these dissimilar men: the encyclopedic mind marshalling generalizations against the specialist marshalling facts; the teacher who wanted his ideas to be acted upon against the scholar concerned only to find out; the interpreter against the legal historian. But though one looked out and the other looked in, they stood upon much the same ground; and it is appropriate that library catalogues should list a book known as 'Pound and Plucknett'. The other memorial is the essay on wager of law which Plucknett contributed to the volume published in honour of Pound in 1962. Although nearly thirty years the younger, he was to outlive Pound by only a few months; and in this, his last printed work, there are signs of struggle.

'Pound and Plucknett' was published in 1927. In 1929 came the Ames Foundation *Year Books of 13 Richard II* and the first edition of the *Concise History of the Common Law*. The Year Book edition follows the pattern which had been worked out by the Selden Society in its Edward II volumes. But the textual problem was simpler because the manuscripts proved to be collatable; and the implications of this and other changes are discussed in an introduction which greatly advanced the study of the Year Books as such. The emphasis of Plucknett's approach to their content shows itself elsewhere in his introduction. Of a substantial commentary on cases which seemed to him interesting, less than a page at the end is devoted to those which played a special part in settling legal doctrine; the rest uses individual cases to light up their social and economic circumstances.

The *Concise History* defies discussion. As such books go it must be a best seller, having run to five editions and been translated into several languages, including Japanese. It grew in size with the years, but even the first edition was over 450 pages; and it was written by dictation in a few weeks. This last is of course a misleading statement. Plucknett did not work by forcing his thoughts into order on paper, disciplining them through successive drafts. A picture formed itself in his mind, and would then go straight down in very much its final form. The *Concise History* must have been taking shape, both in his head and as lecture notes, since he started teaching his Harvard course six years earlier. But the completeness and detailed richness of the panorama he unrolled in a single operation is altogether astonishing; and once again there is Plucknett's quality of immediacy. A rather flat effect is due to the scale of the work and not to any want of originality in the writer's vision. From the first this was far more than the undergraduates' textbook it professed to be; and through the successive editions it became more important for scholars at the expense of its acceptability to students. The accommodation of new knowledge disturbed its balance and flow, and enhanced the difficulties arising from compression. Of these Plucknett tried to take account. 'A concise statement, carefully framed, may be intrinsically accurate, and yet fail to convey to the beginner a true sense of the situation.' The sentence comes from his preface to the fourth edition; and in one reader it still arouses a rueful indignation which would have amused Plucknett, but is not mentioned entirely in fun. The beginner is not alone in his difficulty when there is nowhere else to look, when the words complained of are the only statement of a conclusion derived from a large mass of original materials. It can happen that an answer laboriously won from the sources is afterwards seen to be given in the *Concise History*, but in a way which had not meant much to one reading it before doing the work for himself. But what was lost by economy of words is now only a tantalizing addition to the knowledge inevitably lost on the death of a major scholar.

Plucknett did not go back to the United States after his return to England. Indeed, apart from his visits to France, he was never long away from the house in Wimbledon in which he and Mrs. Plucknett settled soon after his London appointment. They remained there throughout the second half of his life, and his last years were cheered by the presence next door, the width of his pleasant garden away, of their son and daughter-in-law and grandchildren. His study, surrounded by shelves but not nearly large enough for his books, was where he really lived. He was by disposition a methodical man. Files of letters were carefully kept. The page proofs of Selden Society volumes were bound up by himself, so that he could read them without irritation and get the feel of them as books. Finished galley proofs were spiked through at the head and strung together like plea rolls, and then hung up for use as rough paper. But the method did not extend, as it does not with many academic persons, to the accurate estimation and arrangement of his time, and there was generally a rush to get things finished. And after the first onset of his long last illness, when routine for some time continued to deal more or less well with established commitments and old correspondents, there was a growing limbo in which new matters might particularly get lost. For many years the Selden Society and other things involved him in much business over and above his own work. But, although letters except to a few friends particularly tired him, he seems to have found it less distracting to do things himself than to arrange for help. His own dexterity with a typewriter perhaps contributed to this. His books and articles, like his letters, were mostly typed with his own hands, being composed directly on the machine; and after a bout of illness he wrote of his pleasure at being comfortably settled in front of it again.

A survey of the principal works produced in the Wimbledon study, other than those already mentioned, may properly begin with the projects which were not really Plucknett's own. Among reference books and the like, there are many contributions to the *Encyclopaedia of the Social Sciences* and the *Annual Survey of English Law*; there is also the account of legal chronology in the Royal Historical Society's handbooks. The main bulk, however, is in his contributions to books published by learned societies. For the Dugdale Society he made an analytical index to the indictments in a volume of fourteenth-century sessions rolls edited by Dr. Kimball. For the Ames Foundation, of which he was for many years General Editor, he contributed to two volumes apart from his own Year Book: he wrote an elaborate commentary on the indictments in Miss Putnam's volume of proceedings before justices of the peace; and for Miss Thornley's *Year Books of 11 Richard II* he wrote both a commentary on cases and much of the legal annotation accompanying the text.

But the principal beneficiary was the Selden Society, of which he became one of three joint literary directors in 1937 on the death of Pollock. The other two were Holdsworth, who died in 1944, and G. J. Turner, who died in 1946. Although Plucknett edited no complete volume for the Society, and although his name appears on the title-page of only four, he had a hand in getting on for twenty. In some he played a large part, in many a small one; though even then his ministerial function was often arduous, particularly in the difficult period just after the war. There were also, of course, volumes which have not yet appeared, and a few which came to nothing; and some of these involved him in a great deal of work. Of the four volumes to which his name is attached, three are in the Year Book Series. In Volumes XXIII and XXIV of that series, largely the work of Professor Collas, Plucknett discussed the cases and provided their English summaries. Volume X, as its number suggests, had a longer history. It was originally entrusted to Geldart and Turner some time before the first war. Geldart died in 1922, and Turner had got most of the text into proof at least as early as 1933; but there, as happened with Turner, the matter rested. Plucknett completed the editorial work; and the introduction and apparatus are entirely his. The fourth of the volumes carrying Plucknett's name has a longer history still, and for the same reason. This is Turner's edition of *Brevia Placitata*, one of the most important single works the Society has ever published. Finding all the pieces and actually bringing it out were Plucknett's main contribution to this; but he undertook some revision and rearrangement, and added extracts from a later version linked by passages of exceedingly valuable commentary written by himself. It should be added that he had long been working on an edition of *Doctor and Student*, which was far from complete at his death but which the Society hopes to be able to finish. But the matter cannot be left as a discussion of specific books. When he had to give up a few months before his death, Plucknett had been a literary director for more than a third of the Society's existence, chiefly responsible for nearly a quarter; and the Society's aims and Plucknett's subject are that much further forward.

For anyone who feels moved, or able, to attempt a balance-sheet, these things and such activities as Plucknett's work for the History of Parliament, pose a common problem in a pointed way. They add up to a large advance of knowledge, much larger than the library catalogues or a bibliography will show. But from another angle they can be seen as a diffusion of his special talent, or at least as an investment in materials of which, had time been given, he could have made much more. If there is regret, it is for death itself; but at least the extent of his anonymous benefactions must be remembered. This work, with his university teaching, became his daily routine. From it he could and did rescue the time and concentration for many articles. But to produce a book some strong counter-pressure was needed; and the books that he wrote after his return to England were all the products of invitations to give special lectures.

The latest began as the Wiles Lectures in Belfast in 1958 and its rather pedestrian title, *Edward I and Criminal Law*, is misleading. The Wiles Lectures are devoted to the history of civilization, and Plucknett addressed himself to fundamental questions. The approach was characteristic. A society's state of advancement was to be judged by getting inside the mind of a legislator, of Aethelberht and Alfred as well as of Edward I. Was the law seen as a system, or systematic thought seen as desirable? To the extent that it presented itself as a monetary calculus, can considerations of financial advantage be separated from those of good government? And what part was played by what ideas of right and wrong? Such questions are for an historian at the height of his powers; and Plucknett, whose illness had first struck three years before the lectures were given, was too late. His life's learning was brought to bear, but could no longer quite be focused, and by the highest standards his last book must be classed with his first as a failure, though for the converse reason: large ideas are insufficiently fixed in place by detail. But few venture into such dark places, and even a flickering light shows exciting shapes or shadows for other brave men to explore.

Early English Legal Literature began as a series of lectures in Cambridge to celebrate the centenary of Maitland's birth. The first chapter, published also in the *Law Quarterly Review* for 1951, is called 'Maitland's View of Law and History', and it will be mentioned later as the only real expression of Plucknett's view of these things. The rest of the book surveys legal literature from

Henry I to Henry VIII, but its emphasis lies in the thirteenth and early fourteenth centuries. A 'cautious reconnaissance of the Bractonian position' ('there is always the risk of getting caught in the fire of zealous colleagues') is followed by an inspection of more peaceful and ultimately richer ground. The clerical and learned Bractonian tradition ended and, after a little spurt, science with it. A new literary beginning was made in practical tracts and then in the disorderly reporting of cases; and in this dingy new tradition, 'insular, lay, and French (what French!)', the unremarkable English customs were transmuted by men learned in no arts but their own into a great system of law. The real theme is the controlling effect on the law of the education and the cultural background of its practitioners; and this book is the statement for which Plucknett had been feeling in his inaugural lecture in London twenty years earlier.

Just as legal literature was for Plucknett about lawyers, so the law itself was about life. The Ford Lectures in 1947, the *Legislation of Edward I*, and the Creighton Lecture of 1953, *The Mediaeval Bailiff*, are really studies in social history; and they represent his most individual and in one sense his most perfect work. Particular results may of course be open to question: what is conclusively demonstrated, and beautifully, is the method. From the great mass of legal material that survives from the Middle Ages, it will be possible to reconstruct a picture of society as rich and full as any historian could wish for; but it will not be done by chance finds of social detail more or less expressly stated, but by laboriously piecing together lawyer's law.

Plucknett did not often preach, but he was explicit about this message: 'The present trend of medieval studies is happily in the direction of increased use by historians of legal materials as a source for constitutional, economic, and general history, and it is much to be hoped that they will extend their curiosity to the law itself.' If the view suggested earlier of his own metamorphosis is right, namely that he first opened Year Books to look for constitutional statements, these words from his preface to the Ford Lectures must have been deeply felt. The underlying creed was put more characteristically in his Creighton Lecture: 'It is only in text-books that constitutional, economic and legal history are set apart from one another. In real life they are simultaneous, and one man lives all his histories concurrently.'

An important corollary, regarding legal history as sufficiently separate for a person to concentrate on it, is that that person ought to be an historian and not a lawyer. He must know about the other histories his litigants were living. It was this need for completeness of vision, as much as the difficulties of the lawyer in thinking like an historian, that led Plucknett, in his chapter on Maitland at the beginning of *Early English Legal Literature*, to insist that legal historians must be recruited from the history school rather than from the law school. That this is the ideal cannot be doubted, certainly not by one who came from the law school and knows the handicap. But from whichever discipline one starts, the other must always be difficult; and Plucknett did not realize how improbable his own achievement was, or how rebarbative legal technicalities can be to the historian. So far there has been no recruiting and no occasion for choice. The subject's few volunteers have come from either side, and generally by accident.

The value of legal history to lawyers was considered by Plucknett in the same chapter on Maitland and in his presidential address to the Society of Public Teachers of Law; and again the premiss was that the subject must be regarded as history for its own sake. There could be no use in 'obsolete law, repealed statutes, cases overruled, institutions long ago abolished', not even as background knowledge. 'It is still too often said that English law can only be understood historically. Now English law may be bad, but is it really as bad as that?' There was probably conscious exaggeration. Like Maitland before him, Plucknett believed that just as the history which emerges from legal argument is apt to be bad history, so the law which relies on historical justification is apt to be bad law. It is a good working principle. But a system such as ours can never quite be freed from its continuing past; and we do not have to urge that the Chancery Division should be abolished because we cannot well explain its existence without going back in time. Legal history has more workaday relevance than as a diagnostic aid for the law reformer; but reservation about the negative side of Plucknett's proposition does not affect the positive. The history of law, like its philosophy, enables the lawyer to see his subject from the outside, otherwise a very difficult thing for him to do. And if he looks at it as Plucknett did, connecting abstractions not just with other abstractions but with life itself, he may see and judge his own technicalities in their proper place among 'men's attempts to introduce order into their affairs'.

Literally as well as otherwise it was increasingly to historians rather than to lawyers that Plucknett spoke. At the Harvard

Law School his colleagues and his pupils had all been lawyers. But in London he taught constitutional and other history to history students, and legal history but, of course, no modern law to law students; and he had more to do with his colleagues in the history faculty than with those in the law faculty. To lawyers and law teachers he became an honoured but remote figure; and his own sense of pleasant incongruity appears from the beginning of his presidential address to the Public Teachers of Law. A larger task, and an office which meant much to him, was his presidency of the Royal Historical Society. He was given honorary doctorates of laws at Glasgow and Birmingham, and of letters at Cambridge, a variation particularly pleasing to the whole-hearted historian. He also became Fellow of the British Academy, Fellow of University College, London, and Honorary Fellow of Emmanuel College, Cambridge.

Plucknett had to resign his chair in 1963, an old man before his time. He died on 14 February 1965. Outside his home his life had been a solitary one, though not lonely. Having deep reserves, in both senses of that word, he did not seek personal contacts. But there was nothing forbidding about him. Simple and kindly in manner, he went to much trouble for those whom he regarded as having a claim on him, and did it with unaffected enthusiasm. He was incapable of superficial work, however, and the time taken up by such excursions seems to have induced in him a habit of elusiveness to the casual inquirer, which enhanced the withdrawn impression he gave. He came to read mostly around his subject, and his recreations were the unsociable ones of music and, occasionally, mathematical puzzles. Disliking small talk and detesting politics at any level, he appeared to his less intimate colleagues as amiable but uncommunicative and unworldly; and many would have been surprised at the efficiency with which he ordered things that seemed important to him, at the firmness with which he could defend his own interests and those of scholarship, and at the occasional sharpness of his tongue. The two or three friends with whom he would truly relax were all historians of similar interests, and even with them the talk was hardly ever personal; perhaps even they did not fully realize how small was their number, and how unusual such relaxation was for him.

But this was not the withdrawal of melancholy: it was just that Plucknett did not live much of his life in company. He was by nature cheerful, and he remained so through his last illness. He enjoyed dealing with Selden Society proofs, and baby-sitting for his grandchildren while doing so, and looking forward to a glass of wine, and looking back at his own success; and above all he enjoyed making sense of his materials. This deep pleasure in his work was obvious in conversation and in his letters, and it is obvious in much of his writing. Those occasional vivid phrases are not added ornament, but particularly gay flights in a prose in which happy excitement is often discernible. Labour went into it, but not into the composition: things fitted together, and the world which came to life was described with spontaneous delight. Only for Maitland had the dead technicalities of early English law yielded visions so intense.

TABLE OF CASES

I. ENTRIES FROM UNPUBLISHED PLEA ROLLS

The original articles on Trespass and Sale of Goods included references to entries on four rolls which have since been published: KB 26/104 in *Curia Regis Rolls, vol. XIII*; KB 26/117, KB 26/121 and KB 26/123 in vol. XVI. The affected footnotes in Chapters 1 and 3 have been altered to refer to individual entries in these volumes rather than to membranes of the rolls themselves, and the affected entries are included in the second rather than in the first section of this Table.

KB 26/146 (1252)
m.1d	(prisoner abducted)	17
m.9d	(trespass in chase)	12

KB 26/154 (1254)
m.13	*(ejectio firme)*	5
m.31	*(ejectio firme)*	5
m.33	*(ejectio firme)*	5

KB 26/155 (1255)
m.1	(trespass in chase)	12
m.1d	(goods taken from servant)	19, 61
m.2d	(assault and battery)	13
m.3	(ejectment from quarantine)	4
m.3d	(trespass in park)	12, 14
m.3d	(house burnt)	20
m.5	(woman abducted)	17
m.5d	(goods taken)	18, 85
m.6	*(ejectio custodie)*	32
m.9d	(battery)	13
m.9d	(goods taken)	18
m.10d	(goods taken)	18
m.10d	(pound-breach)	37
m.11d	(trespass in park)	12

KB 26/161 (1259-60)
m.1d	(wrongful sale by pledgee)	64
m.3	*(ejectio firme)*	5
m.3d	(trespass: title recited)	35
m.3d	(toll wrongfully taken)	48
m.4	(toll wrongfully taken)	48
m.6	(market picketed)	44, 77
m.9d	(toll collection impeded)	47
m.12	*(ejectio firme)*	5
m.15	*(ejectio firme)*	5
m.17d	(toll collection impeded)	47
m.17d	(wrongful sale by pledgee)	64
m.18d	(market picketed)	44
m.19	(pound breach)	36, 37
m.19d	(rescue)	36, 37
m.22	(servant imprisoned)	16

(KB 26/161 (1259-60, continued)
m.22	(trespass: lease recited)	34
m.22d	(trespass against lessor)	34-35

KB 26/164 (1260)
m.16d	(house burnt)	20, 82

KB 26/167 (1260)
m.1	*(ejectio firme)*	5
m.17	(swan killed)	25
m.19	(market picketed)	44, 77
m.22	(battery)	14

KB 26/168 (1260)
m.1	(principal and accessory)	4
m.2	(battery)	14
m.4	(hunting)	12
m.5d	(battery)	14
m.11d	(fowling)	23
m.16d	*(ejectio firme)*	5
m.16d	(false imprisonment)	16

KB 26/200A (1270)
m.5	(goods taken: duress)	18, 81
m.6	(assault and battery)	14
m.6	(servant wronged)	16
m.6	(goods taken)	18
m.9	(depasturing)	8
m.9d	(market dues taken)	42-43
m.33d	(trespass: title recited)	35

KB 26/201 (1271)
m.7	(prisoner rescued)	14, 16, 17
m.7d	(justification: containing fire)	81
m.8d	*(quare ejecit)*	6
m.9	(jurisdictional franchise)	49, 76
m.19d	(pound-breach)	37

(Entries from Unpublished Plea Rolls, cont.)

CP 40/2A (1273)

m.1	(false imprisonment)	15
m.2	(servant wronged)	16
m.2d	(viscontiel damage formula)	77
m.5	(violent invasion of land)	18
m.6d	*(ejectio custodie)*	32
m.10	(false imprisonment)	15
m.10d	*(ejectio custodie)*	32
m.10d	(market picketed)	44-45
m.11	(act done by night)	75
m.12d	(goods burnt)	20, 77
m.14	(trespass in warren)	12, 79
m.15	(false imprisonment)	15
m.19	(goods taken)	18
m.21d	(trespass: facts recited)	35, 77
m.21d	(rescue)	37
m.22d	(rescue)	36
m.22d	(demise of crown)	74
m.23d	(sea-wall not repaired)	54-55
m.28	(demise of crown)	76

CP 40/4 (1273)

m.2	(battery)	14
m.8	(viscontiel damage formula)	77
m.17d	(pound-breach)	37
m.26	(goods taken)	18
m.29	(viscontiel damage formula)	77
m.30d	(charters burnt)	20
m.31	(market picketed)	44-45
m.35	(false imprisonment)	16
m.40	(viscontiel damage formula)	77
m.41d	*(ejectio custodie)*	32
m.48d	(sea-wall not repaired)	54-55
m.51	(battery)	14
m.52	(battery)	14
m.53d	(battery)	14

CP 40/5 (1274)

m.19d	(depasturing)	8
m.36d	(formedon)	225
m.78	(depasturing)	9
m.89	(market picketed)	44-45
m.98	(trespass: facts recited)	35
m.101d	(viscontiel damage formula)	77

CP 40/7 (1275)

m.9d	(freedom from multure)	34
m.23	(free fold?)	40
m.47	(free boar)	38

CP 40/8 (1275)

m.4	(formedon)	223, 227-8
m.14	*(quare ejecit)*	6

(CP 40/8 [1275], cont.)

m.20d	(bridge broken)	29
m.22	(viscontiel damage formula)	16, 77
m.38	*(quare ejecit)*	6
m.39d	(goods taken)	18
m.48	(free boar)	38
m.53	(formedon)	225, 228-29

CP 40/9 (1275)

m.6	(free fold)	40, 79
m.13	(trespass in warren)	79
m.38d	(viscontiel damage formula)	77

CP 40/13 (1276)

m.1	(demise of crown)	76
m.7	(viscontiel damage formula)	77
m.19	(demise of crown)	76
m.24	(viscontiel damage formula)	77
m.25	(viscontiel damage formula)	77
m.27	(viscontiel damage formula)	77
m.31	(viscontiel damage formula)	77
m.35	(sea-wall not repaired)	54-55, 57, 73
m.38	(viscontiel damage formula)	77
m.49	(viscontiel damage formula)	77
m.50	(principal and accessory)	85
m.61	(viscontiel damage formula)	77
m.71	(viscontiel damage formula)	77

CP 40/17 (1276)

m.13	(easement recited)	40

CP 40/48 (1283)

m.16d	(incidence of *vi et armis*)	12
m.21d	(incidence of *vi et armis*)	7
m.24d	(incidence of *vi et armis*)	12
m.25d	(toll wrongfully taken)	48
m.28d	(swans killed by dogs)	23
m.36d	(incidence of *vi et armis*)	12
m.45d	(false imprisonment)	15
m.51	*(ejectio custodie)*	32, 73
m.57d	*(ejectio custodie)*	32
m.61	(rescue)	37
m.66d	(incidence of *vi et armis*)	12
m.68d	(incidence of *vi et armis*)	12

CP 40/49 (1283)

m.5	(swans taken)	23
m.5d	(false imprisonment)	16
m.6	(jurisdictional franchise)	50
m.11d	(false imprisonment)	16
m.13	(pound-breach)	37
m.17d	(free fold)	39

Table of Cases

(Entries from Unpublished Plea Rolls,
CP 40/49 [1283], cont.)

m.23	(false imprisonment)	16
m.25	(toll wrongfully taken)	48
m.31	(jurisdictional franchise)	50-51, 73, 77
m.45	(market impeded)	45
m.45d	(title recited)	35
m.50d	(false imprisonment)	16
m.51d	(battery)	14
m.54	(battery)	14
m.55d	(false imprisonment)	16

CP 40/50 (1283)

m.16d	(debt: general issue)	115
m.17	(depasturing)	9
m.23	(debt: general issue)	115
m.24	*(ejectio custodie)*	32
m.29d	(general issue and justification)	82
m.40d	(swans killed by dogs)	23
m.52d	(justification: right of common)	79

CP 40/174 (1309)

m.151d	(fraud of market)	46, 73, 92

KB 27/201 (1310)

m.22d	(trespass against bailee)	65

KB 27/215 (1314)

m.4	(trespass: formulation of general issue)	80
m.60d	(trespass: formulation of general issue)	80
m.66d	(trespass: justification)	79
m.69d	(prescriptive right impeded)	40, 53
m.72	(general issue and justification)	82
m.83d	(free fold)	40
m.92	(free fold)	40
m.100	(nuisance to market)	42

KB 27/236 (1319)

m.89	(demise of crown)	74
m.103	(formedon)	225

CP 40/235 (1320)

m.91	(justification: right of common)	79
m.117	(free fold)	40
m.126	(trespass: formulation of general issue)	80

(CP 40/235 [1320], cont.)

m.155d	(protection recited)	53
m.156	(river-banks not repaired)	55
m.160d	(market impeded)	45
m.208	(house broken and goods taken)	66

CP 40/236 (1320)

m.31	(room broken and goods taken)	66
m.100	(freedom from multure)	34
m.103	(trespass against bailee?)	66
m.117d	(river-banks not repaired)	55

KB 27/242 (1320)

m.60	(general issue and justification)	81-82
m.100	(*recordari facias* ignored)	54

CP 40/237 (1321)

m.161d	(river-banks not repaired)	55

CP 40/238 (1321)

m.30d	(horse killed by smith)	86
m.10	(attornies) (river-banks not repaired)	55

KB 27/244 (1321)

m.71	(dogs incited to damage)	22, 23

CP 40/240 (1321)

m.51	(trespass against bailee?)	66

KB 27/279 (1330)

m.51	(market attacked)	43

CP40/291 (1332)

m.42	(collection of market dues impeded)	43
m.52	(free fold?)	40
m.226	(trespass: justification)	79
m.229d	(coal taken and mine damaged)	35

KB 27/300 (1335)

m.8	(market attacked and picketed)	43,44
m.13	(trespass: formulation of general issue)	80
m.17	(horse killed by smith)	86
m.60	(trespass against bailee?)	66
m.93	(trespass against bailee?)	66
m.95d	(trespass: consequential damage	35,62

(Entries from Unpublished Plea Rolls, KB 27/300 [1335], cont.)
m96d	(trespass: justification)	79
m.131	(prohibition)	53

CP 40/312 (1337)
m.47	(beasts killed)	25
m.64	(franchise of estray)	41
m.189	(depasturing)	8,79
m.247	(franchise of wreck)	41

CP 40/320 (1339)
m.334	(franchise of estray)	41,92

CP 40/330 (1342)
m.304	(river wall not repaired)	56,57, 73

CP 40/340 (1344)
m.16	(free fold?)	40
m.62	(franchise of wreck)	41
m.82	(trespass: justification)	79
m.191	(trespass against bailee?)	66
m.257	(jurisdictional franchise)	50
m.286	(collection of market dues impeded)	43
m.375	(trespass against bailee?)	66

KB 27/338 (1344)
m.41	(river wall not repaired)	56

CP 40/350 (1347)
m.1d	(city wall damaged)	53
m.16	(rescue)	36
m.19	(trespass against bailee?)	66
m.56d	(market picketed)	43-44
m.66	(protection recited)	53
m.79	(trespass: justification)	79
m.80d	(trespass:facts recited)	35
m.104	(heriot taken by third party)	41
m.118d	(trespass against bailee?)	66
m.135	(distraint for repair of river-wall)	54,79
m.184	(trespass: formulation of general issue)	80
m.185d	(horse killed by smith)	86
m.251d	(trespass against bailee?)	66
m.302d	*(son assault demesne)*	79

CP 40/360 (1350)
m.4d	(jurisdictional franchise)	52
m.48	(franchise of wreck)	79
m.56d	(king's contractor wronged)	53

(CP 40/360 [1350], cont.)
m.56d	(trespass against bailee?)	66
m.72d	(trespass against bailee?)	66
m.101d	(trespass against bailee?)	66

KB 27/358 (1350)
m.42	(market attacked)	43

CP 40/370 (1352)
m.3	(depasturing)	9
m.12d	(pigs deliberately mutilated)	25
m.22d	(wrongful sequestration)	36
m.26d	(dogs incited to damage)	22
m.35d	(horse killed)	25
m.46	(horse killed)	25
m.49d	(river-walls not repaired)	55,56
m.67d	(gutter not reapaired)	58
m.73d	(horse killed)	25
m.74d	(dogs incited to damage)	22
m.78	(house and goods burnt)	21
m.94	(collection of market dues impeded)	43
m.100	(dogs incited to damage)	22
m.122	(prisoner rescued)	17
m.126d	(bullocks killed)	25
m.137	(protection recited)	53
m.148	(horse killed)	25
m.155d	(dogs incited to damage	22
m.156d	(dogs incited to damage)	22
m.159	(trespass: justification)	79
m.159d	(sheriff's officer wronged)	53
m.165	(trespass against bailee)	68-69

CP 40/371 (1352)
m.2	(horse killed)	25
m.8	(house and goods burnt)	21
m.12	(dogs incited to damage)	22
m.13	(beasts killed)	25
m.25	(depasturing)	10
m.53	(house and goods burnt)	21
m.56	(free fold)	22
m.98	(house and goods burnt)	21
m.122	(dogs incited to damage)	22
m.135	(horse ill shod *contra pacem*)	27,29
m.138	(pigs killed)	25
m.144	(horse killed by smith)	25,27
m.203	(beast killed and servant beaten)	25
m.223	(dogs incited to damage)	22
m.240	(dogs incited to damage)	22

Table of Cases

(Entries from Unpublished Plea Rolls, cont.)

CP 40/373 (1353)
m.1	(house and goods burnt)	21
m.15	(cask of wine destroyed)	27,70
m.17	(son abducted)	16-17
m.39	(trespass against bailee?)	66
m.42d	(house and goods burnt)	21
m.57d	(horse killed)	25
m.60d	(beasts killed and depasturing)	25
m.71	(beasts killed)	25
m.75d	(dogs incited to damage)	22
m.78	(horse driven into marsh)	26
m.94	(horse killed)	25
m.96	(dogs incited to damage)	22
m.97	(dogs incited to damage)	22
m.119	(beasts killed maliciously)	25
m.137d	(trespass against bailee?)	66
m.153d	(malicious damage with dogs)	23-24
m.168d	(beasts killed and goods taken)	25
m.172	(trespass against bailee?)	66
m.185	(beasts killed maliciously)	25
m.189d	(gallows broken)	38

KB 27/380 (1355)
m.7d	(house and goods burnt)	21
m.17	(trespass: justification)	79
m.33d	(depasturing)	9
m.45d	(trespass: justification)	79
m.49d	(jurisdictional franchise)	51
m.71	*(son assault demesne)*	79
m.79	(trespass against carrier)	68

CP 40/391 (1357)
m.11	(replication *de injuria*)	80
m.20d	(house broken and goods taken)	66
m.47	(trespass: justification)	79
m.57	*(son assult demesne)*	79
m.72d	(free fold?)	40
m.117	(replication *de injuria*)	80
m.120	(right of way)	40-41
m.125	(trespass: general issue)	80
m.127	(free fold ?)	40
m.130	(replication *de injuria*)	80
m.155	(jurisdictional franchise)	51
m.213	(customs seal removed)	36
m.236	(goods taken)	66
m.242	(jurisdictional franchise)	51
m.244	(trespass: justification)	79

CP 40/395 (1358)
m.86d	(debt: accountant in credit)	140-41
m.133	*(concessit solvere)*	140,142
m.226d	*(concessit se teneri)*	138

CP 40/399 (1359)
m.11	(franchise of waif)	41
m.19	(beasts killed and servant beaten)	25
m.27	(agisted beast taken without payment)	62
m.28d	(villein abducted)	17
m.35	(horse killed)	25
m.46	(meadow torn up by pigs)	10
m.51	(trespass: justification)	79
m.55	(dogs incited to damage)	22
m.57	(beasts killed maliciously)	25
m.58d	(franchise of wreck)	41
m.62	(villein abducted)	17
m.76d	(franchise of waif)	41
m.80	(beasts killed and land invaded)	25
m.85d	(beasts killed maliciously)	25
m.86d	(villein abducted)	17
m.89	(sheep killed by driving)	22
m.103	(beasts killed and land invaded)	25
m.112	(servant abducted)	17
m.115	*(son assault demesne)*	79
m.120d	(dogs incited to damage)	22
m.135d	(horse killed)	25
m.144d	(villein abducted)	17,82
m.151	(meadow torn up by pigs)	10
m.153d	(dogs incited to damage)	22
m.155	(horse killed)	25
m.155d	(beasts killed and goods taken	25
m.155d	(depasturing)	9
m.158	(rescue)	36
m.161	(beasts killed and depasturing)	25
m.168	*(son default demesne)*	10,80,85
m.185d	(villein abducted)	17
m.188d	(rescue and non-payment of toll)	45
189d	(beasts killed and goods taken)	25
m.204d	(sheep killed by driving)	22
m.210	(horse killed by smith)	25,27
m.215	(dogs incited to damage)	22
m.220d	(documents taken from servant)	19,61

(Entries from Unpublished Plea Rolls, cont.)

CP 40/408 (1362)
m.30	(non-payment of toll)	45
m.76	(franchise of waif)	41

KB 27/405 (1362)
m.2	*(son assault demesne)*	79
m.3d	*(son assault demesne)*	79
m.16d	(mayhem)	84
m.23	(horse killed)	25
m.41d	(villein rescued)	17
m.64	(free fold)	40

KB 27/414 (1364)
m.17d	(servant leaving employment)	52
m.24	(dogs incited to damage)	22
m.37d	(surgeon)	15,71-72, 82
m.50d	(horse killed)	25

KB 27/418 (1365)
m.10	(*scienter* liability: incitement writ)	22-23,24, 81,82

KB 27/419 (1365)
m.24	(battery)	69

CP 40/429 (1367)
m.18	(poisoning by servant)	15
m.79	(franchise of estray)	41
m.86d	(sheep not looked after)	63
m.92	(franchise of waif)	41
m.193d	(collection of market dues impeded)	47
m.232d	(horse killed by smith)	86
m.282d	(leased sheep re-taken)	62
m.295	(rescue)	36
m.357	*(scienter)*	24
m.374d	(profits of fair taken)	42
m.417	(jurisdictional franchise)	51
m.422	(river-walls not repaired)	55,57
m.471	(sheep not looked after)	63,64
m.511d	(franchise of estray)	41
m.552	(leased sheep re-taken)	62
m.576	(dumping mud in which horses perished)	26
m.592	(non-payment of toll)	45,47
m.592	(executioner permitting escape)	64
m.600	(leased sheep retaken)	62

KB 27/430 (1368)
m.26	(river-walls not repaired)	55,56,57
m.33	(trespass against carrier)	69
m.36	(freedom from toll)	76
m.39	(franchise of estray)	41,79

CP 40/440 (1370)
m.61	*(concessit solvere)*	138-39
m.70	(misfeasance: smith)	160-61
m.204d	(misfeasance: bailee)	160-61
m.260	(misfeasance: marshal)	160-61
m.309	(misfeasance: shepherd)	160-61
m.407	(nonfeasance: ploughing and sowing)	160-61
m.520	(misfeasance: tiler)	160-61
m.530d	(debt on private accounting)	141,142
m.630d	(nonfeasance: carriage by water)	160-61

CP 40/443 (1371)
m.20d	(mill not looked after)	63
m.106	(river-walls not repaired)	57
m.124d	(gutter not repaired) chattels)	58 41
m.124d	gutter not repaired)	58
m.188	(wine-cask staved by carrier)	70
m.196d	(jurisdictional franchise)	51
m.232	(river-walls not repaired)	57
m.235	(misfeasance: shepherd)	63
m.237d	(royal grant recited)	35
m.250d	(free fold)	40
m.308	(innkeeper)	58
m.375d	(non-payment of shoppage)	45
m.416	(profits of office taken)	47, 48-49
m.416	(freedom from toll)	76

CP 40/488 (1383)
m.437	(debt: 40s by addition)	107
m.456d	(detinue by buyer)	122

CP 40/521 (1391)
m.28	(debt: verdict for less than 40s)	107
m.96d	(nonfeasance: building house)	161
m.156d	(detinue by buyer)	122
m.174	(warranty on exchange of goods)	129
m.185d	(debt: tender of part)	107
m.201d	(nonfeasance: building

Table of Cases

(Entries from Unpublished Plea Rolls, CP 40/521 [1391], cont.)

m.217	(detinue by buyer)	122
m.249	(debt on account)	134
m.276	(nonfeasance: mowing)	161
m.291d	(nonfeasance: repairing mill)	161
m.300	(debt: 40s by addition)	107
m.340	(nonfeasance: building mill)	161
m.387d	(nonfeasance: repairing mill)	161
m.435d	(debt: verdict for less than claim)	107
m.474	(detinue by buyer)	122, 123
m.481	(nonfeasance: building house)	161

CP 40/574 (1404)

m.89d	(debt: on purchase by wife *dum sola*)	110
m.188	(debt on private accounting)	142
m.195	(warranty: price not paid)	129
m.233d	(debt on private accounting)	142
m.244	(debt; tender of part)	107
m.244d	(debt: wager against executors)	110
m.290	(debt on private accounting)	141, 143
m.367	(debt on private accounting)	141, 143
m.382	(debt: wager against abbot's successor)	110
m.386d	(debt: on sale by wife *dum sola*)	110
m.447d	(debt: tender of part)	107
m.494	(debt: wager against executors)	110

CP 40/632 (1419)

m.102d	(debt on account: examination)	135
m.200	(debt: sale of land)	120
m.304d	(debt on account: examination)	135
m.334d	(debt: sale of land)	120
m.342	(warranty: herring)	127
m.476d	(roast cat served as rabbit)	127
m.492	(warranty: size of oaks)	130

KB 27/639 (1421)

m.69	(warranty: price not paid)	129

CP 40/705 (1437)

m.50d	(case: non-delivery of coal)	125
m.52d	(case: non-delivery of fish)	125
m.115d	(debt: 40s. by subtraction)	108
m.151	(debt: 40s. by subtraction)	108
m.210d	(warranty: size of cloth)	127, 130
m.261d	(debt: 40s. by addition)	107
m.298d	(debt: 40s. by addition)	107, 108
m.431	(debt; 40s. by addition)	107
m.441	(debt: 40s. by addition)	107

KB 27/731 (1444)

m.63d	(case: non-delivery of corn)	125

CP 40/744 (1447)

m.31	(warranty: metal binding of mazer)	129
m.111d	(warranty: size of cloths)	130
m.276	(warranty: growth of wool)	130
m.283d	(warranty: annual value of land)	130
m.358d	(warranty: size of cloths)	130

CP 40/798 (1460)

m.167	(warranty: horse)	127

CP 40/828 (1468)

m.22d	(warranty: growth of wine)	130
m.154d	(warranty: horse)	128

CP 40/875 (1481)

m.133d	(debt: 40s. by addition)	107-08
m.163d	(debt: sale of land)	120
m.420d	(detinue by buyer)	122

CP 40/915 (1491)

m.124	(debt: 40s. by addition)	107
m.166	(warranty: herring)	127
m.411d	(detinue by buyer)	122

CP 40/957 (1501)

m.106d	(detinue by buyer)	122
m.110	(debt: tender by part)	107
m.114d	(detinue by buyer)	122
m.150d	(debt: 40s. by addition)	108
m.173d	(detinue by buyer)	122
m.181	(warranty: metal and music of organ)	129
m.248	(detinue by buyer)	122
m.285d	(debt: 40s. by addition)	107

(Entries from Unpublished Plea Rolls, CP 40/957 [1501], cont.)

m.297	(detinue by buyer)	122
m.297d	(detinue by buyer)	122
m.310	(debt: sale by executors)	106
m.318d	(debt: purchase by wife)	111
m.341	(debt: general issue *modo et forma*)	116
m.342d	(detinue by buyer)	122
m.361	(detinue by buyer)	122
m.475d	(case: non-delivery of goods)	125

KB 27/999 (1511)

m.20d	(detinue by buyer)	122, 125

KB 27/1006 (1513)

m.28d	(detinue by buyer)	122
m.36	(slander)	146-47
m.37	*(praemunire)*	145-46
m.47	(case: non-delivery of goods)	125

CP 40/1064 (1530)

m.139d	(debt: payable *pro rata* on delivery)	120
m.255	(debt: wager against executors)	110
m.307	(debt: tender of part)	107
m.310	(debt: bond for commodity)	122
m.355d	(debt: tender of part)	107
m.421	(debt: verdict for less than 40s.)	107

CP 40/1140 (1549)

m.102	(debt: 40s. by addition)	108
m.248d	(debt: 40s. by addition)	108
m.306d	(debt and detinue: joinder)	105

Sheriffs' Court Roll, 1320
(London – Guildhall Record Office)

m.7	*(concessit solvere)*	137-38
m.7d	*(concessit solvere)*	137
m.15d	*(concessit solvere)*	136-37

II. ENTRIES FROM PUBLISHED PLEA ROLLS

In the paper on Inheritance by Women, here Chapter 12, all the known plea roll entries were given for each case cited; but only the principal entries have been included in this Table.

Three Rolls of the King's Court (1194-95);
Pipe Roll Soc., vol. 14

pp. 30-31	(elder sister against younger)	237, 241, 252

Rotuli Curiae Regis, I (1194-99)

p. 147	(*esnecia* between sisters)	241, 253
p. 359	(curtesy)	256, 257, 258
p. 363	(*esnecia* between brothers)	240
p. 393	(husband's *custodia* of wife's land)	257
p. 432	(curtesy)	255, 256

Rotuli Curiae Regis, II (1199-1200)

p. 56	(dower: marriage denied)	246
p. 65	(curtesy)	256, 257, 258
pp. 88-89	(elder brother against younger)	240
pp. 124-25	(*maritagium*)	256, 258
p. 196	(curtesy)	256, 257, 258
pp. 202-03	(curtesy)	254, 255, 256

"Curia Regis Roll, 9 Ric. I":
Pipe Roll Society, NS. vol. 31, pp. 96-118

pp. 100-01	(*maritagium* claimed from heir)	244
p. 105	(*maritagium*: writ patent to heir)	244
p. 109	(inheritance or purchase)	241, 253
p. 110	(tenure between sisters)	242

"Roll of the Justices in Eyre at Bedford, 1202":
Bedfordshire Historical Record Society, vol. 1,
pp. 144-247

pp. 158-61, pl. 63	(curtesy)	255
pp. 160-61, pl. 65	(curtesy)	255-257

The Earliest Northamptonshire Assize Rolls,
Northamptonshire Record Society, vol. 5
(1202-03)

pl. 450	(husband's *custodia* of wife's land)	257

Pleas before the King or his Justices, I
Selden Society, vol. 67
(pleas 1199-1202; writs 1190-1206)

pl. 3198	(dispute over Barnstaple)	238
pl. 3475	(nature of heiress's right)	260
pl. 3488	(*precipe* between sisters)	242, 244

Pleas before the King or his Justices, II
Selden Society, vol. 68 (1198-1202)

pl. 455	(husband's *custodia* of wife's land	257

Pleas before the King or his Justices, III
Selden Society, vol. 83 (1199-1206)

pl. 860	(mort d'ancestor between sisters)	245

Rolls of the Justices in Eyre for Yorkshire, 1218-19
Selden Society, vol. 56

pl. 22	(curtesy)	255
pl. 167	(curtesy)	254, 256
pl. 292	(husband's customary power to sell)	254
pl. 309	(curtesy)	255
pl. 304	(*esnecia* between sisters)	241, 242
pl. 322	(mort d'ancestor between sisters)	245
pl. 1132	(curtesy)	254, 256

Rolls of the Justices in Eyre for Lincolnshire, 1218-19, and Worcestershire, 1221
Selden Society, vol. 53

pl. 357	(curtesy)	255, 256, 259
pl. 1040	(*maritagium* and hotchpot)	252-53

(Entries from Published Plea Rolls, cont.)

Rolls of the Justices in Eyre for Gloucestershire, Warwickshire and [Shropshire], 1221-22
Selden Society, vol. 59

pl. 534	(curtesy)	255, 256
pl. 1090	(curtesy)	255
pl. 1133	(parage)	243

Curia Regis Rolls, I (1195-1201)

p. 41	(*maritagium* claimed from heir)	244
p. 182	(curtesy)	255, 257
p. 201	(nature of heiress's right)	260
pp. 249-50	(curtesy)	255, 257
pp. 250-51	(inheritance: elder daughter)	240
p. 309	(dower: marriage denied)	246
p. 322	(dower: marriage denied)	246
pp. 330-31	(curtesy)	254, 255, 256
p. 350	(*esnecia* between sisters)	241
pp. 388-89	(grant induced by fraud)	184
pp. 447-48	(*esnecia*)	241, 252

Curia Regis Rolls, II (1201-03)

p. 41	(dower: marriage denied)	246
p. 63	(dower: marriage denied)	246
p. 79	(dower: marriage denied)	246
pp. 112-13	(*maritagium* and right to inherit)	252
p. 218	(nature of heiress's right)	235
p. 221	(husband's *custodia* of wife's land)	257
pp. 223-24	(nature of heiress's right)	235
p. 232	(royal serjeanty granted with younger sister)	237

Curia Regis Rolls, III (1203-05)

p. 66	(curtesy)	255
p. 150	(dower: marriage denied)	246

Curia Regis Rolls, IV (1205-06)

p. 2	(*maritagium*: degrees)	243
pp. 2-3	(dower: marriage denied)	246
pp. 38-39	(dower: marriage denied)	246
pp. 157-58	(co-heiresses and bastardy)	245, 246
p. 162	(*esnecia*: capital messuage)	241, 242
pp. 256-57	(grand assize: same stock)	186

(Curia Regis Rolls, IV (1205-6), cont.)

p. 290	(forerunner of *nuper obiit*)	245

Curia Regis Rolls, V (1207-09)

pp. 46-47	(elder sister's issue against younger sister's)	237, 241, 252
p. 75	(grand assize: same stock)	186
pp. 79-80	(co-heiress made nun)	251
p. 282	(inheritance granted to son of younger sister)	238
pp. 183-86	(co-heiress made nun)	251

Curia Regis Rolls, VI (1210-12)

pp. 11-12	(curtesy)	255, 256
p. 153	(dower: marriage denied)	246
pp. 199-200	(lord choosing between sisters)	237
p. 254	(*maritagium* and hotchpot)	242, 252
pp. 282-83	(*maritagium* and hotchpot)	242, 252
pp. 333-34	(curtesy)	255
pp. 391-92	(dower: two claim as widow)	246

Curia Regis Rolls, VII (1213-15 and, pp. 327-51, 1196-99)

p. 7	(curtesy)	255
p. 41	(dower: capital messuage)	241
p. 99	(dower: marriage denied)	246
p. 101	(dower: marriage denied)	246
p. 109	(curtesy)	254, 255
pp. 110-11	(Mandeville inheritance)	239
p. 180	(curtesy)	254
p. 206	(depasturing)	8
p. 296	(grand assize: grant while insane)	184
p. 298	(*maritagium* and hotchpot)	242, 252
p. 338	(*esnecia*: elder brother against younger)	240

Curia Regis Rolls, VIII (1219-20)

pp. 24-25	(dower: husband having surrendered land)	241
p. 152	(curtesy: *custodia*)	256, 257
p. 204	(goods taken)	18
pp. 213-15	(*esnecia* between parceners)	241, 256
p. 236	(Mandeville inheritance)	238
p. 335	(husband's *custodia* of *maritagium*)	254, 255

Table of Cases

(Entries from Published Plea Rolls, Curia Regis Rolls, VIII [1219-20], cont.)

p. 387	(parage)	241, 242
p. 394	(goods taken)	18

Curia Regis Rolls, IX (1220)

p. 14	(elder sister's line claims from younger)	237
pp. 65-67	(co-heiress put in nunnery)	251
pp. 142-43	(lands of Eleanor of Brittany)	238
pp. 178-79	*(casus regis)*	239-40
pp. 237-38	(lands of Eleanor of Brittany)	238
pp. 268-69	*(casus regis:* nephew against aunts)	240
pp. 284-85	(elder sister's line claims from younger)	237
pp. 381-82	(co-heiress made nun)	251

Curia Regis Rolls, X (1221-22)

pp. 17-18	*(esnecia:* capital messuage)	241, 242
pp. 73-74	(curtesy)	255
pp. 106-08	(co-heiresses: tenant's position)	243
p. 165	(jurisdictional franchise)	49, 73
pp. 166-67	*(esnecia: maritagium* and hotchpot)	241, 242, 245, 253
pp. 281-82	(tenure between sisters)	242
p. 324	(false imprisonment)	15
p. 350	(false imprisonment of plaintiff's men)	16

Curia Regis Rolls, XI (1223-24)

pl. 420	(tenure between parceners)	242
pl. 869	(parage)	242
pl. 891	(freedom from toll)	48, 73
pl. 1065	(tenure between parceners)	242, 253
pl. 1223	(Lucy inheritance)	241, 242, 250
pl. 1460	*(maritagium* and hearth-child)	252
pl. 1743	*(maritagium* excluding inheritance)	252
pl. 1821	(false imprisonment)	15
pl. 2090	(tenure between sisters)	242
pl. 2211	(taking crops)	7
pl. 2303	(false imprisonment of plaintiff's man)	16
pl. 2594	*(quare intruserunt:* lessee against lessor)	5
pl. 2682	*(esnecia:* parage)	241, 243
pl. 2793	*(maritagium* and hotchpot)	253
pl. 2806	(writ *de placito transgressionis)*	7

Curia Regis Rolls, XII (1225-26)

pl. 256	(parage)	241, 243
pl. 360	(Lucy inheritance: *esnecia)*	241, 242, 250
pl. 866	(Lucy inheritance)	241, 242, 250
pl. 1537	*(nuper obiit:* bastardy)	246
pl. 1576	(Lucy inheritance)	241, 242, 250
pl. 1751	(partition: capital messuage)	242
pl. 1771	*(esnecia)*	241, 253
pl. 1839	(inheritance: first-born daughter)	240
pl. 2577	(freedom from toll)	48

Curia Regis Rolls, XIII (1227-30)

pl. 311	(curtesy and wardship)	256
pl. 2350	(trespass: defendant claims title)	8
pl. 2352	(trespass in park)	12
pl. 2444	(trespass in park)	12

Curia Regis Rolls, XIV (1230-32)

pl. 1067	(special tail: curtesy and second husband)	254

Curia Regis Rolls, XVI (1237-42)

pl. 36	(trespass in wood)	7, 73
pl. 127	(battery)	13
pl. 1174	(ejectment of heir)	4
pl. 1180	(taking crops)	7
pl. 1195	(trespass: wager)	78
pl. 1204	(battery of plaintiff's men)	16
pl. 1207	(prisoners abducted)	17
pl. 1234	(battery of plaintiff's men)	16
pl. 1254	(entering marsh and taking trees)	7

(Entries from Published Plea Rolls, Curia Regis Rolls, XVI [1237-42], cont.)

pl. 1308	(depasturing)	8
pl. 1325	(battery of plaintiff's men)	16
pl. 1364	(trespass in warren)	12
pl. 1400	(trespass in park)	12
pl. 1416	(false imprisonment)	15
pl. 1447	(trespass in park)	12
pl. 1457	(false imprisonment)	15
pl. 1532	(wife consenting to be abducted)	17
pl. 1547	(freedom from toll)	48, 73
pl. 1583	(entering wood, felling and taking)	7
pl. 1585	(master's goods taken)	19, 61
pl. 1694	(wife abducted)	17
pl. 1719	(entering wood, felling and taking)	7
pl. 1727	(fraud of market)	46-7, 73
pl. 1732	(false imprisonment)	15
pl. 1744	(trespass and appeal)	84
pl. 1756	(wife abducted)	17
pl. 1764	(fraud of market)	46-7, 73
pl. 1824	(entering wood, felling and taking)	7
pl. 1826	(money taken)	18
pl. 1834	(trespass and appeal)	84
pl. 1879	(sheriff's failure to protect as ordered)	54
pl. 1927	*(de placito debiti catallorum)*	121
pl. 1933	(goods taken from bailee or servant)	19, 61
pl. 2136	*(debet* of chattels)	121
pl. 2241	(pledgee selling beyond amount owed)	30, 64
pl. 2316	(false imprisonment)	15
pl. 2556	*(de placito quare vi et armis)*	13
pl. 2775	(trespass and appeal)	84

Bracton's Note Book (1217-40)

pl. 8	(Mandeville inheritance)	238
pl. 12	(*nuper obiit*; Buckland inheritance)	237, 245, 247
pl. 16	(freedom from toll)	47-8
pl. 61	(*maritagium*: reversion)	223
pl. 85	(goods taken)	18
pl. 86	(*esnecia* between parceners)	241
pl. 137	(capital messuage for elder co-heiress)	242

(Bracton's Note Book [1217-40], cont.)

pl. 145	(freedom from toll)	47-8,
pl. 266	(curtesy and wardship)	256
pl. 287	(trespass: title recited)	34
pl. 302	(elder sister's line claims from younger)	237
pl. 314	(imprisonment of plaintiff's men)	16
pl. 378	(trespass: defendant claims title)	8
pl. 402	(escheat: entry formulation)	223
pl. 462	(escheat: entry through king's committee)	223
pl. 487	(special tail: curtesy and second husband)	223, 2 226, 2
pl. 494	(nuisance: market)	42
pl. 578	(nuisance: market)	42
pl. 597	(escheat: entry through king's committee)	223
pl. 687	("conversion" of crops by ward under age)	179
pl. 786	(nuisance: market)	42
pl. 821	(prisoner abducted and hanged)	17
pl. 835	(trespass in fishery)	10-11
pl. 839	(trespass in fishery)	11
pl. 843	(trespass: denying right of way)	3, 11-1 73
pl. 881	(free bull and boar)	38
pl. 924	(*esnecia*: parage)	241, 2
pl. 934	(*maritagium* and hotchpot)	253
pl. 951	(*maritagium* and hearth-child)	252
pl. 988	(*maritagium* and hearth-child)	252
pl. 1018	(*maritagium* excluding inheritance)	252
pl. 1037	(nuisance: market)	42
pl. 1041	(false imprisonment)	15
pl. 1053	(parage)	241, 2
pl. 1121	(goods of plaintiff's men taken)	16
pl. 1123	(freedom from customary dues)	47-8
pl. 1140	*(quare ejecit)*	6
pl. 1188	(freedom from customary dues)	47-8
pl. 1207	(capital messuage and distraint)	241
pl. 1215	(*precipe* writs of aiel, cosinage)	246-7

Table of Cases

(Entries from Published Plea Rolls, Bracton's Note Book [1217-40], cont.)

pl. 1232	(son abducted: trespass and appeal)	16, 84
pl. 1250	(freedom from toll)	47-8, 73
pl. 1462	*(casus regis)*	239-40
pl. 1596	(tenure between parceners)	242
pl. 1639	(parage)	242
pl. 1720	(freedom from toll)	47-8, 73

Select Cases of Procedure without Writ under Henry III
Selden Society, vol. 60 (1224-69)

p. 23, pl. 19	(depasturing)	8
p. 97, pl. 85	*(ejectio firme)*	5
p. 104, pl. 96	*(ejectio firme)*	5
p. 122, pl. 123	(trespass: specific remedy; wager)	33, 78
p. 127, pl.127B	*(ejectio firme)*	5

Select Cases in the Court of King's Bench, I
Selden Society, vol. 55 (1273-90)

p. 15, pl. 9	(procuring ostracism)	77
p. 29, pl. 20	(procuring imprisonment)	77
p. 30, pl. 21	(battery)	14
p. 34, pl. 25	(sale by sample)	126
p. 65, pl. 45	(deceit: promise of marriage)	163-64, 184
p. 181, pl. 120	(accidental fire)	20-21, 29, 82-83, 180-81

Select Cases in the Court of King's Bench, II
Selden Society, vol. 57 (1290-93)

p. 20, pl. 11	(deceit: promise of marriage)	184
p. 84, pl. 40	(depasturing)	8, 9
p. 113, pl. 44	(consequential loss)	36
p. 115, pl. 45	(false imprisonment)	15, 16
p. 117, pl. 47	(lord suppressing writ of right)	54
p. 135, pl. 53	(free fold)	39
p. 157, pl. 67	(false imprisonment)	15, 16

Select Cases in the Court of King's Bench, III
Selden Society, vol. 58 (1294-1307)

p. 7, pl. 4	(false imprisonment)	15, 16
p. 22, pl. 10	(conspiracy; abduction)	87
p. 78, pl. 46	(false imprisonment)	15, 16

(Select Cases in the Court of King's Bench, III [1294-1307], cont.)

p. 100, pl. 58	(wife abducted)	17
p. 105, pl. 61	(false imprisonment)	15, 16
p. 134, pl. 74	(depasturing)	8, 9
p. 147, pl. 79	(false imprisonment)	15, 16
p. 154, pl. 82	(false imprisonment)	15, 16
p. 179, pl. 97	(false warranty)	126

Select Cases in the Court of King's Bench, IV
Selden Society, vol. 74 (1308-26)

p.1 (at. p. 4), pl. 1	(principal and accessory)	85
p. 24, pl. 7	(trespass: justification)	79
p. 86, pl. 34	(trespass: pardon)	84

Placita Coram Rege, 1297
British Record Society

p. 1	(depasturing)	8, 9
p. 3	(goods taken: *vi et armis*)	18
pp. 6-7	(crops taken: *vi et armis*)	7
pp. 30-31	(goods taken: *vi et armis*)	18
pp. 61-2	(crops taken : *vi et armis*)	7
p. 66	(goods taken: *vi et armis*)	18
p. 94	(goods taken: *vi et armis*)	18
p. 95	(goods taken: *vi et armis*)	18
p. 96	(goods taken: *vi et armis*)	18
p. 104	(pigs killed maliciously)	25
p. 151	(goods taken: *vi et armis*)	18
p. 168	(house and goods burnt)	21
pp. 171-2	(battery)	14
p. 178	(goods taken: *vi et armis*)	18
p. 187	(depasturing)	8, 9
p. 224	(lord suppressing writ of right)	54

Select Cases in the Exchequer of Pleas
Selden Society, vol. 48 (1236-1304)

p. 121	*(ex parte talis)*	133

Placitorum Abbreviatio (1194-1326)

p. 142(a)	(trespass: defendant claims title)	8
p. 151(a)	(freedom from toll)	48
p. 151(b)	(impeding collection of tolls)	47
p. 154(b)	(jurisdictional franchise)	51
p. 160(b)	(freedom from customary dues)	48
p. 174 (a-b)	(freedom from customary dues)	48

(Entries from Published Plea Rolls,
Placitorum Abbreviatio [1194-1326], cont.)

p.194 (a)	(trespass in warren)	79
p. 223(a)	*(de quarentina habenda)*	4
p. 223(b)	(free fold)	39
p. 262(a)	(trespass: defendant claims title)	8
p. 268(a)	(principal and accessory)	4
p. 305(b)	(freedom from toll: specific remedy)	49
p. 306(b)	(rescue)	37
p. 337(b)	(dogs incited to damage)	22
p. 346(b)	(trespass: damages only)	6,33

Select Cases on the Law Merchant, I
Selden Society, vol. 23 (1270-1638)

p. 50	(condition of quality)	126
p. 91	(sale by sample: forfeiture)	126
p. 102	(sale by sample: covenant)	126
pp. 103-04	(building with bad wood)	159
p. 105-06	(false warranty: covenant)	126

Select Cases on the Law Merchant, II
Selden Society, vol. 46 (1240-1632)

p. 28	(seller as bailee; false warranty as trespass)	123,126

The Court Baron
Selden Society, vol. 4 (cases 1285-1327)

p. 140	(misfeasance; covenant)	159

Calendar of Early Mayors' Court Rolls, London,
1298-1307

p. 68	(false warranty: recission)	126
p. 81	(surgeon)	72,159
p. 82	(roofing with substituted lead: trespass)	159
p. 154	(false warranty: trespass)	126
p. 168	(apprentice taken)	86
pp. 170-71	(fraud over payment)	166
p. 181	(private accounting: *concessit solvere*)	136
p. 216	(false warranty: trespass)	126,128
p. 247	(fraud over payment)	166

Calendar of Plea and Memoranda Rolls, London
1323-1364

p. 251	(quality of food)	127
p. 260	(warranty of title)	130

Calendar of Plea and Memoranda Rolls, London,
1364-1381

p. 34	(defective cloth: loss passed to fuller)	126,128
p. 56	(land sold, conveyed to third party)	165
p. 126	(warranty of title: recission)	126,130, 168
p. 236	(surgeon)	72

Calendar of Select Pleas and Memoranda, London,
1381-1412

p. 23	(land sold, conveyed to third party)	164-65
p. 153-54	(value of land warranted)	130

III. CASES FROM YEAR BOOKS

ROLLS SERIES

20 & 21 Ed. I, p. 189	(bailment to married woman)	179
20 & 21 Ed. I, p. 462	(acts done by night)	75
21 & 22 Ed. I, p. 3	(sale of land: wager)	114
21 & 22 Ed. I, p. 28	(waste: accidental fire)	21, 83, 181
21 & 22 Ed. I, p. 74	(prohibition)	53
21 & 22 Ed. I, p. 272	(novel disseisin: *vi et armis*)	74
21 & 22 Ed. I, p. 321	(formedon)	225
21 & 22 Ed. I, p. 482	(pillory knocked down)	37, 43
30 & 31 Ed. I, p. 14	(formedon)	226
30 & 31 Ed. I, p. 282	*(quare ejecit)*	6
30 & 31 Ed. I, p. 391	(debt on sale by executors)	106
30 & 31 Ed. I, p. 454	(prohibition)	53
32 & 33 Ed. I, p. 15	(loan to woman *dum sola*)	110
32 & 33 Ed. I, p. 51	(market picketed)	44
32 & 33 Ed. I, p. 258	(false imprisonment)	15, 28
32 & 33 Ed. I, p. 258	(trees felled)	28
32 & 33 Ed. I, p. 270	(free boar)	38
33-35 Ed. I, p. 151	(debt: payment)	118

SELDEN SOCIETY

1 & 2 Ed. II, vol. 17, p. 39	*(de rationabili parte bonorum)*	121
1 & 2 Ed. II, vol. 17, p. 79	(formedon)	226
1 & 2 Ed. II, vol. 17, p. 170	(formedon)	226
2 & 3 Ed. II, vol. 19, p. 15	(wager against executors)	110
2 & 3 Ed. II, vol. 19, p. 36	(novel disseisin: *vi et armis*)	74
2 & 3 Ed. II, vol. 19, p. 71	(fraud of market)	37, 45-46, 73, 92
2 & 3 Ed. II, vol. 19, p. 195	(examination of *secta*)	113, 175
3 Ed. II, vol. 20, p. 104	(trespass: demise of crown)	74
3 Ed. II, vol. 20, p. 133	(formedon)	226
3 & 4 Ed. II, vol. 22, p. 10	(formedon)	226
3 & 4 Ed. II, vol. 22, p. 21	(wager against executors)	110
3 & 4 Ed. II, vol. 22, p. 26	(debt and detinue)	121
3 & 4 Ed. II, vol. 22, p. 27	(formedon)	226
3 & 4 Ed. II, vol. 22, pp. 29, 208	(formedon)	13, 28
3 & 4 Ed. II, vol. 22, p. 40	(formedon)	225
3 & 4 Ed. II, vol. 22, p. 112	(statements about formedon)	224, 225, 226
3 & 4 Ed. II, vol. 22, p. 195	(replevin called trespass)	75
4 Ed. II, vol. 26, p. 11	*(concessit se teneri)*	138
4 Ed. II, vol. 26, p. 13	(loan to woman *dum sola*)	110
4 Ed. II, vol. 42, p. 181	*(quare ejecit)*	6
5 Ed. II, vol. 63, p. 76	(formedon)	226
5 Ed. II, vol. 63, p. 208	(free bull, boar)	38
5 Ed. II, vol. 31, p. 49	*(ejectio custodie)*	32
5 Ed. II, vol. 31, p. 120	(fee tail: dower)	226
5 Ed. II, vol. 31, p. 215	(writing delivered for inspection, taken)	65
5 Ed. II, vol. 33, p. 94	(ravishment of ward, *vi et armis*)	78, 87
5 Ed. II, vol. 33, p. 125	(trespass: justification)	79
5 Ed. II, vol. 33, p. 141	(free bull, boar)	38
6 Ed. II, vol. 34, p. 43	(fee tail: dower)	224, 225, 226
6 Ed. II, vol. 34, p. 99	(free boar)	38

(Cases from Year Books, Selden Society, cont.)

6 Ed. II, vol. 34, p. 142	(trespass and replevin)	67, 75
6 Ed. II, vol. 34, p. 153	(purchase by married woman)	110, 111
6 & 7 Ed. II, vol. 36, p. 1	(trespass: justification)	79
6 & 7 Ed. II, vol. 36, p. 16	(goods taken)	66
7 Ed. II, vol. 39, p. 14	(sold goods adulterated *contra pacem*)	67, 126
7 Ed. II, vol. 39, p. 104	(account against receiver: wager)	109
9 Ed. II, vol. 45, p. 10	(formedon)	225
9 Ed. II, vol. 45, p. 28	(daughter and heiress abducted)	16
9 Ed. II, vol. 45, p. 49	(franchise of wreck)	41, 79, 80
9 Ed. II, vol. 45, p. 52	(rescue)	36
9 Ed. II, vol. 45, p. 69	(trespass: no specific remedy)	33
10 Ed. II, vol. 52, p. 102	(loan to monk while secular)	110
10 Ed. II, vol. 52, p. 132	(cosinage: entail before *de donis*)	224, 225, 226
10 Ed. II, vol. 54, p. 109	(account against receiver, wager)	109
10 Ed. II, vol. 54, p. 140	(sold wine adulterated *contra pacem*)	67, 68, 123, 155
11 Ed. II, vol. 61, p. 34	(formedon)	226
11 Ed. II, vol. 61, p. 220	(prohibition)	53
11 Ed. II, vol. 61, p. 290	(writing delivered for inspection destroyed)	65
12 Ed. II, vol. 70, p. 146	(account against receiver: wager)	109, 139
Eyre of Kent, II, vol. 27, p. 46	(loan to married woman)	111

MEMOIRS OF THE AMERICAN ACADEMY OF ARTS AND SCIENCES

Eyre of London, 14 Ed. II, p. 44	(note on deposit and custody)	65
Eyre of London, 14 Ed. II, p. 74	(trespass: bailor against bailee)	64-65

BLACK LETTER

Trin.	16 Ed. II, p. 490	(detinue: *devenit ad manus*)	100
Hil.	19 Ed. II, p. 655-56	(debt on account)	139
Hil.	1 Ed. III, pl. 4, f.1	(free fold)	39
Hil.	1 Ed. III, pl. 10, f.2	(account, trespass: demise of crown)	74
Pasch.	1 Ed. III, pl. 19, f.9	(ravishment of ward: demise of crown)	74
Hil.	2 Ed. III, pl. 20, f.7	(market picketing discussed)	44
Trin.	2 Ed. III, pl. 11, f.24	(tolls taken)	47, 50
Trin.	2 Ed. III, pl. 13, f.26	(duties of repair)	56
Mich.	2 Ed. III, pl. 9, f.15	(market picketed)	44
Hil.	3 Ed. III, pl. 7, f.3	(free fold)	22, 39, 40
Mich.	3 Ed. III, pl. 2, f.31	(formedon)	225
Mich.	3 Ed. III, pl. 17, f.39	*(ejectio custodie)*	32
Pasch.	4 Ed. III, pl. 5, f.15	(pound-breach)	36
Mich.	5 Ed. III, pl. 7, f.35	(formedon)	225
Mich.	5 Ed. III, pl. 31, f.41	(act done by night)	75
Mich.	5 Ed. III, pl. 49, f.46	(pillory knocked down)	37-38
Mich.	5 Ed. III, pl. 91, f.59	(franchise of wreck)	41, 42
Mich.	6 Ed. III, pl. 10, f.38	(principal and accessory)	85
Pasch.	7 Ed. III, pl. 2, f.12	(debt: accountant in credit)	139
Pasch.	7 Ed. III, pl. 23, f.19	(rescue)	36
Trin.	7 Ed. III, pl. 1, f.23	(superior orders)	82
Pasch.	8 Ed. III, pl. 48, f.37	(free fold)	39, 40
Mich.	9 Ed. III, pl. 17, f.29	(principal and accessory)	85
Pasch.	10 Ed. III, pl. 36, f.21d	(act done by night)	75

Table of Cases 311

(Cases from Year Books, cont.)

ROLLS SERIES

11 & 12 Ed. III, p. 38	(taking market profits)	43
11 & 12 Ed. III, p. 51	*(ejectio custodie)*	32
11 & 12 Ed. III, p. 500	(*recordari facias* ignored)	53
11 & 12 Ed. III, p. 516	(*recordari facias* ignored)	53
13 & 14 Ed. III, p. 134	(franchise of estray)	41, 79, 92
14 Ed. III, p. 230	(*recordari facias* ignored)	53
14 Ed. III, p. 232	(*recordari facias* ignored)	53
14 & 15 Ed. III, p. 88	(jurisdictional franchise)	44, 50
14 & 15 Ed. III, p. 195	(wager against executor)	110
14 & 15 Ed. III, p. 246	(sea-walls not repaired)	55-56
15 Ed. III, p. 86	(river-walls not repaired)	55-56, 94
16 Ed. III, (vol. I), p. 256	(river-walls not repaired)	55-56
16 Ed. III, (vol. II), p. 25	(account: receiver by third hand)	109
16 Ed. III, (vol. II), p. 246	(trespass: demise of crown)	75
17 Ed. III, p. 2	(*contra pacem*: contrary to statute)	78
17 Ed. III, p. 7	(wager against executors)	110
17 Ed. III, p. 141	(detinue and debt)	121, 177
17 & 18 Ed. III, p. 73	(examination of *secta*)	113, 175
17 & 18 Ed. III, p. 212	(jurisdictional franchise)	50, 77
17 & 18 Ed. III, p. 355	(debt by executors)	106
17 & 18 Ed. III, p. 466	(trespass: wager)	78
17 & 18 Ed. III, p. 511	(detinue, debt: formulation of general issue)	115
18 Ed. III, p. 234	(sea-walls not repaired)	55-56
18 & 19 Ed. III, p. 14	(trespass and indictment)	84
18 & 19 Ed. III, p. 325	(account: socage wardship)	87
20 Ed. III, (vol. I), p. 17	(debt in exchequer)	113
20 Ed. III (vol. II), p. 146	(debt: local claims for 39s 11¾d)	106

BLACK LETTER

Mich.	17 Ed. III, pl. 37, f.56	(jurisdictional franchise)	50
Mich.	17 Ed. III, pl. 105, f.73	(debt; novel disseisin *vi et armis*)	74
Trin.	18 Ed. III, pl. 6, f.23	(river-walls not repaired)	55-56
Hil.	21 Ed. III, pl. 26, f.9	(trespass between co-tenants)	87
Pasch.	21 Ed. III, pl. 2, f.11d	(buyer losing goods to third party)	119, 121
Mich.	21 Ed. III, pl. 8, f.29	(trespass between co-tenants)	87
Trin.	22 Ed. III, pl. 16, f.8	(debt: purchase by monk)	112
Mich.	22 Ed. III, pl. 48, f.15	*("trespas sur son case")*	87-8
Trin.	24 Ed. III, pl. 12, f.28	(jurisdictional franchise)	52, 73
Trin.	24 Ed. III, pl. 44, f.56d	(jurisdictional franchise)	52, 73
Mich.	24 Ed. III, pl. 72, f.66d	*(son assault demesne)*	79
Trin.	25 Ed. III, pl. 4, f.80d	(trespass: justification)	79
Mich.	25 Ed. III, pl. 2, f.48	(debt: purchase by monk)	112
Hil.	29 Ed. III, f.21	(market picketing discussed)	44
Pasch.	29 Ed. III, f.18d	(fair picketed)	44
Pasch.	29 Ed. III, f.25d	*(concessit se teneri, solvere)*	138, 139-40
Pasch.	29 Ed. III, f.32d	(river-banks not repaired)	56, 57, 73
Trin.	29 Ed. III, f.36d	(sale involving servant: wager)	110
Trin.	29 Ed. III, f.38d	(detinue: *devenit ad manus*)	99, 100
Hil.	30 Ed. III, f.2d	(detinue: heir's chattels)	121

(Cases from Year Books, Black Letter, cont.)

Mich.	30 Ed. III, f.11	(agisted beasts retaken without payment)	62, 84
Mich.	30 Ed. III, f.18d	(sale by servant)	110, 111
Mich.	30 Ed. III, f.25	(de rationabili parte bonorum)	121
Hil.	38 Ed. III, f.5d	(labourers: trespass)	52
Trin.	38 Ed. III, f.12d	(labourers: trespass)	52
Mich.	38 Ed. III, f.33d	(ejectio firme)	6
Hil.	39 Ed. III, f.6	(detinue: heir's chattels)	121
Pasch.	39 Ed. III, f.6d	(labourers: trespass)	52
Pasch.	39 Ed. III, f.9d	(detinue: heir's chattels)	121
Pasch.	39 Ed. III, f.13d	(freedom from toll)	48
Trin.	39 Ed. III, f.18d	("bref sur son case")	88
Mich.	39 Ed. III, f.37d	(servant taken from service)	17, 86
Hil.	40 Ed. III, pl. 19, f.10	(franchise of waif)	41, 42
Pasch.	40 Ed. III, pl. 27, f.24d	(debt: payment)	118
Mich.	40 Ed. III, pl. 2, f.35	(labourers: trespass)	52
Hil.	41 Ed. III, pl. 15, f.7	(debt: private accounting; satisfaction)	118, 142
Trin.	41 Ed. III, pl. 3, f.13d	(debt against executors)	112
Mich.	41 Ed. III, pl. 1, f.17	(labourers: covenant)	161
Mich.	41 Ed. III, pl. 4, f.20	(labourers: covenant)	161
Mich.	41 Ed. III, pl. 17, f.24	(freedom from multure: *sur le case*)	33-4, 44
Mich.	41 Ed. III, pl. 30, f.29d	(trespass: scope of general issue)	82
Pasch.	42 Ed. III, pl. 13, f.11	(innkeeper)	58, 59, 94
Mich.	42 Ed. III, pl. 10, f.25d	(debt: separate counts)	106
Hil.	43 Ed. III, pl. 3, f.1d	(debt on account)	134
Mich.	43 Ed. III, pl. 14, f.29d	(freedom from toll)	49
Mich.	43 Ed. III, pl. 16, f.30	("especial bref sur le cas")	88
Mich.	43 Ed. III, pl. 38, f.33	(horse dying after negligent cure)	86
Hil.	44 Ed. III, pl. 16, f.4	("bref ...sur vostre case")	88
Pasch.	44 Ed. III, pl. 28, f.13d	(*vi et armis* writ against lord)	75
Trin.	44 Ed. III, pl. 16, f.20	(*vi et armis* writ against lord)	34, 76
Mich.	44 Ed. III, pl. 6, f.27d	(sale: condition)	117, 125
Hil.	45 Ed. III, pl. 5, f.2d	(franchise to have deodands)	41
Trin.	45 Ed. III, pl. 6, f.17d	(river-banks not repaired)	57
Mich.	45 Ed. III, pl. 13, f.14d	(private accounting as plea)	144
Mich.	45 Ed. III, pl. 15, f.15	(labourers: covenant)	161
Hil.	46 Ed. III, pl. 10, f.4d	(labourers: covenant)	161
Hil.	46 Ed. III, pl. 16, f.6	(debt: payment)	107, 117
Pasch.	46 Ed. III, pl. 2, f.8d	(river-banks not repaired)	57
Pasch.	46 Ed. III, pl. 7, f.10	(purchase by monk, wife etc. discussed)	111
Pasch.	46 Ed. III, pl. 9, f.11d	(trespass: scope of general issue)	82
Trin.	46 Ed. III, pl. 19, f.19	(farrier)	26, 29, 86
Mich.	46 Ed. III, pl. 16, f.27	(river-banks not repaired)	57
Mich.	46 Ed. III, pl. 21, f.28d	(trespass in fishery)	35
Mich.	46 Ed. III, pl. 32, f.31	(waste: tenant for life or years)	87
Mich.	46 Ed. III, pl. 40, f.32d	(trespass: scope of general issue)	82
Mich.	47 Ed. III, pl. 7, f.10d	(trespass in park)	52, 84
Mich.	47 Ed. III, pl. 10, f.12	(goods taken from bailiff)	61
Mich.	47 Ed. III, pl. 15, f.14	(labourers: trespass)	52
Mich.	47 Ed. III, pl. 23, f.16	(labourers: covenant)	52, 161
Mich.	47 Ed. III, pl. 54, f.22d	(trespass between co-tenants)	87
Mich.	47 Ed. III, pl. 56, f.23d	(judgment debt against woman *dum sola*)	110

Table of Cases

(Cases from Year Books, Black Letter, cont.)

Hil.	48 Ed. III, pl. 10, f.5d	(*vi et armis* writ against freeholder)	76
Hil.	48 Ed. III, pl. 11, f.6	(surgeon)	71, 72, 78, 159
Hil.	48 Ed. III, pl. 12, f.6d	(*ejectio firme*)	6
Trin.	48 Ed. III, pl. 8, f.20d	(trespass: bailee against third party)	61
Mich.	48 Ed. III, pl. 8, f.25	(trespass: accidental fire)	21, 83, 87, 181-82
Hil.	49 Ed. III, pl. 6, f.2d	(debt on account)	134
Hil.	49 Ed. III, pl. 10, f.6	(freedom from toll)	49
22 Lib. Ass., pl. 41, f.94		(misfeance: Humber ferry)	70-71
22 Lib. Ass. pl. 42, f.94d		(*son default demesne*)	80, 85
22 Lib. Ass. pl. 48, f.95d		(depasturing)	9
22 Lib. Ass. pl. 51, f.96		(depasturing)	10
22 Lib. Ass. pl. 56, f.98		(battery: justification; necessity)	81
22 Lib. Ass. pl. 59, f.98d		(principal and accessory)	85
27 Lib. Ass. pl. 56, f.141		(depasturing: escape)	9-10
27 Lib. Ass. pl. 64, f. 143		(impounded horse kills itself)	66-7, 82
38 Lib. Ass. pl. 9, f.223d		(*ejectio custodie*)	32, 85
38 Lib. Ass. pl. 13, f.224d		(sheriff sued in exchequer)	54
42 Lib. Ass. pl. 8, f.259d		("appeal": sale without title)	84, 130
42 Lib. Ass. pl. 9, f.259d		(house burnt)	21, 83, 86, 181
42 Lib. Ass. pl. 17, f.260d		(innkeeper)	58, 59

AMES FOUNDATION

11 Ric. II, p. 4	(false warranty)	127
12 Ric. II, p. 46	(*scire facias*: entail)	226
13 Ric. II, p. 95	(debt on account)	134, 141

BLACK LETTER

Mich.	2 Hy. IV, pl. 9, f.3d	(nonfeasance: building house)	160, 192
Hil.	2 Hy. IV, pl. 12, f.14d	(debt: compellable service)	113
Hil.	2 Hy. IV, pl. 15, f.15	(debt: immediate law)	114
Trin.	2 Hy. IV, pl. 1, f.21	(bailment to monk)	111
Mich.	3 Hy. IV, pl. 8, f.2	(debt: separate counts)	106
Mich.	3 Hy. IV, pl. 12, f.3	(deceit: conveyance to third party)	164
Pasch.	3 Hy. IV, pl. 14, f.17d	(debt: subsequent bond)	118
Hil.	6 Hy. IV, pl. 28, f.6	(debt on account)	134
Pasch.	7 Hy. IV, pl. 19, f.14d	(bad wine sold)	127, 128
Mich.	11 Hy. IV, pl. 60, f.33	(nonfeasance: building house)	160, 192
Hil.	11 Hy. IV, pl. 27, f.50	(detinue: redelivery in foreign county)	108, 118, 186
Hil.	11 Hy. IV, pl. 38, f.55	(debt: separate counts)	106
Pasch.	11 Hy. IV, pl. 17, f.64	(debt on account)	112
Trin.	11 Hy. IV, pl. 21, f.79d	(debt on account)	108, 118
Trin.	11 Hy. IV, pl. 48, f.91d	(debt on account)	112
Mich.	13 Hy. IV, pl. 4, f.1	(warranty: quantity)	128, 130
Mich.	13 Hy. IV, pl. 38, f.11d	(trespass, debt: separate counts)	106
Hil.	14 Hy. IV, pl. 21, f.19	(debt on account)	109
Hil.	14 Hy. IV, pl. 33, f.25	(London customs discussed)	106
Hil.	14 Hy. IV, pl. 35, f.27	(debt: satisfaction)	118
Hil.	14 Hy. IV, pl. 37, f.27d	(detinue: *de debito*)	121, 177
Pasch.	1 Hy. V, pl. 5, f.4d	(debt: separate counts)	106
Trin.	1 Hy. V, pl. 1, f.6	(debt: separate counts; payment)	106, 118
Hil.	5 Hy. V, pl. 26, f.11	(labourers: rehearsal of statute)	161
Hil.	8 Hy. V, pl. 14, f.3d	(debt: immediate law)	114
Pasch.	9 Hy. V, pl. 14, f.5	(debt: immediate law)	114

(Cases from Year Books, cont.)

SELDEN SOCIETY

    1 Hy. VI, vol. 50, p. 12   (debt on lease of sheep: wager)   108

BLACK LETTER

Mich.	1 Hy. VI, pl. 3, f.1	(debt on lease of sheep: wager)	108
Mich.	1 Hy. VI, pl. 31, f.7d	(account; debt: subsequent bond)	118
Mich.	3 Hy. VI, pl. 16, f.13d	(debt: immediate law)	114
Hil.	3 Hy. VI, pl. 26, f.33d	(debt: compellable service)	113
Hil.	3 Hy. VI, pl. 33, f.36d	(nonfeasance: building mill)	160, 163
Hil.	3 Hy. VI, pl. 38, f.37d	(debt: separate counts)	108
Pasch.	3 Hy. VI, pl. 13, f.42	(debt: compellable service)	113
Trin.	3 Hy. VI, pl. 6, f.48	(debt: separate pleas)	106
Trin.	3 Hy. VI, pl. 12, f.49d	(debt, 40s.: part tendered; immediate law)	106, 107, 114
Pasch.	4 Hy. VI, pl. 3, f.17d	(debt on account)	134
Pasch.	4 Hy. VI, pl. 5, f.19d	(debt against executors: compellable service)	113
Trin.	4 Hy. VI, pl. 3, f.25d	(debt on account)	135
Mich.	7 Hy. VI, pl. 9, f.5	(debt against jailer)	105, 114
Mich.	8 Hy. VI, pl. 13, f.5d	(debt: when cause traversable)	115
Mich.	8 Hy. VI, pl. 24, f.10	(detinue: buyer counts on bailment)	117, 123
Mich.	8 Hy. VI, pl. 25, f.10d	(debt on account)	109, 143
Mich.	8 Hy. VI, pl. 36, f.15d	(debt on account)	109, 143
Hil.	8 Hy. VI, pl. 23, f.29	(debt: when cause traversable)	115
Mich.	9 Hy. VI, pl. 37, f.53d	(warranty of wine: sale by servant)	110, 111, 127, 128, 129
Hil.	9 Hy. VI, pl. 4, f.58	(detinue of charter: *devenit ad manus*)	100
Pasch.	9 Hy. VI, pl. 24, f.9	(detinue of charter: redelivery in foreign county)	117
Trin.	9 Hy. VI, pl. 7, f.16	(debt: 40s. by addition)	108
Mich.	10 Hy. VI, pl. 17, f.5	(debt: separate counts)	106
Mich.	10 Hy. VI, pl. 67, f.20d	(debt on account)	143
Mich.	10 Hy. VI, pl. 84, f.24d	(debt on account: by executor)	112, 140
Mich.	11 Hy. VI, pl. 9, f.5	(replevin; debt: separate counts)	106
Mich.	11 Hy. VI, pl. 12, f.7d	(debt against administrator: conversion)	126
Hil.	11 Hy. VI, pl. 9, f.16	(debt against administrator: conversion)	126
Hil.	11 Hy. VI, pl. 10, f.18	(lawyer's misconduct of purchase)	164
Pasch.	11 Hy. VI, pl. 1, f.24	(lawyer's misconduct of purchase)	129, 164
Pasch.	11 Hy. VI, pl. 16, f.30	(purchase by predecessor, monk, wife)	111
Pasch.	11 Hy. VI, pl. 30, f35d	(debt against administrator: conversion)	126
Trin.	11 Hy. VI, pl. 5, f.48	(debt against executor: compellable service)	113
Trin.	11 Hy. VI, pl. 6, f.48d	(debt, detinue: joinder)	105
Trin.	11 Hy. VI, pl. 26, f.55d	(lawyer's misconduct of purchase)	164
	14 Hy. VI, pl. 66, f.22d	(sale by sample)	129, 130
	14 Hy. VI, pl. 71, f.24d	(debt: accountant in credit)	140
Mich.	19 Hy. VI, pl. 19, f.8d	(trespass, debt: verdict less than 40s.)	106
Mich.	19 Hy. VI, pl. 25, f.10	(debt: victualler)	113
Mich.	19 Hy. VI, pl. 47, f.23d	(trespass: sale of land discussed)	120
Hil.	19 Hy. VI, pl. 5, f.49	(horse dying after negligent cure)	127
Hil.	19 Hy. VI, pl. 17, f.54	(bailiff hearing case over 40s.)	106

Table of Cases

(Cases from Year Books, Black Letter, cont.)

Mich.	20 Hy. VI, pl. 9, f.3	(replevin: payment in debt discussed)	117
Mich.	20 Hy. VI, pl. 14, f.4d	(debt on account by executor)	106, 119
Hil.	20 Hy. VI, pl. 2, f.16	(debt on account: examination)	135, 143
Hil.	20 Hy. VI, pl. 4, f.16d	(debt on account: examination)	135
Hil.	20 Hy. VI, pl. 19, f.21	(debt: loan to abbot's predecessor)	111, 118, 126
Pasch.	20 Hy. VI, pl. 6, f.24	(debt on account)	108
Trin.	20 Hy. VI, pl. 4, f.34	(deceit: land sold, conveyed to third party)	120, 123, 125, 127, 163, 164
Trin.	20 Hy. VI, pl. 17, f.41d	(debt on account)	135
Hil.	21 Hy. VI, pl. 3, f. 23	(debt: sale to abbot's predecessor)	99, 110, 111, 112
Pasch.	21 Hy. VI, pl. 2, f.35	(detinue, debt: scope of general issue)	115, 116, 174
Pasch.	21 Hy. VI, pl. 26, f.43	(trespass: sale of goods and property)	123
Trin.	21 Hy. VI, pl. 12, f.55d	(case: seller not delivering)	123, 125
Mich.	22 Hy. VI, pl. 18, f.13d	(debt for board: wager)	113, 114
Mich.	22 Hy. VI, pl. 50, f.33	(detinue by buyer)	117, 123
Hil.	22 Hy. VI, pl. 1, f.36	(debt on account: payment in foreign county)	118, 186
Hil.	22 Hy. VI, pl. 13, f.41	(debt on account)	135
Hil.	22 Hy. VI, pl. 28, f.43d	(debt: sale of land)	107, 114, 117, 120, 125
Pasch.	22 Hy. VI, pl. 32, f.55d	(debt on account: subsequent bond)	118
Mich.	28 Hy. VI, pl. 21, f.4d	(debt by jailer for food)	113, 118
Mich.	32 Hy. VI, pl. 21, f.14	(trespass: payment in debt discussed)	118
Mich.	33 Hy. VI, pl. 17, f.38d	(traversability of cause in debt discussed)	115, 117
Mich.	33 Hy. VI, pl. 23, f.43	(debt: sale to woman *dum sola*)	111, 115, 117, 118
Mich.	33 Hy. VI, pl. 32, f.47	(debt: conditional bond)	174
Hil.	33 Hy. VI, pl. 3, f.1	(debt against jailer for escape)	178
Trin.	33 Hy. VI, pl. 12, f.26d	(detinue: trover)	100
Mich.	34 Hy. VI, pl. 42, f.22d	(debt against executors: conversion)	112, 126
Pasch.	34 Hy. VI, pl. 13, f.42	(debt: when place of contract traversable)	117
Mich.	35 Hy. VI, pl. 5, f.5	(debt on account: examination)	135
Mich.	35 Hy. VI, pl. 33, f.25d	(*devenit ad manus* discussed)	100
Mich.	37 Hy. VI, pl. 18, f.8d	(debt: consideration of marriage; many contracts discussed)	119, 120
Mich.	38 Hy. VI, pl. 14, f.5d	(debt: accountant in credit)	139, 140
Mich.	38 Hy. VI, pl. 30, f.13d	(debt: compellable service)	113
Hil.	38 Hy. VI, pl. 4, f.22	(debt: compellable service)	112, 115
Pasch.	38.Hy. VI, pl. 12, f.29d	*(concessit solvere)*	136, 141
Mich.	39 Hy. VI, pl. 46, f.34d	(debt: subsequent bond)	105, 118
Hil.	39 Hy. VI, pl. 1, f.36	(detinue: bailment and trover discussed)	123
Mich.	1 Ed. IV, pl. 13, f.5d	(debt, London: board, *concessit solvere*)	136
Trin.	2 Ed. IV, pl. 1, f.10	(debt: part tender discussed)	106
Mich.	2 Ed. IV, pl. 2, f.14	(debt: private accounting)	141, 143
Pasch.	4 Ed. IV, pl. 6, f.6	(private accounting as plea)	141
Mich.	4 Ed. IV, pl. 15, f.32d	(debt: failure of part discussed)	106
Pasch.	5 Ed. IV, pl. 20, f.2d	(lien of innkeeper, tailor, seller)	123, 124
	Long Quinto, f. 70d	(debt: purchase by provost's predecessor)	111, 115
	Long Quinto, f. 140d	(debt on account: examination)	135, 141

Studies in the History of the Common Law

(Cases from Year Books, Black Letter, cont.)

Mich.	7 Ed. IV, pl. 2, f.15	(note on purchase of *res sua*)	119
Mich.	8 Ed. IV, pl. 9, f.9	(purchase by agent discussed)	111
Pasch.	9. Ed. IV, pl. 1, f.1	(debt: separate counts)	108
Trin.	9 Ed. IV, pl. 32-33, (note) f.24d	(debt: purchase by woman *dum sola*)	110
Trin.	9 Ed. IV, pl. 34, f.25	(debt: mortgage taken)	117, 118
Mich.	9 Ed. IV, pl. 14, f.36d	(debt: separate counts; satisfaction)	105, 117, 118, 120
Mich.	9 Ed. IV, pl. 32, f.45	(account, debt: when place traversable)	117
Hil.	9 Ed. IV, pl. 10, f.50d	(debt: subsequent bond discussed)	118
Mich.	49 Hy. VI, pl. 23, f.18d	(debt, service: seller's lien discussed)	123, 124
Trin.	11 Ed. IV, pl. 10, f.6	(warranty: size of cloths; sale by servant)	127, 128, 129, 130
Mich.	12 Ed. IV, pl. 2, f.11d	(detinue, trover: scope of general issue)	112, 115, 118
Mich.	12 Ed. IV, pl. 14, f.14	(detinue, trover: scope of general issue)	115, 118
Mich.	13 Ed. IV, pl. 9, f.4	(debt: loan to abbot's predecessor)	115
Pasch.	15 Ed. IV, pl. 7, f.25	(debt against executor)	112
Mich.	15 Ed. IV, pl. 4, f.2d	(debt: purchase by woman *dum sola*)	110
Mich.	15 Ed. IV, pl. 5, f.2d	(annuity; buyer's liability in debt discussed)	119
Hil.	15 Ed. IV, pl. 3, f.16	(debt for board: against executor)	113
Mich.	16 Ed. IV, pl. 7, f.9d	(deceit: land sold, conveyed to third party)	125
Hil.	16 Ed. IV, pl. 3, f.10d	(debt: separate counts; compellable service)	107, 113
Pasch.	17 Ed. IV, pl. 2, f.1	(trespass: seller's lien discussed)	123, 124
Pasch.	18 Ed. IV, pl. 30, f.5d	(debt: sale of *res aliena*)	119, 120
Hil.	18 Ed. IV, pl. 1, f.21d	(debt: sale of *res aliena*)	119, 123, 124
Hil.	18 Ed. IV, pl. 5, f.23	(case: conversion by bailee)	101
Pasch.	20 Ed. IV, pl. 14, f.3	(debt on account: against executor)	112
Pasch.	20 Ed. IV, pl. 17, f.3d	(debt: consideration of marriage)	120
Pasch.	21 Ed. IV, pl. 2, f.21d	(debt: general issue *modo et forma* discussed)	116
Pasch.	21 Ed. IV, pl. 24, f.28d	(debt: bed and board)	115, 116, 117
Pasch.	22 Ed. IV, pl. 8, f.2	(debt on sale: weight or value mis-stated)	116
Mich.	22 Ed. IV, pl. 10, f.29d	(debt: when cause traversable)	115
Hil.	1 Hy. VII, pl. 29, f.13d	(debt on sale: pleading of condition)	117
Pasch.	1 Hy. VII, pl. 17, f.24d	(free fold)	39
Pasch.	1 Hy. VII, pl. 18, f.25	(debt: purchase by abbot's predecessor)	110, 112
Hil.	5 Hy. VII, pl. 10, f.16d	(warranties discussed)	129
Trin.	5 Hy. VII, pl. 7, f.41d	(warranty given after sale)	96, 129
Hil.	9 Hy. VII, pl. 21, f.21d	(warranty: unpaid seller liable)	129
Trin.	9 Hy. VII, pl. 4, f.3	(trespass, debt: separate counts)	106
Mich.	10 Hy. VII, pl. 4, f.4	(debt: payment in foreign county, etc.)	118, 174, 186
Mich.	10 Hy. VII, pl. 14, f.7	(various sales discussed)	113, 124
Mich.	11 Hy. VII, pl. 16, f.4d	(debt: payment in foreign county)	118, 186
Trin.	11 Hy. VII, pl. 9, f.26d	(debt against executors: *quo minus*)	113
Mich.	13 Hy. VII, pl. 2, f.2d	(debt: purchase by prior's predecessor)	111, 112

(Cases from Year Books, Black Letter, cont.)

Hil.	14 Hy. VII, pl. 5, f.15	(process by *capias*)	74
Mich.	16 Hy. VII, pl. 7, f.2d	(seller of goods as bailee)	123
Trin.	16 Hy. VII, pl. 8, f.14	(debt: 40s. by addition)	108
Mich.	20 Hy. VII, pl. 5, f.2d	(debt: position of executors)	113
Mich.	20 Hy. VII, pl. 18, f.8d	(case against seller for conversion)	122, 126
Mich.	21 Hy. VII, pl. 45, f.36	(debt on sale: mis-statement of subject-matter discussed)	116
Mich.	21 Hy. VII, pl. 64, f.40d	(purchase by wife discussed)	111
Mich.	21 Hy. VII, pl. 66, f.41	(misfeasance: building house; conveying land)	125
Hil.	21 Hy. VII, pl. 4, f.6	(effect of sale before payment)	124
Mich.	12 Hy. VIII, pl. 3, f.11	(case against executors: guarantee by testator)	98
Hil.	14 Hy. VIII, pl. 1, f.15d	(effect of sale before payment)	124
Hil.	14 Hy. VIII, pl. 7, f.18d	(effect of sale before payment)	124
Mich.	18 Hy. VIII, pl. 15, f.3	(debt, account: third hand and wager)	109
Pasch.	27 Hy. VIII, pl. 35, f.13	(detinue: bailment and trover)	99, 100, 179
Trin.	27 Hy. VIII, pl. 21, f.23	(case against executors for debt)	113
Mich.	27 Hy. VIII, pl. 3, f.24	(*assumpsit* for money: third party contracts discussed)	110, 111

FITZHERBERT'S ABRIDGMENT

Accion sur le case 32	(freedom from toll)	49
Accion sur le case 34	(river-banks not repaired)	57
Briefe 597	(river-banks not repaired)	57
Briefe 674	(franchise of estray)	42
Ley 63	(sale by servant: wager)	110
Ley 70	(debt by executors, tally: wager)	110
Rescous 12	(rescue)	37

BROOKE'S ABRIDGMENT

Accion sur le case 35	(bad wine sold)	127
Accion sur le case 113	(conversion: count in trover; bailment pleaded)	100, 101
Contract bargen & achate 29	(debt on contract: subsequent bond)	118
Contract bargen & achate 41	(debt: purchase by servant, wife)	111
Ley Gager 8	(debt by jailer for food)	113
Ley Gager 55	(debt for board: against executors)	113
Ley Gager 69	*(concessit solvere)*	136
Ley Gager 93	(debt: general issue *modo et forma*)	115, 116, 174
London 15	*(concessit solvere)*	136
Nonsuite 52	(debt: immediate law)	114
Nonsuite 55	(debt: immediate law)	114
Quod permittat 5	(freedom from multure)	34

IV. CASES FROM REPORTS

References are given only for Anonymous cases and for cases cited by reference and without name in the original footnote.

Anon (1563) Dalison 49 (pl. 13)	174
Anon (1573) Dalison 84 (pl. 35)	98
Anon (1537) Dyer 29(b)-30	117, 124, 125
Anon (1505) Keilway 69 (pl. 2)	122, 126
Anon (1505) Keilway 77 (pl. 25)	122, 126
Anon (1507) Keilway 91 (pl. 16)	127, 128
Anon (1510) Keilway 160 (pl. 2)	101
Anon (1516) Keilway 180 (pl. 3)	112
Anon (1590) 1 Leon 208 (pl. 290)	154
Agar v. Lisle (1613)	102
Baxter and Read's Case (1584)	98
Beecher's Case (1608) 8 Co. Rep. 58a, at 59b	74
Bonham's Case (1608)	283
Candler v. Crane Christmas & Co. (1951)	103
Central London Property Trust Ltd. v. High Trees House Ltd. (1947)	194
Coggs v. Bernard (1703)	27
Core's Case (1536)	101
Donoghue v. Stevenson (1932)	220
Edwards v. Burre (1573), Dalison 104 (pl. 45)	97
Entick v. Carrington (1765)	200
Fowler v. Lanning (1959)	157
Gibbons v. Pepper (1695)	82
Gordon v. Harper (1796)	102
Gumbleton v. Grafton (1600)	101, 102
Hollins v. Fowler (1875)	102
Hudson v. Leigh (1589) 4 Co. Rep. 43a, 1 Leon. 318	84
Isaack v. Clark (1615)	102, 158
Letang v. Cooper (1964)	157
London County Council v. Allen (1914)	166-67
Maleverer v. Spinke (1537), Dyer 35b (at 36b)	81
Marshalsea, Case of the (1612)	158
Milles v. Gage (1507) Keilway 95 (pl. 1)	84
Mounteagle v. Countess of Worcester (1555) Dyer 121a Benloe 41	100
Mouse's Case (1608) 12 Co. Rep. 63	81
National Provincial Bank v. Hastings Car Mart (1965)	166
Norwood v. Read (1558)	112
Oakley v. Lyster (1931)	102
Oxford's Case, Chancellor of	102
Pinnel's Case (1602)	144, 174, 188
Reynolds v. Clarke (1725)	92
Roscorla v. Thomas (1842)	96
Rylands v. Fletcher (1866, 1868)	217, 220
Shortridge and Hill's Case (1623) Godbolt 426 (pl. 492)	78
Shrewsbury's Case, Countess of (1600) 5 Co. Rep. 13b	87
Shrewsbury's Case, Earl of (1610) 9 Co. Rep. 42a (at 50b)	78
Slade's Case (1602)	97, 98, 174, 214-15
Walgrave v. Somerset (1587) Gould 72, 4 Leon. 167	87
Ward v. Macauley (1791)	102
Willion v. Berkley (1562)	226
Winsmore v. Greenbank (1745)	18

TABLE OF STATUTES AND DOCUMENTS

1100	1 Hy. I: Coronation Charter		
	c.2	(relief)	234
	c.3	(marriage of daughter, heiress, widow; widow's dower; *maritagium*)	234, 236, 252, 258, 259
	c.4	(widow's dower, *maritagium*; wardship of children, land)	234, 235, 258
1176	22 Hy. II: Assize of Northampton c.4 (mort d'ancestor)		246
1215	17 John: *Magna Carta*		
	c.2	(relief)	234
	c.3	(no relief after wardship)	234
	c.4	(wardship: waste)	234, 235
	c.5	(wardship: maintenance, stock)	234, 235
	c.6	(marriage: no disparagement)	234
	c.7	(widow's quarantine, dower, *maritagium*, inheritance)	234, 258
	c.8	(marriage of widow)	234, 258
	c.34	(writ called *precipe*)	244-48
1236	20 Hy. III: Merton, c.1 (widow's quarantine, dower)		4
1259	43 Hy. III: Provisions of Westminster c. 9 (damages in mort d'ancestor)		246
1267	52 Hy. III: Marlborough		
	c.3	(lord distraining within fee)	75, 76
	c.16	(damages in mort d'ancestor)	246
	c.23	(account: process)	156
1275	3 Ed. I: Westminster I		
	c.6	(amercements)	158
	c.13	(ravishment of women)	17
	c.20	(trespass in parks)	84
1278	6 Ed. I: Gloucester, c.8 (trespass: jurisdiction)		30, 75, 76, 78, 88-9, 106, 125
1284	12 Ed. I: Wales, c.10 (covenant)		163
1285	13 Ed. I: Westminster II		
	c.1	*(de donis)*	223-27
	c.11	(account: committal by auditors)	133, 156
	c.24	*(in consimili casu)*	1, 6, 89-90, 91
	c.34	(ravishment of women)	17
	c.35	(ravishment of ward; *ejectio custodie*)	32
1327	1 Ed. III: statute 1, c.6 (attaint)		85
1328	2 Ed. III: Northampton		
	c.3	(going armed: fairs and markets)	43
	c.13	(trespass: demise of crown)	74-5
1335	9 Ed. III, statute 1, c.3 (process against executors)		121
1344	18 Ed. III, statute 2, c.5 (trespass: process)		75
1351	25 Ed. III, statute 2: Labourers		17, 52, 161
1352	25 Ed. III, statute 5, c.17 (debt, detinue, replevin: process)		75, 156, 163
1382	6 Ric. II, statute 1, c.3 (petty nuisance)		156
1403	5 Hy. IV, c.8 (debt on feigned account)		108-09, 134-35, 142-43
1504	19 Hy. VII, c.9 (actions on the case: process)		156, 158
1536	27 Hy. VIII, c.10: Uses		283
1585	27 Eliz. I, c.8 (error in king's bench)		97
1601	43 Eliz. I, c.6 (small cases)		106
1660	12 Charles II, c.24 (military tenures)		199, 274-75
1873	36 & 37 Vict. c.66: Judicature Act		273
1875	38 & 39 Vict. c.77: Judicature Act		273
1897	60 & 61 Vict. c.65: Land Transfer Act		201

INDEX

A page number may refer to matter appearing only in a footnote on that page; but names appearing only in footnotes have not been indexed.

A

ACCIDENT
bailee's liability 177-79
trespass, in 82-3, 173-74, 180-82, 212, 216

ACCOUNT
accountant in credit 139-40, 142
auditors, status and function 134, 139
debt on 108-09, 112, 133-44, 186
"equity" in 139
fictitious 108-09, 112, 135
guardian in socage 87
insimul computaverunt 141-44
pleas 109
process 156
trading in partnership 136
wager of law 109, 113

ACCOUNT STATED
133-44

ACTIO NEGOTIORUM GESTORUM
139

ACTIO REDHIBITORIA
126

ACTIONS ON THE CASE: *See* CASE

ADMINISTRATIVE LAW
222

AGISTMENT
62

AIEL: *see* COINAGE

AMES, J.B.
91, 93, 95, 98, 99, 101, 165, 167

ANIMALS: *see also* ESTRAY
damage by 8-10, 21-26, 85
damage to 24-27
hiring of 62

ANSON ON CONTRACT
261

APPEAL OF FELONY
indictment and 273
trespass and 1, 20, 84

ASSIZE: *see* GRAND ASSIZE, MORT D'ANCESTOR, NOVEL DISSEISIN

ASSUMPSIT
bailees, by 63-64, 70, 101
buyers of goods, by 125
buyers of land, by 125, 163
deceit and 93-96, 160, 163-65, 195, 214
indebitatus 97-99, 133, 165, 214-15
misfeasance 158-59
negligence and 168-69
nonfeasance 93-96, 160-66, 191-92
not guilty 157
reliance and 191-92
services, for 161

ATTAINT
85

B

BAILEY, S.J.
224

BAILMENTS
bailee's liability 177-79
detinue and 99-100, 176-79
Jones on 205-06, 207
legal analysis 176-79
sale of goods and 122-23
trespass actions and 61-67, 68, 86

BARONIES, ETC., INHERITANCE OF
Aldington 238
Buckland, William de 236-37, 248, 252
Henry I, Coronation Charter on 236
Mandeville 235, 237-38, 239
Redbourne 235, 238, 239

BATTLE, TRIAL BY
champion as witness 183
grand assize and 172, 183, 184, 186-87
ordeals and 172

BATTLE, TRIAL BY – *continued*
  parties of same stock 186-87
  questions lost in 176, 186-87

BENDLOWES, W.
  226-27

BENTHAM, J.
  98, 199

BILL, PROCEEDINGS BEGUN BY
  2-3

BLACKSTONE, W.
  addressing laymen 198-99,
    201-04, 208
  Analysis 197
  Commentaries, arrangement 198,
    202-03
  Commentaries, influence 197-99
  Commentaries, longevity 197,
    273-74
  Gaius and 206-07
  his predecessors 203-04
  his use of "tort" 158
  his use of "trespass" 89
  lectures 197
  legal literature following 205-6
  new kind of exposition 200, 205-06
  on abolition of military tenures 199
  on bailments 206
  on contract 203
  on inheritance 201
  on land law 201

BOND: *see* CONDITIONAL BOND

BRACTON
  Bracton's Note Book 265, 268, 276,
    277
  Brevia Placitata and 173, 182
  influence on Maitland 276-77
  literary tradition 289-90
  on accidental fire 20
  on bailee's liability 177
  on battery 13, 16
  on curtesy 253, 257
  on dower *unde nichil* 246, 247
  on process 73
  on *quare ejecit* 5-6
  on remainderman's remedy 224, 225
  on trespass and rights in land 4, 13
  Roman influence and 182

BREVIA PLACITATA
  compared with Bracton 173, 182
  Selden Society edition 288

BRITTON
  on bailee's liability 177-78
  on battery of servant 5, 6
  on formedon 224
  on terms of years 5, 6
  on trespass and appeal 84

BUCKLAND, W.W.
  262, 266

C

CAM, H.M.
  262

CAPIAS: see PROCESS

CAPITAL MESSUAGE
  241, 242

CARRIERS
  68-71

CASE, ACTIONS ON THE
  "deceit on the case" 93-94, 95
  development of law and 185
  early actions so called 33-34
  formulations of writs 46, 87, 92
  in consimili casu clause and 1, 89-90
    91-92
  trespass, relationship with 1-2, 29-30, 42,
    75, 91-94, 156-57

CATALLA FELONUM
  41

CATTLE TRESPASS
  8-10, 85

CHALLIS, H.W.
  223

CHARTERS OF LIBERTIES, NATURE OF
  235-36

CHURCH COURTS
  defamation and 146-47
  maritagium and 233, 248

Index

CLASSIFICATION, LEGAL: *see* LEGAL CHANGE

COALMINES
35

COKE, E.
auditors as judges of record 134
his use of "trespass" 157, 158
Littleton's *Tenures* and 201, 206
on formedon in the descender 225

COLOUR IN PLEADING
187

CONCESSIT SOLVERE
133-44

CONDITIONAL BOND
95, 144, 162, 174

CONSIDERATION
debt precedent 98
deceit and 95-96, 165, 167, 214-15
estoppel and 167, 193-94
moving from plaintiff 96
past consideration 96
promise under seal and 167, 194

CONTRACT: *see also ASSUMPSIT,* COVENANT
Blackstone's treatment 203
"death" of 191-96
early sense of word 154, 195
early treatises on 195-96
nature of early law 175
reliance 191-92
status and 161-62, 203
theory of 194-95
under seal and promissory estoppel 194

CONVERSION
against bailees 101-02
against sellers of goods 125-26
"altering property" 102
debt and 125-26
denial of title 102
detinue and 100-01, 178-79
indebitatus assumpsit and 102
sense of word 126, 179

COPYHOLD
274

CORBIN, A.L.
192, 196

COSINAGE, AIEL, BESAIEL
246-47

COVENANT
case and 96, 159-65
disuse 162-63, 192
lease and 5
seal required 30, 89, 138, 153-54, 159, 165, 192
trespass and 71, 94-95

CRIMINAL LAW, EARLY
273

CRUISE ON FINES
205

CRUISE'S *DIGEST OF REAL PROPERTY*
205

CURTESY
conditional fee and 259-60
dower and 254
homage and 254, 258
litigation concerning 254-57
maritagium and 253, 259
mort d'ancestor and 255, 256
name 253, 256-57
novel disseisin and 255, 257, 258, 259
second husband 254, 258
wife's inheritance and 253, 259
wardship and 254, 258

CUSTOM AND LAW
201, 210-11, 236, 274

CUSTOMS
collection 77
payment 36

D

DAMAGES
for future 7
in debt 137
inscrutability of award 95-96, 214-15

DEBT
abbot, against 99, 112, 115
accountant in credit 139-40, 142

DEBT – *continued*
   concessit solvere 133-44
   contract made abroad 136
   contract misstated 115-16
   conversion and 125-26
   damages in 137
   debet and *detinet* 99, 105-06, 112, 121, 176, 179
   detinue, relationship with 121-22, 131, 176-79
   executors, by 110
   executors, against 112-13, 121, 137, 153
   formulation of general issue 114-16
   forty-shilling rule 106-08, 143
   indebitatus assumpsit and 97-99, 165, 214-15
   joinder of claims 105
   jurisdiction over 106-08, 132
   London, in 137
   non-delivery 119-20, 121-26
   on account 108-09, 112, 133-44, 186
   on lease 114, 115, 120, 143, 186
   on sale 105-20
   pleading payment 107-08, 117-18, 186
   pleading subsequent obligation 118
   pledge taken 118
   price contested 106-07
   process 156
   quid pro quo 98, 119, 120, 131, 138
   smaller sum accepted 118, 174
   viscontiel writs 106
   wager of law 96, 108-14, 115, 174-75, 186, 214

DECEIT
   assumpsit and 93-96, 160, 163-65, 167-68, 195, 214
   "deceit on the case" 93-94, 95
   jurisdiction over 163-65, 168
   legal change and 168
   rescission and 126, 168
   sale of land 120, 164-65
   tort of 167
   warranty and 96, 126, 128, 168

DEFAMATION
   appearance in royal courts 214
   church courts and 146-47

DEMISE OF THE CROWN
   74-75, 78, 88

DEMURRER
   146-47

DE NATIVO HABENDO
   175

DEODANDS
   41

DEPOSIT
   65

DE QUARENTINA HABENDA
   4

DE RATIONABILI PARTE BONORUM
   121, 131

DE RATIONABILI PARTE TENEMENTI
   243-44

DETINUE
   bailment 99-100, 131, 176-79
   charters 114, 177
   conversion and 100-01, 178
   debt, relationship with 121-22, 131, 176-79
   devenit ad manus, trover 99-100, 131, 176-79
   misdescription of object 116
   process 156
   sense of general issue 179

DISTRESS
   capital messuage 241
   damage feasant 9, 10, 38, 66, 79, 82
   suit of court, for 49
   wrongs arising from 36-37

DIX, E. J.
   1

DOWER
   Bracton on 246, 247
   capital messuage and 241
   curtesy and 254
   early nature and protection 231-32, 243-44
   frequency of litigation 254
   Glanvill on 247
   maritagium and 231-32, 244
   marriage denied 246
   tenurial bearing 247
   unde nichil 245-47

DUE PROCESS
   judgment of peers and 200, 210, 222

Index

DUE PROCESS – *continued*
   rules of natural justice and 200, 222

E

EASEMENTS AND PROFITS
   3, 11-13, 33, 30-41, 79

ECONOMIC DAMAGE
   35-36, 42, 89

EJECTIO CUSTODIE
   32, 73

EJECTIO FIRME
   4-7, 32, 74, 75

ENTAIL
   gift to younger son and 233
   origin 233
   protection 223-29

ERROR, WRIT OF
   188-89

ESCAPE OF PRISONER
   64

ESCHEAT
   formedon in the reverter and 223, 225
   writs of entry and 223, 225

ESTRAY
   41, 79, 92

EVESHAM, BATTLE OF
   35

EXCHEQUER
   113

EXECUTORS
   debt against 112-13, 121, 137, 153
   debt by 110
   exchequer, sued in 113
   liability in debt in London 136-37
   testator's pledgee sued by 30, 64
   wager of law against 110
   wager of law by 109, 112, 137, 153

EX PARTE TALIS
   133

F

FAIRS AND MARKETS
   customary rights 77
   fixtures damaged 43, 44
   fraud on, by selling outside 45-47, 59, 60,
   measures 77
   nuisance to 42
   picketing 43-45
   pillory and 37
   tolls 42, 45-47
   wrongs to 42-47, 59, 60, 73

FAMILY PROVISION: *see* CURTESY; DOWER; ENTAIL; *MARITAGIUM*; YOUNGER SON

FARRIERS: *see* SMITHS

FEARNE ON CONTINGENT REMAINDERS
   205

FERRIES, FERRYMEN
   70-71, 159

FET ASAVER
   73

FICTIONS
   attention drawn to 204
   change by reclassification and 152
   judges and 213, 215
   juries and 214-15

FIFOOT, C.H.S.
   1, 91, 93-94, 120

FINCH, H.
   203-04

FIRE
   19-21, 29, 82-83, 86-87, 180-82, 184

FLETA
   on bailee's liability 177
   on formedon 224

FORMEDON
   223-29

FORMS OF ACTION
   153-54, 195, 272-73

FORMULARY SYSTEM
   jury direction compared 202

FORMULARY SYSTEM – *continued*
  substantive law and 171, 202

FRANKPLEDGE, VIEW OF
  49, 51

FREE BOAR, BULL
  32, 37-39

FREE FOLD
  32, 33, 37 - 40, 79

FULLER, L.L.
  192

G

GAIRDNER, J
  145

GAIUS
  172, 207

GALLOWS
  51

GENERAL ISSUE
  criminal law and 188
  detinue, possible senses in 179
  formulation in debt 114-16
  formulation in deceit on warranty 128
  formulation in trespass 80
  inscrutability 81, 107, 108, 177-79, 180-82, 187-88
  law, questions of 111
  modo & forma 116
  principles of liability and 81, 82-83, 180-82, 216
  special pleading and 185-89

GILMORE, G.
  191-96

GLANVILL
  on bailee's liability 178
  on curtesy 253, 257
  on dower 247
  on grand assize 183, 186
  on marriage of daughter 236
  on *precipe* writs 247
  on warranty of goods 126
  on writ of right patent 243

GRAND ASSIZE
  battle and 172, 183, 184, 186-87

GRAND ASSIZE – *continued*
  Glanvill on 183, 186
  introduction 172
  parties of same stock 186-87
  special mise 184
  special verdict 183
  tender of demi-mark 187
  trespass, in 11

H

HALE, M.
  203-04

HALL, G.D.G.
  2, 3, 48, 133

HARDING, A.
  3

HAZELTINE, H.D.
  281-82

HERESY
  145-47

HERIOT
  41

HOLDSWORTH, W.S.
  121, 225, 288

HOLLOND, H.A.
  262

HOLMES, O.W.
  151, 194, 196

HOMAGE: *see also* LORD AND HEIR
  consequences 232
  curtesy and 254, 258
  heiress's husband doing 234, 236
  inheritance and 231-33, 234, 258-59
  maritagium and 232
  parage and 241-42, 243
  significance of word 233
  wardship and 233-34

HUMPHREYS, W.H.
  224

HUNNE, Richard
  145-47

Index

HURNARD, N.D.
  244

I

IN CONSIMILI CASU
  1, 89-90, 91-92

INDICTMENT
  proof and 273
  trespass and 3

INFANT: *see* WARDSHIP

INHERITANCE
  Blackstone on 201
  by (or through) women 231-60
  casus regis 238-40
  changing nature 201, 210-11, 233-40
  formation of canons 187
  homage and 231-33, 234, 258-59
  lord and heir 232-33
  lord's part in early 201, 210-11, 231-49
  maritagium and 251-53
  parage 237, 241-49, 252, 254
  purchase and 252-53
  widow's 235, 239, 258, 260

INNKEEPERS
  58-59, 73, 94

J

JAILERS
  79, 113, 178

JEFFRIES DAVIS, E.
  145, 280

JONES ON BAILMENTS
  205-08

JUDGE-MADE LAW: *see also* LEGAL CHANGE; LEGAL DEVELOPMENT; PRECEDENT
  changing nature 217-21
  contract, tort, crime 201-02, 212-16
  control of administration 222
  descent into detail 218-22
  disuse of juries 218-20
  expense 218
  fictions and 152, 213, 214-15
  jury direction 182, 202, 212, 215-16, 218-19
  legislation and 169-70, 209, 220-21

JUDGE-MADE LAW – *continued*
  making or finding law 207-08, 216-17, 220
  moral authority 221-22
  new actions 213-15
  property 201, 210-13
  single judge 218
  special pleas 212-13

JUDGMENT OF PEERS
  due process and 200, 210, 222
  rules of natural justice and 200, 222

JURISDICTION: *see also* LEGAL CHANGE
  inheritance and 201, 210-11, 231-49
  forty-shilling rule 106-08, 143, 213
  property in land and 201, 210-11, 240, 274
  tenant's tenure and 210
  trespass and 1-2, 29-30, 31, 57-60, 64, 65, 66, 75-78, 85, 88-89, 155-56, 180-81

JURY
  alternative to wager 114, 188
  colour and 187
  consequences of disuse 218-20
  damages 95-96, 214-15
  directions 182, 188, 202, 215-16, 218-19
  fictions and 214-15
  foreign county 118, 186
  insurance and 219-20
  legal development and 171-89, 202, 212-16, 218-19
  moral force of law and 219-20
  reasonable man 216, 219
  special pleading and 185-87, 188, 202, 213, 276
  special verdict 22-23, 81, 186, 243

JUSTIFICATION
  appearing in verdict on general issue 81-82
  law made by pleas 202, 212
  replication *de injuria* 79-80, 157
  sicut ei bene licuit 79-81

K

KING'S PEACE: *see* DEMISE OF THE CROWN; TRESPASS (s.v.v. jurisdiction, process, wager of law); WORDS AND PHRASES (s.v. *contra pacem regis*).

KIRALFY, A.K.R.
26, 59, 63, 88

L

LANGDELL, C.C.
194-95

LEASE: *see* TERM OF YEARS

LEGAL CHANGE
artificiality resulting from
reclassification 202-03, 204
classification and
reclassification 70-71, 93-103, 149,
191-96, 202-03, 214, 270, 271
deceit and 168
fiction 152, 204, 213, 214-15
imperceptibility 271, 275
jurisdiction, effect of shift 88-90,
155-56, 213, 274
jurisdiction, effect of superior 201,
210-12, 240, 274
legislation 150, 152
mixed economy and 199
negligence and 168-69
perception by historians 166, 197, 271,
275
private rights and governmental
allocations
199, 201, 210-12, 274-75
property and lordship 199-200,
210-12, 273-75
social change and 149-50, 197, 275
statements and promises 152, 191-92
status and contract 161-62, 203
words changing meaning 271, 275

LEGAL DEVELOPMENT: *see also*
JUDGE-MADE LAW; JURY
actions on the case 185
analogy and 2, 157
battle and 172, 176
early modes of proof and 171-80, 212
explanation to laymen 198-99, 202-03,
208, 218-19
exposition, alphabetical 198, 202
exposition, procedural 202
exposition, substantive 198-99, 202-04,
207, 216-17
facts emerging in law suits 171-89
formulary system 171, 202
jury directions 182, 188, 202, 212, 215-17
218-19
jury disused 218-20

LEGAL DEVELOPMENT – *continued*
jury trial and 171-89, 212-17, 276
new actions 183-85, 213-15
nineteenth century systems 193-95,
207-08, 216-17
property and obligation 176-79
reflection in legal formalities 176-77,
184
special pleading and 183-89, 202, 213,
276
text books and treatises 200-04, 207,
212, 217
wager of law and 174-75, 186, 188

LEGIS ACTIONES
legal discussion and 172
per sacramentum 172

LEGISLATION
directness of change 150, 152
judge-made law and 169-70, 209, 220-21

LICENCES 166

LITTLETON'S *TENURES*
201, 264, 273

LONDON
concessit solvere 133-44
debt in 137
executors liable in debt 136-37

LORD AND HEIR
232-33

LORDSHIP
copyhold and freehold 274
discretionary power lost 199-200, 201,
210-12, 222, 273-75
judgment of peers 210
military tenures, abolition 199, 274-75
remainders and 210-11
seisin and 275

LÜCKE, H. K.
133

M

MAITLAND, F.W.
aims of legal history 149, 277
Bracton's influence on 276-77
Bracton's Note Book 265, 268,
276, 277
Constitutional History 272

Index

MAITLAND – *continued*
  English Law and the Renaissance 272
  Gloucestershire Pleas of the Crown 268
  longevity of his work 261-77
  marriage 268
  on curtesy 253, 258
  on early pleaders 267
  on formedon 223-25
  on grand assize in trespass 11
  on history of contract 276
  on "injunction" in trespass 46
  on lawyers as legal historians 265, 269
  on legal tradition 271, 272
  on medieval land law 274-75
  on modern land law 211-12, 273-74
  on origins of trespass and case 1, 2
  on remainders 224
  on women's degrees 266-67
  on Year Books 276
  "Pollock and Maitland" 261, 273, 276
  practice at the bar 268-70
  quality as a lawyer 269-70
  Selden Society 268
  The Court Baron 276
  The Forms of Action 272-73, 276
  undergraduate days 264-66

MARITAGIUM
  capital messuage and 241
  coheiresses and 251-53
  curtesy and 253, 259
  degrees in 243
  dower and 231-32, 244
  early nature 231-33
  homage and 232
  parage and 241-42, 252, 254
  protected in heir's court 232, 233, 244
  protected in church courts 233, 248

MARKET OVERT
  128-29

MARKETS: *see* FAIRS AND MARKETS

MEASURES, ENFORCEMENT OF
  77

MARRIAGE
  coheiresses 250-51
  daughter 236
  heiress 234
  widow 234-35, 239, 258

MERCHANTS, CUSTOM OF
  64

MILITARY TENURES, ABOLITION OF,
  199, 274-75

MILLS, MILLERS
  33, 34, 63

MORE, THOMAS
  145-47

MORT D'ANCESTOR
  by heir in tail 224, 226
  by or between coheiresses 245
  curtesy and 255, 256
  damages 246
  extension of principle 246-47
  nuper obiit and 245
  original role 246

MORTUARY
  145

N

NARRATORES
  176

NECESSITY
  81

NEGLIGENCE
  agent of change 168-69
  specific tort 169

NEGLIGENT MISSTATEMENT
  103

NIGHT, ACTS DONE BY
  12, 34-35, 75

NISI PRIUS
  182, 218

NONFEASANCE
  assumpsit 93-96, 160-66, 191-92
  trespass 54-60, 91-103

NONSUIT
  114

NOVEL DISSEISIN
  curtesy and 255, 257, 258, 259
  early nature 275
  pasture 9
  process 74, 76, 78
  special verdict 243

NOVEL DISSEISIN – *continued*
   trespass and 1, 4

NUISANCE
   fairs and markets 42
   royal jurisdiction 156

NUPER OBIIT
   bastardy and 246
   dower *unde nichil* and 245-48
   Magna Carta and 246-48
   mort d' ancestor and 245-47
   origin 263-49
   ostensurus quare formulation 249

O

OGLE, A.
   145

ORDEALS
   172, 212, 276

P

PARAGE
   capital messuage and 241, 242
   changing interest of lord 242
   degrees in 243
   disputes arising from 242-43
   homage and 241-42, 243
   maritagium and 241-42, 252, 254
   nature 241
   protection of 243-49
   subinfeudation and 248

PARDON, EFFECT UPON PLAINTIFF
   84

PASTURE
   8-10, 79

PERKINS, *PROFITABLE BOOKE*
   119

PERSONS, LAW OF
   203

PETTY TREASON
   15

PILLORY
   37-38

PLEDGE
   30, 64, 118

PLUCKNETT, T.F.T.
   Brevia Placitata 288
   Concise History 285, 286
   constitutional history 281-83
   contributions 149
   Early English Legal Literature 289-90
   Edward I and Criminal Law 289
   education 279
   external degree 279
   Legislation of Edward I 290
   marriage 284
   on formulation of writs 96
   on lawyers as legal historians 265,
      269, 290-91
   on legal history 290-91
   on Maitland 289, 291
   on origins of trespass 29, 84, 91, 93
   Selden Society 287-89
   Statutes and their Interpretation 281
   The Medieval Bailiff
      290

POLLOCK F.
   261, 273

POTHIER, R.J.
   195

POUND, R.
   280, 284, 285

POUND-BREACH
   36-37

PRECEDENT: *see also* JUDGE-MADE LAW
   expense of litigation and 218
   increasing detail 218
   in England and U.S.A. 169-70, 194-95,
      208
   report "not law" 113
   single hierarchy 194, 218
   single judge 218

PRECIPE writs
   cosinage, aiel, besaiel 246-47
   covenant, debt, detinue 96
   for land 244-45
   Glanvill on 247
   Magna Carta and 244-45, 247
   ostensurus quare and 96-97, 249
   performance ordered 162-63
   quia dominus remisit curiam 245
   writs of entry 245

PREMUNIRE
   145-47

Index

PRESTON ON ESTATES
265

PRINCIPAL AND ACCESSORY
4, 85

PRIVATE LAW
  economic and social basis 199-200
  private rights and governmental
    allocations 199-201, 210-12,
    274-75
  Roman law and common law 200
  status and contract 161-62, 203

PROCESS
  attachment and trespass 72-74
  Bracton on 73
  capias and *contra pacem regis* 71, 72-75,
    84-85, 89
  capias and demise of the crown 74-75
  capias and outlawry 75
  capias and power to make attorney 75
  debt and detinue in 75
  Fet Asaver on 73
  summons and property 56-57, 72-75
  vi et armis and novel disseisin 74, 84

PRODUCT LIABILITY
  169, 192, 219-20

PROMISSORY ESTOPPEL 192-94

PROTECTIONS 52-53

PROOF, EARLY MODES OF
  and forms of action 273
  and legal development 171-80, 212, 277
  and medieval legal system 273

PROPERTY LAW
  how it came into being 199-201, 210-12,
    274
  how it is being superseded 199, 200,
    221, 275
  Maitland on 211-12, 273-75
  property and management 200, 221-22,
    275
  property and obligation 166-67, 176-79

Q

QUARE EJECIT INFRA TERMINUM
  5-7

QUID PRO QUO
  98, 119, 120, 131, 138

QUOD PERMITTAT
  free bull 39
  free fold 39
  pasture 8-9
  trespass and 33-34
  view of frankpledge 51

QUO JURE
  8, 11

QUO MINUS
  113

R

RELIEF
  234

RASTELL'S *ENTREES*
  on estray 42
  on failures to repair 58
  on *scienter* 24
  on wrongs concerning tolls 49

RECORDARI FACIAS
  53-54

REEVES, J.
  225

REMAINDERS
  origin 210-11
  puzzle about early 224

REPAIR OF RIVER WALLS etc
  54-58, 60, 73, 94

REPARARI FACIAS
  54, 56, 58

REPLEVIN
  67, 75, 87

RESCUE
  36-37, 59

RESTATEMENT OF CONTRACTS
  193-94, 196

RICHARDSON, H.G.
  8

ROMAN LAW
  development parallel with common
    law 200, 207
  importance of lay *iudex* 202

ROMAN LAW – *continued*
  influence on Bracton 177-78,
    275-76
  influence on English law 176, 178, 182
  influence on English legal historians
    275-7
  institutional arrangement 204
  why Roman law and common law 200
  working of law suits 171-72

S

SALE OF GOODS
  abbot, by 112
  bailment, and 122-23, 231
  case, actions on 125-26
  conditions 116-17, 123, 132
  constructive delivery 122
  defective goods 67
  different county 116-17
  exchange and 105-06
  goods damaged 67-68
  market overt 128-29
  married women 110-11
  necessaries 111
  passing of property 121-26, 130-32
  payment, conditional upon 123-25
  real or consensual 105, 130-32, 174-75
  res aliena 119, 120
  res extincta 119, 120
  res sua 119
  seller resells 124, 232
  seller retakes 119
  seller's lien 124, 132
  servant or agent, by 110, 128-29
  servant or agent, to 110-11
  specific or unascertained goods 121-22,
    131, 176-77

SALE OF LAND
  120, 125, 164-65, 175

SANDERS ON USES AND TRUSTS
  205

SAYLES, G.O.
  8, 77

SCIENTER
  21, 24, 26, 81, 82, 86

SEISIN
  275

SEQUESTRATION
  36

SHEEP, SHEPHERDS
  22, 39-40, 62-64

SHIPS, BOATS
  35, 40, 62, 68-71

SIDGWICK, H.
  265-66, 268, 269

SLANDER: *see* DEFAMATION
  47

SMITHS
  26-27, 66, 70, 86

SON ASSAULT DEMESNE
  79

SON DEFAULT DEMESNE
  79-80

SPECIAL VERDICT
  22-23, 81, 183, 186, 243

STATUS AND CONTRACT
  161-62, 203

SUIT, *SECTA*
  de nativo habendo
    175
  examination 113, 175
  nature 175

SUIT OF COURT
  49-50

SUMMONS, TRESPASS ACTIONS
    STARTED BY
  56-57, 72-74

SURGEONS
  15, 71-72, 82, 159

T

TENANCY IN COMMON
  87

TERM OF YEARS
  debt for rent 114, 115, 120, 143,
    186

Index

TERM OF YEARS – *continued*
   protection 4-7
   recited 34-35

TEXT-BOOKS AND TREATISES
   contract 195-96, 212
   crime 212
   importance 200, 206, 217
   land law 201, 205, 212
   tort 158, 195, 212

THORNE S.E.
   263

TOLL
   distraint for 45
   fairs and markets 45-47
   freedom from 47-48, 73
   wrongs concerning 47-49

TORT, EARLY TREATISES
   158, 195

TOURN
   51-52

TRESPASS
   abduction of apprentice 82, 86, 87
   abduction of prisoner 17
   abduction of son 16-17
   abduction of villeins or servants 17-18, 82, 86
   abduction of wards 84, 250-51
   abduction of wife 17, 18, 85
   accident 82-83, 173-74, 180-82, 212, 216
   against freeholder 6-7, 8
   against surgeon 15
   animals, damage by 21-24
   animals, damage to 24-27
   appeal of felony and 1, 20, 84
   assault and battery 13-15
   bailments and 61-67, 86
   battery of servant 16
   cat among pigeons 181
   cattle trespass 8-10, 85, 157
   classical view of nature and origin 1, 39, 90
   contra pacem regis: see Words and Phrases
   damages for future 7
   de bonis asportatis 18-19, 36
   distress and 36-37
   easements and profits 11-13, 33, 40-41

TRESPASS – *continued*
   estray 41-42
   executors, by 30, 32
   failures to repair 54-58, 73, 85, 94
   fairs and markets 42-47, 73
   false imprisonment 15-16
   fire 19-21, 29, 82-83, 86-87, 180-82, 184
   fishing rights and 10-12, 35
   formulation of general issue 80-83
   franchises and 41-52, 73
   game, taking 12-13
   general and special writs 3, 31, 41-42, 49, 64-68, 87-88, 92-93
   grand assize in 11
   indictment and 3, 84-5, 155
   jurisdiction 1-2, 29-30, 31, 57-60, 64, 65, 66, 75-78, 85, 88-89, 155-56, 180-81
   justification 79, 81-82
   land, to 3-13
   malice 23, 25, 70, 86
   mistake 82
   necessity 81-82
   novel disseisin and 1, 4, 84
   pasture rights and 8-10, 79, 85
   pleading in 78, 83
   poisoning 15
   possession and 41-42
   process 57, 72-75, 84-85, 155
   property rights and 11-12, 32-34, 39, 56-57, 59, 72-74
   protections recited 52-54
   royal commands recited 52-54
   sense of word: *see* Words and Phrases
   specific remedies 5, 6, 33-34, 44, 46, 48-49, 56
   statutes recited 52
   toll 47-48, 73
   vi et armis: see Words and Phrases
   view and 57
   viscontiel writs 30, 64, 65, 69, 76, 77, 78
   wager of law 47, 72, 78
   wardship and 32, 84
   weapons specified 9, 28, 67, 155
   wreck of the sea 41

TROVER: *see* CONVERSION; DETINUE

TUNSTALL, CUTHBERT
   145

TURNER G.J.
   288

V

VICTUALLERS
113

VINER'S *ABRIDGMENT*
198

W

WAGER OF LAW
abbot's successor, by 99, 112, 115
account before auditors 108-09, 133-44
account, in 190-10, 113
admonition and examination 174
debt and detinue, in 96, 152
defendant's choice 114
detinue of charters 114
equitable interference 114
Exchequer and 113
executors, against 110
executors, by 109, 112, 137, 153
jury alternative to 114, 138
king, against 78, 113
land involved 114
law made at once 114
law, questions of 118
legal development and 176-75, 186, 188
local custom and 175
notice of countryside 109-10, 113
ouster 108-13, 115, 133-35, 136
rent on lease 108, 114
safety in conscience 115, 116, 174, 175
secta and 175
service compellable 112-13
third hand 109-12
trespass in 47, 72, 78
witnesses ousting 136

WAIF
41

WARDSHIP
curtesy and 254, 258
of heiress 234
of infant male heir 233, 275
of socage tenant 235, 258
of widow 234-35

WARRANTY
classification of remedy 126
deceit and 96, 126, 168

WARRANTY – *continued*
food 127
Glanvill on 126
misfeasance and 129
patent defects 128
payment and 129
present facts 129
sale by servant or agent 128-29
seller's knowledge 127-28
size, weight, value 130
title 130

WASTE
fault 21, 83
tenant at will 21, 86-87, 181-82
wardship 235

WAY, RIGHTS OF
3, 40-41

WESTMINSTER, PALACE OF
53

WIDOWS: *see also* **DOWER**
custodia of 234-35
inheritance 235, 239, 258, 260
remarriage 234, 258

WILLIAMS, GLANVILLE
8-10, 21

WILLISTON, S.
194, 196

WINFIELD, P.H.
158

WITNESSES
136

WOOD, T.
203-04

WOODBINE, G.E.
1

WORDS AND PHRASES
case, on the 33, 87-88, 156
concessit se teneri 138, 140
concessit solvere 133-44
contra pacem regis 29-30, 57-60, 63, 65, 67, 68-69, 72-78, 84-85, 86

WORDS AND PHRASES – *continued*
    contract 154, 195
    covenant 94-95, 153-54, 159, 176, 191, 195
    conversion 126, 179
    curtesy 256-57
    custodia, custos 231-2, 233-5, 244, 256-57, 259, 260
    dampnum non modicum et gravamen 69, 76-77
    debet and *detinet* 99, 105-06, 112, 121, 176, 179
    esnecia, aesnecia, antenatio 238, 240-41, 242, 250, 252
    estoppel 193
    insimul computaverunt 140-44
    per quod servitium amisit 16, 41
    reckoning 136, 141-44
    seisin, seised, disseised 275
    simplex dictum 79
    sine licencia 7, 12
    tort 157-58, 195
    transgressio super casum 156
    trespass, *transgressio* 1, 30, 31, 36, 46, 52-60, 64, 69, 71, 72, 73, 75, 89-90, 91-93, 125, 154-60, 176, 191, 272
    vi et armis 4, 6-7, 9, 12-13, 14, 16, 18, 28, 30, 64-65, 67-68, 75-78, 89
    years and terms 146-47

WRECK OF THE SEA
    41, 79

WRIT OF RIGHT PATENT
    addressee 243-44, 248
    Glanvill on 243
    nature 176, 246
    precipe and 243-45
    suppression 54

WRITS OF ENTRY
    causa matrimonii prelocuti 164, 184
    dum non compos mentis 184
    escheat and 223, 225
    formedon in the descender and 226
    formedon in the reverter and 223, 225

WRITTEN PLEADINGS
    189

Y

YEAR BOOKS
    decline 189
    nature of discussion 185-89

YOUNGER SON, GIFT TO
    entail and 233
    lord and heir 233
    permissibility 233, 251